HANDBOOK ON
MASS MEDIA
IN THE
UNITED STATES

HANDBOOK ON
MASS MEDIA
IN THE
UNITED STATES

The Industry and Its Audiences

Edited by ERWIN K. THOMAS
and BROWN H. CARPENTER

GREENWOOD PRESS
Westport, Connecticut • London

Library of Congress Cataloging-in-Publication Data

Handbook on mass media in the United States : the industry and its
    audiences / edited by Erwin K. Thomas and Brown H. Carpenter.
        p.   cm.
    Includes bibliographical references and index.
    ISBN 0-313-27811-3
     1. Mass media—United States—Handbooks, manuals, etc.
  I. Thomas, Erwin Kenneth. II. Carpenter, Brown H.
  P92.U5H36   1994
  302.23'0973—dc20   93-30984

British Library Cataloguing in Publication Data is available.

Library of Congress Catalog Card Number: 93-30984
ISBN: 0-313-27811-3

First published in 1994

Greenwood Press, 88 Post Road West, Westport, CT 06881
An imprint of Greenwood Publishing Group, Inc.

Printed in the United States of America

The paper used in this book complies with the
Permanent Paper Standard issued by the National
Information Standards Organization (Z39.48–1984).

10 9 8 7 6 5 4 3 2

CONTENTS

ILLUSTRATIONS

PREFACE

This handbook on mass media in the United States is intended for college and university students and for general readers. It is a review and synthesis of information about the various industry sectors and their audiences and offers succinct surveys of the history, organization, role, current issues, and outlook for the future of different segments of the industry.

An introduction provides a brief overview of the growth and development of mass media and communications in the United States and points to a few key issues and problems facing producers and audiences today. Part I surveys the industries in the following order: advertising, books, cable, films, magazines, newspapers, public relations, radio, recordings, and television. Part II analyzes several audiences: minorities, women, children and youth, disabled, religious, and sports. Selected bibliographies accompany each chapter, and a short bibliography on the topic as a whole and a general index complete the volume.

ACKNOWLEDGMENTS

We express our appreciation to the contributors: Maurine H. Beasley, Shirley S. Carter, Robert G. Finney, Bruce Garrison, Barbara Bealor Hines, James Phillip Jeter, Kevin L. Keenan, Marilyn Kern-Foxworth, Katherine C. McAdams, Randy E. Miller, Lawrence N. Redd, M. Kent Sidel, Lowndes F. Stephens, Alice A. Tait, and Ronald J. Zboray.

In addition, we are grateful for the support of our wives, Mary Barta Thomas and Linda H. Carpenter. Finally, we thank our editors, Lynn Taylor, Mildred Vasan, and Arlene Belzer.

INTRODUCTION

The first written medium of communication following scrolls was a short book printed with movable type. The *Diamond Sutra,* the teachings of Buddha, was probably the first and was published in China in 868. The next world landmark was Johannes Guttenberg's *Bible,* printed in Germany in 1456. Almost 200 years later, the first printing press in North America was established in 1639 at Harvard College in Cambridge, Massachusetts, with the publication of the *Whole Booke of Psalmes.* The publication and distribution of books grew dramatically with the development of urbanization and literacy. And dispersion of the written word opened yet new avenues of thought, stimulating public debate and impacting, in a major way, the democratization of the nation.

Newspapers in America go back to the first days of the colonies. Historically, they resisted organizational change. By 1921, there were 2,042 local newspapers in existence in this country. The newspaper industry exploded in 1933 with the publication of Benjamin Day's *New York Sun,* which was followed by other newspapers that sold for "one penny."

During the 1970s and 1980s, newspapers and the rest of the print media experienced traumatic changes in production with the use of the computer. And in the 1990s, organizational plans for newspapers changed in structure.

Magazines hit the scene in the eighteenth century and represent some of the first institutions in America. Quite diverse in their appeal, they have proved themselves to be a formidable force culturally, politically, and educationally. By the year 2000, their total ad revenue should hit $13.6 billion.

Mass media became more diversified and more widely available through the development of new technology. In 1835, Samuel Morse's telegraph transmitted dots and dashes as codes for sending messages. And in 1848, news wire service became a reality when six New York newspapers agreed to share the telegraphy costs of transmitting foreign news from Boston where many European ships docked first. In 1895, Guglielmo Marconi invented the first wireless telegraphy and sent a signal across the Atlantic Ocean, which paved the way for the creation of international news services. In 1907, E. W. Scripps established the United Press (UP) Association; in 1909, William Randolph Hearst set up his International News Service (INS); and in the 1920s, Kent Cooper organized the Associated Press (AP).

Alexander Graham Bell perfected the telephone with its capacity for voice communication. Other developments followed, including the transmission of voice and music by Reginald Fessenden's alternator and Lee De Forest's audio tube (audion) in the early 1900s.

The first voice was heard on radio in 1892 in Murray, Kentucky, and belonged to Nathan B. Stubble. The National Broadcasting Company (NBC) began broadcasting on Red and Blue networks, and by 1929, sales of radio receivers reached $19 million. Al Jarvis was the first disc jockey on radio in the 1930s, and Franklin D. Roosevelt's "fireside chats" were heard nationwide during the depression years. David Sarnoff's National Broadcasting Company (NBC) was famous for its "music box." In the 1940s, William S. Paley's Columbia Broadcasting System (CBS) became well known for its World War II coverage by Edward R. Murrow and others.

In 1890, the first television feasibility study in America was undertaken by Charles F. Jenkins. Experimenters such as Philo T. Farnsworth and Vladimir Zworykin developed the process further, and the first TV prototype was demonstrated in 1925. In 1927, closed-circuit pictures of Herbert Hoover were sent from Washington, D.C. to New York, and an experimental TV station was built there in the Empire State Building in 1932. In 1936, the Radio Corporation of America (RCA) began extensive field tests of TV signals, and by 1937, seventeen experimental stations were in operation. The Midwest was linked by coaxial cable by the end of the 1940s, and CATV (community antenna television) systems were in operation in seventy communities in 1950. In 1991, some 98 percent of TV households in the United States had color, 71 percent of American households had cable, and 15 million households had videos.

In 1893, Thomas Alva Edison patented the kentograph and the kinetoscope. D. W. Griffith, referred to as the "Father of Film," released masterpiece *The Birth of a Nation* in 1915. The silent movies saw the emergence of the comedic genre of Charlie Chaplin in 1913–1916. During the 1920s and 1930s, the film industry came of age, and the 1930s and 1940s gave birth to major studios. A rating system of the audience followed in the 1990s.

Some authors trace the origins of advertising to 3000 B.C. Five thousand years ago, ads consisted of carvings. In 1704 the *Boston Newsletter* became the first American paper to carry advertisements, and in the early nineteenth century, the invention of photography introduced a different form of advertisement.

The American Association of Advertising Agencies (AAAA) was formed in 1917. A decade of tremendous growth for advertising occurred in the 1950s, and by 1960, advertising was a $12 billion enterprise. Public relations began during World War II. In the 1990s, some 1,600 public relations firms existed.

The Public Relations Society of America (PRSA) has done much to improve this industry.

New technology is continuing to transform audiences. Technology, which has been revolutionizing American society since the beginning of the nineteenth century, has seen a marriage of print and broadcasting. In four decades, Americans have witnessed:

1. Since the 1950s, the coming of CATV;
2. Since the 1960s, the arrival of communications satellites;
3. Since the 1970s, the development of viewdata, compact disc (CD), videodisc, laser disc, camcorder, low-power TV (LPTV), teletext, and videotex; and
4. Other developments including data banks, CD-ROM (compact disc read-only memory), and fiber optics.

Pundits can look for the following: First, there will continue to be technological changes that will alter the face of industries and their audiences. Second, the media will have the effect of reaching its audiences with more diversified information at the touch of a button or the turn of a knob. Third, according to trends, audiences can expect a multiplicity of media sources, although conglomerates may always risk shrinking the marketplace. And finally, audiences will continue to become more and more selective in what they choose to view or read. Most likely, they will do so at a price—for example, through pay-per-view channels. At this juncture, Americans will be witnessing an advance form of the "global village," since worldwide information will be accessed routinely, heavily, and with amazing speed.

Part I

THE INDUSTRY

1

ADVERTISING

Kevin L. Keenan

As the major revenue source for the mass media in the United States, advertising plays an important role in most areas of commerce and society. Consumers rely on advertising for information about products and services and increasingly as input in making decisions about political elections and issues outside of the traditional marketing framework. Interest groups and government regulators express serious concern about the content and effects of advertisements.

The advertising industry is complex and requires expertise and endless hours and billions of dollars to plan, develop, and place messages. Newspapers, magazines, and radio and TV stations compete with each other and with outdoor advertising (billboards), direct mail, and other media forms in trying to attract advertisers. Volumes of literature exist on different aspects of advertising practice and theory. Professional associations, trade journals, and lengthy undergraduate and graduate university programs devote themselves to advertising specializations today.

This chapter provides an overview of the advertising industry, its history, present-day arrangements, and role in the future. This survey describes the responsibilities of the distinct functional areas of advertising and the relationship of advertising to other segments of the media and to different audiences. The bibliography ("For Further Reading"—see the end of the chapter) suggests sources for further reading and of interest to those considering a career in advertising.

HISTORY

Some writers trace the origins of advertising to archeological findings and events as far back as 3000 B.C. Others point out that modern advertising, "calling something to the attention of the public, especially by paid announcements," has developed just in the last one hundred years. Clearly, systems for communicating with customers and audiences since the earliest marketplaces and many early techniques have contributed to the evolution of today's practices.

Signs carved in stone for ancient Greek and Roman merchants 5,000 years ago were simple graphic ads with no words or copy. The forerunner of modern-day billboards informed the mostly illiterate community about a business, its purpose, and its location. During the Middle Ages, a sign in front of the local cobbler might show a boot or shoe; a sign used to indicate the dairy might picture a cow. In time, merchants customized symbols so that their signs were distinct from their competitors'—perhaps the first instance of the now-common use of trademarks and logos in advertising.

Another practice from the same period involved the use of street criers to promote goods and services, much like barkers soliciting business today outside restaurants and businesses or employees offering free samples in supermarkets. Occasionally, the crier might shout his message in rhyme or was accompanied by a musician, giving rise to the first advertising jingles. "Sandwich men" with signs draped over their shoulders, with one in front and one behind, developed also as a method of delivering advertisements during this period as they strolled a town's streets, spreading information and extolling a merchant's offerings.

With the invention of movable type and printing in the midfifteenth century, advertising went in new directions. As literacy rates increased, printed handbills became popular, and signs began to include copy as well as visuals. By the early seventeenth century, the first examples of newspaper advertising appeared in England, and in 1704 the *Boston Newsletter* was the first American paper to carry advertisements.

These initial newspaper ads were quite primitive by today's standards. The format was simply column after column of straight black and white text without illustrations or headlines. They were informative, rather than persuasive, promoting books, tobacco, some household products, and retail businesses. There was much classified advertising, including auction listings, employers seeking servants, and personal announcements.

Benjamin Franklin is often regarded as the father of American advertising. As publisher of the *Pennsylvania Gazette,* he was responsible for many innovations in the mideighteenth century, making regular use of artwork and white space in designing advertisements and setting headlines in type larger than the rest of the ad. He also handled advertising sales for what became the largest circulation newspaper of its time.

Early in the nineteenth century, the invention of photography introduced a different form of illustration to the design and layout of advertisements. Newspaper advertising evolved further, with increasing attention to creativity and persuasive appeals. The rise of the penny press during this period resulted in papers with much larger audiences. The first magazines in the United States represented another new outlet for advertisers to consider, although the use of magazines as a major advertising channel didn't occur until the last half of the century.

In 1841, Volney Palmer began what is generally recognized as the very first advertising agency, though others that soon entered the business were nothing like the full-service advertising specialists who write, produce, and place advertisements today. Instead, they were brokers who bought quantities of newspaper advertising space and sold it to advertisers in smaller units, earning a commission paid by the paper. Ad agencies took on greater responsibility and developed various areas of expertise, while the Industrial Revolution changed the structure of society and of the advertising industry in important ways. Some of the most successful ad agencies of the twentieth century trace their origins back to the days of space brokers, and the main system of advertising agency compensation is still a commission paid by the media.

Since the beginning of the twentieth century, advertising practices have undergone significant changes. Growth in population and consumer affluence, improvements in production and transportation technologies, and shifts from a rural/agricultural economy to an urban/industrial one contributed to an environment establishing advertising as a crucial element of business and culture in the second half of the nineteenth century. Brand-name products grew in importance and in distribution nationally in large part due to advertising. Magazines became the first truly national advertising medium, their pages often filled with ads describing the miraculous benefits of patent medicine potions so popular during this era. Mail-order catalogs and newspaper advertising flourished as total spending on advertising more than tripled between 1850 and 1900.

In the 1870s the N. W. Ayer advertising agency was the first to expand beyond the traditional agency role of space brokerage by offering clients assistance with the planning and creation of entire advertising campaigns. The full-service agency became established and respected as central in the operations of the advertising industry. The structure and functions of contemporary advertising were mostly in place at the end of the nineteenth century. Relationships between advertisers, agencies, and the media existed in the same basic arrangement that is common today. The role of advertising as an information and marketing device was clearly established.

The advertising industry prospered during the early part of the twentieth century. The boom climate that characterized general economic conditions in the United States was evident as advertising became further entrenched as a primary method of communicating with consumers and as an accepted element of media content. In 1917 the founding of the American Association of Advertising Agencies (AAAA) lent stability and recognition to the business as the major agency trade group, a status it still holds today.

The Roaring Twenties included the introduction and growth of radio as a very popular source of entertainment. While some questioned whether radio should even carry advertisements in its earliest days, by the end of the decade, it had become a major advertising medium, and whole new approaches to advertising were developed to take advantage of the unique characteristics that radio offered.

When the depression began in 1929, the growth of advertising came to an abrupt halt. Advertising was a common scapegoat. Advertising spending, which had reached $3.4 billion in 1929, was less than half that amount by 1933. The rise of consumerism and accusations that many advertisements were exploitative and deceptive led to increased government and industry regulation. The depression also changed certain advertising practices. Copy concentrated on the hard sell—on appeals to thrift—and emphasized explicit, straightforward reasons for buying. Ads also began to include mention of contests, special deals, and various forms of promotion. Research became important when advertisers insisted on ways to measure the effectiveness of spending limited ad dollars.

Advertising underwent a series of recovery stages through the last part of the 1930s; only in the late 1940s did total spending on advertising rise to predepression levels.

During World War II, patriotic themes became major copy for all advertisers. The Advertising War Council, made up of representatives of advertising agencies, their clients, and the media, donated time and services in creating and running campaigns with ads to sell bonds, to build military enlistment, and to assist in the war effort. Renamed simply the Advertising Council after the war, the same industry group continues to provide volunteer advertising services in the form of public service messages today.

With the invention of television and a healthy postwar economy, the 1950s signaled a period of tremendous growth for advertising. Special TV opportunities led to big spending in the new medium and to a rethinking and repositioning of the established advertising media. During the decade, the agency business also increased in size and importance. Many agencies added public relations, marketing research, and customized assistance with promotion and communication strategies in expanding the range of services and expertise provided to clients.

By 1960, advertising was a $12 billion enterprise, and the decade has often been characterized as the most creative period in the advertising business. Comfortable with the range of options offered by television and a general philosophy that stressed originality and imagination, advertising from this era used humor and a soft-sell approach to produce messages and campaigns that remain memorable three decades later. During the 1960s, Ronald McDonald, the Marlboro Man, Charlie the Tuna, and Morris the Cat became part of American culture.

The 1970s represented a return to hard-sell copy and increased attention to how advertising adds to a company's bottom line. Budget considerations led to advertisements that used straightforward appeals and fewer of the subtleties that marked the previous decade. The seventies also were the beginning of a trend that has continued into the 1990s in the agency end of the ad business. Through these years, mergers and acquisitions produced huge agency conglomerates that accounted for more and more of total advertising spending. As of 1992, the WPP Group has become the largest conglomerate with international billings of over $16 billion per year.

Advertising now is firmly established as a crucial component of our business and communication systems and is a pervasive element of life in the United States. Changes in consumer life-styles, social trends, media technology, and reactions of government and the trade will continue to affect advertising processes and uses.

ORGANIZATION, SIZE, AND SCOPE

It is difficult to provide any single, concise description of the modern advertising business. Unlike most other industries, advertising involves people and operations that not only are diverse but in many cases represent extremes and opposites in terms of their backgrounds, skills, and purposes. In one sense, advertising is a management-oriented profession guided by discipline and organized decision making. In another, it is an art form without boundaries or formality. Advertising products often consist of amorphous ideas and images, and yet advertising entails precise quantification in budgetary and evaluative decision making.

To show how the advertising industry is set up and how it operates, it is useful to identify the major parties involved in an ad campaign or project. Most commonly, the advertising business consists of the advertisers, the advertising agencies retained as experts to handle an advertiser's account, and various suppliers whose materials and services are used in conducting a campaign. By far, the largest such suppliers are the mass media whose time and space are available for carrying advertising messages to their intended audiences.

The structure is often quite flexible, and there are many variations in function. There are exceptions and overlaps whereby an advertiser may perform many of the tasks usually assigned to an agency, media may play a role considered that of the advertiser or agency, the agency may take on work beyond its generally accepted parameters, or advertising may be done by complete outsiders. This same flexibility occurs when advertising professionals are employed by the client (advertiser), agency, or the supplier at different points in their careers and is common.

Almost every company or organization advertises to some extent. Product manufacturers and retailers have been big users of advertising for some time. Today's advertisers include services of all types—hospitals, political parties, the military, charities, and literally every cause and seller with an appeal or message it wants to communicate to the public. Advertisers range in size from the smallest corner store or local business to huge multinational corporations. In 1992, the Procter & Gamble Company was the single largest advertiser in the United States, spending $2.15 billion on advertising. Philip Morris Companies were a close second, with $2.05 billion spent advertising their tobacco, beer, and food brands.

With smaller, local advertisers, budgets are usually limited, and agencies are not always involved. Advertising decisions and operations are handled internally. Local or regional retail chains often use an in-house department to plan and operate their advertising programs. Or the advertising work may be done by someone with responsibility for sales, in-store displays, and other promotion areas as well as advertising. In the smallest businesses, the advertising job is commonly handled by the store manager or proprietor.

Local advertisers sometimes make use of freelance advertising specialists (artists, writers, or production people) to work on some aspect of an ad or campaign. Assistance is often available through the media and through the manufacturers whose products a local store might carry. Media sales representatives often help to design or write an advertisement and give advice about strategy when businesses lack experience and the resources to employ agency or freelance specialists.

On occasion, product manufacturers provide artwork or funding to cover a portion of local retailer advertising costs through cooperative (co-op) advertising. In exchange the retailer features the manufacturer's item in retailer-placed advertisements. Co-op arrangements improve manufacturer relations with their dealers, inform consumers of locations where the product is available, and run manufacturer advertisements at local rates, which, in many cases, are much less than charges for national advertisers.

With larger advertisers—most consumer goods firms, automobiles, grocery products, and the fast-food industry—the structure and duties of the advertising department vary in relation to whether an outside agency is used and to the division of responsibilities between advertiser and agency. In rare cases where no agency is involved, an elaborate in-house organization is likely to include all the functional areas of advertising more commonly associated with the agency end of the business. Usually when a full-service agency is used, the client's advertising department will be streamlined so that an advertising manager and some assistants serve as important contacts but leave the actual work of creating and placing advertisements to the agency. In both situations, advertising is generally considered a marketing function under a marketing director or vice-president in the organization.

On the agency side of the business, jobs tend to be arranged according to a specific area of advertising work. Some small advertising agencies use a "jack-of-all-trades" approach, with one person handling every aspect of an account; more commonly, agencies are structured into separate account management, creative services, research, and media departments.

The account management department serves as the primary contact between an agency and its advertiser clients. Account executives work with advertisers to set goals and to develop the overall strategy guiding an advertising campaign. They oversee the hands-on jobs of other departments in servicing an account and are responsible for making presentations and securing approval of concepts and finished advertisements from the client. In addition, account people often solicit new business opportunities for the agency. Those in account management are often referred to as "the suits," a reference to their role as an agency's business representatives who usually dress the part.

The creative services department of an advertising agency develops and produces ads. Working together closely under the supervision of a creative director are copywriters, largely responsible for the copy of an ad, and art directors, who are visual experts.

In print advertising, most departments include production artists to prepare the finished version of an advertisement, following the layout and instructions of the account's art director and copywriter. For television and radio ads, an agency may have broadcast producers on its staff or may contract with outside production houses. The scheduling and routing of ads through the different stages and areas of a creative services department is usually the job of the agency's traffic manager.

An agency's research department provides the data used in planning a campaign and for measuring the effectiveness of proposed creative themes or completed ads. Advertising research projects include consumer surveys, focus group discussions, market tests, analyses of secondary information, and anything else needed to help the client or account team with decision making. Large agencies may conduct full research studies on their own, but in many situations, the research department calls on independent suppliers and syndicated sources for much of the labor and resources required.

The media department of an ad agency decides where advertisements should run and negotiates and purchases advertising time or space in the mass media. In some agencies, these are distinct jobs with media planners evaluating different media vehicles (TV programs, magazines, newspapers, etc.) and media buyers handling negotiation and purchase. The largest portion of an advertiser's budget is usually spent on media, with careful attention to cost efficiency in reaching the desired audience and buyers attuned to availabilities and bargains in the media marketplace. Some advertising professionals view the media department as a stepping stone into account management, whereas others treat media work as a rewarding career of its own.

The relationship of advertising agencies to their clients is a very close one, because advertisers must share intimate details of their business, customers, and areas of operation that are highly secret and proprietary. In turn, agencies must respect the confidentiality of their dealings with a client, mindful that final approval of all elements of a campaign rests with the client.

In selecting an agency to handle their accounts, advertisers look for specific areas of expertise and experience and an agency not working on other accounts in the same product category or industry in order to avoid potential conflicts and ensure that full effort within a category is devoted to a single advertiser. The recent trend of advertising agency mergers has led to problems in terms of account conflicts.

Advertising agency compensation comes in several different forms. The commission system remains the major source of agency revenue; commission income is based on media allowing agencies a discount (usually 15 percent) off their established advertising rates. Alternative compensation arrangements include fee systems whereby an agency bills clients on an hourly or project basis, markups of the costs and materials used on an account, or some combination of these methods.

To this point, the discussion of advertising agencies and their organization and functions has involved full-service agencies, those that handle all the advertising needs of a client. In recent years a few advertisers have adopted an "à la carte" approach, using different agencies for different services. This has led to some agencies establishing themselves as specialists in one or more of the departmental areas covered above and to some separate organizations only providing assistance in a single advertising area. The latter are "creative boutiques" whose forte is copy and design and "media-buying services."

Advertising agency headquarters are located throughout all fifty states of the country because many advertisers choose to work with an agency that is in their own state or market. However, New York City has long been the center of the advertising business, and it remains so today. In addition to offices of the largest agencies in the world, New York is home to several advertising-related trade associations and most of the major media organizations.

Mass media is the third principal party in the advertising process and in the structure of the overall industry, and mass media is where the effort and spending of advertisers and agencies culminate. Each medium has its own unique characteristics. Large-scale campaigns usually involve a mix of media, but occasionally an entire advertising budget is spent in a single medium. In terms of total advertising revenue, newspapers are the largest medium in the United States, followed by broadcast television, magazines, radio, and out-of-home media, such as billboards and transit vehicles. Some newer media are becoming increasingly important, including cable television, electronic news services, point-of-purchase devices, and a variety of direct-response mechanisms.

Both structurally and functionally, the position of advertising within media organizations is one that emphasizes sales. The primary role of the advertising department within a newspaper, magazine, radio station, TV network, or other media outlet is to sell advertising to advertisers and agencies.

In most cases a distinction is made between local and national accounts, with separate departments and "sales reps" responsible for each type of advertiser. Network television and some magazines are exceptions to this arrangement in that they are strictly national media and thus are not used by local advertisers. In the case of newspapers, classified advertising is usually a third category, with its own operation and sales force.

Whereas broadcast stations, newspapers, and media with a local presence will have their own sales staff for dealing with local advertisers, national accounts are often handled by outside "media representative" organizations. These consist of individuals who serve as sales agents for many papers or stations from different geographic markets. Most national media representatives are located in New York, Chicago, and metropolitan areas where the largest agencies and clients are found. The rationales for using independent media representatives include the knowledge and expertise they offer and the fact that their cost is shared by several noncompeting stations or papers.

In addition to their critical position as message carriers for others, the media are themselves advertisers. Media organizations make use of their own resources and often buy time or space in other media to run ads for the purpose of building their audience size and attracting advertising business. As with other advertisers, the media may use an agency or handle advertising work on their own. When done internally, advertising is usually the job of a "promotions department," separate from the advertising department whose responsibilities and expertise are more in the area of media sales.

Beyond the advertisers, advertising agencies, and media that make up the core of the industry, other people and businesses contribute to advertising in peripheral ways. Printing companies, talent agents, mailing list specialists, outdoor plants, and those who directly or indirectly supply services and materials used in planning and producing advertisements are all part of the advertising community. Viewed as a trade or a profession, as an art or a science, as an irritant or a valuable information source, advertising is a multifaceted industry with a structure that is extensive in both breadth and depth.

ISSUES

Questions have long been raised about the value and contribution of advertising to the American market system and to society. As advertising has become an established institution, controversies involving certain types of advertisements and different practices and roles of the industry have grown. The most common criticism suggests that advertising causes certain economic and social problems. Although detractors and defenders of advertising present arguments damning or praising it, and academics employ multiple theories and research methods in examining the social and economic implications of advertising, few decisive conclusions have been reached.

Some concerns center broadly on the relationships of advertising to competition, monopolistic practices, and market structure. Others involve such specifics as the influence of advertising on prices or consumer purchasing behavior. The interest in macro- and microeconomic issues is another indication of the field's far-reaching status and importance in contemporary America.

A basic economic consideration is market concentration and whether advertising promotes or inhibits competitive conditions. Those who feel advertising leads to highly concentrated markets dominated by one or a few brands say that smaller brands are at a disadvantage, unable to afford the advertising expenditures necessary to compete with large advertisers. In the case of new brands, some see advertising as a "barrier to entry," which increases the costs to introduce a product and discourages new competitors. Supporters of advertising counter that through advertisements new or smaller brands can most efficiently make themselves known to consumers and argue that advertising actually advances competition and reduces market concentration.

Opinions and evidence are divided on the question of whether advertising raises or lowers prices. Those who claim it increases prices point out that advertising is a cost that must be covered eventually. They see advertisers passing this cost along to their customers in the form of higher prices. Others point out that advertising lowers prices by stimulating price competition and through economies of scale. The economies-of-scale argument is based on the notion that certain production and distribution costs remain constant regardless of the quantity of sales, and by increasing demand for a product, advertising reduces the cost per unit and savings are reflected in lower prices.

Concerns about advertising's social roles and effects cover a gamut of topics and viewpoints. Some critics see only negative ramifications and place some or all of the blame for assorted societal troubles on advertising. Others worry about social issues related to a specific audience or the content of specific advertisements. Some are critical of advertising as an institution for promoting materialism and unrealistic portrayals of social life. Others are more narrow in questioning the ads or campaigns of individual advertisers and product categories.

One area of particular concern and general agreement involves deception in advertising. Almost everyone agrees that including blatant lies in an advertisement or intentionally deceiving an audience is wrong, but there is disagreement in defining what constitutes deception. Some critics feel that any deviation from verifiable facts is misleading. Others allow that a certain amount of "puffery" or overstatement of product qualities is appropriate. Children seem especially susceptible to deceptive advertising and other questionable practices and deserve special protections. Recently criticism has risen about cigarette and liquor advertising targeted at minority audiences. Those who single out certain populations as particularly vulnerable believe that they may be less experienced or unfairly dealt with as message receivers and as consumers.

Advertising has also been accused of creating or reinforcing stereotypes of different groups and settings. Concerns range from charges that advertisements depict women and blacks in unrealistic and unflattering situations to the feeling that Hispanics, handicapped people, the elderly, and nontraditional families are underrepresented in ads. Some problems attributed to advertising stereotypes include eating disorders among those who perceive advertising models as the ideal body type, negative self-images or insecurity as a result of comparisons with advertising norms, and social prejudices of several types caused by continued exposure to advertising characterizations.

Underlying many of these issues is the question whether advertising reflects reality and, if not, whether it should do so. Several studies have shown differences in actual population characteristics and the demographic or economic worlds portrayed in advertisements. The possible harm of these discrepancies is a topic of debate and interpretation. Some are disturbed by the possibility that ads will serve to shape audience perceptions and behaviors. Others contend that the influence of advertising is not so great because it is recognized as an attempt to persuade, and advertising content reflecting people or conditions somewhat unlike the real world provides aspirational points of reference no different than other forms of salesmanship.

Further criticisms of advertising focus on specific questions about *what* is advertised, *how* it is advertised, or *where* it is advertised. For example, in recent years, alcohol, condoms, certain personal care items, and "adult" businesses have all received attention as inappropriate advertisers in the opinions of some. Others have no problems with the advertising of such products and services per se but are disturbed by what they see as offensive or suggestive features of particular ads. Such concerns include nudity and eroticism in advertisements, the linking of unhealthy products with healthy settings, and insufficient attention to warnings and disclaimers.

Still other critics find nothing wrong with the advertisers or the content of advertising but take issue with scheduling, placement, or delivery. In television, some feel that ads that would be perfectly acceptable later in the evening should not be run during prime time or that messages for certain kinds of products should not air on children's programming or during dinner hours. Others consider outdoor advertising a form of visual pollution or believe that publicly funded facilities such as stadiums and school classrooms should be free of all advertising. Direct-mail and print advertising have been criticized by environmentalists for wasting natural resources and contributing to landfill problems. Advertising is like many other areas of modern existence in that it is seen in different ways by different people with different interests and concerns. Whereas some are satisfied with current advertising methods and systems, others are dissatisfied and endorse major reforms or the abolishment of certain practices. Feelings about advertising range from those who see it as a contributing and useful element of business and society to the opinion that it is a device detrimental to general social and economic well-being.

RESPONSIBILITY AND REGULATION

In response to criticism and concern and as a means to maintain fairness and integrity, various advertising guidelines and regulations have been offered by sources within the industry, by concerned parties from outside, and by government bodies.

Most advertisers recognize that it is in their own best interest to consider the feelings and wishes of their customers in all facets of the business process. Accordingly, many companies have policies regarding the content and placement of their advertising. For instance, some advertisers insist that wedding rings be visible in ads alluding to romance or that magazines containing nudity not be included in their plans. Others do not buy time on television programs that they find distasteful or that might offend their customers. While such practices are voluntary and vary from advertiser to advertiser, they represent a sense of responsibility and self-regulation. Generally, advertisers take special care in setting and meeting standards of their own.

The media also determine the propriety and acceptability of advertising. They have the right to reject any advertisement they deem unsuitable, and through a process known as *clearance,* television networks, magazines, newspapers, and other media screen ads before they are run. If an ad is untruthful, offensive, or otherwise short of their standards, the advertiser will be asked to modify it or be informed that it will be dropped. In addition to considering the content of individual ads, sometimes networks, stations, or publications make it a rule not to accept certain types of advertisements, such as those for tobacco products, gambling services, or X-rated movies.

Some advertising agencies also have policies regarding the kinds of work that they will do and the types of clients that they will accept. It is not uncommon for an agency to decline the opportunity to pitch an account for a product that it does not believe in or to resign an account over matters of principle. In other cases, agencies will work for advertisers or causes that they especially endorse on a pro bono basis. An ad agency is guided by its conscience in much the same way that individuals and other organizations are.

Beyond the efforts of individual advertisers, media, and agencies, several trade associations include advertising codes and guidance. Groups such as the United States Brewers Association, the American Medical Association, and the Toy Manufacturers of America provide instructions and standards about advertising that their members are expected to follow. Within the advertising industry, the Association of National Advertisers (ANA), the American Advertising Federation (AAF), and the American Association of Advertising Agencies (AAAA) are the major trade groups, and each is active in establishing and monitoring adherence to their own guidelines and codes of conduct.

The most rigorous example of self-regulation in advertising is a system developed through the network of Better Business Bureaus in the United States along with the ANA, the AAF, and the AAAA. Begun in 1971, the National Advertising Review Council (NARC) is a two-tiered mechanism for dealing with false and improper advertising. The first level of this system is the National Advertising Division (NAD) of the Council of Better Business Bureaus. The NAD consists of a full-time staff whose job it is to investigate complaints registered by consumers, competitors, and local Better Business Bureaus and to attend to advertising practices. When the NAD finds merit in a complaint, the offending advertiser will be asked to voluntarily modify or stop running the advertisement. If the advertiser refuses to comply, the case will be sent to the second tier of the NARC setup, the National Advertising Review Board (NARB). The NARB, made up of representatives from advertisers, agencies, and the general public, will hear the complaint and the accused advertiser's position and make its own recommendation that the ad be allowed to continue or that it be changed or stopped. In the rare event that an advertiser refuses to cooperate with NARB findings, the case is likely to be referred to the appropriate government agency or office.

Government regulation of advertising exists at the local, state, and federal levels. Jurisdictions and powers differ according to the perceived importance of advertising problems and general philosophies about regulation and government intervention. Locally, some communities may not involve themselves in regulating advertising, but others may have complete bans on billboards or other forms of advertising. State and federal regulation varies with different administrations; some are quite strict, and others take the position that less regulation is better.

The majority of those in the advertising industry acknowledge the need for some form of government regulation and are supportive and cooperative. Disagreement or friction surfaces in determining what amount of government regulation is necessary and at what levels it is most beneficial. For instance, many advertisers worry that too much regulation at the state level will lead to fifty different and possibly contradictory sets of rules that would make national advertising campaigns nearly impossible. Another concern regarding state regulation is the taxing of advertising services, a revenue device proposed in several state legislatures since the late 1980s.

At the federal level, regulation covers many similar efforts by industry regulatory structures, but with an added note of authority and without the stigma of self-interest that some associate with internal regulation. Responsibilities for advertising regulation are divided among several federal agencies, with occasionally overlapping or conflicting policies, procedures, and duties.

The U.S. Patent Office oversees the use of protected trademarks, and the Library of Congress handles the copyrighting of advertisements. The U.S. Postal Service has regulations regarding what may be advertised through the mail, and the Treasury Department's Bureau of Alcohol, Tobacco, and Firearms deals with the advertising of guns, cigarettes, and alcoholic beverages. The Food and Drug Administration establishes and enforces rules on the labeling and advertising of products under its jurisdiction.

Probably the most important federal regulator of advertising is the Federal Trade Commission (FTC). Established in 1914 to guard businesses from unfair practices of competitors, the FTC powers were extended to include advertising with the Wheeler-Lea amendments of 1938. The primary area of FTC concern is deception in advertising. Over the years the FTC has developed various definitions and policies regarding deceptive advertising and shifted focus from advertisements with the *"capacity* to mislead" to those considered *"likely* to mislead." The FTC has paid particular attention to testimonials, comparative ads, product demonstrations, and the use of words such as *free, light, new,* and *fresh.*

FTC investigators typically allow advertisers to present their cases and substantiate questionable claims. If the FTC decides that an advertisement is deceptive, it may first seek a "consent order" whereby the advertiser agrees to discontinue the advertising but does not necessarily admit to any wrongdoing or issue a court "cease-and-desist order" requiring that the practice in question be stopped. Orders may include conditions that must be met or may call for punitive action. The FTC has the authority to require that future ads contain "affirmative disclosure" in the form of disclaimers or explanations or to make an advertiser pay for "corrective advertising."

Industry and government regulations both treat children's advertising as a special category. The NARC self-regulatory structure includes a separate division, the Children's Advertising Unit, charged with developing standards for such ads, and the FTC has given detailed attention to the advertising of cereals and other products aimed at children.

FUTURE OUTLOOK

Certain trends and changes in business practices, in communication technologies, and in social priorities and life-styles provide suggestions about the future of the advertising industry.

Developments in marketing indicate that traditional media advertising may play a slightly diminished role for some companies in coming years. For reasons of cost, efficiency, and effectiveness, many advertisers place more emphasis on forms of promotion such as sweepstakes, rebates, in-store messages, and sampling programs. Although these activities usually complement other advertising programs, they are often funded from budgets that might have been devoted entirely to media spending in the past.

As more and more women work outside the home, catalogs and other forms of direct marketing will become more important. Home shopping channels may be a convenient way for busy households to save time and a significant outlet for advertisers. Daytime soap operas are no longer the best way to reach female consumers. New media programs will be designed with working women in mind.

Technologies like the videocassette recorder (VCR) have presented advertisers with both opportunities and difficulties in the past and will certainly offer challenges in the times ahead. While the ability to record television material for playback at a later time has resulted in advertisements reaching a larger audience, the VCR phenomenon of fast-forwarding through commercials lessens an ad's effectiveness substantially. A similar problem involves the use of remote control units and "zapping" from station to station to avoid advertising while watching television. Advertising professionals must address these and similar areas as consumer and media technologies grow more sophisticated.

Cable television is an accepted advertising medium and offers interesting opportunities for the future. Many cable systems plan to develop interactive capabilities so that viewers can select information and advertising options and order merchandise right over their television sets. Pay-per-view events are a new phenomenon that may provide especially attentive audiences when used for advertising purposes.

Advances and changes in other media also affect advertising. Newspapers have been concerned with declining readership and promise improved color quality, specialized sections, and zoned editions as incentives to attract advertisers in the future. Electronic newspapers, videotex, and teletext transmitted via home computer have been tested in some markets and may be a direction the medium takes. Magazines may enable advertisers to communicate with narrower and narrower audiences as they become increasingly specialized. In some parts of the country, outdoor advertising is assuming new formats, including signs that rotate to provide advertising space for several different advertisers on a single billboard.

Examples of new advertising media include video shopping carts, "in-flight radio" spots on airplanes, and "bathroom billboards." There has even been talk of postage stamps and dollar bills carrying advertising someday.

Numerous social and demographic changes influence advertising as well. The increasing concern about the environment is likely to result in advertising copy that stresses the environmental qualities of an advertiser's product or corporate behavior. It may also cause trouble for media and advertisers perceived to contribute to pollution. Increased use of public transportation systems may reduce the audiences of in-car radio and outdoor advertising but be a boon for poster advertising in train and bus stations and advertisements on the inside or outside of subway cars and buses.

Advertisers interested in reaching the large percentage of the population that is Spanish speaking will need to develop new strategies. There will probably be more Spanish-language newspapers, television stations, and magazines in the future, and advertising agencies that specialize in the Hispanic market will be needed.

Clearly, advertising will undergo interesting and important changes in the years to come. As an occupation or a field of study, advertising is demanding, dynamic, and exciting. Involvement of individuals with so many different perspectives and talents, government, the mass media, and organizations internal and external to the industry makes advertising a unique American business and cultural institution.

KEY PERIODICALS

Advertising Age is a weekly publication that calls itself the "International Newspaper of Marketing." It covers all aspects of advertising and is recognized as the leading trade journal in the field. *Editorial Offices:* 740 Rush Street, Chicago, IL 60611–2590; *Subscription Information:* 965 E. Jefferson, Detroit, MI 48207–3185.

Adweek is another useful weekly trade publication. In addition to national advertising news, *Adweek* includes more local coverage in six regional editions. *Editorial Offices:* 49 East 21st Street, New York, NY 10010; *Subscription Information:* Route 22—Robin Hill Road, Patterson, NY 12563.

American Advertising is a quarterly publication put out by the American Advertising Federation for its members. It includes industry profiles, legislative issues, and other topics of interest to those in the advertising business. 1400 K Street, NW, Suite 1000, Washington, DC 20005.

The *Journal of Advertising* is a quarterly research journal published by the American Academy of Advertising, a group of academic and industry representatives interested in advertising education, theory, and research. It reports studies related to various aspects of advertising. *Editorial Offices:* Department of Marketing, University of Houston, Houston, TX 77204–6283; *Subscription Information:* CtC Press, P. O. Box 1826, Clemson, SC 29633–1826.

FOR FURTHER READING

Berman, Ronald. (1981). *Advertising and social change.* Beverly Hills, CA: Sage Publications.

Cohen, Dorothy. (1988). *Advertising.* Glenview, IL: Scott, Foresman.

Dunn, S. Watson, Barban, Arnold M., Krugman, Dean M., & Reid, Leonard N. (1993). *Advertising: Its role in modern marketing.* Chicago: Dryden Press.

Fox, Stephen. (1984). *The mirror makers.* New York: William Morrow.

Millman, Nancy. (1988). *Emperors of adland.* New York: Warner Books.

Norris, James D. (1990). *Advertising and the transformation of American society, 1865–1920.* Westport, CT: Greenwood Press.

Patti, Charles H., & Frazer, Charles F. (1988). *Advertising: A decision-making approach.* Chicago: Dryden Press.

Rotzoll, Kim B., Haefner, James E., & Sandage, Charles H. (1990). *Advertising in contemporary society.* Cincinnati, OH: South-Western.

Russell, J. Thomas, & Lane, W. Ronald. (1993). *Kleppner's advertising procedure.* Englewood Cliffs, NJ: Prentice-Hall.

Sandage, C. H., Fryburger, Vernon, & Rotzoll, Kim. (1989). *Advertising theory and practice.* New York: Longman.

Schudson, Michael. (1984). *Advertising, the uneasy persuasion.* New York: Basic Books.

Sissors, Jack, & Bumba, Lincoln. (1993). *Advertising media planning.* Lincolnwood, IL: NTC Publishing Group.

Wells, William, Burnett, John, & Moriarty, Sandra. (1989). *Advertising principles and practice.* Englewood Cliffs, NJ: Prentice-Hall.

2

BOOKS

Ronald J. Zboray

HISTORY

Books hold a unique place among other media in the development of the United States. The settlement of the country began in the wake of the Protestant Reformation that used the power of print to spread new religious and humanitarian ideas throughout Western Europe. Books carried news of the Enlightenment to the British colonies and popularized the Whig political ideology that shaped the course of the revolutionary and early national eras. Book distribution followed the trails of westward pioneers and assured a relative cultural homogeneity in the expanding nation. The high literacy rates in the middle of the nineteenth century and the easy availability of books—especially instructional aids and technical manuals—encouraged the rapid spread of industrial capitalism.

From the founding of the first press in Britain's North American colonies in Cambridge, Massachusetts, in 1639, the main production unit of publishing has been the "house." The word reveals the origin of publishing, literally in houses for printing, that emerged in the fifteenth century in Germany first and then throughout most of Europe. An artisan way of life characterized the printing houses. A master artisan owned most or all of the business, employing journeymen, usually young men on their way to starting their own houses, and apprentices, boys from seven to fourteen years old who served as trainees, and combining under one roof all the modern operations of book production and selling: editing, typesetting, printing, and in fewer shops over time, bookbinding, retail, and distribution.

By the early nineteenth century as the scale of book production increased dramatically, editorial activities split off into the separate business of publishing. The publisher handled and copyedited the manuscripts and made the financial arrangements for publishing and distributing them; the printer produced the printed sheets that composed the book. Although printers in some areas of the country continued in the traditional manner, by the early twentieth century, this new pattern of industrial organization could be found everywhere. The publisher decided what was published, in what form, and, usually, determined its marketing strategy.

While a few smaller houses worked on one title at a time, most large publishing firms worked simultaneously on several projects. The inventory of finished products constituted the house's "list."

Professional publishing began in early nineteenth-century America as a highly personalized business with few full-time professional positions. The publisher himself reviewed manuscripts, contracted writers, suggested the design of the book, arranged for printing and binding, devised advertising campaigns and other marketing techniques, and took responsibility for distribution. Most publishers even did their own elementary double-entry bookkeeping. A clerk or secretary might help out with these various tasks, but the "house" felt the hand of the publisher in every aspect of the business. A few family members (e.g., the Harper brothers in the early 1800s) or partners often shared managerial responsibility.

Toward the end of the nineteenth century, publishing houses increasingly divided tasks among several workers, as would-be authors besieged publishers with a flood of manuscripts that strained the ability of an individual house to screen them. The burgeoning common schools of the period opened a vast market for books, as did innovations in transportation. Publishers sent out more books and titles to booksellers and distributors, and the scale of their business operations increased correspondingly. Periodicals with mass circulations opened a complex maze of advertising opportunities. The number of booksellers scattered throughout the country exceeded the capability of the already burdened publisher to establish personal contact through correspondence. The adaption of the Adams steam press (c. 1836) for some types of publishing assured cheap, quickly printed large editions that required dozens of laborers and supervisors to watch them. Electrotyping and stereotyping created an extensive backlog of books that could be called into print at any time in response to the shifting market; before this time, each edition had its type recomposed, an arduous and expensive process. New marketing techniques, like the extensive use of canvassers and book agents in the field, sometimes placed the number of employees of the publisher in the thousands. Publishers experimented throughout the late nineteenth century with a division of work that became characteristic of the twentieth-century publishing industry, as described in the next section.

ORGANIZATION, SIZE, AND SCOPE

Labor within a publishing house is generally divided into five areas: (1) editorial, (2) art, (3) production, (4) marketing and advertising, and (5) management and financial.

Editing

Editorial tasks encompass the full range of manuscript handling and responsibility for the content of the text. Job titles and tasks within editing vary with the individual house. Generally, editorial assistants accumulate at the bottom of the job structure, followed by a scale of editors ranging in seniority from assistant, associate, editor, and senior editor through to executive or managing editor.

Editorial work begins with manuscript acquisition. Junior editors may screen unsolicited manuscripts or proposals, while those that arrive with special recommendation or through a literary agent may go to senior staff. Acquisitions editors may also seek out manuscripts from writers and work to suit the needs of the house. Academic or professional manuscripts are sometimes reviewed by paid outside experts who may make suggestions for improvements. In larger houses the editor sponsoring a particular manuscript may argue its case before senior staff members and those from other departments, such as marketing or design. Upon approval, the sponsoring editor offers the writer a contract (often one that promises royalties ranging from 6 percent to 10 percent) for publication.

The sponsoring editor's work continues after the writer signs with the house. At this stage, many editors may intervene, and in some houses, editors may act the role of a silent partner in literary creation, or they may leave most of the detailed work to the copyeditor.

Copyeditors (manuscript or line editors) closely examine a writer's text. They correct obvious problems of grammar, spelling, and typographical errors. They also deal with matters of style, word choice, paragraphing, consistency and accuracy of information, and in some cases, the way the writer presents the material.

Art

Usually, the production department designs the book as the work moves through the editing process. The sponsoring editor provides the designer (or in larger houses, the art department) with information about the book, its size, format, and intended market. The designers occasionally may read the manuscript to get their own ideas about the best physical presentation. Working within the art budget granted the book by the house, the designer determines the look of the book, the typefaces, how they will appear on the page, the size of pages, the type of paper used, and the cover. The designer presents ideas in the form of a sample "layout." It is the editorial staff's or production editor's task to merge the design specifications with the final corrected copy of the manuscript.

Production

Depending on the size and type of house, the production department either schedules the work of outside jobbers or coordinates and supervises an in-house department. The production department typesets the book from the marked manuscript. Today typesetters do not touch cold type but instead key in instructions on a typewriterlike keyboard. Sophisticated machines either photo-compose or generate the text digitally. The output of these machines resembles the finished typeset page, but on photosensitive paper, and with or without page formatting, depending on the complexity of the typesetting machinery. The production department next generates a first copy, called either a proof or a galley. An editorial staff member may read the output against the now-called "dead" copy of the corrected manuscript, and the house sends the proof to the writer for final approval.

The final, corrected proof forms the basis for printing, in most cases done by an outside jobber. The workers in the printing plant transfer a photographic image of the proof to a grain metal plate (or for most paperback production, a continuous plastic plate). The vast majority of modern printers use offset lithography in one form or another to produce the printed sheets. Either the department or a bindery cuts and binds the sheets into a finished book. The books are then stored, ready for dispatching by a shipping department or wholesaler.

Marketing and Advertising

Most publishers have marketing departments responsible for advertising, publicity, and sales. Depending on the house, this department may influence editorial and design decisions. But just as commonly, marketing personnel do not become involved until the first printing is completed; only then do they face the challenge of making sure the book sells to whatever audience by whatever means.

Marketing departments favor advertising and publicity to reach potential buyers. Printed advertisements, in the form of brochures or space ads in literary or professional periodicals, subtly shape readers' expectations of the book and its meaning.

The task of stimulating sales falls to staff whose specific tasks and titles vary among houses. These departments usually contain several levels of sales representatives and managers, who in one form or another try to market books directly to purchasers or to vendors. A publicity subdepartment (few small houses have these) may arrange for public appearances of authors, send out books for review, or try to generate media interest in other ways. The complex subdivision of advertising includes specializations such as advertising director, promotion manager, copy chief, art director, copy and design supervisors, copy writers and designers, ad space writers, and various types of assistants. The "copy" in the descriptions refers to the text of the advertising materials, while artists and designers create the visual context of the book that the marketing department wants to convey to readers. Advertising managers must coordinate word and image in their marketing campaigns.

Management and Financial

Because the personal style of most publishing houses held sway well into the twentieth century, separate managerial and financial departments developed slowly. Eventually, some staff members specialized in examining the long-run performance and objectives of the house with an eye to increasing scale and ever-maximized profits. This long view implied a concern not only for the bottom line but for efficiency and viability within selected markets. As larger houses have expanded and often merged with large communications corporations, management and financial departments have increased their independence from the other divisions of the house.

The overall trend in publishing has been toward ever-greater business concentration. However, a record number of small presses also cultivate their own special markets. With thousands existing in the early 1990s, they devote their efforts to topics ranging from vegetarianism to feminist science fiction. These presses represent the most contemporary expression of the rich history of racial, religious, ethnic, and political minority publishing in America.

Smaller houses usually follow one of three trajectories. First, they remain a small minority voice in the market. Second, they see their peculiar niche in the market co-opted by the larger house, and thus they are forced out of business. Or third, they merge with a larger firm that may gobble them whole or keep the name of their imprint and even their editorial autonomy while retaining distribution rights and profits. Because of the personal style of management of the smaller house, this last course prevails for many successful small presses.

Whether large of small, a house usually must define a publication specialty. The industry, with net annual receipts in the early 1990s of over $16 billion, encompasses five general categories of publications: (1) trade, (2) educational, (3) professional, (4) mass market paperbacks, and (5) mail-order and subscription reference.

Trade publishers are responsible for most of the books that stock the shelves of local consumer-oriented bookstores. Their products range form novels to cookbooks. With varied lists and high advertising budgets, they maintain the highest public profile, speculate more than any part of the business, and seek to find books that will sell broadly. However, trade publishers account for just under a quarter of net receipts in any given year (sales through book clubs might add another 7 or 8 percent to this total). Trade publishers often diversify their lists with sure-fire sellers, books destined to find a small but relatively certain market as well.

Most sales in the book trade come, as they have since the early nineteenth century, from educational books (elementary, secondary, and college, including academic titles). These make up about a third of net annual receipts. Although publishers in this area strive to get the biggest possible share of their markets, the greater market planning and controlled conditions of distribution (mass purchases by school boards and college bookstores) free them, relatively, from trade publishers' dependence on best-sellers.

The best-seller syndrome carries little weight in professional publishing, an area that accounts for about 16 percent of net receipts. These medical, business, technical, and scientific books address a limited audience willing to pay a fairly high price for information necessary to their fields.

Best-sellers, however, define the fourth major category of the industry, the mass market paperbacks (10 percent of net receipts) that can be found everywhere from drugstores to supermarkets. Usually books in this category have proved themselves already in hardcover, thus somewhat limiting the risk for publishers. But other titles, especially romance novels and some self-help books, make their appearance only in paperback.

A final category that combines mail-order publishing with subscription reference works accounts for most of the remainder of the annual net receipts (under 13 percent). The nature of publishing in this category produces tightly controlled advance and in-publication marketing studies that minimize potential losses.

Although some publishers specialize only in trade, educational, professional, mass market, or subscription and mail-order, others have divisions devoted to several or even all categories. Larger communications companies that have bought out other publishing houses often retain the specialized function of their acquisitions and build highly varied and diverse corporate structures. Some of these giants even maintain formerly competing divisions, though corporate managers eventually tend to remove such internal overlaps in the name of rationalization and efficiency.

OVERVIEW OF THE LITERATURE

Book publishing, perhaps because of its importance to American cultural development, attracts scholarly interest from many quarters. Professionals in library science, communications, journalism, education, religion, literature, and cultural and intellectual history all contribute to the field. The scholarship also benefits from work outside academe, from antiquarian book dealers to amateur bibliophiles, from practicing librarians to professionals in the book trade itself. The varied literature on book publishing may be broken down into historical and contemporary studies of varying sorts, although obviously with the passage of time, current observations become the primary sources that historians draw upon.

Historical Studies

Most early histories of American publishing described the accomplishments of individual firms but seldom analyzed the larger workings of the trade (Thomas, 1810; Oswald, 1937; Wroth, 1938). These works have relied on a long-standing tradition that equates printing with progress; they assume that as long as the books get published, only social good (and profits) will follow. A separate but related trend has grown out of the many studies of the first presses on America's several, evolving frontiers (McMurtrie, 1936). These presses, according to these authors, stand as inescapable signs of progress and cultural maturation. While these studies have left a solid legacy of detail upon which future historians can build, they dwell too much on origins and early progress at the expense of later significant developments.

Though under the influence of European bibliography, there had been increasingly sophisticated studies of the history of American publishing in the early years of the twentieth century, the field came of age only in 1937 with the publication in Germany of the magisterial *Das amerikanische Buchwesen* (Lehmann-Haupt, Graniss, & Wroth, 1937), translated for American audiences two years later as *The Book in America* (rev., 1951). In a work of scope and vision that retains its value as an introduction to the field, the authors set a high standard indeed for the history of publishing in the United States.

The 1940s and 1950s brought a new emphasis on popular literature in studies of the history of publishing. Frank Luther Mott's *Golden Multitudes* (1947) and James D. Hart's *The Popular Book: A History of America's Literary Taste* (1950) were written for a general audience but contained much of value to scholars. Frank L. Schick's *The Paperbound Book in America* (1958) drew on the time period's fascination with its "second paperback revolution" to explore the roots of affordable literature for the masses.

The late 1950s through the mid-1970s saw publishing take a keener, more analytical and academic turn. Much of this was the work of a handful of scholars representing several different disciplines such as literature, library science, history, and journalism (Charvat, 1959, 1968; Kaser, 1966; McLuhan, 1968; McMullen, 1966; Sutton, 1961; Tanselle, 1965; Tebbel, 1972, 1987; Tryon, 1947, 1963). In 1972, John Tebbel began publishing his landmark multivolume synthetic history of American book publishing, which remains the standard source for the topic.

Some writers of this generation continued to make contributions from outside the university. Charles A. Madison produced overviews of publishing and author-publisher relations (Madison, 1966, 1974). Madeleine B. Stern, began her series of contributions of short biographies of individual publishers (Stern, 1956, 1978).

Until the late 1970s and early 1980s, American historians of publishing had taken little notice of new trends in European publishing history, especially in Britain, Germany, and France. Ironically, it was an American scholar of early modern French intellectual history, Robert Darnton (1971, 1979), who helped bring these new currents to the attention of the public in the United States. In general, this European scholarship stressed the cultural significance of publishing and employed innovative quantitative and qualitative approaches.

Influenced by these currents, the history of publishing in America widened during the 1980s to include a variety of disciplinary perspectives and fields of interest. The Library of Congress, the American Antiquarian Society, and several other institutions sponsored programs and conferences of differing sorts in the history of the book. Several important studies appeared that consider the role of books and other printed materials in various aspects of American culture (Baym, 1984; Coultrap-McQuin, 1990; Davidson, 1986; Denning, 1987; Douglas, 1977; Hall, 1989; Kelley, 1984; Warner, 1990—to name but a few). None of these are histories of publishing per se, but they, in very different ways, draw upon and add to the scholarship of that field. A separate but related area of scholarly interest has been the history of reading (Brown, 1989; Davidson, 1986, 1989; Gilmore, 1989; R. A. Gross, 1987; Nord, 1986, 1988; Zboray, 1993).

Between the general interpretive studies of books in American culture, on the one hand, and the monographs on reading, on the other, however, can be found few efforts in the direction of revising the course set for the history of publishing by the previous generation of Charvat and Tebbel. And, also in keeping with that tradition (with the notable exception of Tebbel), the scholarship of the 1980s has focused almost exclusively on the period through the middle of the nineteenth century. Undoubtedly, as detailed studies accumulate on the history of publishing, scholars will augment, if not overturn, the work of the 1960s. And as historical models are developed to deal with the meaning of mass communications in the consumption-oriented society of the twentieth century, future historians of publishing will increasingly focus on recent topics.

Contemporary Analyses

Contemporary observations of book publishing date back at least to Isaiah Thomas's *The History of Printing in America* (1810); a few articles on the topic had appeared even earlier. Most of this sporadic commentary merely described the progress of the industry. This latter quality naturally characterizes the many reminiscences of participants in the book trade, although some of these, such as Samuel Goodrich's *Recollections of a Lifetime* (1855), contain analyses (see also Derby, 1884; Moore, 1886). Occasionally, publishing plays a role in general contemporary surveys of arts or industries (e.g., Dunlap, 1834; Freedley, 1856; and various federal and state census reports).

Trade papers devoted to publishing emerged in the 1820s and sometimes carried analyses of the contemporary publishing scene. The best of these were *Norton's Literary Advertiser* (1851–1855) and its successor, *American Publishers' Circular* (1855–1858). Eventually, Frederick Leypoldt founded *Publishers Weekly* (1872), which remained the predominant organ of the industry throughout the twentieth century. Other important trade papers include *The American Bookseller* (1876–1893), *Inland Printer* (1833–), and *American Bookmaker* (1885–). Related to these are the various trade directories and annuals—such as *Literary Marketplace* (1940–) and *International Literary Marketplace* (1965–) —that periodically emerged from the publishing industry.

Some of the most valuable sources on book publishing have been the "how-to" books, meant as introductions to the trade. Numerous guides to printing were published in the early nineteenth century, beginning with C. S. Van Winkle's *The Printer's Guide* (1818). Only in the second half of the nineteenth century did such books appear with specific reference to publishing as opposed to printing (Harrington, 1879; Putnam & Putnam, 1883). In the 1980s, the annual *Writer's Market*, style books such as *The Chicago Manual of Style*, and a number of self-help books performed a similar function (e.g., Fry, 1987).

The rise of modern sociology in the early twentieth century encouraged more analytic contemporary observations on book publishing (Yard, 1913; Leacock, 1914; Sinclair, 1927; Hungerford, 1931; Gill, 1940; Link & Hopf, 1946; Innis, 1949). Several published series of lectures on the contemporary trade added to this research (Bowker Company, 1943; Simmons College, 1954). A few significant books blended the sociological perspective with an instructional purpose (e.g., Graniss, 1967; G. Gross, 1961). By far, the most enduring of the sociological surveys of publishing was Coser, Kadushin, and Powell's *Books: The Culture and Commerce of Publishing* (1982). The sociology of book publishing has produced, in addition to these more general considerations, occasional commentary on two perennial issues: copyright (e.g., Bowker, 1912; Rogers, 1960) and censorship (e.g., Haney 1960; Kilpatrick, 1960).

In the future, studies of contemporary publishing will probably benefit more and more from the pioneering work of the industry's historians. Janice Radway, in particular, has effectively applied models derived from this scholarship to produce highly nuanced considerations of women's reading of romantic literature (1984) and the fiction offered by book clubs (1989).

ISSUES

The marketing of knowledge under capitalism (Coser, Kadushin, & Powell, 1982) leads to several perennial questions: Can ideas flow freely under a price system? Doesn't purchasing power dictate the creation and dissemination of the kind of information desired by those who have such power? Do groups with questionable tastes (e.g., users of violent pornography) have the right to produce materials considered by some communities injurious to the general public welfare? What if communities see potential damage to "the common good" in the printed expression of minority opinions such as those voiced by oppressed racial and ethnic groups? The issues these questions raise are becoming more complex with the increasing globalization of communications. For example, the death warrant Iran placed upon Salmon Rushdie in 1987 for his "heretical" *Satanic Verses* shows that even internationally recognized writers are not immune from outraging local, tradition-bound cultures; and the reluctance of publishers to produce the paperback version of the book demonstrates the chilling effect of such controversies on the freedom of the press.

Given the physical durability of books, the above questions are important historically. American publications and the importation of foreign books accumulate as part of our cultural legacy. The long story of censorship can be seen in this light as a struggle for cultural representation and for the nurturing of a diversity of viewpoints. Sometimes market forces have promoted this diversity, as in the case of the paperback revolution after World War II, which brought an unprecedented number of titles at very low prices to wide audiences. At other times the economic weight of the more homogeneous mass market has all but silenced diversity. In any case the nature of American democracy requires equal and representational access to media and never strays very far from public discourse about books.

In a capitalist democracy, the book publishing industry has the responsibility for ensuring the free flow of ideas and the diversity of opinion upon which the legitimation of the political system depends. The contradictions inherent in publishing that discourage the achievement of this goal are treated below.

EFFECTIVENESS

The effectiveness of the publishing industry in reaching its audience has traditionally been limited by overproduction. At first glance, an overabundance of books would seem to guarantee a wide variety of viewpoints on most readers' shelves. The point at which books begin to repay the cost of producing them seems low: from net sales of about 500 to 1,000 copies in the colonial era to more than a few thousand in the early 1990s. Because the United States has had near-universal white adult literacy since the midnineteenth century, the potential market of millions would seem to ensure that most books would break even. Indeed, the low cost of business entry and the low break-even point have encouraged a continuous stream of small presses throughout American history and ensured some measure of diversity.

The vast majority of books, about 80 percent, however, never find their market, and thus publishers fall short of recouping their production expenses. This remarkably high failure rate distinguishes publishing from just about every other form of business enterprise in modern America. The blame for this has been passed back and forth among writers, publishers, booksellers, other distributors, and readers since the beginnings of the industry. Although vigorous discounting, the sale of remaindered titles, and the maintenance of a backlist of older titles sometimes narrow the margin of loss, publishers still produce too many books that cannot be given away at any price. Owing to tax laws that disallow publishers from claiming depreciation on remaindered books, they have taken on a wholesale destruction of "failures" once these books have exhausted their limited market.

Publishers have resisted undertaking formal studies of the market for particular books, preferring to rely on instinct and savvy. Many publishers have viewed themselves as more than "mere" businessmen and have exalted their roles as guardians of culture. As a consequence, they have developed criteria of "literary quality" in which marketability may play only a limited role. Many publishers have felt it right to publish a worthy book even if it may not make money. The willingness of publishers to accept a high failure rate has meant that many books see publication with small chance of finding a market. This has helped book publishing retain at least an outward appearance of diversity in the face of the homogenization of nearly all other types of print and electronic media. Of course, the stakes are not as high as in other media; a typical press run of the 1990s of 7,000 copies cost about $25,000 to produce.

Within trade and best-seller-oriented categories, there are certainly many non-speculative ventures. So, by value in net receipts, only about one-third to one-half of the industry engages in the type of risk taking that an 80 percent failure rate of new titles implies. The segments of the industry that take risks simply publish numerically more titles at cheaper prices than other divisions of the industry.

The variety of titles that results from overproduction in the book trade should not be confused with diversity. The number of books published only for their intrinsic quality in spite of market considerations cannot be very high and hardly accounts for the vast majority of failures. Most publishers pursue a market strategy behind each book they publish; they often lose out to competition from very similar books of other publishers, usually due to the rival's superior marketing strategy.

The high failure rate in publishing makes it a very speculative venture. Publishers protect themselves in two ways. First, sometimes publishers accept the failures as part of a larger overall strategy. And second, generally, the few successes of any publishing house must underwrite the costs of the many failures. Houses must rely on, on the one hand, works that have proven their marketability and, on the other, best-sellers.

The relative permanence of books influences publishers' larger strategies to cope with the high failure rate. Many houses try to build up a writer's reputation over time and will be willing to sustain one or two losses at the beginning of a career in return for increasing critical notice and, eventually, acclaim (at which point the house will make money on reissuing the writer's earlier works). Even the house itself can gain, after a string of losses in a subject area or genre, a reputation for publishing "a certain type of book of a certain level of quality" and attract, on this basis, writers in the subject area with more market potential.

Most books with proven markets have fallen traditionally into the category of reference or other standard works. In the colonial and early national period, most publishers relied on this type of book to sustain their businesses. They often issued a pirated edition of an European work outside American copyright law jurisdiction. Early American publishers avoided speculation and sometimes asked authors of new and more risky books to help subsidize the potential losses their books might incur.

As nineteenth-century railroad development began to open a national market for publishers, they came to rely more and more on "decided hits"—books that in the 1850s sold over 10,000 copies. Interestingly, books in the late twentieth century have to sell only about five times that number in hardcover to qualify as best-sellers (publishers will reap handsome rewards for paperback editions that could sell hundreds of thousands or millions of copies). A best-seller in whatever area pays dividends beyond the receipts for the book itself. It enhances the reputations of the writer and, more rarely, the house; the publisher can realize additional profits from selling rights to adapt the book to other media or to reprint it in a different format.

If the overproduction of books and the creeping homogenization of their content can be discounted, the publishing industry in the United States has been remarkably effective at reaching at least a large portion of its potential audience. It has also tended to avoid a narrow capital-provincial dichotomy that characterizes book distribution in other countries, even though the industry has been centralized in New York City.

Today the book industry disseminates information alongside various electronic and other print media, but given its historical role in American development, the book industry influences the overall structure and sociocultural context of all publishing. At the center of that influence lies the dual nature (material versus ideational) of information dissemination in a capitalist society: the marketing of knowledge (Coser, Kadushin, & Powell, 1982). Prior to the rise of capitalism and the emergence of the printed word, societies transmitted nearly all information by word of mouth, gratis—outside the shaping force of the marketplace. The "coming of the book" (Febvre & Martin, 1976) gave material form and a market price to great amounts of information but did not erase the older cultural expectations of oral traditions: that the system of signs and the meanings they conveyed in the minds of readers transcend the physical substance of the book.

In a capitalist system of the marketing of knowledge, the organization of the publishing industry reflects the changing currents of diversity within the marketplace of ideas. While no American publishing firm has achieved a true monopoly in even a few topic areas, book publishers have never operated under purely free market conditions, either. Historically, American publishing has wavered between these two extremes largely because of contradictions that inhere in the marketing of knowledge. Economics and culture exert their own sometimes opposing pulls on the industry. As economic forces have driven book publishers, like other businessmen, toward increasingly larger units of production and toward addressing an ever-widening market, a countertrend has persistently developed to redress the cultural needs of those left out of definitions of the American reading public at large.

The theoretical potential for diversity with the organization of book production thus may begin with writers. Seemingly anyone with a typewriter can become a writer. Usually, however, a more discernible path of socialization through reading leads individuals to try their hands at writing.

Writing, however, for the American system of book production is above all a speculative venture that has inherent tendencies to compromise the goal of diversity. The writer creates, hoping to (1) find a publisher; (2) convince a publisher that the book will reach a large enough market to pay a profit beyond the costs of publication; (3) elicit at least some favorable reviews; and (4) in the best of all possible worlds, find a receptive readership. The first two aspirations pull the author toward the largest possible and least diverse market. The critical establishment tends to mirror the demographic biases of the reading public and publishers and thus reinforces them. And an author may simply eschew voicing diversity in order to reach a greater number of readers.

Discouragement to diversity, however, may be in place before a person even imagines becoming an author. Not all groups have had equal access to the education, books, leisure, or role models that have traditionally encouraged Americans to turn to writing. Moreover, the primary markets American writers have addressed have been urban and suburban and middle- to upper-middle-class. The demographics of the primary audience have naturally encouraged a predominance of writers with a similar profile.

Yet because authorship has not always been a profession the dominant American middle class has honored, it has occasionally remained open to some members of minority groups with few other alternatives. How much the process of writing for a market, its rejections, and the inevitable editorial interpositions alter the degree to which these individuals' creations truly represent their minority origins remains open to question.

Such acceptance, under rare conditions and for specific groups, of minority writers operates only within limited areas of the book production industry, mostly for novels and other belles lettres. As for the rest of the area of trade publications (with notable exceptions for nonfiction relating to women's traditional roles, such as juvenile literature and cooking) and the remainder of the industry, little openness to different viewpoints exists.

Even if a minority author gets into print, the marketing and advertising efforts of publishing houses by their very drive to find the largest market obviously cannot strongly encourage diversity. A book that speaks for a minority viewpoint may be "mainstreamed" through advertising with a calculated guess that the reader may either never read or truly understand the book anyhow beyond the homogenized context created by the publicity.

Nor does the trend toward business concentration augur well for diversity. Corporate influence and the predominance of management and financial departments will reshape book publishing along the lines of other communications businesses: toward the mass market and away from catering to different minority needs. With large national book chains driving smaller general bookstores out of business or into very limited specialized market niches (e.g., ones with a focus on "feminist" issues), the chances for plural viewpoints in book distribution are further lessened.

OUTLOOK FOR THE FUTURE

Thus, discussions of the future of the book industry take on an ideological aspect. Some observers see the book industry as the beacon of a great Western tradition and fear the imminent demise of both. Newspapers, magazines, movies, radio, television, and most recently, the computer have all posed, according to critics, threats to books. However, the book industry has consistently renegotiated its role in society and continued on as an important force and will not disappear. On the other hand, since Johannes Gutenberg, other seers have heralded the book as an unstoppable machine of (at first Protestant and then nonsecular) liberal democratic progress. According to this view, modernization will always push societies toward greater and greater educational levels in the long run and toward more democratic cultural participation. The lack of diversity, the problems of the mass market, and falling literacy rates among certain groups are all short-term stumbling blocks, not inherent in the processes of information dissemination in a capitalist society.

The contradictions regarding homogeneity and diversity within the book publishing industry certainly give enough ammunition for both the naysayers and yeasayers. The consolidation and integration taking place within the industry, matched by the ever-increasing costs of books, suggest that a quantitative limit upon diversity may already be in place. For most Americans, the mass book market will prevail perhaps more than it ever has in publishing history. The high cost of books will put them in reach of fewer, wealthier buyers able and willing to afford them and will leave out many minorities, since diversity tends to cluster at the bottom of the socioeconomic scale. At the same time, the very weight of the mass market puts a premium on difference, if not diversity, and can qualitatively influence expressions of diversity.

Minority writers, small presses, and alternative bookstores may express their diversity more purely. For example, the public visibility of the various gay/lesbian literary communities might not be possible if they contended for a mass market audience. Will ''purer'' rather than mainstreamed expressions of diversity more effectively promote social change? Or will their heightened visibility simply make them targets for future campaigns of censorship and harassment?

A countervailing technological trend may help to promote diversity in book production: publishing and printing using microcomputers. Microcomputers and the networks and bulletin boards that they can access have already provided a new form of ''publication.'' The development of desktop publishing along with laser printers in the mid-1980s gave a new lease on life to the printed word. Laser printers now achieve ''book-quality'' resolution for the images they produce and encourage publishers to use this output as a camera-ready replacement for traditional typesetting (a more sophisticated extension of xerographic or photographic reproduction of typewritten materials, like dissertations, in book form). Various publishing programs have already greatly reduced typesetting costs for small publishing houses. The sum effect of microcomputer publishing will be to dramatically lower overhead and business entry costs within the industry and to encourage more smaller houses.

Technological innovations alone will not assure diversity within publishing, however, for the machines that bring the new technology to the masses are themselves commodities, and their distribution throughout society will roughly match the maldistribution of wealth. Those in power may simply become more powerful through superior control of the new technology.

In the final analysis, the future of diversity within the book publishing industry hinges not on technological or organizational change but on societal goals. If diversity is seen as a value to be upheld and cherished as part of the American cultural legacy, then this will ipso facto create a need for more knowledge about human differences. The book product will follow the market opened up by that need to know. But the value of diversity must be applied across the full spectrum of literary production and consumption. It is not enough to have a handful of minority authors published by a mainstream publishing industry for a homogenized audience. Only when writers, publishers, booksellers, and readers come to represent and give voice to the highly varied, geographically dispersed, multiracial, multiethnic, socially stratified American population will true diversity in book publishing be achieved. And only then will the publishing industry fulfill its full responsibility to the American public.

SELECTED BIBLIOGRAPHY

Anderson, Charles B. (Ed.). (1975). *Bookselling in America and the world.* New York: Quadrangle/New York Times Book Co.

Baym, Nina. (1984). *Novels, readers, and reviewers: Responses to fiction in antebellum America.* Ithaca, NY: Cornell University Press.

Bowker, Richard Rogers. (1912). *Copyright: Its history and its law.* Boston: Houghton Mifflin.

Bowker Company. (1943). *Bowker lectures on book publishing.* New York: Typophiles.

Brown, Richard D. (1989). *Knowledge is power: The diffusion of information in early America.* New York: Oxford University Press.

Charvat, William. (1959). *Literary publishing in America, 1790–1850.* Philadelphia: University of Pennsylvania Press.

Charvat, William. (1968). *The profession of authorship in America,* with Matthew Bruccoli (Ed.). Columbus: Ohio State University Press.

Cheney, O. H. (1931). *Economic survey of the book industry, 1930–1931.* New York: National Association of Book Publishers.

Cole, John Y. (Ed.). (1987). *Books in our future: Perspectives and proposals.* Washington, DC: Library of Congress.

Compaine, Benjamin M. (1978). *The book industry in transition: An economic study of book distribution and marketing.* White Plains, NY: Knowledge Industry Publications.

Comparato, Frank. (1971). *Books for the millions: A history of the men whose methods and machines packaged the printed word.* Harrisburg, PA: Stackpole.

Coser, Lewis A., Kadushin, Charles, & Powell, Walter W. (1982). *Books: The culture and commerce of publishing.* New York: Basic Books.

Coultrap-McQuin, Susan. (1990). *Doing literary business: American women writers in the nineteenth century.* Chapel Hill: University of North Carolina Press.

Darnton, Robert. (1971). Reading, writing, and publishing in eighteenth-century France: A case study in the sociology of literature. *Daedalus, 100,* 214–256.

Darnton, Robert. (1979). *The business of enlightenment: A publishing history of the encylcopédie, 1775–1800.* Cambridge, MA: Harvard University Press.

Davidson, Cathy N. (1986). *Revolution and the word: The rise of the novel in America.* New York: Oxford University Press.

Davidson, Cathy N. (Ed.). (1989). *Reading in America: Literature and social history.* Baltimore: Johns Hopkins University Press.

Denning, Michael. (1987). *Mechanic accents: Dime novels and working class culture in America.* London and New York: Verso.

Derby, James Cephas. (1884). *Fifty years among authors, books, and publishers.* New York: G. W. Carlton.

Douglas, Ann. (1977). *The feminization of American culture.* New York: Alfred A. Knopf.

Dunlap, William. (1834). *The history of the rise and progress of the arts of design in the United States.* New York: G. P. Scott.

Febvre, Lucien, & Martin, Henri Jean. (1976). *The coming of the book: The impact of printing, 1450–1800.* London: New Left Books.

Freedley, Edwin T. (Ed.). (1856). *Leading pursuits and leading men: A treatise on the principal trades and manufactures of the United States.* Philadelphia: E. Young.

Fry, Ronald W. (Ed.). (1987). *Book publishing career directory.* Hawthorne, NJ: Career Press.

Gaskell, Philip. (1972). *A new introduction to bibliography.* New York: Oxford University Press.

Gill, Robert S. (1940). *The author, publisher, printer complex.* Baltimore: Williams and Wilkins.

Gilmore, William. (1989). *Reading becomes a necessity of life: Material and cultural life in rural New England, 1780–1830.* Knoxville: University of Tennessee Press.

Goodrich, Samuel G. (1855). *Recollections of a lifetime.* New York: Orton, Miller, and Mulligan.

Grannis, Chandler B. (1967). *What happens in book publishing?* (2nd ed.). New York: Columbia University Press.

Gross, Gerald (Ed.). (1961). *Publishers on publishing.* New York: Grosset & Dunlap.

Gross, Robert A. (1987). Much instruction from little reading: Books and libraries in Thoreau's Concord. *Proceedings of the American Antiquarian Society, 97,* 129–188.

Hall, David D. (1984). *On native ground: From the history of printing to the history of books.* Worcester, MA: American Antiquarian Society.

Hall, David D. (1989). *Worlds of wonder, days of judgment: Popular religious belief in early New England.* New York: Alfred A. Knopf.

Hall, David D., & Hench, John B. (Eds.). (1987). *Needs and opportunities in the history of the book: America: 1639–1876.* Worcester, MA: American Antiquarian Society.

Haney, Robert W. (1960). *Comstockery in America: Patterns of censorship and control.* Boston: Beacon Press.

Harrington, Bates. (1879). *How 'tis done: A thorough ventilation of numerous schemes conducted by wandering canvassers.* Chicago: Fidelity.

Hart, James D. (1950). *The popular book: A history of America's literary taste.* New York: Oxford University Press.

Hungerford, Herbert. (1931). *How publishers win.* Washington, DC: Ransdell.

Innis, Harold Adams. (1949). *The press: A neglected factor in the economic history of the twentieth century.* London: Oxford University Press.

Kaser, David (Ed.). (1966). *Books in America's past: Essays in honor of Rudolph H. Gjelsness.* Charlottesville: University Press of Virginia.

Kaufmann, William. (1977). *One book/five ways: The publishing procedures of five university presses.* Los Altos, CA: William Kaufmann.

Kelley, Mary. (1984). *Private woman, public stage: Literary domesticity in nineteenth-century America.* New York: Oxford University Press.

Kilpatrick, James J. (1960). *The smut peddlers.* Garden City, NY: Doubleday.

Leacock, Stephen. (1914). *The methods of Mr. Sellyer: A book store study.* New York: Lane.

Lehmann-Haupt, Hellmut, Graniss, Ruth Shepard, & Wroth, Lawrence C. (1937). *Das amerikanische Buchwesen.* Leipzig: Karl W. Hiersemann. Rev. and enl. as *The book in America: A history of the making and selling of books in the United States.* New York: R. R. Bowker, 1951.

Link, Henry Charles, & Hopf, Harry Arthur. (1946). *People and books: A study of reading and book-buying habits.* New York: Book Industry Committee, Book Manufacturers' Institute.

Madison, Charles A. (1966). *Book publishing in America.* New York: McGraw-Hill.

Madison, Charles A. (1974). *Irving to Irving: Author-publisher relations, 1800–1974.* New York: R. R. Bowker.

Maitland, Sara, & Appignanesi, Lisa. (Eds.). (1990). *The Rushdie file.* Syracuse, NY: Syracuse University Press.

McLuhan, Marshall. (1968). *The Gutenberg galaxy.* Toronto: University of Toronto Press.

McMullen, Haynes. (1966). The use of books in the Ohio Valley before 1850. *Journal of Library History, 1,* 43–56, 73.

McMurtrie, Douglas C. (1936). *A history of printing in the United States* (Vol. 2). New York: R. R. Bowker.

Moore, John W. (1886). *Moore's historical, biographical, and miscellaneous gatherings.* Concord, NH: Republican Press.

Mott, Frank Luther. (1947). *Golden multitudes: The story of bestsellers in the United States.* New York: Macmillan.

Nord, David Paul. (1986). Working class readers: Family, community, and reading in late nineteenth-century America. *Communication Research, 13,* 156–181.

Nord, David Paul. (1988, May). The evangelical origins of the mass media in America. *Communications Monographs, 88.*

Oswald, John Clyde. (1937). *Printing in the Americas.* New York: Gregg.

Putnam, George Haven, & Putnam, John Bishop. (1883). *Authors and publishers: A manual of suggestions for beginners.* New York: Putnam.

Radway, Janice. (1984). *Reading the romance: Women, patriarchy, and popular litera-*
    ture. Chapel Hill: University of North Carolina Press.
Radway, Janice. (1989). The Book-of-the-Month Club and the general reader: The uses
    of 'serious' fiction. In Cathy N. Davidson (Ed.), *Reading in America: Literature*
    and social history (pp. 259–284). Baltimore: Johns Hopkins University Press.
Rogers, Joseph W. (1960). *U.S. national bibliography and copyright law.* New York: R.
    R. Bowker.
Schick, Frank L. (1958). *The paperbound book in America: The history of paperbacks*
    and their European antecedents. New York: R. R. Bowker.
Silver, Rollo. (1967). *The American printer, 1787–1825.* Charlottesville: University Press
    of Virginia.
Simmons College. (1954). *Books and book publishing.* Boston: Simmons College School
    of Library Science.
Sinclair, Upton. (1927). *Money writes!* New York: A. & C. Boni.
Stern, Madeleine B. (1956). *Imprints on history: Book publishers and American frontiers.*
    Bloomington: Indiana University Press.
Stern, Madeleine B. (1978). *Books and book people in nineteenth-century America.* New
    York: R. R. Bowker.
Sutton, Walter. (1961). *The western booktrade: Cincinnati as a nineteenth-century pub-*
    lishing center. Columbus: Ohio State University Press.
Tanselle, G. Thomas. (1965). The historiography of American literary publishing. *Studies*
    in Bibliography, 18, 3–39.
Tanselle, G. Thomas. (1971). *Guide to the study of United States imprints.* Cambridge,
    MA: Harvard University Press.
Tebbel, John. (1972). *A history of book publishing in the United States, volume I: The*
    creation of an industry, 1630–1865. New York: R. R. Bowker.
Tebbel, John. (1987). *Between covers: The rise and transformation of book publishing*
    in America. New York: Oxford University Press.
Thomas, Isaiah. (1810). *The history of printing in America.* Worcester, MA: Thomas.
Tryon, Warren S. (1947). Book distribution in mid-nineteenth century America: Illus-
    trated by the publishing records of Ticknor and Fields. *Publications of the Bib-*
    liographical Society of America, 41, 210–230.
Tryon, Warren S. (1963). *Parnassus corner: The life of James T. Fields, publisher to*
    the Victorians. Boston: Houghton Mifflin.
Van Winkle, C. S. (1818). *The printer's guide.* New York: Van Winkle.
Warner, Michael. (1990). *The letters of the Republic: Publication and the public sphere*
    in eighteenth-century America. Cambridge, MA: Harvard University Press.
West, James L. W., III. (1988). *American authors and the literary marketplace since*
    1900. Philadelphia: University of Pennsylvania Press.
Whiteside, Thomas. (1981). *The blockbuster complex: Conglomerates, show business,*
    and book publishing. Middletown, CT: Wesleyan University Press.
Wilson, Christopher P. (1985). *The labor of words: Literary professionalism in the pro-*
    gressive era. Athens: University of Georgia Press.
Wroth, Lawrence C. (1938). *The colonial printing press: A chapter from the 'Colonial*
    Printer.' Portland, ME: Southworth-Anthoensen Press.
Yard, Robert Sterling. (1913). *The publisher.* Boston: Houghton Mifflin.
Zboray, Ronald J. (1993). *A fictive people: Antebellum economic development and the*
    American reading public. New York: Oxford University Press.

USEFUL PERIODICALS

American Bookmaker
The American Bookseller
Booklist
Book Research Quarterly
Colophon
Inland Printer
International Literary Marketplace
Journal of Library History
Libraries and Culture
Literary Marketplace
Papers of the Bibliographical Society of America
Proof
Publishers Weekly
Publishing History
Publishing Research Quarterly
Studies in Bibliography
Writer's Market

3

CABLE

James Phillip Jeter

Cable television is the oldest of the "new" communications technologies. Although direct broadcast satellite (DBS), high-definition television (HDTV), and multichannel multipoint distribution service (MMDS) have yet to demonstrate that they are ongoing effective telecommunications delivery systems, cable television has become THE alternative television delivery system (ATDS) in America. The 1991 Persian Gulf war left no doubt that cable has arrived. According to one published report, nearly one-half of Americans watched most of their war news on Cable News Network (CNN), the world's first twenty-four-hour television news service. More than six of every ten American households with television in 1993 had cable.

From a passive delivery system operated by a few entrepreneurs in the 1950s, cable television by 1993 had grown into an industry that provided original programming, accounted for over 130,000 jobs, and had a subscriber base worth over $125 billion. Although the bulk of material carried on cable is devoted to entertainment programming, cable television can provide many services not possible with over-the-air (OTA) television, for example, interactive education, entertainment and shopping, home security, emergency alert, municipal utilities monitoring, opinion polling, and data transmission. In 1993, these services had seen minimal development and were not available on a large scale.

HISTORY

The site of the first actual cable system is a matter of debate with communities in the states of New York, Ohio, Oregon, Pennsylvania, and Washington, the leading candidates. Each community had a common desire to get television reception in the late 1940s when there were only a few television stations on the air, mostly in distant markets. Throughout its first years of operation, cable television was viewed as an adjunct service to broadcasting capable of extending the coverage of licensed stations to areas that could not otherwise receive these signals.

Known now as simply "cable," cable television started out as community antenna television (CATV). This referred to a way of making television reception possible to communities in which OTA reception was limited because of mountains or distance. Because OTA television uses the very high frequency (VHF) and ultra-high-frequency (UHF) bands for transmission, the television signal does not bend or bounce like amplitude modulation (AM) radio transmissions. Consequently, factors such as distance, curvature of the earth, and intervening terrain affect the strength of the television signal.

To remedy this situation, a single (master) antenna for a community was placed atop a mountain to access existing OTA signals. A special coaxial cable was run from this antenna to homes in the area. With entrepreneurs providing this service for a fee, the early days of cable were a classic marketing match. Entrepreneurs provided a wanted service for a fee customers felt reasonable; CATV subscribers received the new television phenomenon, and television broadcasters sold commercial time to advertisers who reached expanded audiences. The harmony of this arrangement did not last long. By the mid-1950s, broadcasters and cable system operators started squabbling in the first of a series of arguments that have continued ever since.

The Freeze

The television "freeze" on new broadcast stations that lasted from 1948 to 1952 also helped cable television to develop. The demand for television station licenses after World War II proved too great for the method of license allocation first devised by the Federal Communications Commission (FCC) in 1941. Initially, television broadcasting was only authorized for the VHF band (channels 2 to 13). In an attempt to prevent television reception from becoming the chaotic confusion that characterized the early days of radio, the FCC "froze" television in its tracks in 1948 and stopped granting television station applications until the agency could come up with a method by which more television stations could be available. While this moratorium on new stations existed, the demand for television continued to grow. This demand/supply imbalance provided the opportunity for cable operators, who extended the signals of existing stations to the delight of television station owners.

When the freeze was lifted in 1952, the CATV industry generated revenues of less than $1 million and consisted of approximately seventy community antenna systems serving 14,000 subscribers (see Table 3.1). After the freeze, CATV started its metamorphosis from a passive delivery system into one distinct from OTA television. Using available technology, CATV operators started to expand the function of a community antenna. Microwave relay stations were used to bring into the communities television station signals from hundreds of miles away, as well as the local or nearest television signals. As CATV started

Table 3.1
Cable Television Industry Growth

Year	Operating Systems	Subscribers	TV Homes (%)	Revenues (Millions)
1952[a]	70	14,000	.1	$.5
1960[a]	600	750,000	1.6	$35
1970[b]	2,490	4,498,030	7.5	$700
1980[c]	4,225	17,671,490	22.6	$2,603
1990[d]	9,500	52,300,080	57.1	$15,230
1992[e]	11,254	55,576,390	60.1	$20,039[f]

Sources: [a]Le Duc, D. R. (1973). *Cable television and the FCC.* Philadelphia: Temple University Press, pp. 69, 70, 86, and 114.
[b]National Cable Television Association, *Cable television developments* 13(52) (December 1989): 4.
[c]National Cable Television Association, *Cable television developments* 13(52) (December 1989): 4.
[d]Summary of broadcasting and cable. (1990, February 19). *Broadcasting,* p. 10.
[e]Summary of broadcasting and cable. (1992, December 21). *Broadcasting,* p. 57.
[f]National Cable Television Association, *Cable television developments* 16(58) (May 1992): 8A.

to change from merely being a passive delivery system and convenient method of extending the nearest or local television station, the relationship the fledging industry had enjoyed with OTA broadcasters changed from one of harmony to friction. Broadcasters turned to the FCC for help—an action that threw down the gauntlet between the two industries. Since then, cable system operators and OTA broadcasters have taken turns accusing the other of being protected by the federal government.

Federal Regulation

The FCC first sided with the cable industry, deciding in 1959 that it had no basis for regulating cable. However, the broadcasting industry marshaled its forces and successfully lobbied the FCC to reconsider its decision. A series of FCC rules and legal decisions followed that "protected" broadcasters from cable system operators for nearly twenty years (see Table 3.2), keeping cable out of the major markets or severely limiting the manner in which it could operate.

Table 3.2
Significant Cable Television Judicial Rulings and Legislation

Year	Case/Law	Effect
1958	<u>Frontier Broadcasting</u> <u>Co. v. Collier</u>	FCC would not regulate cable directly.
1962	<u>Carter Mountain</u> <u>Transmission Corp. v.</u> <u>FCC</u>	FCC can regulate cable if CATV uses microwaves for distant signal importation and causes economic injury to broadcasters.
1968	<u>United States v.</u> <u>Southwestern Cable Co.</u>	FCC can regulate cable because it is related to broadcasting.
1972	<u>U. S. v. Midwest Video</u> <u>Corp. (Midwest I)</u>	FCC rules requiring certain cable systems to create programming upheld.
1978	<u>Midwest Video Corp.</u> <u>v. FCC (Midwest II)</u>	FCC 1976 cable programming rules outside FCC jurisdiction.
1979	<u>FCC v. Midwest Video</u> <u>Corp. (Midwest III)</u>	FCC cable access rules struck down.
1980	Report and Order FCC 80-443	FCC abolishes syndicated exclusivity and distant signal importation rules.
1984	Cable Communications Policy Act	Deregulated cable television.
1992	Cable Television Consumer Protection and Competition Act	Regulated cable television.

Political, social, and economic forces must often react to technological reality. Nowhere was this more evident than with the developments in the cable industry in the 1970s. In 1973 the FCC approved the use of domestic communications satellites, and *Westar I,* the first geosynchronous domestic satellite, was launched in 1974.

Geosynchronous satellites orbit 22,300 miles above the equator at a pace that keeps in step with the earth's rotation. The practical result is that the satellites "hang" at one point in space and can serve as continuous communications relay devices. Because they can cover up to one-third of the earth with their signal, called a *footprint,* domestic communications satellites offer tremendous cost and efficiency advantages over wire and microwave signal distribution.

Home Box Office (HBO) gained early success as a regional network by offering to cable subscribers programming they could not get from OTA signals. After three years as a regional network, HBO went national in 1975, using the RCA *Satcom I* satellite to distribute its signal. Later that year, R. E. "Ted" Turner gave birth to the "superstation" by making the signal from WTBS-TV, the independent UHF television station he operated in Atlanta, Georgia, available on the same satellite. Once satellite delivery of cable programming services began, the development of cable television into a national alternative television delivery service was able to start. Using microwave relay, then satellites and now increasingly fiber optics, the cable television industry has relied on early use of nontraditional technology to provide a marketing advantage against OTA television. These technologies have been the basis by which cable television operators can offer a range of programming that local broadcasters, restricted to one signal channel per market, are hard-pressed to match.

Legal developments also helped create a better operating environment for cable television. The Supreme Court's ruling in the Midwest II case (1978) that the FCC's 1976 cable rules exceeded the FCC's jurisdiction liberated cable television. This ruling established an environment for cable television to change from a passive broadcast programming relay system to a true alternative delivery system to OTA television. The Court's ruling in the 1978 Midwest II case also created an absence of federal cable regulation by eliminating the set of rules that had applied on this level. Cable television regulation at the local level became the next arena of contention.

During the 1970s the cable industry evolved from one of individual entrepreneurs ("mom and pop") operations to an industry dominated by multiple system operators (MSOs), companies that own and operate cable systems in different cities and states. Faced with a multiplicity of city, county, and state rules, regulations, and procedures, the cable industry turned to the federal government for help. The result was the Cable Communications Policy Act of 1984, which deregulated cable television rates and prohibited cable from being regulated as a common carrier or utility service.

Reregulation

The success of the cable television industry after 1985 would cost it. Although the 1984 legislation allowed municipalities to govern educational, governmental, public access, and leased channels and collect franchise fees from cable operators, areas of concern developed. Consumers and Congress, responding to constituent complaints, perceived that the cable television industry had become a greedy monopoly, with price increases and customer service topping the list of complaints.

The Cable Communications Policy Act of 1984 virtually deregulated most of the systems because they operate in cities with three or more broadcast stations. As the industry continued to become dominated by a few big players since the 1984 landmark legislation, cable television rate increases exceeded the annual rate of inflation. A General Accounting Office (GAO) study showed cable television rates increased nearly one-third in the two years after deregulation in 1984. With the 1990 average monthly cost of basic service approaching $18 (double the 1983 average), consumers complained to Congress, which then took up the issue.

Broadcasters were also asking Congress for protection from cable, alleging that cable television had become an unregulated monopoly that enjoyed an unfair competitive advantage. Although Congress made several attempts after 1990 to deal with these complaints, it finally passed the 1992 Cable Television Consumer Protection and Competition Act.

ORGANIZATION, SCOPE, STRUCTURE, AND SIZE

The 1993 cable industry structure represented a 180-degree shift from the industry that started during the 1940s. Now dominated by large corporations (see Table 3.3), MSOs serve 80 percent of America's cable homes. Cable systems may be bought or sold like any business, changing hands for between $1,500 and $3,000 per subscriber. Valuing each subscriber at an average of $2,250 yields a national cable industry worth approximately $125 billion.

Company Organization

Cable television operations are called *systems*. The purpose of any cable system is for a fee to distribute to subscribers programming received from OTA television stations, satellites, and other sources by means of a coaxial or fiber optic cable. Figure 3.1 shows the organizational structure of an MSO.

No matter what the ownership structure, a cable system must address the normal operational functions of any for-profit telecommunications entity, that is, management, programming, engineering, business, and sales. Figure 3.2 shows the organizational structure of a cable system at the local level. Under the MSO structure, the system manager reports to the appropriate geographic vice-president.

Management

Supervising the entire operation of a cable system is the chief duty of the system manager. In addition to the normal planning, monitoring, and supervisory functions of this position, a key area to which management must pay close

Table 3.3
Ten Largest Multiple System Operators, 1992

Rank	Company	Subscribers (Millions)
1	Tele-Communications	10.06
2	Time Warner	6.71
3	Continental Cablevision Inc.	2.81
4	Comcast Cable	1.70
5	Cox Cable	1.68
6	Cablevision Systems	1.66
7	Storer Communications	1.65
8	Jones Intercable	1.50
9	Newhouse Broadcasting	1.30
10	Adelphia Communications	1.15

Source: National Cable Television Association, *Cable television developments* 16(58) (May 1992): 14A.

attention is government relations. Because cable systems operate under franchises (agreements with local governments that allow the companies to operate in certain geographical areas), someone at the cable system must maintain a liaison with the municipality involved. This is usually a function of the system manager. In MSOs a person or an entire department may perform this function. Duties include appearing before city council/commission meetings and monitoring the franchise agreement.

Programming

Although cable systems in Rochester, New York, and Toledo, Ohio, have created the "cable independent" by offering a combination of syndicated and locally oriented programming on their own cable channels, such efforts in 1993 were the exception rather than the rule. Although cable systems can program their own channels by buying their own programs from film and television program distributors, there is usually little system-originated programming on most of the operating cable systems beyond what is mandated in the local fran-

Figure 3.1
MSO Organizational Chart

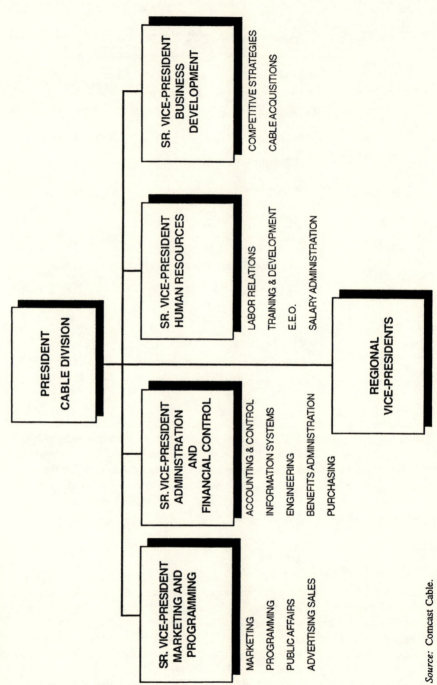

Source: Comcast Cable.

46

Figure 3.2
Cable Television System Organizational Chart

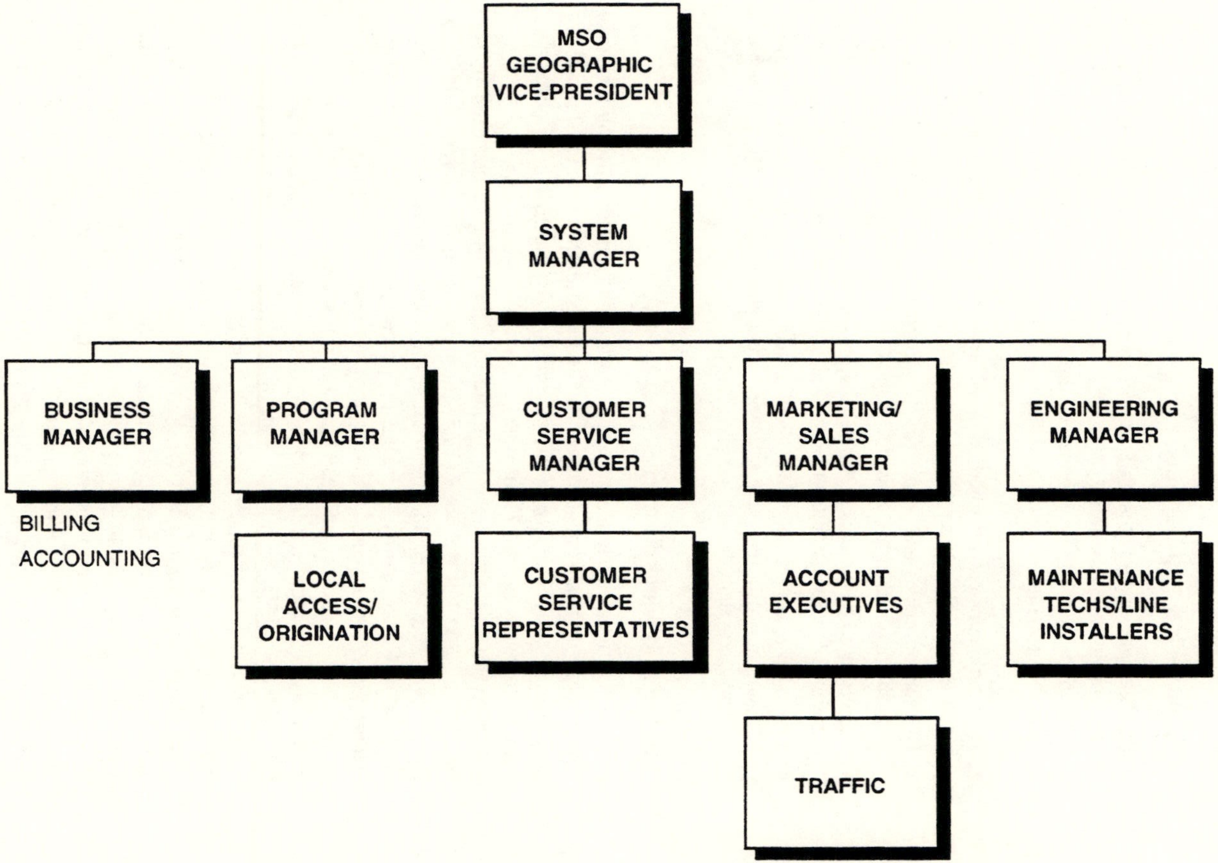

chise agreement. The person responsible for programming deals mostly with the system's local origination efforts and access programming.

Engineering and Service

Persons working in this area are responsible for maintaining the cable distribution system and installing, disconnecting, and maintaining service. The division of labor depends on the size of the system and staff, but someone must be responsible for maintenance and repair of the following:

1. Headend equipment—the portion of the system that receives, processes, and distributes the video signals on the cable system
2. Distribution cables and amplifiers—the portion of the system that gets the signals from the headend to the individual homes
3. Subscriber converter boxes, remote controls—the equipment that goes into individual subscriber homes that allow them to access the cable service for which they pay
4. Television production equipment—all the equipment (audio, video, microwave) used in connection with the cable system's access efforts/requirements and whatever production the system does

Sales and Marketing

Although more systems are selling time to advertisers, the bulk of cable system revenue comes from subscribers who pay monthly fees for the cable services they choose to receive. In 1991, advertising accounted for 15 percent of cable television revenues (see Figure 3.3)

Persons in this area are responsible for attempting to persuade persons who could get cable but do not have it (homes passed) to buy it. Adding a home passed by cable is technically the cheapest and easiest type of customer base expansion. Consequently, hooking up homes passed to the cable system is the primary sales strategy and one that does not require inordinate company expense to extend the subscriber base. In some instances, apartment complexes are treated as individual entities wired by the owner as a marketing differentiation for the property. Other landlords allow cable operators to wire only those apartment units that want the service in its various configurations.

Cable system operators use a combination of advertising media (newspaper, radio, direct mail, flyers left on doors or mailboxes), telemarketing, and face-to-face methods to get new customers. As more and more homes become cable homes, the need to "sell" cable diminishes. System operators then become more interested in moving customers up to the next tier (level of service) to maximize revenue or to add additional services to accomplish the same purpose. One sales tactic used for this purpose is the "preview." Under this method, pay/premium channels are descrambled for a few days, giving existing cable subscribers a look at what they have thus far chosen not to pay for.

Figure 3.3
1991 Cable Television Industry Revenues

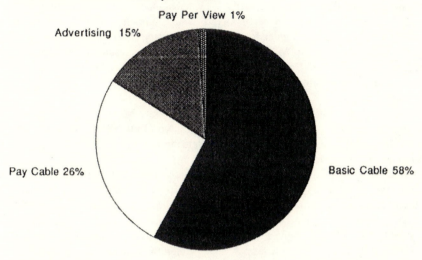

Pay Per View 1%

Advertising 15%

Pay Cable 26%

Basic Cable 58%

Source: National Cable Television Association, *Cable television developments* 16(58) (May 1992):
8A–9A.

ISSUES

Horizontal Integration

Horizontal integration (one company controlling its competitors) is virtually unknown in the cable business, which is considered a natural monopoly because economies of scale can be demonstrated or are particularly pronounced and competition is impractical because of natural barriers against entry and the large financial investment needed. The communications industry's best example is the local telephone company. Under the natural monopoly theory, one company is given an exclusive franchise to operate by a governing municipal body, which reserves the right to regulate the monopoly to prevent abuses.

Because cable television uses existing streets to distribute its signal, local municipalities generally grant one system the right to operate in a specific geographic area. Whereas cable subscribers get the benefit of cable television service, the municipality gets a franchise fee payment in exchange for this exclusive right.

Vertical Integration

As MSOs became major players in the cable industry, vertical integration (the ability to control raw materials, production, distribution, and exhibition of cable television programming) became more pronounced and more of a public policy concern. Vertical integration in the cable industry dates back to the industry's infancy. By building and operating cable systems, electronics manufacturer Jerrold Electronics was able to get involved in new markets for its products. In addition to being the dominant force in cable industry electronics, Jerrold serviced systems and was an MSO before it stopped as the result of a Justice Department investigation. Because the details of the 1992 Cable Act have not been established, in 1993 the question of vertical integration in the cable industry remained an issue.

Tele-Communications, Inc. (TCI) and Time Warner Inc. are often raised as the specters of the less desirable realities that have resulted from the evolution of cable television as a major player in the telecommunications industry and the dominance and power of the large MSOs.

As the largest MSO, TCI in 1993 had nearly one-fifth of all cable subscribers. Using values of $2,250 per subscriber, TCI's 10 million subscriber base may be valued at $23 billion. Clearly, any cable programming service needed TCI to be profitable. Of far more concern to critics is the shadow TCI casts across the cable industry with its partial ownership interest in such cable programming services as American Movie Classics, Black Entertainment Television, The Discovery Channel, and Turner Broadcasting System.

To broadcasters, the precedent set by American Television and Communications' (ATC) Rochester, New York, cable television system was troubling. In 1989, this system created the "cable independent" by offering a cable channel that patterns itself as an independent television station (one without network affiliation). The channel was identified as WGRC-TV (a standard broadcast call sign method of identification—four letters beginning with *W* and the *TV* suffix), offered a programming lineup consisting of popular syndicated programming (e.g., game shows, off-network reruns, etc.), sought to acquire sports rights to professional baseball games, was run by individuals with expertise and experience in broadcast management, and provided local news.

Because the line between cable television programming services and OTA broadcasting had blurred, independent television station owners joined the chorus of voices who wanted cable television reregulation. Table 3.4 illustrates their concern.

ATC's majority owner is Time Warner, the largest communications company in the world and the second largest MSO. ATC has the major franchise for Rochester, America's seventy-fourth-ranking television market. In addition, Time Warner owns controlling or partial interest in several of the cable programming services carried by Greater Rochester Cablevision, Inc. Time Warner's Lorimar and Warner Communications subsidiaries are major producers of television programming.

Critics—most notably independent television station operators—of this arrangement argued that with the Time Warner connection the Rochester cable system had an unfair advantage and was in a position to engage in real and

Table 3.4
Time Warner Inc. Cable/Television Interests

Entity	Ownership Level
Cable MSOs	
American Television and Communications Corp.	Majority
Warner Cable	Total
Cable Programming Services	
Black Entertainment Television	Minority
Courtroom TV	Minority
E! Entertainment TV	Minority
Turner Broadcasting System	Minority
Cinemax	Total
Comedy Central	Total
Home Box Office	Total
Other Media	
Warner Bros. Films	Total
Warner Bros. Television	Total
Lorimar	Total
Warner Music Group (Warner, Elektra, Asylum, and Atlantic Labels)	Total

Source: Time Warner Inc. *1991 Annual report.*

potential abuses that would harm the local independent television stations. Early audience surveys suggested the early success of the WGRC-TV channel was coming at the expense of local independent stations. Negotiations began to make the WGRC-TV channel available to other Rochester area cable systems.

The prospect of cable independents led INTV, the trade organization for independent television station operators, to petition the FCC to adopt rules that would prevent many alleged real and potential abuses possible with vertical integration. Specifically, the independent television station owners are concerned about the following issues:

1. Cable operators giving their locally offered programming channel(s) favored dial/tuner positions. (ATC's WGRC-TV service was placed on Channel 5. One Nielsen study found that cable services on lower channel positions have the highest ratings [Nielsen Study, 1990]).
2. Cable operators controlling the availability of competing television programming. (This is a particularly troubling prospect to local television station operators if the must-carry issue is resolved in favor of cable system operators.)
3. Cable operators using other cable channels to cross-promote their own "cable independents."
4. Cable operators cross-subsidizing operation of "cable independents." (Cable operators get revenues from cable subscribers. Consequently, cable operators can charge significantly lower advertising rates than single channel OTA television station operators, particularly independents.)

ISSUES AND FUTURE OUTLOOK

The exact nature of the cable television industry of the future is murky because numerous issues related to the environment in which cable television will operate remain unsettled. Although the 1992 Cable Act exists, many aspects of the law have not been clarified, and it may be some time before this happens. Turner Communications and Time Warner were among the first to file suits against the 1992 Cable Act. In addition, the legislation charged the FCC with establishing rules for certain areas. If history is any indication, the FCC action should generate litigation from a number of parties taking exception to these rules.

Among the matters to be resolved are questions related to the future of basic and pay cable services, pay-per-view, sports rights, marketing, must-carry, HDTV and fiber optics, overbuilds, and competition—particularly from telephone companies.

Basic and Pay Cable

For all its promise, cable television has not yet become the glue that holds American lives together. Although it is possible to use cable television for banking, home security, interactive instruction and shopping, medical alert emergencies, and data access, these capabilities are not the reasons America is moving toward becoming a wired video nation. The main selling point of cable is the entertainment programming services it offers in addition to OTA television, cable's core business over the years. Consumers seem to want to pay for the entertainment and informational programming not available on OTA television.

The history of cable franchising is one in which "pie in the sky" promises were made to get franchises, and once the franchise was awarded, the winner often went back to renegotiate because too much had been promised based on what the cable operator could afford to provide. The 1992 Cable Act requires the FCC to determine which cable franchises exist in a competitive environment. For those systems that do not, the law requires the FCC to develop formulas for pricing basic cable service (OTA television and public, educational, and governmental channels), installation, and monthly reception equipment rental fees. The law also allows the FCC to directly regulate franchises if the FCC has determined the franchise operator has been charging "excessive" rates.

Cable rates and customer service were the issues about which consumers complained most to Congress. The cable industry said its research revealed that although consumers felt the price paid for cable was reasonable, consumers were unhappy about dealing with the cable system when a problem arose and trying to get a sympathetic customer service representative. The industry was slow to realize the depth of consumer feeling on this matter. Although a cable industry group adopted a voluntary set of service standards in 1990, the 1992 Cable Act will require the establishment of minimum standards for billing and refunds, office hours, service call response times, and telephone operator availability.

Pay-Per-View/Interactive

As more homes get cable, the task of the cable operator becomes one of maximizing revenue from each home. For this reason, pay-per-view (PPV) programming is one growth area many cable operators are viewing closely, historically involving movies, prizefights, rock concerts, and special performances for which subscribers pay on a one-time basis. Although not a big earnings area now (see Figure 3.3), this area has tremendous growth possibilities because the cash flow PPV generates makes this level of cable service a potentially lucrative revenue source. Under PPV, a cable subscriber "orders" a programming event with a handheld remote control or gets a special converter unit and pays a fee in addition to the other cable services received.

The cable operator faces the problem here of perceived value on the part of the subscriber. For example, major boxing matches are available on PPV for between $30 and $35. Even if prices come down, why would subscribers pay $3 per event for PPV when for, say, $10 a month they can get unlimited pay service such as HBO or Cinemax? Conversely, the potential revenue from PPV is substantially higher to the cable operator because two or three PPV events even at $3 each bring in revenue equivalent to one pay cable service. The success of the cable home shopping networks is such that one might believe that if the cable industry could solve the problems of home selection units with sufficient addressability and sophistication, billing methods, and enough big pay events, PPV is the next growth area that will generate large revenues for cable television operators in the future. The interest in this area is best typified by

Barry Diller, the former Fox Broadcasting Company television executive, who in 1993 left network television to devote his energy to the home television shopping/events programming.

Sports Rights

Perhaps no area of television programming generates the type of public interest that sports programming does. ABC, CBS, and NBC paid nearly $4 billion for rights to their professional and collegiate baseball, basketball, and football programming for the early 1990s. They did so in an environment in which network audience viewing shares were decreasing. There was also concern about "sports siphoning" by the cable industry. Although National Football League (NFL) Commissioner Paul Tagliagbue promised a 1989 U.S. Senate hearing to keep the Super Bowl on OTA television until the year 2000, some regular season NFL games are now available only on cable.

Major League Baseball and the National Basketball Association also have cable deals that make some of the regular season games available only on cable. In 1990, professional baseball, basketball, and football for the first time made some games available only on cable. The issue here is whether sports rights that had long been the dominion of independent television stations will become available on cable television only and the public's access to these events limited. Some collegiate conferences (the Big Ten, PAC 10, and Southeast) already have exclusive cable deals. The deal that raised the issue of sports "siphoning" to congressional attention was the deal between the New York Yankees and a cable system that results in cable getting all Yankee games exclusively for twelve years even though only about half of the homes in the New York area are wired for cable.

Cable operators argue that the bulk of sports on cable consists of events ignored or abandoned by the networks so the cables are performing a public service. The 1992 Cable Act calls for a study of all sports on all levels on all forms of television, with a report due in 1994.

Overbuilds

As indicated previously, the exact title of the 1992 Cable Act is the 1992 Cable Television Consumer Protection and Competition Act. Some have begun to challenge the notion of cable as a natural monopoly and have started the process of overbuilds, a geographic area with two competing cable systems. In one small Georgia community, an overbuild resulted in competition for TCI (the largest MSO), and cable customers wound up with rate cuts of more than a third, the reverse of the national trend for cable customers. However, many cities have decided that overbuilds are not worth the construction disruptions and that competition in the form of cable overbuilds has not worked in enough other cities. However, a 1990 federal court ruling struck down a Los Angeles rule against overbuilds.

Living with Reregulation

The major challenges to the cable industry under the 1992 Cable Act center around four areas: (1) cable rates, (2) competition, particularly from the telephone companies, (3) ownership stakes in program suppliers, and (4) competing delivery systems for video signals and must-carry/retransmission consent.

Rates

Once they are developed, the FCC's rate formulas are likely to wind up in long-term litigation because of the unlikelihood that all interested parties will agree to the formula. The issue here relates to which tiers (levels of service) will be available to which subscribers at what price.

Competition

In the 1980s, a list of potential competitors to cable television (MMDSs, telephone companies, and other entrepreneurs who want to pursue overbuilds) joined the chorus of critics calling for cable industry reregulation or the opportunity to compete with cable television operators for viewers. If given the opportunity to compete, these entities argued they could provide more choice, better service, and lower prices. The emerging potential chief competitor is the telephone company.

Telephone Companies

The regional Bell operating companies (RBOCs) that provide local telephone service were spun off from American Telephone and Telegraph (AT&T) in the company's 1980 consent decree with the Justice Department. The RBOCs were interested in getting into the home video delivery business, but they were barred from doing so. Although exceptions were made for some rural areas, the 1984 Cable Act prohibited telephone companies from owning cable systems in their service areas, and the modified final judgment of the 1980 consent decree bars the RBOCs from offering information services. A crack in the ban appeared in 1991 when a federal judge ruled the RBOCs must be allowed to offer cable television and information services. That same year, the FCC adopted its "video dialtone" concept that would allow telephone companies to distribute video on a common carrier basis without having to get local franchises. The rules would also allow the telephone companies to loan money to programmers and have a maximum 5 percent ownership interest in the programming. The RBOCs are beginning to move in this area; deals have already been announced for cities in California and New Jersey.

Cable operators clearly are quite concerned about the entry of telephone companies into the cable business. Phone companies argue they could keep down costs and improve customer service—the chief consumer complaints against cable. The RBOCs also argue that with their economic resources they can install fiber optic cable that can make HDTV and other information and nonentertainment video services a reality. Although some cable system rebuilds and expansions have begun, most cable systems in 1993 do not have such an ability. The telephone industry has sided with local broadcasters on one key issue—must-carry. The telephone industry has said that if allowed to provide video services, they would provide distribution for all local television signals. The issue of mandatory signal carriage has caused friction between cable operators and local broadcasters since the 1950s. Over the years, several plans to solve the problem have been announced, only to be scrapped.

Cable operators have warned of the potential for predatory pricing tactics by the telephone companies. The RBOCs have billions of dollars that could be used to cut prices and cross-subsidize any cable television efforts until the current group of cable owners are out of business.

James Mooney, president of the National Cable Television Association, cautioned OTA broadcasters not to be taken in by the telephone industry promise of must-carry. In 1989, Mooney characterized any deal the OTA broadcasters would make with the telephone companies as one that would make "Faust's deal with the devil pale in comparison" ("Must Carry Negotiations," 1989). The initial beneficiaries of the debate will be the coffers of members of Congress and law firms as OTA broadcasters, the cable industry, and the telephone industry participate in the various FCC rule makings and litigation associated with those rule makings as the 1992 Cable Act is transformed from policy to practice.

Must-Carry/Retransmission Consent

These have been the fighting words between broadcasters and cable system operators since the 1950s. The debate on which signals a cable operator must carry is one that dates back to the television freeze era. Over the years, broadcasters argued cable systems were getting a free ride because cable operators did not pay for the privilege of carrying local television signals. Cable system operators countered they carry local signals as an accommodation to broadcasters, many of whom have less-than-desirable UHF signals, and should not have to pay for what broadcasters send out for free.

Over the years, legal challenges and negotiations failed to reach an agreement by all parties on the subject. Cable operators argued that rules requiring the mandatory carriage of signals prevent the cable systems from offering alternative services that would make their product unique. Broadcasters argue that without the local signals cable television's "product" would be less attractive to consumers and cable penetration and renewal rates would drop significantly.

The 1992 Cable Act gives a victory to OTA broadcasters. The law provides them with the right to negotiate a fee with cable systems that carry their signals or simply require the cable systems to carry their signal. This must-carry/ (signal retransmission consent) aspect of the act has raised other considerations. Some program producers have raised copyright royalty questions, and bills on the subject have already surfaced in Congress. The earliest cable industry lawsuits challenging the 1992 Cable Act targeted the must-carry/retransmission consent question on First Amendment infringement grounds.

Integration

The 1992 Cable Act in principle limits the market share of MSOs and MSO ownership in competing telecommunications delivery systems, for example, wireless cable systems and SMATV (Satellite Master Antenna Television) systems, in a signal geographic area. The law also prohibits exclusive contracts between cable program suppliers and cable system operators. However, as a practical matter, limits have yet to be set, and some existing situations have been grandfathered (allowed to continue because they existed before the law was passed).

SUMMARY

To its credit, the cable television industry is attempting to adapt to the new environment. The trade press is full of announcements of the industry's plans to compete with the telephone company to offer nonvideo services such as long-distance telephony and personal communications services (mobile telephones). There is a flurry of activity related to digital signal compression. This technology will significantly increase the program/information capacity of cable systems. While it may be some time before the plus-200-channel cable system is widespread, the cable systems of the year 2000 are likely to be used differently and offer significantly more communications options than the system found in operation in most places in mid-1993.

BIBLIOGRAPHY/FURTHER READING

Magazines

INTV asks FCC to rein in cable. (1990, January 15). *INTV Journal,* p. 68.
Kuhl, C. (1990, January 15). Cable will contribute $42 billion to nation's GNP this year, report says. *Cablevision,* p. 4.
Must carry negotiations at a standstill. (1989, November 6). *Broadcasting,* p. 35.
Nielsen Study. (1990, January 8). Lower dial position equals higher ratings. *Broadcasting,* p. 12.
On the brink of war, NAB tells cable: It's cash or carry time. (1989, December 4). *Broadcasting,* p. 35.

Books

Baldwin, T., & McVoy, D. S. (1983). *Cable communication.* Englewood Cliffs, NJ: Prentice-Hall.

Cable franchising and regulation: A local government guide to the new law. (1985). Washington, DC: National League of Cities.

Deschler, K. (1987). *Cable television technology.* New York: McGraw-Hill.

Garay, R. (1988). *Cable television: A reference guide for information.* Westport, CT: Greenwood Press.

Hunter, C., & Greenberg, B. S. (1988). *Cableviewing.* Norwood, NJ: Ablex.

Le Duc, D. R. (1973). *Cable television and the FCC.* Philadelphia: Temple University Press.

Quigley, J. (1985). *Cable job guide* (2nd ed.). Alexandria, VA: Cable Television Information Center.

Ricks, J., & Wiley, R. E. (1985). *Cable Communications Policy Act of 1984.* San Diego: Harcourt Brace Jovanovich.

Sloan Commission on Cable Communications. (1971). *On the cable: The television of abundance.* New York: McGraw-Hill.

PERIODICALS

Broadcasting & Cable (formerly *Broadcasting*) a weekly magazine focusing on broadcasting and cable television.

Cablevision, a weekly publication focusing on the cable television industry.

Variety, a weekly newspaper covering the entertainment industry.

Wall Street Journal, Section B. "Marketing & Media" column.

ORGANIZATIONS

Because of its potential and growing pervasiveness, many constituencies are interested in the cable industry. The Cable Television Information Center is consumer oriented. The principal trade organization of the cable television industry is the National Cable Television Association (NCTA). It holds an annual convention in the spring in various cities around the United States. The broadcasting industry has more than a passing interest in cable television. Since franchises are granted by local government, the National League of Cities has maintained an interest in the cable industry over the years. Each has a variety of information (brochures, pamphlets, position papers, speeches by executives, and studies) available on request. They may be contacted at the following addresses:

Cable Television Information Center
1500 N. Beauregard St., Suite 265
Alexandria, VA 22311

National Association of Broadcasters (NAB)
1771 N Street, NW
Washington, DC 20036

National Cable Television Association (NCTA)
1724 Massachusetts Avenue, NW
Washington, DC 20036–1969

National League of Cities
1301 Pennsylvania Avenue, NW
Washington, DC 20004

SELECTED ANNOTATED BIBLIOGRAPHY

Because cable television has a history of being regulated as a utility, a variety of scholars from business, economics, engineering, law, mass communications, political science, and public administration have been attracted to the topic as an area of study. The most widely read mass communications journals are *Journal of Broadcasting & Electronic Media, Journal of Communication, Journal of Media Economics,* and *Journalism Quarterly.*

For an examination of early local origination and public access television, see Royal D. Colle, "Television at the Grassroots: CATV," *Journal of Broadcasting* 7 (Winter 1962–1963), pp. 3–10; and Ralph Engelman, "The Origins of Public Access Cable Television 1966–1972," *Journalism Monographs* 123 (October 1990).

An excellent collection of materials on the infancy and adolescence of cable television can be found in Don R. Le Duc, "A Selected Bibliography on the Evolution of CATV 1950–1970," *Journal of Broadcasting* 15 (Spring 1971), pp. 195–234.

For a discussion of the state of cable television in the preboom days of the 1970s, see Anne W. Branscomb, "The Cable Fable: Will It Come True?" *Journal of Communication* 25 (Winter 1975), pp. 44–56; and Monroe E. Price, "The Illusions of Cable Television," *Journal of Communication* 4 (Summer 1974), pp. 71–76.

For data and a discussion of the consolidation of ownership in the cable industry from the 1970s through the mid-1980s, see Herbert H. Howard, "Ownership Trends in Cable Television, 1972–1979," *Journalism Quarterly* 58 (Summer 1981), pp. 288–291; idem, "An Update on Cable TV Ownership: 1985," *Journalism Quarterly* 63 (Winter 1987), pp. 706–709; and Sylvia M. Chan-Olmsted and Barry R. Litman, "Antitrust and Horizontal Mergers in the Cable Industry," *Journal of Media Economics* 1 (Fall 1988), pp. 3–28.

An account of the political machinations surrounding the 1972 cable rules is found in Harvey Jassem, "The Selling of the Cable TV Compromise," *Journal of Broadcasting* 17 (Fall 1973), pp. 427–436.

The issue of cable television as a natural monopoly versus overbuilds is taken up in Rolland C. Johnson and Robert T. Blau, "Single Versus Multiple-System Cable Television," *Journal of Broadcasting* 18 (Summer 1974), pp. 323–346; Thomas W. Hazlett, "The Policy of Exclusive Franchising in Cable Television," *Journal of Broadcasting & Electronic Media* 31 (Winter 1987), pp. 1–20; Robert T. Blau and Michael O. Wirth, "Forum," *Journal of Broadcasting & Electronic Media* 31 (Winter 1987), pp. 95–101.

The question of whether local governments have the knowledge to regulate cable is the subject of Vernone Sparkes's "Local Regulatory Agencies for Cable Television," *Journal of Broadcasting* 19 (Spring 1975), pp. 221–233. For a case study of how the policy definition of cable television evolved, see Patrick R. Parsons, "Defining Cable Television: Structuration and Public Policy," *Journal of Communication* 39 (Spring 1989), pp. 10–26.

For economic analyses of cable programming, see Thomas F. Baldwin, Michael O. Wirth, and Jayne W. Zenaty, "The Economics of Per-Program Pay Cable Television,"

Journal of Broadcasting 22 (Spring 1978), pp. 143–154; David Waterman, "The Failure of Cultural Programming on Cable TV: An Economic Interpretation," *Journal of Communication* 36 (Summer 1986), pp. 92–107; Michele Siemicki, David Atkin, Bradley Greenberg, and Thomas Baldwin, "Nationally Distributed Children's Shows: What Cable TV Contributes," *Journalism Quarterly* 63 (Winter 1987), pp. 710–718.

Information on viewer behavior effects and patterns can be found in Leo W. Jeffres, "Cable TV and Viewer Selectivity," *Journal of Broadcasting* 22 (Spring 1978), pp. 167–178; Stuart J. Kaplan, "The Impact of Cable Television Services on the Use of Competing Media," *Journal of Broadcasting* 22 (Spring 1978), pp. 155–166; and James A. Danowski and Gerhard J. Hanneman, "Aging and Preferences for Interactive Cable Services," *Journal of Broadcasting* 24 (Summer 1980), pp. 337–345. For a discussion of cable television's impact on other media, see Don Agostino, "Cable Television's Impact on the Audience of Public Television," *Journal of Broadcasting* 24 (Summer 1980), pp. 347–365; and James G. Webster, "Cable Television's Impact on Audience for Local News," *Journalism Quarterly* 61 (Summer 1984), pp. 419–422.

Discussions of the First Amendment issues related to cable can be found in Howard M. Kleiman, "Indecent Programming on Cable Television: Legal and Social Implications," *Journal of Broadcasting & Electronic Media* 30 (Summer 1986), pp. 275–294; and Michael O. Wirth and Linda Cobb-Reiley, "A First Amendment Critique of the 1984 Cable Act," *Journal of Broadcasting & Electronic Media* 31 (Fall 1987), pp. 391–407—an essay on how cable television should handle programming containing sex and nudity.

A study by Wenmouth Williams, Jr., and Kathleen Mahoney, "Perceived Impact of the Cable Policy Act of 1984," *Journal of Broadcasting & Electronic Media* 31 (Spring 1987), p. 193, found cable system operators and local regulators were generally satisfied with the Cable Communication Policy Act of 1984.

For data on consumer sentiment about cable television, see Vernone M. Sparkes and NamJun Kang's "Public Reactions to Cable Television: Time in the Diffusion Process," *Journal of Broadcasting & Electronic Media* 30 (Spring 1986), p. 213, a five-year study on viewer attitudes toward cable television.

4

FILMS

Shirley S. Carter

THE GROWTH AND DEVELOPMENT OF FILM

The development of film in America may be traced to Thomas Alva Edison's patent of the kentograph camera and kenetoscope viewer in 1893. Shortly thereafter, Fred Ott, a protégé of Edison, produced the earliest whole film, *Sneeze* (Mast, 1981, p. 35). The first public showing of a projected motion picture in the United States for a paying audience was on April 23, 1896, in New York City, for *The Vitascope.*

These earliest innovations in film led the way for the first well-developed film, the narrative. Edwin S. Porter produced *The Life of an American Fireman* in 1903 and *The Great Train Robbery,* which is considered the most popular American film prior to 1912.

D. W. Griffith, often referred to as the "father of film" because of his consolidation and expansion of film technique, released the masterpiece feature-length film *The Birth of a Nation* in 1915, which was based on Thomas Dixon's novel *The Clansman.* Film historians describe the record-breaking $125,000 spectacular as a brilliant use of film techniques such as classical cutting—editing for dramatic intensity and emotional emphasis. He also used close-up and split screen shots and realistic and impressionistic lighting. With its glorified view of the Old South and its portrayal of Ku Klux Klansmen as heroes, the film presented in dramatic fashion how a movie can create powerful emotional and propagandistic effects. Griffith made good use of stereotypes, the displaced family of the South, and "carpetbaggers" from the North, and President Woodrow Wilson proclaimed, "It's like writing history in lightning." However, the film caused the National Association for the Advancement of Colored People (NAACP) to boycott, protesting the film's negative, stereotypical portrayal of blacks. Contemporary film scholars often refer to *The Birth of a Nation* as a "classic, racist masterpiece" (Bogle, 1988).

At about the same time, from 1913 to 1916, the comedic genius of Charlie Chaplin began to emerge as a new film form. Chaplin viewed the comic world as the means to examine the serious world of human needs and societal structures (Mast, 1981, pp. 85–86). Chaplin has often been characterized as the most popular and critically admired player of the silent cinema, from his inventive use of pantomime to his ability to blend comedy with pathos. The image of Chaplin as the little clown with the bowler hat, the baggy pants, reedy cane, and floppy shoes was perhaps one of the most enduring of the silent film era.

The film industry came of age in the 1920s and 1930s because of the rise of Hollywood film stars like Rudolph Valentino, Mary Pickford, Lillian Gish, Douglas Fairbanks, and of course, Chaplin—and through the introduction of sound. Three significant aspects of filmmaking that also marked this era were the tiny budgets required to produce films, production times of two to three weeks to shoot a full-length film, and the requirement of relatively few people in the production crew (Gilbert & McCarter, 1988, pp. 254–255). The two films credited with introducing sound to film, bringing in the "talkie" era, were Al Jolson's *The Jazz Singer* (1927) and *The Singing Fool* (1928). Both films were released by Warner Brothers and achieved box office success. In fact, Warner Brothers is credited with pioneering the use of sound (Gomery, 1990).

Although some historians view *The Jazz Singer* as the first sound film, it merely perfected the technique of synchronization as a form of storytelling. *The Singing Fool,* on the other hand, is thought to be the biggest box office success during the 1920s and 1930s, second only to *Gone with the Wind* (1939). The film cost an estimated $200,000 to produce but grossed $5 million. *The Singing Fool* also helped to establish the criteria for profit making in the film industry: top stars, a gripping story, spectacular special effects, and a first-rate production team.

ORGANIZATIONAL STRUCTURE AND SIZE

The film industry reached its peak during the 1930s and mid-1940s. More than 500 feature films had been produced by 1937, and in 1938, 80 million people went to the movie theaters every week.

The increasing size of the film audience also created a need for more theaters and a greater number of film releases to meet the demands, thus supporting the studio system, which was geared for production in quantity (Mast, 1981, p. 225).

Films that characterize the successful studio years are Chaplin's *Modern Times* (1936), David O. Selznick's *Gone with the Wind* (1939), and Orson Welles's *Citizen Kane* (1941). *Gone with the Wind* is commercially acclaimed as the all-time box office leader, with revenues of more than $300 million if one adjusts for inflation.

The film has also been praised for its brilliant use of color and received artistic accolades. Hattie McDaniel's portrayal of Mammy in *Gone with the Wind* earned for her an Oscar as Best Supporting Actress and the distinction of being the first African-American female to receive an Academy Award.

Although judged neither as a critical success nor as a commercial success when RKO released *Citizen Kane* (1941), contemporary film scholars and consumers invariably include Welles and *Kane* among the lists of the ten best filmmakers and films. The film's innovations included the use of narration, newsreel, and camera technique to weave a gripping and probing tale. Welles has been called an *auteur,* a film director with maximum control over a film's production and an individual style.

Major studios of the 1930s and 1940s included Warner Brothers, MGM (Metro-Goldwyn-Mayer, Inc.), RKO, Paramount, Twentieth Century Fox, Universal, and Columbia. Warner Brothers was the studio most committed to depicting contemporary social problems; MGM was the studio of stars such as Greta Garbo, Jean Harlow, Joan Crawford, Katharine Hepburn, Clark Gable, Spencer Tracy, and James Stewart; RKO featured the Fred Astaire–Ginger Rogers musicals and Orson Welles; Paramount was a studio of writers and directors such as Cecil B. DeMille, Preston Sturges, Billy Wilder, Mae West, and W. C. Fields; Twentieth Century Fox excelled in historical and adventure films directed by John Ford and Henry King and featured such stars as Tyrone Power and Henry Fonda; Universal's specialty was the Frankenstein horror films and the later comedies of W. C. Fields; and Columbia attracted Frank Capra and George Cukor (Mast, 1981, pp. 231–233). Together these studios released more than 312 feature films during 1930–1931; 326 in 1935–1936; and 363 during the period 1940–1945. The film industry peaked in 1946 when it grossed more than $1 billion.

Ratings and Distribution Systems

Filmmakers and distributors prior to the 1960s belonged to the Motion Picture Producers and Distributors of America (MPPDA), which adhered to the strict codes of the Production Code Administration (PCA) established in 1930. Among its guidelines, the PCA restricted the depiction of sexual promiscuity and the glamorization of crime and brutality in gangster movies. As a historical document, the PCA tried to regulate cultural mores and determine what was suitable for public view. Otto Preminger's release of *The Moon Is Blue* (1953) without the PCA's seal of approval obliterated its effectiveness.

The PCA was replaced in 1968 by the industry's rating system, which placed the burden of determining what is morally acceptable in film content on the film audience. In fact, this tactic proved to be a lure in providing sexual relationship themes and social criticism in film content as one way of competing with television (Mast, 1981).

Films and Profit

The top ten global box office leaders for 1993 include *Jurassic Park,* a Universal release, with combined domestic and foreign earnings of more than $868 million; *The Fugitive,* a Warner Brothers' release at $349 million; Disney's

Aladdin, which earned a combined $303 million; *The Bodyguard,* a Warner Brothers' release with combined earnings of more than $290 million; Paramount's *Indecent Proposal,* $258 million, and *The Firm,* $254 million; Tri-Star's *Cliffhanger,* $223 million, and *Sleepless in Seattle,* $189 million; and Columbia's *In the Line of Fire* at $171 million, and *A Few Good Men* at $146 million (*Variety,* Jan. 3–9, 1994, pp. 1, 42).

Since De Fleur and Dennis's 1988 study, the leading domestic moneymakers are now *Jurassic Park,* $338 million; *Gone with the Wind,* more than $300 million; *E.T.* (1982), $229 million; *Star Wars* (1977), $193 million; *The Fugitive,* $179 million; *Return of the Jedi* (1983), $168 million; *Batman Returns* (1992), $162 million; *The Firm,* $158 million; *Batman* (1989), $150 million; *Beauty and the Beast* (1992), $144.9 million; and *Lethal Weapon 3* (1992), $144.6 million (Intelligence Report 1993).

The film industry is still controlled by the studios, which handle production, distribution, and exhibition. The top film studios in the late 1980s were Warner Brothers, Universal, Twentieth Century Fox, Columbia, Paramount, Tri-Star, and Disney (all studios' domination continued into the 1990s).

Although the major studios dominate the business, independent filmmakers are making significant strides. In 1984, the majors produced 200 of the 500 films produced in Hollywood. Independents produced the rest, a trend that has become more prominent since 1984 when 172 of the 316 films produced were by independents who can produce films at a fraction of the cost of majors. Independents still rely on the major studios for financing and distributing their films. Notable examples of independent film producers in the 1980s include David Puttnam, *Chariots of Fire* (1981); Robert Townsend, *Hollywood Shuffle* (1987), which cost $1 million to produce compared with the studio average of $20 million; Spike Lee, whose *She's Gotta Have It* (1986) cost $200,000 to produce but earned $7 million, and his critically acclaimed and controversial *Malcolm X* (1992), which drew audiences in spite of its three and a half hour length; and John Singleton, who produced *Boyz in the Hood* (1991) at a cost of $4 million.

The success of independent filmmakers such as Lee and Singleton helped to usher in a new cinematic wave in the 1990s, according to film writer Janet Maslin (1992). Maslin cited several of 1992's best American independently made films: *The Waterdance,* codirected by Neal Jimenez and Michael Steinberg; Carl Franklin's *One False Move;* Allison Anders's *Gas Food Lodging;* Gregg Araki's *Living End;* Tom Kalin's *Swoon;* Quentin Tarantino's *Reservoir Dogs;* Tim Robbins's *Bob Roberts;* and Julie Dash's *Daughters of the Dust.* Two other African-American female film directors, Ruby Oliver and Leslie Harris, had debut films in early 1993, *Love Your Mama,* and *Just Another Girl on the IRT,* respectively. According to the *New York Times,* in 1991 and 1992, nearly thirty films directed by African-American males were released, and a dozen by white women in 1991 (Maslin, 1992). The ranks of women directors have expanded to include Penny Marshall, Barbra Streisand, Jodie Foster, and Nora Ephron.

According to Maslin (1992), these films succeeded in dispensing with the something-for-everyone blandness of big studio efforts. While not necessarily box office smashes, these films did succeed in targeting specific audiences by "race, politics or general outlook and showing those audiences characters they wanted to see" (pp. H-1, H-26). Maslin considers risk taking or "taking chances that would be out of the question in mainstream Hollywood" (pp. H-1, H-26) one of the defining characteristics of independent filmmakers. Part of their appeal to the film audience may also be attributed to the diminishing popularity of "formula filmmaking" that characterizes the Hollywood, major studio product. Other factors that contribute to the commercial viability of independent films include the decline in quality and popularity of foreign films, the rise in independent film audience sophistication, and their "particularization of experience" or idiosyncracy, such as Dash's *Daughters of the Dust,* which depicted the experiences of a turn-of-the-century Gullah family in the Carolina Sea Islands.

Facing down the major studios may no longer be an obstacle for the more established independent film producers such as Lee and Robbins. Still others must contend with such industry features as major studios that collect at least 90 percent of the total income of movie distributors, which they share with independent producers and directors. The theater must generate its income from concessions because of the high percentage of ticket sales that must go back to the distributor. According to Biagi (1994) the number of motion picture theaters in the United States grew from 19,489 silent theaters in 1926 to 20,755 sound and 2,800 outdoor theaters in 1988, but dropped to 25,105 in 1992. The top five American theater chains in 1992 were United Artists, Cineplex Odeon, American Multi-Cinema, Carmike, and General Cinema (pp. 520-522).

As more film companies have come under the ownership of conglomerates such as Gulf+Western and Coca-Cola, it is little wonder that the film industry operates like a conglomerate. Thus, the goal of the film industry seems to be to maximize its profits while minimizing the product—or as critics claim, produce formula films. According to Jeffrey Katzenberg, chairman of Walt Disney Pictures, "Commerce has overwhelmed art, which is why Hollywood movies aren't as good as they used to be. The process has been corrupted. It is too much about money and not enough about good entertainment" (Maslin, 1992, p. H-1).

Television, cable, and videocassette have provided other distribution channels for films. The industry's smaller, more sociological film projects are made specifically for television, such as *The Autobiography of Miss Jane Pittman* or *Sara: Plain and Tall.* The narrative form has given way to the miniseries, a medium pioneered by *Roots* and *Rich Man, Poor Man,* for example, and the last of the Haley family sagas, *Queen.* Films that have limited runs in movie theaters may be rereleased for video sales; indeed, it is not uncommon for a studio such as Disney to release a box office success such as *Beauty and the Beast* and then make it available to consumers on videocassette.

DeFleur and Dennis (1988) cite film scholar John Fell's seven stages or elements in the filmmaking process:

1. Conceptualization: the idea for a film
2. Production: stages that include fund-raising, organizing the crew and cast, and putting the film on screen
3. Direction: director chooses the script and solves problems
4. Performance: actors must be chosen and their performances calibrated to the script and other film personnel
5. Visualization: the planning and execution of the actual film involves cinematographers, lighting technicians, and others
6. Special Effects: camera and action devices
7. Editing: achieving artistic success to shape the director's vision

The film industry still relies on theater box office receipts for its revenues. According to DeFleur and Dennis, the following formula illustrates a successful film: expenditures (negative cost factors), $20 million (production), $8 million (marketing); and revenues, $16 million (domestic film rentals), $7 million (foreign releases), and $17 million (home video, pay TV, network TV syndication). The industry primarily relies on newspapers for advertising spending almost 70 percent in this medium and 27 percent in television. According to *USA Today,* the average studio movie cost $55 million to make in 1993 and $11.2 million to market, up 5 percent from 1991.

RESPONSIBILITY AND EFFECTIVENESS: THE FILM AUDIENCE

Film audience profiles have dramatically changed since the 1980s, when Hollywood was justified to play to a young audience since roughly 76 percent was under forty in 1992 (Crumpler, 1993). In 1990, teens spent an estimated $79 billion, ostensibly to watch a new Hollywood subgenre of films that featured comedies or drama set in a middle-class high school (Aufderheide, 1991). According to Aufderheide, 1980s films set in high school reflected disturbing social realities—about the power of commercial youth culture, about authority, about the powerful dividers of class and race. And they could make you feel downright sorry for the teacher. *Ferris Bueller's Day Off* (1986) and *Bill & Ted's Excellent Adventure* (1989) typify this film type. Such "kidpix" underscored an important part of the youth film audience as Hollywood shaped its products to reflect their values, interests, styles, themes, music, and moral codes. For them, film became an essential part of the socialization process, to get out of the house, away from their parent's society, and into a society of their own peers (Mast, 1981, p. 313).

But the audience is changing, according to Jack Valenti, president of the

Motion Picture Association of America. In 1992, 30 percent of all tickets in 1992 were bought by an audience over age forty, up from 14.2 percent in 1985. Valenti also reported a decline in the number of tickets sold in 1992, a drop of 1.8 percent; the number of films viewed by the typical moviegoer decreased from 8.4 in 1985 to 5.7 in 1992. According to other statistics, Hispanics are the fastest-growing movie audience in the 1990s. Mark Canton, chairman of Columbia Pictures, said more than half of films made are R-rated, while PG films are three times more likely to gross $100 million (Spillman, 1993).

The film industry vacillates in its portrayal of women. In 1991, the newest generation of female stars suggested positive role models for women in their portrayal of realistic characters, unlike the stereotypes of earlier years. One of the most provocative films to explore the woman's perspective is *Thelma & Louise* (1991). In both politics and film, 1992 was supposed to have been the "Year of the Woman." While 1992 was a watershed year for women in politics, it was a virtual shutout when it came to nonstereotypical roles for women in film. According to *New York Times* film writer Caryn James, the most dominant Hollywood film role for women in 1992 was a "crazed killer updated from the wicked women in 1940's films noirs," as seen in *Basic Instinct, The Hand That Rocks the Cradle,* and *Single White Female.*

Meaningful roles for black women were even less abundant. Although the film industry appears to target the black film audience in the 1990s, black women have received only 3 percent of the 29 percent of all roles in film and television that went to women (Horowitz, 1991).

One notable exception among black actresses is Whoopi Goldberg, who won the 1991 Academy Award for best supporting actress for *Ghost* (1990) and starred in *Sister Act* (1992). Two other black actresses had prominent starring roles in films in 1992 and 1993, respectively: Angela Bassett, who played Malcolm X's wife, Betty Shabazz, in *Malcolm X,* and Alfre Woodard, featured in *Passion Fish* (1993).

CRITICISM OF FILM

The criticism of the film industry revolves around two issues: The first issue deals with the somewhat diminished role of the film critic, and the second issue concerns the role of film as a transmitter of culture and values in society. Film critics predictably lament the trend toward blockbuster films as meaning that films no longer have to be well made but merely well sold. In their view, media hype has replaced art, and the movies are deader than ever as a meaningful and cultural experience (Mast, 1981). But unlike other forms of artistic expression, films target the audience, as word of mouth becomes a more effective marketing tool than the critical review.

Nonetheless, the film critic has a place in modern society. Magazines and newspapers feature movie reviews. "The Today Show" has a resident film critic in Gene Shalit, and Gene Siskel and Roger Ebert have their own syndicated review program that appears on several commercial television stations.

The film industry has been criticized for its role in portraying negative stereotypes of women and minorities, and its depiction of violent and sexual themes. The industry responds to this type of criticism by maintaining that its critics expect it to serve as a beacon, rather than as a mirror of societal problems, and that this is an unrealistic role for film. Still, the Motion Picture Association has released statistics that support the contention that the industry should reexamine its bottom line and story line. The most successful Hollywood films at the box office are those rated G or PG.

THE FUTURE OF FILM

Film endures both as a form of visual communications and as a form of mass communication. As a financial institution the industry will remain profitable even as it undergoes change.

As a medium of mass communication and in its role as a transmitter of culture, film has the opportunity to explore societal issues and trends more effectively than other more traditional media such as newspapers and network television. For example, the industry can probe controversial issues surrounding contemporary themes such as sexual orientation, gender and cultural diversity, AIDS and other health care crises, politics, and the environment. The industry can also recapture aesthetic qualities in old movie genres such as the Western, such as Clint Eastwood's Oscar-winning *Unforgiven* (1992).

The competition of the new technology that further fragments a sophisticated audience will pose other challenges that the film industry will not ignore. For instance, some films are already produced with an expected short life at the box office but a longer run at Blockbuster Video. Some releases are made for television; others are created especially for cable. Not too far off in the future is the likelihood that we may all become auteurs—the newest film technology is interactive films. The low-budget, good-humored, twenty-minute interfilm *I'm Your Man* debuted in 1993 in New York and Lakewood, California, and allowed audiences to direct the plot by pushing green, orange, or red buttons connected to the armrest of every seat in the theater.

An increasingly diverse film audience will suggest other changes in the industry. As independent black filmmakers have recognized the need to produce their own movies, so will other ethnic and cultural groups such as Latinos, Asian Americans, and Native Americans. Hollywood cannot ignore the population increase among these groups that will constitute a majority by the mid-2000s. Films will be more narrowly targeted in order to achieve the same kind of appeal that "particularizes experiences" of diverse audiences.

The film industry will also be affected by environmental and global constraints, particularly as they impact production, distribution, and exhibition.

A BRIEF HISTORY OF BLACKS IN FILM IN THE UNITED STATES

The history of blacks in film is provided for the 1900s through 1980 by the outstanding works of film historian and scholar Donald Bogle (1988), traced from Hollywood's "race" movies and classics like *The Birth of a Nation* and *Gone with the Wind* to later films casting blacks other than as actors in blackface and featuring easily defined black themes, such as *Stormy Weather, Carmen Jones,* and *A Raisin in the Sun. Lady Sings the Blues, Beverly Hills Cops, Do the Right Thing, She's Gotta Have It,* and *Boyz in the Hood* are more contemporary examples.

The history corresponds with prevailing themes that characterized a particular period.

1. 1903–1928—The First Twenty-five Years: Depravity and Decadence: 1903, *Uncle Tom's Cabin;* 1915, *The Birth of a Nation;* 1916–1918, black films produced by independent filmmakers outside Hollywood: *The Realization of a Negro's Ambition, Trooper K of Troop K,* and *The Homesteader.*

2. 1929–1940—The Black Performer: The all-talking, all-singing, all-colored major studio productions of *Hearts in Dixie,* and *Hallelujah.* The 1930s decade was called the Golden Age for black performers, who introduced film audiences to a new timing, rhythmic thrust, and comic assertiveness. Best example: Bill "Bojangles" Robinson in *The Little Colonel* (1934). Other notable characters included Butterfly McQueen's unique comedy and "patheticism" and Hattie McDaniel's high-flung sense of superiority in *Gone with the Wind. Stormy Weather* (1943) and *Cabin in the Sky* (1943) were much heralded as two films that depicted the enormous talents of black Americans as performers: Lena Horne, Ethel Waters, Bill "Bojangles" Robinson, Eddie "Rochester" Anderson, Cab Calloway, Louis Armstrong, and Katherine Dunham.

3. 1945–1955—The Emergence of the Black Actor and Social Themes: This era focused on so-called problem films that touched on racial issues confronting the nation at the time and featured prominent black characters and themes. 1949: *Home of the Brave; Pinky; Lost Boundaries;* and *Intruder in the Dust.*

4. 1950–1960—The Noble Black Actor: One actor personified this era: Sidney Poitier— intense, urban, introspective. Other noble actors of this period: James Edwards, Ruby Dee, Juano Hernandez, Ossie Davis, Claudia McNeil, Diana Sands, and Louis Gossett, Jr.

5. 1960–1980—Blaxploitation and Searching for an Identity: The 1960s audience demanded, but didn't get, films that conveyed the national mood of militancy and cultural nationalism. The 1970s produced such contradictory fare as Melvin Van Peebles's *Sweet Sweetback's Baadasssss Song* (1971) and *Sounder* (1972). According to Bogle, more often than not, blaxploitation films (those that played on the needs of the black audience for heroic figures but did not deliver in realistic terms) were the norm. The sensitive films of the 1970s were those with strong black female characters: *Buck and the Preacher* (1972), *Lady Sings the Blues* (1972), and *Claudine* (1974).

6. 1980– —The Hollywood Shuffle to Do the Right Thing: The 1980s featured black

actors in background roles in what Bogle labels as the theme of interracial male bonding, or the "Huck Finn" fixation—the tough, assertive white male learns about emotion from his good black male friend. This genre featured such actors and films as Billy Dee Williams in *Star Wars* (1977), *The Empire Strikes Back* (1980), *The Return of the Jedi* (1983), and *Nighthawks* (1981); Richard Pryor in *Stir Crazy* (1980) and *Superman III* (1983); Eddie Murphy in *Beverly Hills Cop* (1984), *48 Hrs.* (1982), and *Trading Places* (1983); Gregory Hines in *White Nights* (1985) and *Running Scared* (1986); and Louis Gossett, Jr., in *Enemy Mine* (1985), *Iron Eagle* (1986), and *Firewalker* (1986).

The 1980s also produced memorable yet controversial films such as Steven Spielberg's adaptation of Alice Walker's *The Color Purple* (1985) and independent filmmaker Spike Lee's *She's Gotta Have It* (1986). The controversy in each film centered around the complex relationships between men and women, with underlying themes in *The Color Purple* of relationships in general, the needs of women in particular. *The Color Purple* also depicted black women in roles other than the "scary, high-flung exotics" that characterized earlier films. On the other hand, *She's Gotta Have It* managed to perpetuate the black female stereotype.

Lee's debut in the 1980s helped to usher in a fresher perspective for the black film audience in the 1990s. Following *She's Gotta Have It* were Lee's *School Daze* (1987), *Do the Right Thing*, and in 1991, *Jungle Fever*. Lee's success has helped to sensitize the film industry to such independents as Robert Townsend and newcomer John Singleton. Other up and coming independent filmmakers include Melvin Van Peebles, whose film *Possee* (1993) is the first of a new wave of films about black cowboys. But perhaps most interesting is the promise of Julie Dash, whose *Daughters of the Dust* (fall 1991) has been described as the first screen translation of the sensibility found in contemporary black women's literature.

Strong images of black women in film are conspicuously absent, even from such films by Lee, Peebles, and others, including black and white producers. In fact, of the 400 movies Hollywood produces annually, African-American women have found few that depict their personal experiences (Hruska & Rayman, 1993). Another criticism of the film industry is that when it comes to portraying ethnic minorities, some studios "can't seem to see beyond the ghetto." Helaine Head, the director of *Simple Justice*, a recent PBS docudrama about the *Brown v. Board of Education* Supreme Court decision, laments that a "lack of violence, drug use and unmarried pregnancies in her scripts were definite drawbacks, and that black projects without those elements are not bankable" (quoted in Hruska & Rayman, 1993). Leslie Harris said she produced *Just Another Girl on the IRT* because she was tired of the same old images of African-American women in movies: She's on someone's arm, she's a sex object, or she's a drug dealer's girlfriend.

BIBLIOGRAPHY

Books

Berger, Arthur Asa. (1989). *Seeing is believing: An introduction to visual communication.* Mountainview, CA: Mayfield.

Biagi, Shirley (1994). *Media impact.* Belmont, CA: Wadsworth.

Bogle, Donald. (1988). *Blacks in American films and television.* New York: Garland.

Cripps, Thomas. (1990). Sweet Sweetback's Baadasssss Song and the changing politics of genre film. In Peter Lehman (Ed.), *Close viewings: An anthology of new film criticism.* Tallahassee: Florida State University Press.

DeFleur, Melvin L., & Dennis, Everette E. (1988). *Understanding mass communication.* Boston: Houghton Mifflin.

Gianetti, Louis. (1990). *Understanding movies.* Englewood Cliffs, NJ: Prentice-Hall.

Gilbert, Rita, & McCarter, William. (1988). *Living with art.* New York: Knopf.

Gomery, Douglas. (1990). The Singing Fool. In Peter Lehman (Ed.), *Close viewings: An anthology of new film criticism.* Tallahassee: Florida State University Press.

Kaminsky, Stuart M. (1974). *American film genres.* Dayton, OH: Pflaum.

Lehman, Peter (Ed.). (1990). *Close viewings: An anthology of new film criticism.* Tallahassee: Florida State University Press.

Luhr, William. (1990). Tracking the Maltese Falcon: Classical Hollywood narration. In Peter Lehman (Ed.), *Close viewings: An anthology of new film criticism.* Tallahassee: Florida State University Press.

Mast, Gerald. (1981). *A short history of the movies.* New York: Bobbs-Merrill.

Periodicals

Aufderheide, Patricia. (1991). Hollywood High. *Gannett Center Journal, 5* (1), 61.

Crumpler, David. (1993, March 28). Going for the gold, Oscar-style. *Florida-Times Union,* p. G-1.

Horowitz, Joy. (1991, June 4). New York Times News Service. *Florida-Times Union,* pp. D-1, D-6.

Hruska, Bronwen, & Rayman, Graham. (1993, February 23). On the outside looking in. *New York Times,* pp. H-17, H-26.

Intelligence Report. (1993, January 10). Battered batmobile wins race, even on flat tires. *Parade,* p. 22.

James, Caryn. (1993, February 7). Look, Ma, I'm an auteur! *New York Times,* p. 2.

Kady, Leonard. (1994, January 3–9). Top 100 pix take $8 bil globally. *Variety,* pp. 1, 42.

Maslin, Janet. (1992, December 13). Is a cinematic new wave cresting?'' *New York Times,* pp. H-1, H-26.

Spillman, Susan. (1993, March 10). Moviegoing slips; audiences growing older. *USA Today,* p. D-1.

Tate, Greg. (1991, June). Cinematic sisterhood. *The Village Voice Film Special.*

Tate, Greg. (1991, June). Of homegirl goddesses and geechee women. *The Village Voice Film Festival.*

5

MAGAZINES

Marilyn Kern-Foxworth

Anyone searching today for a magazine to read has 11,092 from which to make a selection. These magazines offer diverse reading that is targeted to selected audiences according to age, occupation, sex, hobby, and life-styles. Magazines are one of America's great institutions. The first national medium for mass communication, magazines have played an important role in American politics, education, culture, acculturation, and socialization. Magazines not only have informed but also have provided entertainment and recreation to countless isolated families during times when these pleasures were few and far between.

One would be hard-pressed to visit any American home and not find a magazine of some kind. According to the Magazine Publishers Association (MPA), each reader spends an average of sixty-one minutes on each copy read (Guthrie, 1988). Nearly all Americans, 94 percent, read magazines during the average month. The middle-class and highly educated consumers are the best readers.

Although the magazine lacks the immediacy of the broadcast media and the newspaper, it nevertheless is timely enough to deal with the continuous flow of news events. Its timeliness and continuity set it apart from the book. As a continuing publication, it has several noted advantages over other mediums, including:

- It can provide a form of discussion by carrying responses from its audience
- It can sustain campaigns for indefinite periods
- It can work for cumulative rather than single impact
- Its available space and the reading habits of its audience enable it to give fairly lengthy treatment to the subjects it covers
- Magazines offer a 50-50 ratio of advertising to news, whereas newspapers have traditionally offered 60 percent advertising and 40 percent news

Moreover, magazines, like other print media, appeal more to the intellect than to the senses and emotions of their audiences. Magazines became volatile commodities with the advent of television but were able to sustain their territory because they were not as transient as the broadcast media. They are more permanent than newspapers, with a longer readership span; and magazines remain in readers' homes for weeks, months, and sometimes even years. The *National Geographic,* well known for its writing and photography, is a medium of instruction and interpretation for the leisurely critical reader and boasts an 84.2 percent renewal rate among subscribers in seventy countries. American magazines have survived many revolutions and technological advances during their 253-year existence.

In 1860, 260 magazines were published in America; by 1865, the number had increased to 700; and by 1885, the number had surged to 3,300. A downswing occurred, and by 1900, there were 1,800. However, the number of magazine subscribers increased dramatically and continued to do so. "From 1900 to 1950, the number of 'magazine families' subscribing to one or more periodicals rose from 200,000 to more than 32 million" (Whetmore, 1987, p. 71.)

HISTORY

Pioneering magazines in England were storage places for many literary items of prose and poetry. Thus, the term *magazine* originated from the French term *magasin,* the Italian *magazzino,* and the Arabic *makhazin* and originally meant "storehouse." The top of a typesetting machine is a flat container in an inclined position that stores matrices, and it, too, is referred to as a magazine (Wolseley, 1969). In colonial times, the word *magazine* meant warehouse or depository, a place where different kinds of provisions were stored under one roof (Dominick, 1987).

Magazines had their beginnings on the European continent after the introduction of the printing press. Prior to the introduction of magazines, there existed pamphlets, broadsheets, ballads, chapbooks, and almanacs. The first magazine was *The Review,* which was published in London by Daniel Defoe, author of *Robinson Crusoe,* in 1704 (Berger, 1988). The four-page publication, a newspaper and magazine hybrid and the first British periodical, contained articles on domestic affairs, national policies, and commentary on news events. It appeared three times each week at first and as a biweekly in later years. Later, departments highlighting literature, manners, and morals were added (Wolseley, 1969). Defoe published *The Review* for nine years.

The term *magazine* was used for the first time as a part of a periodical by a London-based publication entitled *Gentleman's Magazine,* which was published by Edward Cave in 1731. The first magazines published in the United States came with the introduction of Andrew Bradford's *The American Magazine or a Monthly View of the Political State of the British Colonies* on February 13, 1741, and the debut of Benjamin Franklin's *General Magazine and Historical*

Chronicle for the British Plantation in America on February 16, 1741, both issued in Philadelphia. The periodical press did not begin to flourish until the nineteenth century. During the early years, American periodicals experienced the typical hardships endured by any publication emerging in a developing country.

In the 1900s, astute journalists attacked corruption in the cities and illegal and immoral practices by big business. Theodore Roosevelt expressed disdain for them by labeling these crusaders as "muckrakers," when he likened them to the "Man with the Muckrake" in *Pilgrim's Progress,* who spent so much time raking the manure on the barnyard floor that he didn't look up to see the good things even when he was offered a glittering crown (DeFleur & Dennis, 1987, p. 139).

Samuel Sidney McClure, who founded *McClure's Magazine* in 1893, recognized that twenty-five to thirty cents was too high for most consumers, so he priced his magazine at fifteen cents. With a large number of readers, he profited more from advertising. His strategy was to produce an entertaining, easy-to-read magazine for the masses, but he revolutionized magazine publishing when he printed Ida Tarbell's "History of the Standard Oil Company" and Joseph Lincoln Steffens's "Shame of the Cities," an exposé detailing bribery, fraud, unfair business practices, and violence. Shocking stories on political corruption in big cities and another series on crooked practices in the railroad industry succeeded Tarbell's original story.

Munsey's Magazine, published by Frank Munsey, was McClure's chief rival. To compete with McClure, Munsey dropped the price of his magazine to ten cents in 1893. Munsey acquired a reputation as a ruthless and shrewd character who would stop at nothing to increase readership of his magazine (Whetmore, 1987, p. 71).

In 1906, Ida Tarbell, Lincoln Steffens, and William Allen White joined the staff of the *American Magazine* to continue the reform. Also in 1906, other magazines joined the bandwagon and initiated their own investigations of big business corruption.

By 1912, muckraking was no longer in vogue and had all but disappeared, but it was rejuvenated briefly in 1914 with the inauguration of *The New Republic,* featuring the political ideology of Walter Lippmann. By World War I, muckraking was a style of journalism no longer practiced by most magazines. Magazines that specialized in scrutinies of these kinds died by the wayside, and by 1990, only a handful still existed, including *The Nation, The New Republic,* and *Mother Jones,* which first gained national notoriety for its charges that the Ford Pinto was a potentially dangerous automobile.

ORGANIZATIONAL STRUCTURE AND SIZE

"The recent history of the magazine business indicates this is a very volatile industry, one that is extremely susceptible to social change as well as to economic fluctuations'' (Wright, 1987, p. 480). Owing to personnel turnover and the number of magazines that fold each year, it is difficult to determine, but the best estimates are that there are about 95,000 people employed in the magazine industry. Additionally, Weaver and Wilhoit (1986) estimate that news magazine journalists make up only 1.1 percent of the full-time editorial work force in the American news media.

Competitive salaries guarantee that there will always be someone waiting in the wings hoping to be a director, editor, or staff writer. The average salary for editorial directors and their equivalents in top management is $66,444. This represents 2.6 percent less than the average reported in 1992. Editors reported an average salary of $46,893, which is 6 percent less than 1992. Managing editors averaged salaries of $41,052, an increase of 5.1 percent in 1992. Senior editors earned $43,441, an increase of 5.9 percent over 1992 (Angelo and Drucker, 1993, p. 41).

The divisions of labor for a magazine are categorized into four areas: (1) editorial, (2) advertising sales, (3) circulation, and (4) production. The publisher is responsible for the key areas of advertising sales, newsstand circulation, subscriptions, production, promotion, and finance. On most magazines, the publisher is also responsible for budgeting, financial projections, and the preparation of profit-and-loss statements for the board of directors. The publisher's primary concern is keeping the publication financially stable through subscriptions, single-copy sales, and advertising.

The Editorial Department handles the nonadvertising content of the magazine. The person in charge may be called the executive editor, the editor-in-chief, or simply the editor. On most publications, the job of editor is primarily one of administration, and much of the editor's time is spent in supervising the editorial staff, planning topics that might be used in upcoming issues, and informing the advertising department about plans.

The editor-in-chief is responsible for the editorial content of the magazine. The managing editor is usually in charge of the daily business of getting the magazine in finished form to the printer, making sure all articles are completed on time, selecting artwork, writing titles, changing layouts, and shortening stories. Assisting the managing editor are other editors dealing with various departments within the magazine. All editors work closely with art, graphics, and photography directors to design not only the articles appearing in the magazine but the magazine's cover and logo as well.

Staff writers write the stories, and many may be expected to write two or three stories a week. Yet at some of the major magazines, a staff writer may spend weeks or months researching, developing, and writing a story, especially if the focus of the story or the principal characters are located far from the magazine's headquarters.

The Advertising Department is responsible for selling advertising space in the magazine. Including farm and business publications, magazine advertising revenue in 1988 was $8.9 billion, approximately 7.5 percent of all advertising dollars (Fink, 1990).

The advertising director reports directly to the publisher and directs all advertising sales on a magazine, supervising all salespeople, branch office operations, and out-of-town representatives, as well as the activities of those working in promotion and research necessary for increasing sales. The advertising director also makes calls on the sales staff, develops strategic plans for increasing sales, and analyzes the results of reports submitted weekly by the house staff and the branch offices. The advertising director consults with editors concerning advertising programs that can be tied in with future magazine stories. The director is also responsible for overseeing and approving the format and layout of all advertisements. The director collaborates with the sales promotion manager concerning all marketing material.

Research specialists augment this effort by compiling information about the magazine's target markets. The top 300 magazines drew 57 percent of their revenue from advertising, or $9.9 billion (Endicott, 1992).

The Circulation Department, under the supervision of the circulation director, is responsible for getting new readers and retaining current subscribers. If the magazine is losing readers, the circulation director must find out why. If the research director sees untapped consumer markets, the circulation director must devise creative and innovative ways to garner those markets. Responsible to the circulation director are the heads of three divisions: (1) the subscription manager, who attempts to increase the number of people on the magazine's subscription list; (2) the single-copy sales manager, who works with the national distributors, wholesalers, and retailers; and (3) the subscription-fulfillment director, whose division is responsible for making sure the magazine gets to subscribers by taking care of matters ranging from address changes, renewals, new subscribers, and complaints.

Magazines use more than fourteen methods to increase their subscriber lists. These methods include, but are not limited to, "cash-field" agencies, with salespeople who make house-to-house calls to sell subscriptions directly to consumers; direct-mail campaigns by the publishers; "blow-in cards," those small nuisance cards inserted in magazines that fall out when the magazine is opened; and direct-marketing companies.

The Production Department is concerned with printing and binding the publication. The person who oversees this department is the production manager, who purchases paper, handles contracts with printers, orders new typesetting equipment, and makes frequent visits to printing plants to supervise the printing of the magazine.

MAGAZINE CLASSIFICATION

Codification of magazines becomes more difficult as they become more specialized and cater to more segmented audiences. According to *Writer's Market*, there are one hundred categories into which magazines can be placed. The magazines that have captured the top spots in terms of circulation are *Modern Ma-*

turity and *NRTA/AARP News Bulletin,* with circulations of 22,450,003 and 22,270,390, respectively, magazines that are targeted to senior citizens and are a part of the organizations' membership fees.

General Consumer Magazines

"A consumer magazine is one that can be acquired by anyone through a subscription or a single-copy purchase or by obtaining a free copy" (Dominick, 1987, p. 211). They are so called because consumers can purchase the goods and services advertised in the magazines. Also called *slicks* because of the smooth paper on which they are printed, consumer magazines approximated 1,200 in 1992, and according to Standard Rate and Data Service (SRDS), there are approximately fifty categories into which consumer magazines can be placed. Increasingly, newly created consumer magazines specialize in order to attract and retain their audiences, and special interest magazines account for over 90 percent of the magazines published today. The consumer magazine with the largest circulation is *Reader's Digest,* with a circulation of 16,258,476. The magazine resisted selling advertising for more than thirty years until rising costs finally forced it to give in ("Circulation Leaders," 1993). *Reader's Digest* appears in fifteen languages and has 100 million readers (Inside Track, 1990, p. 10). Other examples of such magazines include such notables as *People, Time,* and *TV Guide,* the fourth largest circulating magazine with a circulation of 14,498,341.

Secondary categories of consumer magazines include *newsmagazines,* a term coined by Henry Luce and Briton Hadden when they founded *Time* in 1923. *Time* boasted a circulation of 4,203,991 in 1992. Serving a function similar to that of national television newscasts, newsmagazines also include *Newsweek,* with a circulation of 3,240,131, owned by the Washington Post Company; and *U.S. News & World Report,* with a pro-business orientation.

City Magazines

Publications such as *New York, The Washingtonian, New West,* and *Houston Downtown Magazine* exemplify the city magazines, or what are sometimes called *metropolitan magazines,* which came to maturity in the 1960s and tend to concentrate on the activities of a particular city or region. American magazines that have chosen to focus on a particular geographic region have been in existence since 1743 when America's third magazine, the *Boston Weekly Magazine,* made its debut. Most major cities and many smaller ones (e.g., *Insite Magazine,* published in Bryan–College Station, Texas, twin cities with a combined population of approximately 100,000) now have city magazines that both investigate public affairs and try to monitor what happens in the city, especially the local entertainment.

Sex Magazines

With a wide range of sometimes controversial articles, these publications have high circulations and provide lucrative incomes for the owners. This group includes such general interest magazines as *Playboy, Playgirl,* and *Penthouse,* which have become increasingly respectable over the years. *Playboy* was counted among the top twenty magazines in 1992 with a circulation of 3,402,630. Sex magazines take pride in their fiction and nonfiction articles and interviews as well as in their suggestive photographs. Contrary to popular belief, the editorial material contained in these publications is generally well written and addresses timely issues affecting politics, education, and the American economy.

Sports Magazines

To say that America is full of sports buffs would be an understatement. To satisfy the curiosity of these fans, scores of magazines dedicated to covering every sport imaginable have surfaced. Such magazines include *Sports Illustrated,* which reports on all sports, and many, more specialized magazines covering golf, tennis, skiing, weightlifting, and so on. In 1992, *Sports Illustrated* had a circulation of 3,432,044.

Opinion Magazines

These include some of the oldest and most well-respected journals in America and include the *National Review,* a conservative magazine founded in the 1950s by columnist William F. Buckley, Jr. Some others are the liberal *New Leader, The New Republic,* and the *Progressive,* which received national attention in 1979 when it refused to cease publication of an article describing how an H-bomb is made over the objections of the federal government.

Intellectual Magazines

Such publications as *Commentary, American Scholar,* and *Partisan* are very similar to the opinion magazines, but they usually have denser copy and are aimed at a more highly educated consumer market. Both the opinion and the scholarly periodicals are proud of the high quality of their audiences and their ability to have an impact with such influential subscribers.

Quality Magazines

Although these magazines are similar to opinion and intellectual magazines, they usually have slightly larger circulations, approximately 500,000, and reach a more general audience than the scholarly journals. Some examples are the

Atlantic Monthly, Harper's, the *Saturday Review,* the *Smithsonian,* and *National Geographic.*

Men's Interest Magazines

These periodicals often overlap with sex and sports magazines and include *True: The Man's Magazine, Argosy,* and *EM/Ebony Man.* Targeted toward black males, *EM* is one of several magazines published by John Johnson of the Johnson publishing empire.

Women's Interest Magazines

Since the beginning of magazines, those with the highest circulation have been aimed at female audiences. Traditional women's magazines—*Godey's Lady's Book, Ladies' Home Journal, Family Circle, Woman's Day,* and *McCall's*—emerged from 1850 to 1900. In 1850, *Godey's Lady's Book* had a circulation of 40,000, the largest circulation of any magazine at that time (Busby, 1988). Moreover, the first American magazine in the nineteenth century to have a circulation of more than a million was *Ladies' Home Journal,* founded in 1881 by Cyrus Curtis. Today there exists a core of magazines directed toward female audiences known as the "Seven Sisters": *Better Homes and Gardens, Good Housekeeping, Redbook, Ladies' Home Journal, Family Circle, Woman's Day,* and *McCall's.* At least six of these magazines was listed in the top twenty list of magazines as determined by the Audit Bureau of Circulations in 1992: *Better Homes and Gardens,* 8,002,585; *Family Circle,* 5,283,660; *Good Housekeeping,* 5,139,355; *McCall's,* 4,704,772; *Woman's Day,* 4,810,445; and *Redbook,* 3,395,029 (Garland, 1993).

A women's interest magazine that differs from the rest is *Ms.,* founded in 1972, which reflects a moderate feminist point of view. *Ms.* ceased publication in 1989 amidst speculation that its editorial content was being directed by the advertising it received. In an attempt to correct the situation, the publication was suspended and restarted during the spring of 1990. The editors announced they would no longer depend on advertising for economic support; instead, they solicited private donations.

Ethnic Publications

Critics of ethnic media have suggested that they condone polarization of the races rather than their unification. However, proponents of ethnic media point out that their publications aid in the promulgation of ethnic culture and heritage; offer advertisers, marketers, and promoters excellent vehicles for reaching the multiracial consumer markets; and provide the only means for members of ALANA (African, Latin, Asian, Native American) groups to keep abreast of what is happening in their communities on local, regional, and national scales.

Social issues affecting multiracial and multiethnic communities in America are not adequately addressed by the mainstream press.

The African-American magazine publishing industry is on a steady rise, with more than two dozen magazines aimed at the black consumer market. John Johnson, president of the Johnson Publishing Company, began in 1945 with $500 and built a publishing empire. *Ebony* has a circulation of 1.7 million, formatted in the style of *Life,* and contains general interest stories and profiles of successful personalities. Johnson also publishes *Jet,* which has a circulation of 850,000. According to *Folio,* "John Johnson's publishing creed has been simple—emphasize the positive achievements of African Americans with his Chicago-based *Ebony* and *Jet*"("Celebrating 250 Years," 1991, p. 75).

Other black magazines include *Essence,* a popular women's magazine with a circulation of 800,000; *Players,* a men's interest magazine with a circulation of more than 200,000; and *Black Collegian,* a publication geared toward black college students, with a circulation of 180,000. *Black Enterprise* has a business orientation and a circulation of more than 250,000.

In 1989, Time, Inc., became the first major publisher to venture into the ethnic market, obtaining a 19 percent interest in a publication. *Emerge,* targeted toward upwardly mobile blacks, was promoted as the black consumer's equivalency of *Time* or *Newsweek* and promised coverage of news events, health and features, business, and social and cultural trends from a black perspective (Landro, 1988).

Recognizing a void in publications directed toward black teens, Black Entertainment Television (BET), a cable network reaching 30 million households, scheduled a periodical with just that purpose in July 1991. *YSB (Young Sisters and Brothers)* initially hoped to attract 200,000 subscribers. BET has allocated $1.5 million worth of airtime to promote the magazine. "Our research shows black teens spend a lot of money," commented Debra Lee, publisher and vice-president and general counsel for BET (Rich, 1991).

Latin American Magazines

Spanish-oriented magazines have proliferated to an all-time high. Special interest magazines targeted toward or published by Latin Americans include *Data Digest, Mr. Te Ve* (television and entertainment), *Industria Internacional* (plant management and engineering), *Aboard* (an in-flight airline magazine), *Dinero* (business and investing), and *Fotonovela Pimientia* (adult photo magazine). *Nuestro—The Magazine for Latinos,* is a general interest publication with a circulation of more than 200,000. Another publication is *Cosmopolitan en Espanol,* which has a monthly circulation of 30,000.

Hispanic is one of the most recent publications to capture the attention of Latin American consumers. Launched in 1986 by former governor Jerry Apoda of New Mexico with an initial distribution of 150,000, the magazine's publishers touted it as the only nationally circulated Hispanic magazine. Aimed at the

Hispanic middle class, the publishers targeted the top thirty-three Hispanic markets in the country.

Business Publications/Trade Publications

These are designed to provide information to specific businesses, industries, and professions. Not available to the general public, they are read primarily by the targeted audiences. Although many business magazines are provided free of charge to the readers, advertising is an essential factor, and attaining a high level of readership is imperative for maintaining and attracting advertisers. The readership is specialized and tailor-made—for example, 375 different publications catering to specific areas of medicine. About a dozen large publishing companies dominate the business/trade publications.

There are 4,000 periodicals that can be classified as business publications. The majority are published by publishing companies that have no affiliation with the fields they are serving. Other business publications are provided by professional organizations, either free of charge or the cost is included with membership.

Literary Reviews and Academic Journals

These are mostly produced by nonprofit corporations, including associations and organizations. The cost of production is usually funded or subsidized by universities, foundations, or professional organizations. The nonprofit magazines often do not publish as frequently as commercial magazines, averaging four issues a year. Circulation for these magazines is much lower than for traditional magazines, and readership may vary from a few hundred to several thousand.

Sponsored Publications

These are the internal publications of organizations, unions, or other groups. They include publications of the Elks and American Legion as well as the magazines that airlines publish and distribute during their flights, such as *American Way* (American Airlines), *Sky Magazine* (Delta Airlines), and *Continental Profiles* (Continental Airlines). Also included are college and university magazines; customers' publications; magazines aimed at a company's dealers, agents, and franchisers; and various employee magazines.

Farm Publications

Ranging from *Farm Journal,* a rather general, family-oriented farm magazine, to *Southern Hog Farmer,* agricultural magazines are given a category of their own because of their large number and the degree of specialization within the farm press.

RESPONSIBILITY AND EFFECTIVENESS

Magazines have been responsible for the dissemination and proliferation of information to masses of people for over 250 years. As the first national medium, magazines have been at the forefront of the transmission of ideas, information, and attitudes from person to person, city to city, state to state, country to country, and continent to continent. Magazines appear in many forms and formats.

Magazines have been so successful in their attempts to communicate with the masses that other media have often emulated them. Newspapers have become more like magazines in marketing methods, writing style, and format. Every year for the past decade there has been the creation of television programs promoted as newsmagazine shows. The most popular of these is CBS's long-running "60 Minutes."

Theodore Peterson (1964), author of *Magazines in the Twentieth Century,* describes the contributions that magazines have made to improving the quality of life in society:

First, magazines certainly were responsible in some measure for the social and political reforms made during the century. . . . Second, magazines not only interpreted issues and events but put them in national perspective. . . . Third, the national viewpoint of magazines no doubt fostered what might be called a sense of national community. . . . Fourth, magazines provided millions of Americans with low-cost entertainment. . . . Fifth, for millions of Americans the magazine was an inexpensive instructor in daily living. . . . Sixth, magazines were an educator in man's cultural heritage; and . . . Finally, one of the most reassuring strengths of magazines was their variety in entertainment, information and ideas (quoted in DeFleur and Dennis, 1987, pp. 147–148).

Magazine Criticism

Major criticism of the magazine industry revolves around ownership, which changes so frequently, making it exceptionally difficult to track such information. As is common with most media, the magazine industry is owned largely by a small number of media conglomerates. Most of the consumer magazines are owned by eleven publishers: Time Warner; Triangle Publications; Hearst Corporation; CBS, Inc.; Washington Post Company; Reader's Digest Association, Inc.; Newhouse (Conde Nast); New York Times Company; Meredith Corporation; Ziff-Davis Publishing Company; and Playboy Enterprises Inc. In 1985, CBS acquired five magazines from Ziff-Davis, increasing the number of magazines owned by CBS to twenty-two. The merger of Capital Cities Communication and ABC, Inc., created a $1 billion per year publishing empire. Additionally, the New York Times Company Magazine Group purchased *McCall's* for $80 million, while Rupert Murdock paid Gerry Ritterman $70 million for *Soap Opera Digest* (Selinger, 1990, p. 8). Murdock also took part in the year's largest deal, selling his travel publishing group to Reed International for $825 million. In a joint venture, Macfadden Holdings and Boston Ventures paid $412.5 million for the *National Enquirer,* with a circulation of 4,019,187, and *Weekly World News* ("Magazine," 1990, p. 93).

Media critics often argue that large concentrations of media ownership stagnate growth and give too much power to those whose ideas influence masses of people. However, "the magazine industry as a whole is characterized by a less concentrated ownership pattern than the broadcasting, newspaper, and film industries" (Gamble & Gamble, 1989).

MAGAZINE INDUSTRY PROJECTIONS

Advertisers and readers were expected to spend $21.4 billion on magazines in 1992. Circulation dollars will continue to outpace advertising sales dollars over the next five years. Gross expenditures on consumer magazines were expected to climb to $17.7 billion in 1992, with circulation accounting for $10.2 billion. Additionally, although circulation spending is projected to grow 11.2 percent annually, advertising will grow only 6.3 percent. Business titles will lag behind, growing at an annual rate of 5.9 percent. Advertising, the only revenue stream for many business titles, is expected to reach $3.3 billion in 1992, and circulation spending will be $400 million.[1]

Greg Daugherty (1990), an editor at *Consumer Reports,* interviewed editors, writers, and other magazine industry leaders and made "10 Bold Predictions" for the 1990s. One of his predictions was that general interest magazines will make a comeback. Samir Husni, a professor of journalism at the University of Mississippi who publishes an annual guide to new magazines, forecasts that an influx of audience-specific general interest magazines with circulations in the 250,000 to 500,000 range will surface during the 1990s. He further asserts that special interest magazines will become even more specialized and that desktop publishing will contribute to the resurgence of fiction (Daugherty, 1990, p. 30).

Daugherty (1990) further suggests that with major technological advances in publishing magazines will come in new shapes and guises. Hybrids of magazines are becoming more and more common, and during the 1990s there will continue to be a myriad of magazines presented in different formats. Among some of the more formidable of these are:

• Videozines: Videocassette alternatives to print magazines are still relatively new. An example of such a format is the sixty-minute *Sailing Quarterly,* a television formatted magazine for boat enthusiasts that can be purchased for an annual fee of $99.95. Also included in this category are videozines created for small-business owners by conventional magazines. For example, *Inc.* has produced a series of employee-training tapes, and *Sports Illustrated* now provides a video version of its highly publicized swimsuit issue. In 1988, publishing mogul Rupert Murdock invested $50 million for research and development of electronic publishing.

• Magalogs: Existing since the early 1980s, this is a cross between a catalog and a magazine. More specifically, the product is a catalog containing some editorial material to make it more appealing to readers. For example, a clothing outlet catalog selling washable silk items may contain a story about the origins and benefits of washable silk as opposed to raw silk. The magalog will continue to become more pervasive in the 1990s and well into the twenty-first century as mail-order houses become more competitive.

- Magazettes: Still in an embryonic stage, these are magazines that are published on computer diskettes and feature programs, games, articles, and miscellaneous entertaining information. In 1990, *Uptime,* a monthly magazine-on-a-disc sold in bookstores for $11.95 an issue. Magazettes have not enjoyed the widespread appeal of other magazine hybrids but are still trying to become a recognized form. There are many ordinary magazines to which a consumer can subscribe for an entire year for $11.95, so paying that amount per month is exorbitant to many people and will generally not appeal to consumers.

Daugherty concludes his predictions by noting that the per-copy cost of magazines will rise. He bases his prediction on the fact that the per-copy cost of magazines rose consistently from 1976 to 1986 at a rate of two to three times faster than the U.S. consumer price index. Every year, between 250 and 300 new magazines are started, and only 1 in 10 survives, which means that 25 to 30 new magazines are successful. Almost half of the new starts never publish a single issue.

Failures of magazine startups occur as a result of undercapitalization (the average cost of starting a magazine is $1 million), incorrectly targeting or identifying a market, and lack of knowledge about how a magazine should be operated. Another factor can be rise in postage. Changes in postal rates in previous years almost made the magazine an extinct commodity.

Conrad Fink, author of *Inside the Media* (1990), outlines three reasons why economic stability will remain an imperative concern for magazines: First, a main appeal of most magazines is high-quality color photography and layout. Readers like it and so do advertisers (full-page color photos of new autos and other products really sell). To compete against television, color is an imperative. Also, with the introduction of *USA Today*'s bright-colored format, more daily and weekly newspapers have added color to their format. To compete, magazines must provide more slick, high-quality paper, which is much more expensive than the $650-per-ton newsprint used by newspapers.

Second, most magazines have national or even international circulation and must use the expensive U.S. Postal Service for delivery to readers who are widespread over many geographical locations.

Third, except for a few well-known magazines that have readers who border on cult loyalty, most magazines have high rates of subscriber turnover. Readers are very fickle, and many subscribe to a magazine for only a short period of time. The more subscribers, the more a publication can charge for advertising. The per-copy costs of creating, selling, and distributing magazines is so expensive that without advertising the more copies a magazine sells, the more money it will lose. The sporadic loyalty of subscribers keeps magazines in constant circulation peril, and to offset such erratic actions, they constantly engage in expensive sales campaigns involving giveaways, sweepstakes, and contests.

Despite the concerns for magazines outlined above, most analysts project that magazines will continue to be lucrative ventures, reaching possible revenues of $13.6 billion by the year 2000.

During the 250th anniversary of the American magazine in 1991, there was not a lot of celebrating taking place, as the industry experienced its toughest year since 1975. "The number of advertising pages sold in magazines in the first half of this year [1991] is down nearly 11% from 1990, which itself was not a good year" (Guy, 1991, pp. 1B–2B). Magazine publishers and editors are optimistic about the future of magazines and are looking forward to utilizing the new technology to increase circulation and to entice more advertisers. Noting that magazines have faced critical times before, the editors of *Folio* remarked, "It's not that we've never been without critical issues and challenges. All magazine managers, since the days of Benjamin Franklin 253 years ago, have been confronted by changes in the business climate of their times. They responded and flourished—or failed and were replaced by other, more enlightened individuals" ("Celebrating 250 Years," 1991). This positivism was eloquently reinforced in an advertisement:

In the year 2091, when the travel-weary passenger on a moonshuttle has had his fill of: Dinner on the anti-gravity magnetic tray, three dimensional television. Intergalactic weather reports and conversational banter with the flight attendants, as they float by— he'll then settle back in his contour couch, and return to that important, private activity each of us does alone. Reading. (It will be, we trust, a magazine) (Fink, 1990, p. 153).

BIBLIOGRAPHIC ESSAY

Although magazines have always been considered one of the major mass media, scholars and researchers have not dedicated time and energy commensurate with that given to television, newspapers, and radio. Gerlach (1987) offers the following reasons for the paucity of research that exists pertinent to magazines: (1) Only a handful of universities include research about magazines in their graduate programs or encourage it as an area of exploration; (2) journalism faculty with expertise or knowledge about magazines cannot be found on the faculties of most journalism and mass communication programs; (3) faculty who were veteran professionals within the magazine industry are probably not as interested in publishing research about the industry as those who have gone through doctoral programs that emphasize research; and (4) the lack of published research about magazines has prevented other researchers from having a literature base upon which to build.

Lyon Norman Richardson (1931) was one of the first scholars to study the historical origins of magazines during the years 1741–1789, from the time the first two magazines appeared in America through the year of George Washington's election to the presidency.

Richardson scrutinized thirty-seven periodicals, noting the contributions of such publishers as Benjamin Franklin, Andrew Bradford, Jeremy Gridley, Thomas Prince, Jr., William Livingston, William Smith, Noah Webster, Thomas Coke, and Mathew Carey.

James Playsted Wood (1971) reviewed the early history of magazines from 1741, when the first American magazines were published, to 1955, when the *Saturday Evening Post* appeared in new type and layout. "He stressed the magazines' roles as national educators and as literary and crusading forces. He pointed out that the vast improvements in the appearance of modern-day magazines were due to the rise in advertising revenue and better printing, and in the reproductions of illustrations. More efficient methods of magazine distribution also contributed" (Rankin, 1980).

The economic history of consumer magazines from 1900 to 1950 was explored in the work of Theodore Bernard Peterson's doctoral dissertation "Consumer Magazines in the United States, 1900–1950, a Social and Economic History" (1955). He emphasized the importance of the Audit Bureau of Circulations in changing the attitude of magazine publishers toward circulation.

One of the most comprehensive studies conducted relative to general consumer magazines was done by Calvin Ellsworth Chunn in 1950. Chunn began his analysis by surveying the history of general consumer magazines, beginning in 1741. He chronicled the activities leading up to the publication, in 1855, of the first newsmagazine, *Leslie's Weekly*.

One of the most popular books written about the early days of magazines is Frank Luther Mott's *A History of American Magazines 1741–1850* (1930). It is by far the most complete compendium of information on early magazines and presents detailed descriptions of the more prolific publications. A scholarly assessment of the American magazine industry from 1900 to the early 1960s is presented in Theodore Peterson's *Magazines in the Twentieth Century* (1964). One of the most comprehensive overviews of the magazine industry was written by Roland E. Wolseley, *Understanding Magazines* (1969), which addresses editorial and business operations of consumer, business, and specialized publications. Roland Wolseley's *The Changing Magazine: Trends in Readership and Management* (1973) traces trends in readership and management. The Medill School of Journalism's *Magazine Profiles* (1974) presents studies by twelve graduate students of nearly fifty current magazines. John Tebbel's *The American Magazine: A Compact History* (1969) is a readable and entertaining synopsis of major events in the history of magazines. Benjamin M. Compaine's *The Business of Consumer Magazines* (1982) provides a thorough examination of the magazine industry including such factors as size, circulation, advertising, research, entrepreneurship, ownership, and the future.

A classic analysis of specialized magazines is provided by Julien Elfenbein's *Business Journalism* (1960). Other books pertinent to designing and editing magazines include Ruori McLean's *Magazine Design* (1969), Jan V. White's *Designing for Magazines* (1982), and Don Gussow's *The New Business Journalism* (1984).

A definitive supplement to the magazine field texts is Leonard Mogel's *The Magazine: Everything You Need to Know to Make It in the Magazine Business* (1979). William H. Taft's *American Magazines for the 1980s* (1982) is a state-of-the-art summary. So is *Handbook of Magazine Publishing*, compiled in 1983 by the editors of *Folio* magazine, a publication for those in magazine management. The manual is a compilation of more than 160 major articles and features that originally appeared in *Folio*.

Textbooks on magazine editing and writing include Roy Paul Nelson's *Articles and Features* (1978); Betsy P. Graham's *Writing Magazine Articles with Style* (1980); J. T.

W. Hubbard's *Magazine Editing* (1982), a how-to-do-it manual; William L. Rivers' *Magazine Editing in the '80s* (1983); J. William Click and Russell N. Baird's *Magazine Editing and Production* (1986), which covers the responsibilities of magazine editors from concept to production; and Myrick Land's *Writing for Magazines* (1987).

One of the latest articles pertinent to magazine publishing was a paper presented by Kathleen L. Endres (1989) at the annual convention of the Association for Education in Journalism and Mass Communication in Washington, D.C. The paper, "New Technology Ancillary Products in Magazine Publishing," examined video and computer-based ancillary products being used by magazine publishing companies. The author concluded that video and computer ancillary products of magazines are potentially very lucrative ventures, noting the phenomenal success of the *Cosmopolitan* magazine exercise/makeover series and the blockbuster sales of *Sports Illustrated*'s swimsuit video.[2] In the first six months that the *Cosmopolitan* video was available to the public, thousands of tapes were sold (Endres, 1989). Magazine industry leaders are optimistic about the potential of these ancillaries because it is projected that by 1995 one in three homes will have a computer (Boyd, 1989), and some magazine publishing companies have found that 80 percent or more of their readers own at least one video cassette recorder (VCR) (Harbert, 1989). One of the most interesting facts uncovered by the study was that business publishers tend to concentrate on computer-based products, while consumer magazine companies focus on the video market.

NOTES

1. These calculations are based on projections given in a "Five-Year Communications Industry Forecast," released by Veronis & Suhler, a media brokerage and investment banking firm.

2. On March 17, 1989, the *Beacon Journal* reported that *Sports Illustrated*'s video was the fifth largest selling video the previous week.

BIBLIOGRAPHY

Agee, Warren K., Ault, Phillip H., & Emery, Edwin. (1988). *Introduction to mass communications* (9th ed.). New York: Harper & Row.

Agee, Warren K., Ault, Phillip H., & Emery, Edwin. (1989). *Maincurrents in mass communications.* New York: Harper & Row.

Angelo, Jean Marie, & Drucker, Rachel. (1993, August). Editors Report Stalled Earnings. *Folio: The Magazine for Magazine Management, 22,* pp. 41-46.

Berger, Arthur Asa (Ed.). (1988). *Media USA: Process and effect.* New York: Longman.

Boyd, Robert S. (1989, February 12). Information age hitting high gear: Satellite transmissions transforming the way we work, play, learn. *Akron Beacon Journal.*

Busby, Linda J. (1988). *Mass communication in a new age: A media survey.* Glenview, IL: Scott Foresman.

Celebrating 250 years of magazines. (1991, March). *Folio: The Magazine for Magazine Management, 20* (3), 69–149.

Chunn, Calvin Ellsworth. (1950). *History of news magazines.* Unpublished doctoral dissertation, University of Missouri, Columbia.

Circulation leaders: Top 100 ABC and BPA audited magazines by total circulation. (1993). *Folio: Special Sourcebook Issue,* p. 159.

Click, J. William, & Baird, Russell N. (1986). *Magazine editing and production.* Dubuque, IA: William C. Brown.

Compaine, Benjamin M. (1982). *The business of consumer magazines.* White Plains, NY: Knowledge.

Critical issues in magazine publishing. (1991, October). *Folio: The Magazine for Magazine Management,* p. 62.

Daugherty, Greg. (1990). Writing into the year 2000. Part II: The changing magazine market. *Writer's Digest, 70* (1), 30–34.

DeFleur, Melvin L., & Dennis, Everette E. (1987). *Understanding mass communications* (3rd ed.). Boston: Houghton Mifflin.

Deming, Caren J., & Becker, Samuel L. (1988). *Media in society: Readings in mass communication.* Glenview, IL: Scott Foresman.

Dominick, Joseph R. (1987). *The dynamics of mass communication* (2nd ed.). New York: Random House.

Elfenbein, Julien. (1960). *Business journalism.* New York: Harper & Row.

Endicott, Craig. (1992, June 15). *Ad Age* ranks the nation's largest magazines. *Advertising Age,* p. S-1.

Endres, Kathleen L. (1989, August). *New technology ancillary products in magazine publishing: A pilot study.* Paper presented to the Magazine Division of the Association for Education in Journalism and Mass Communication, Washington, DC.

Ferguson, Rowena. (1976). *Editing the small magazine.* New York: Columbia University Press.

Fink, Conrad C. (1990). *Inside the media.* New York: Longman.

Ford, James L. (1969). *Magazines for millions: The story of specialized publications.* Carbondale, IL: Southern Illinois University Press.

Gamble, Michael W., & Gamble, Teri Kwal. (1989). *Introducing mass communication.* 2nd ed. New York: McGraw-Hill.

Garland, Eric. (1993, March). Mind writers: The public's latest obsessions have driven the country's hottest magazine. *Adweek,* p. 22.

Gerlach, Peter. (1987). Research about magazines appearing in *Journalism Quarterly. Journalism Quarterly, 64* (1), 179–182.

Graham, Betsy P. (1980). *Writing magazine articles with style.* New York: Holt, Rinehart & Winston.

Gussow, Don. (1984). *The new business journalism.* San Diego: Harcourt Brace Jovanovich.

Guthrie, James R. (1988, June 29). A letter. *Wall Street Journal,* p. 23.

Guy, Pat. (1991, August 9). Recovery might not rescue some. *USA Today,* pp. 1B–2B.

Handbook of magazine publishing. New Canaan, CT: Folio Publishing Corporation, 1983.

Harbert, Ted. (1989, March 2). Telephone interview by Kathleen Endres with Ted Harbert, executive producer, *New York Times Magazine.*

Hubbard, J. T. W. (1982). *Magazine editing.* Englewood Cliffs, NJ: Prentice-Hall/Spectrum.

Inside track: What is hot, what is new, what is happening. (1990, February 12). *Adweek,* p. 10.

Johnson, Sammye. (1990–1991, Fall/Winter). Magazine industry salary and status survey: Limitations and difficulties as a mass communications research area. *Southwestern Mass Communication Journal, 6* (2), 1–13.

Kobak, James B. (1990, March). 25 Years of change. *Folio: The Magazine for Magazine Management, 19*(3), 82–89.

Land, Myrick E. (1987). *Writing for magazines.* Englewood Cliffs, NJ: Prentice-Hall.

Landro, Laura. (1988, June 8). Time to buy 19% of new magazines aimed at blacks. *Wall Street Journal.*

McLean, Ruori. (1969). *Magazine design.* London: Oxford University Press.

Magazine: 1989 mergers and acquisitions. (1990, February). *Folio: The Magazine for Magazine Management,* pp. 93-100.

Medill School of Journalism. (1974). *Magazine profiles.* Evanston, IL: Northwestern University.

Mogel, Leonard. (1979). *The magazine: Everything you need to know to make it in the magazine business.* Englewood Cliffs, NJ: Prentice-Hall.

Mott, Frank Luther. (1930). *A history of American magazines 1741–1850.* New York: D. Appleton.

Nelson, Roy Paul. (1978). *Articles and features.* Boston: Houghton Mifflin.

Pember, Don R. (1987). *Mass media in America* (5th ed.). Chicago: Science Research Associates.

Peterson, Theodore. (1955). *Consumer magazines in the United States, 1900-1950: A social and economic history.* Unpublished doctoral dissertation, University of Illinois, Urbana-Champaign.

Peterson, Theodore. (1964). *Magazines in the twentieth century* (2nd ed.). Urbana and Chicago: University of Illinois Press.

Prior-Miller, Marcia R., & Esch, Kellie L. (1990). A census and analysis of journals publishing research about magazines, 1977–1987. Paper presented at the annual convention of the Association for Education in Journalism and Mass Communication, Minneapolis, Minn.

Rankin, W. Parkman (1980). *Business management of general consumer magazines.* New York: Praeger.

Rich, Cary Peyton. (1991, March). BET wagers on black teen title. *Folio: The Magazine for Magazine Management, 20*(3), 37.

Richardson, Lyon Norman. (1931). *A history of early American magazines, 1741–1789.* New York: Thomas Nelson & Sons.

Riley, Sam G., & Selnow, Gary W. (1989, August). *U.S. regional interest magazines, 1950–1988: A statistical overview.* Paper presented to the Magazine Division of the Association for Education in Journalism and Mass Communication, Washington, DC.

Rivers, William L. (1983). *Magazine editing in the '80s.* Belmont, CA: Wadsworth.

Selinger, Iris Cohen. (1989, October). Consumer magazines. *Adweek,* pp. 8–12.

Selinger, Iris Cohen. (1990, February 12). Sugar daddies. *Adweek,* pp. 4–8.

Taft, William H. (1982). *American magazines for the 1980s.* New York: Hastings House.

Tebbel, John. (1969). *The American magazine: A compact history.* New York: Hawthorn.

Weaver, David H., & Cleveland, G. Wilhoit. (1986). *The American journalist: A portrait of U.S. news people and their work.* Bloomington: Indiana University Press.

Whetmore, Edward Jay. (1987). *Mediamerica: Form, content, and consequence of mass communication.* Belmont, CA: Wadsworth.

White, Jan V. (1982). *Designing for magazines* (2nd ed.). New York: R. R. Bowker.

Wilson, Harold S. (1970). *McClure's Magazine and the muckrakers*. Princeton, NJ: Princeton University Press.

Wolseley, Roland E. (1969). *Understanding magazines*. Ames: Iowa State University Press.

Wolseley, Roland E. (1971). *Magazines in the United States* (3rd ed.). New York: Ronald Press.

Wolseley, Roland E. (1973). *The changing magazine: Trends in leadership and management* (2nd ed.). New York: Hastings House.

Wood, James Playsted. (1971). *Magazines in the United States* (3rd ed.). New York: Ronald Press.

Wright, John. (1987). *The American almanac of jobs and salaries* (1987–1988 ed.). New York: Avon Books.

newscopy when it debuted in 1982. In the darkroom, photographers and photo editors are also in the middle of a transition from film to electronic, digital photography. In the newsroom, reporters have new tools such as cellular telephones, "palmtop" computers, and portable fax machines that did not exist a generation ago to assist them in gathering, organizing, analyzing, and presenting news to readers.

This is also a time of great opportunity for minorities and women as newspaper companies attempt to diversify their staffs through increased hiring and special hiring programs focused on minority groups and women. It is also an era when newspaper companies are attempting—although not at a speed entirely to the satisfaction of everyone—to bring more minorities and women into middle and upper-level management and policy-making positions. Another reason for diversity is that it brings different perspectives and insights to news coverage often overlooked in the past.

Organizationally, the newspaper industry continues to be dominated by large public corporations that own a growing number of the nation's major publications. There are fewer family-owned and privately operated newspaper companies in the 1990s than in previous generations. In fact, four-fifths of all U.S. dailies are now group owned. A major reason for this has been efficiency in operation and greater availability of capital for growth and expansion. At the turn of the twentieth century, the proportion was only one-tenth, and at the end of World War II, only two-fifths were group owned. These large information-oriented corporations have become more than just newspaper companies, emerging at the end of this century as communication and information mega-businesses. They have been purchasing and operating other news media companies in addition to their daily and weekly newspapers—branching into television and radio station ownership, cable channels and cable systems ownership, entertainment interests such as professional sports teams, and other information distribution businesses. While these companies earn millions, and even billions, of dollars a year in a wide variety of businesses, their heart and soul and, often, most of the profits remain largely with the metropolitan daily newspapers.

Competition is being redefined in the newspaper industry as the century comes to an end. At the beginning of the century, competition was daily newspaper against daily newspaper in most communities. But as the new century nears, daily newspapers are more and more alone in publishing the news in a given metropolitan area. However, weekly and specialized newspapers are getting a new life by targeting specific audiences and through the use of less-expensive production and printing systems. Multidaily newspaper cities are mostly a thing of the past, leaving a new type of news media competition both for audiences and for advertising dollars. Instead of one daily newspaper competing against another in a metropolitan area, newspapers are now competing against other forms of news media, such as weekly newspapers, specialized or topical newspapers, local broadcast television, cable television, radio, magazines, specialized newsletters, point-of-purchase advertising, direct mail, and free "advertiser" publications aimed at the leisure time of potential readers and the dollars of potential advertisers. But newspapers are finding new ways to offer information alternatives to the speed of radio and television and the market specificity of other printed competition. Newspapers are refining ways to more effectively use the permanence and depth of printed mass communication.

The technological revolution brought on by rapidly evolving computers that began in the 1960s and 1970s has reached full intensity in the 1990s with powerful personal computers, sophisticated accounting, word processing, desktop publishing software, portable systems, cellular telephone communications, and facsimile (fax) transmission systems. Not only is communication more efficient; it is faster, with lower costs in many cases. Technology of the sort discussed above has affected both the content and the distribution of news by newspapers. This has encouraged larger newspapers to accomplish more with their resources and made smaller newspapers more economical to operate and, thus, able to continue to compete at lower costs in ever-challenging economic times.

Because of all of these influences, newspapers are reorganizing. How a newspaper organization exists, functions, and prepares the product are being reinvented. This chapter will review many of these major developments to paint a picture of an industry with a history of success and domination in information gathering and distribution that is in transition. It is an industry with some serious problems but an industry with a future in the next century.

GROWTH AND DEVELOPMENT

At one time, of course, newspapers were the only mass communication news source for many Americans. But that seems like thousands of years ago. Most Americans these days cannot remember when newspapers dominated the information marketplace. In fact, most ''baby boomers'' (born in the post–World War II era of 1945–1960) grew up with television, as have their children and, soon, their grandchildren. Newspapers dominated information distribution in the United States and the world until the rapid development of commercial AM radio in the 1920s and 1930s. But it was not until commercial television began its amazing growth immediately after World War II that newspapers began to lose their dominance. Since the mid-1960s, audience research about media use has consistently shown that television has been the major source of news and information for most Americans. However, recent research has shown that most people use newspapers primarily for *local* news and use television for *national* and *international* news (Stempel, 1991). This, Ohio University researcher Guido Stempel says, raises the question of which type of news is most important to individuals. It is clear that local news is very important to newspapers in the visually oriented contemporary world.

Approximately 62 to 63 million copies are read daily by about 113 million adults. Those copies are sold by about 1,600 morning and evening daily newspapers. This is an average circulation of about 38,000 copies per daily news-paper. On Sundays, the figures are somewhat higher. Americans devote more time to read the Sunday newspaper and more readers buy a Sunday newspaper for its special contents. A total of just under 900 Sunday editions circulate an average of approximately 72,000 copies each week. There are far more weekly newspapers, of course. In 1993, there were about 7,400 weekly newspapers with an average circulation of about 7,500 copies (Okola, 1993). Newspaper read-ership figures will vary slightly from year to year, but they have not changed significantly since the mid-1960s.

Some industry estimates show six in ten adults read a newspaper daily, but most Americans get their news elsewhere in the 1990s. Research over the past three decades shows a decline in daily *readership* habits among all adults. As the American population continues to shift from urban centers to the suburbs, suburban-oriented newspapers are growing, and metropolitan dailies are shrink-ing and sometimes failing. Not only is population movement important, but the demographics of the shift are a concern to newspaper managers. Often referred to as "white flight," the shift has been dominated by affluent whites who have left their increasingly racially and ethnically diverse neighborhoods behind. And the metropolitan dailies have followed those with the income and life-style dem-ographics that advertisers prefer. Many metropolitan newspapers are still head-quartered in the center of the city but are reaching out to meet the market shifts by creating new sections, segmenting the market with zoned editions for specific neighborhoods. Some have even built new printing plants and distribution cen-ters out of the center city, closer to the circulation growth areas and closer to more convenient transportation.

Segmenting audiences and markets for advertisers has caught on. A trend begun in the late 1970s and early 1980s, edition "zoning" has become a feature of most metropolitan dailies in the mid-1990s. It is common to find these news-papers, featuring the special sections two or three times a week, and perhaps as often as daily, in areas surrounding Baltimore, Miami, St. Petersburg–Tampa, Chicago, Milwaukee, Los Angeles–Anaheim, New Orleans, and Philadelphia, to name just a few examples.

But segmenting has problems. Some critics argue this marketing strategy may keep advertisers happy, but it has also helped keep newspapers oriented to the white middle class. But efforts to diversify newspapers may change all that in the future. The need for more minorities in all departments of newspapers, not just newsrooms, will make the newspaper more appealing to all racial and ethnic groups.

Despite recent difficult economic times, some newspapers have enjoyed growth and success. While size of a publication is not the only measure of achievement, it is one indicator. The largest newspapers in the nation in the mid-1990s are *USA Today,* the *Wall Street Journal,* the *Los Angeles Times,* the *New York Daily News,* the *New York Times,* the *Washington Post,* and the *Chicago Tribune.* Several of those newspapers market themselves as national newspapers, while the others are the dominant newspapers in their regions.

Most American newspapers that were originally published in the afternoons for evening consumption have been closed, merged with morning editions, or converted to morning cycle newspapers. Changing life-styles and work styles, growing leisure time for some individuals, the impact of more sophisticated evening news on broadcast television, growth of twenty-four-hour cable news sources such as Cable News Network (CNN), and other factors have meant that afternoon newspapers are less valuable to readers than ever before. Thus, the large majority of newspapers in the mid-1990s are published for morning consumption, but research shows they are actually read throughout the day. Many metropolitan areas that once had morning and afternoon newspapers, not necessarily owned by the same company, are served by only one daily newspaper in the mid-1990s.

Despite the continuing shift in their role, newspapers have remained important to many Americans. But their importance and relevance will depend on their ability to satisfy entertainment needs, that is, mixing entertainment with news. One way newspaper companies have done this is to diversify financial interests. As *information* companies instead of *newspaper* companies, these organizations serve the public by providing information in a variety of forms—from traditional newspapers and magazines to radio, television, and cable systems, to more recently developed computer-based "on-line" information services. But the core has remained the newspaper and its information-gathering strengths. Reporters, news services, out-of-town bureaus, photographers, and graphic artists create a team that provides depth and breadth to continue to compete with other forms of news media.

Technology is helping tear down walls in the newspaper industry. Previously sharp organizational divisions, with clearly defined areas of responsibility, are not so distinct these days. Newspapers of all circulation sizes and publication cycles are affected by this era of reorganization. American Newspaper Publishers Association (ANPA)—renamed in 1992 as the Newspaper Association of America (NAA)—president Jerry W. Friedheim (1990) says this decade could be a time of real change in the newspaper industry. He wrote: "There is a sense that for our newspaper companies the '70s were 'On, your mark,' the '80s were 'Get set,' and the '90s are 'Go!' " (p. 19). Why? He argues that the industry has worked for many years to understand its mission in this decade, to know its competitors, and to know how to do what the industry does in a better manner. He also says newspaper people can adapt.

The 1990s are the decade of high technological impact on the newspaper. How a newspaper is produced will impact on the organization of the institution known as a newspaper. Technology is already redefining how newspapers are structured because it has changed how employees in all divisions get work done and even changed the work they do. What technological advancement is responsible for the most change?

Newspaper companies had historically resisted organizational change, "confronting change only when environmental forces require it," stated Polansky and Hughes (1986, p. 1). These companies have traditionally responded only to market or economic pressure. During the 1970s and 1980s, newspapers, and the rest of the print media, experienced traumatic changes in production technology. These changes centered on how a news story found its way into the newspaper the next day. Leaving 1960s-era typewriters and glue pots behind, journalists have become dependent on computers as a more efficient means for getting the day's news to readers (Aumente, 1989).

At the heart of this change was computer-based word processing and information storage systems, informational and design graphics systems, and digital photographic systems. The computer, combined with photocomposition systems, revolutionized production and distribution in the newspaper industry. The computer has found application in the business office for accounting applications. It has aided circulation by storing subscriber accounts and nonsubscriber listings. It has reorganized the mailroom, where product packaging and distribution begin. It has become a part of production through color separation and printing processes. And it has become a part of advertising in billings and advertisement layout and design.

The two-plus decades of technological innovation forever changed the industry. These developments forced unexpected internal reorganization. The number of employees dropped, and the duties of the remaining employees were redefined. With the computer, newspapers can still be gigantic businesses of thousands of employees in dozens of departments. Or they literally can be one-person operations. Goltz (1989a, 1989b), an industry labor expert, says that Labor Department statistics show these changes in dramatic fashion. In 1970, 49 percent of all newspapers jobs were production oriented. By 1990, the figure was 36 percent. The industry has experienced a remarkable redefinition of the responsibilities of the business. "[S]ome departments, like news-editorial, just ballooned as they incorporated new duties and new responsibilities. Another factor was the creation of entirely new departments and new areas of expertise inside the newspaper plant itself," Goltz wrote (1989b, p. 18).

Many of these changes have been initiated by changing social structure, Goltz says. He points to three major shifts that have reorganized the newspaper industry: (1) change from a blue-collar to white-collar work force, (2) growth of the size of the service sector, and (3) emergence of the working woman and the two-income family.

He also attributes the change to competition from television, a declining newspaper industry share of national advertising, growth of direct-mail advertising, and loss of young readers to other media. But this change is only the beginning, industry experts predict. The recent changes have been remarkably fast, considering that virtually the same former technology and organization of the industry existed for over a century until the 1970s. Technological changes have forced publishers and other newspaper executives to rethink how their companies are organized. "Technical experts believe the combination of cooperation among newspaper departments and computerization of processes such as inserting and bundling is making possible ever-more-sophisticated newspaper zoning," says

Rosalind Truitt (1989), a newspaper technology expert. There is more departmental interdependency and communication than ever before.

Publishers and department heads now talk about the "total" newspaper, the
concept of interaction of the previously autonomous departments in planning
and in production through regular meetings, temporary job reassignment and
exchanges, and training seminars. The newspaper of the midtwentieth century
that had little or no interaction of department functions and employees is an
anachronism. Even the newsroom, which has always seemed to have barriers
keeping it from regular interaction with advertising, production, circulation, and
other departments, has softened its desire for complete independence.

ORGANIZATIONAL STRUCTURE AND SIZE

Newspapers were rather simply organized until the computer and other new
technology of the past two decades were developed (Aumente, 1989). There are
three main functions performed by a newspaper company: business, production,
and news-opinion reporting (Hynds, 1980). Rucker and Williams (1969) described the five traditional departments of any newspaper:

1. News-editorial: news, opinion, copy desk, photography, and library
2. Business: advertising, circulation, and job printing
3. Mechanical/production: typesetting, platemaking, and the press room
4. Promotion: education, sales, and public service
5. Administrative: personnel, payroll, and benefits

Sohn, Ogan, and Polich (1986) described the modern organizational approach
with five divisions:

1. Publisher's office and general management
2. Advertising
3. Circulation
4. News-editorial
5. Production

Sohn, Ogan, and Polich argue that "although demographics and philosophies
may differ, most newspapers have a fairly similar departmental structure" (p.
4). However, there is no doubt that the internal organizational plan for the
newspaper of the mid-1990s is changing. Scholars such as Powell (1982, p. 35)
have concluded that "alterations in the institutional and organizational contexts
in which mass communicators work affect the nature and type of work they
do." Even the names of the departments have changed in startling fashion. For
instance, fewer contemporary newspapers have "composing rooms." Instead,

"prepress" functions are often controlled through the newsroom and a computer center. The personnel department has grown to become an increasingly important human resources service responsible for, among other things, hiring and training, communication, testing and evaluation, child day care, workplace quality, health care, and continuing education.

By the end of the 1990s, most newspapers will eliminate the remaining portions of their operations that were formerly composing rooms. With pagination systems and desktop publishing devices to compose pages, the production process will become even more efficient and require even fewer people. Desktop publishing has had its biggest impact on small publishing operations such as weekly newspapers and newsletters (Rykken, 1989; Genovese, 1987). These personal computer–based systems have strengthened weekly newspapers by lowering production and labor expenses. Combined jobs and responsibilities have led to fast growth for many weeklies. Desktop publishing has also led to consolidated production facilities for companies that produce more than one newspaper such as community weeklies. By using telephone-computer-modem links as well as facsimile machines, publishers have reorganized and cut operation costs. Now production, circulation, and business/accounting departments at different locations can work more efficiently through a centralized facility linked in a network by computer and telephone lines (Aumente, 1989).

Technology has also weakened organized labor (Smith, 1980), although it is still strong in some parts of the industry such as major daily newspapers in the Northeast. Unions have lost membership and influence in the organizational structure of newspapers (Newsom, 1986). The industry has created new departments and divisions in response to the changing technology and labor factors. New graphics departments reflect expansion beyond basic photography in the news department, for instance. Information systems departments have been created as the home for the computer operations of the entire company. Other departments that have evolved in recent years include:

1. Education departments for programs such as Newspapers in Education

2. Customer service departments for a variety of public needs such as back copies, photographs, and literacy programs

3. Research departments for market, advertising, and news readership research, and public opinion polls and surveys (Veronis, 1989)

The size of a newspaper organization presents varying advantages and disadvantages (Polansky & Hughes, 1986). Small organizations are more flexible, dynamic, and responsive to change, but they suffer from lack of scale in capital, human resources, and economies of production and distribution. Large newspaper organizations have obvious financial advantages and can be more innovative because of greater resources. Yet large organizations may experience bureaucratic delays and long-term capital investments that discourage willingness to change.

Newspaper organization of the mid-1990s is quite different from the approaches described by pioneer newspaper management scholars Rucker and Williams (1965) and Barnhart (1952). Contemporary newspapers represent a wide variety of approaches to organization. Despite different sizes, there remains common ground. Each size newspaper retains similar divisions with similar functions. However, the differences that appear as newspapers grow in size and responsibilities may be divided into additional departments and subdepartments. Lines of authority also vary, but each leads to the chief executive officer of the company that publishes the newspaper. Key positions include these titles and general duties (Fink, 1988):

1. Publisher and chief executive officer: responsible for overall business and news-editorial performance of the newspaper
2. General manager: directs the daily business, not news, operations of the newspaper including circulation, advertising, promotion, production, and human resources (personnel) departments
3. Chief financial officer: maintains the financial relations of the newspaper with outside financial constituents such as banks and investors; internal financial planning is also part of this job
4. Editor: responsible for the daily news production of the newspaper
5. Marketing director: analyzes the market and promotes sales of the newspaper
6. Advertising director: coordinates sales of all local and national advertising
7. Human resources director: responsible for hiring, firing, motivating, and training employees and for adherence to all labor, employment, and antidiscriminatory practices
8. Circulation director: responsible for marketing and sales strategy
9. Production chief: directs technical production of the newspaper, including page preparation, platemaking, and printing

The major divisions of daily newspapers may be categorized as:

1. Advertising: Because about 80 percent of a newspaper's revenue comes from sales of advertising (Fink, 1988), this division is critical to the financial success of the company. Advertising divisions are frequently divided into classified, retail, and national advertising departments. Other important areas include advertising art, creative, customer service, and ad composition.
2. Business: Business divisions are responsible for administration of the newspaper. Common departments include accounts payable, paper control, cashier, payroll, benefits, general accounting, budgeting, financing, purchasing, shipping and receiving, and cost control (Hynds, 1980).
3. Circulation and marketing: This division is responsible for sales and distribution of the newspaper. From the mailroom department, where the newspaper's parts such as

news and preprinted advertising sections are assembled, to the loading docks, where trucks deliver it to distribution points, this department makes the most direct regular contact with customers. Circulation divisions are often divided into mailroom, city circulation, regional circulation, and single-copy sales departments. Other areas include carrier insurance, bonding, the loading dock operation, mail binding, insertions, subscriptions operations, and transportation.

4. Human resources: This division has been traditionally known as the personnel department. The name reflects the philosophy of many newspapers: using people as important resources for the success of the company. Departments often include personnel and employee records, loss prevention, safety and health, day care, benefits, training, security, quality circles, general compensation, labor relations, worker's compensation, and intracompany communication.

5. Information systems: One of the newest divisions, this area serves many other divisions internal to the newspaper. This division maintains and operates computer and other systems for data processing and production of the newspaper. It often includes a systems engineering department as well.

6. News-editorial: The news-editorial division focuses on two areas of news gathering. The news department includes the traditional reporting and editing sections of the newspaper such as foreign, national, metro/city, sports, news features (life-style, arts, entertainment), business, Sunday magazine, food, and the functions such as the newspaper's reference, photographs, and clippings library and the graphics (photography and art) departments. The editorial department, although smaller, reflects the opinion functions of the newspaper such as editorials, columns, letters to the editor, and special news analyses and interpretations.

7. Physical plant: The physical plant division is responsible for maintenance of the building, grounds, and equipment of the newspaper. This division cleans, repairs, builds, and monitors the facilities of the newspaper. As many newspapers are twenty-four-hour operations, the work of this division never ceases.

8. Production: Production divisions are often divided into departments according to functions. Typesetting and paste-up of pages are the duties of the composition department. The photographs and other art work of the newspaper are prepared by the engraving department. A third subdepartment, the platemaking department, is responsible for preparation of press plates. Larger newspapers maintain production support systems such as electrical and machine shops, as well as in-house parts departments.

9. Promotion: This division works to keep the newspaper's name, its leading journalists, and its products before the public. Promotion includes departments focusing on advertising, charities and public programs, public relations (publicity), community service (speakers and seminars), Newspapers in Education (schools), and even public tours of the newspaper plant.

10. Research: This is a relatively new division in the newspaper industry. More and more management decisions are based in part on original and secondary research by these comparatively small divisions. Research divisions include market research, news story research, and readership research (Veronis, 1989).

The newspaper industry's work force is also changing. It is an older and more heterogeneous group than in decades past (Newsom, 1987a). In the 1990s, as many as 85 percent of individuals joining the newspaper industry work force are women, minorities, and immigrants (Blodger, 1990). John D. Blodger, a newspaper industry human resources expert, believes that newspapers should adapt to these major changes in the makeup of the industry's work force by recognizing that individuals have unique talents, aptitudes, desires, and needs. Other human resources experts point to five major personnel trends that will affect how newspapers will function in the mid-1990s (Newsom, 1985b, 1986, 1987a; Giles, 1988):

1. An aging work force and a shortage of younger workers

2. More women, more single parents in the work force, and more dual-career families

3. More minority workers

4. Different attitudes and policy demands from younger workers

5. Less membership in, and influence by, organized labor

The industry will continue to be fairly labor-intensive, Newsom found in talking to industry experts. These employees will cost more in wages and benefits as they become older, and there may be a shortfall of workers who can offer computer skills. The presence of women and minorities will be the most noticeable change. The white male-dominated industry will slowly yield to greater demographic balance as the new century nears. American Society of Newspaper Editors studies show the most women are found in business office, advertising, and administrative departments. These three divisions have women employees in the majority. Other departments, such as news with about one-third of its employees women, are dominated by men.

Unions, which represent typesetters, delivery truck drivers, press operators, and even reporters and photographers, have lost much of their influence due to various national labor trends. Experts point to economic, political, social, and technological reasons for this decline. Unions have less influence in the organization of the contemporary newspaper because management is more responsive to employee needs (Newsom, 1986; Smith, 1980). There is an indication, however, that unions and newspaper management are beginning to cooperate rather than to continue as adversaries due to fast-changing technology and globalization of the economy (Goltz, 1989a).

The newspaper industry, which did not invest in training as much as other industries until it experienced the technological revolution of the past two decades, now finds training essential to success (Newsom, 1987b). Until the American Press Institute opened its doors in New York City in 1946, there was virtually no training of newspaper personnel conducted outside the plant, according to Newsom. Even the Newspaper Association of America, the nation's leading newspaper organization, began its first program in 1964 when it was known as the American Newspaper Publishers Association. The Poynter Institute for Media Studies in St. Petersburg, Florida, began its educational programs as recently as 1975.

Training is not limited to management. Rank-and-file employees are getting more and more attention for retraining and for new training, especially as departments are created, eliminated, and reorganized. Training of employees is provided by both internal and external sources. Numerous institutions and organizations provide opportunities for midcareer education. Patricia Renfroe (1990), a personnel relations and training services expert, maintains that the newspaper industry of this decade must spend more of its financial resources on training and retraining of employees to be successful. A key ingredient in employee retraining is to adjust to new technology. While large newspapers spend most on personnel training, smaller companies are also turning resources toward training. The commitment by small newspapers is growing, and training is no longer the first budget cut when economic problems occur.

There still is, however, the industry's old-fashioned approach emphasizing on-the-job training. Journalism professors John Lavine and Daniel Wackman (1988) argue that this type of training is most important when found in a daily, one-on-one form. A unique twist to the on-the-job approach, following the "total newspaper" approach, is job exchange programs (Newsom, 1985b). In these programs, managers and employees change jobs with employees in other departments for brief periods.

For young adults and other individuals seeking to enter the industry, the value of college and university educations has grown considerably for the past two decades. Many newspapers now assume that applicants for newsroom positions have a college education, often from an accredited journalism or mass communication program. For certain, larger numbers of applicants are college educated, making this a necessary or highly recommended achievement for the most competitive positions. For individuals seeking a management career, not only is an undergraduate degree from a college or university required, but often an advanced degree such as a master of business administration, a law degree, or a master of arts or master of science in communication or journalism is expected by potential employers.

Management is attempting to enhance the role of employees within the organization through measurement of employee attitudes (Newsom, 1985a). This growing application of survey research is not limited to large newspapers, either. "The goal is to identify strong and weak areas within the newspaper," Newsom found. "An attitude survey can raise employees' expectations that problem areas identified will be addressed" (p. 22). These studies reveal interdepartmental problems such as lack of communication and cooperation. They also focus on the role of the individual in the larger structure of the organization.

Media organizations offer another form of organizational diversity in terms of management structure. *Vertical* and *horizontal relationships* refer to the organizational chart the newspaper company uses for its division of responsibilities. Lavine and Wackman (1988) state that vertical media company structure

entails a number of layers of management, but there are fewer layers in hori-
zontally structured companies. Vertical firms have few employees who report
to any specific department manager. Horizontal companies have more employees
who report to a single manager. Yet there is no particular reason to prefer one
approach over the other when it comes to setting up media companies, Lavine
and Wackman contend. Most media companies follow a horizontal plan rather
than a vertical plan (Lavine & Wackman, 1988; Fink, 1988). Horizontal relationships are taking on increasing importance in the newspaper industry. Newspapers are forced to complete more interdepartmental projects or tasks that force
interdepartmental cooperation. The independence of a single department is no
longer as strong as it once was, resulting in less focus on vertical strengths and
the flow of responsibility downward. The changes in the industry in this decade
will only create new avenues of interaction in a horizontal fashion and in both
formal and informal relationships.

The organization of the newspaper impacts on the content of its products. De
Sola Pool (1983) describes a convergence in the news media that blurs the lines
between the news media. The blurring changes the content of the media and
how consumers use the media. Media no longer have a singular purpose for
users. The reason for this, de Sola Pool says, is electronic technology, specifically the digital computer.

A number of communication theorists have written extensively that technology influences how people communicate (McLuhan, 1964; Carpenter, 1960;
DeFleur & Ball-Rokeach, 1975; Innis, 1972). These scholars argue that technological innovations change the *process* of communication. The *processing* of
news and advertising will also continue to change because of technology.
Greater quantities of information, different forms, and more frequent updates
will force continuing reorganization of production and distribution schedules
(Garrison, 1979). Perhaps the biggest single change is the gradual transfer of
many production responsibilities to the news and advertising departments as
these departments become more sophisticated in computer technology (Garrison,
1979; Smith, 1980). As pagination systems, which allow newspaper editors and
advertising managers to assemble entire pages on a computer screen, increase
in use for production for news and advertising, changes in production will occur.
Responsibility for production will transfer to the news division from the production division. As digitalization of graphics continues to develop in the mid-
1990s, the "engraving" division will be phased out. Eventually, even
platemaking will be computer and robotics driven. Fewer and fewer persons will
be involved in production of the newspaper.

The most obvious places where organization affects content are in the advertising and the news-editorial departments. The subdivisions of these departments
in many ways determine the priorities of space and of financial and human
resources of the organization. Gans (1979) studied major national news organizations and found significant organizational influences in news selection judgment, for instance. He wrote: "When journalists make news judgments, they do

not, of course, take the organization itself into account, but some of its requirements are, in effect, organizational considerations'' (p. 93).

Reorganization of departments and their subdivisions within news and advertising in recent years has been clearly due to technological changes. The change of most newspapers' "photography" departments to "graphics" departments reflects the increased integrated use of color, the use of computer-generated illustrations, informational graphics (such as boxes, tables, maps, or charts), digital photography, computer-based picture editing, and other technology-based (even photocopying equipment) graphics.

Creation of computer "czar" positions in news and advertising departments in the 1980s also points to the value placed on technology and the need to adjust the flow of authority in the organization. Many newspapers hired editors with advanced computer skills, or retrained those who did not have them, to help solve programming, formatting, and other software-related production problems. Some of these individuals serve more than one department.

THE LITERATURE ABOUT NEWSPAPERS

Newspaper publishing has a long and rich tradition of literature. Until this century, much of the newspaper literature was devoted to biography, history, and development issues. Many of the early books focused on biographies of leading individuals in the industry or chronological histories of institutions such as newspaper companies. In the past century, a more diverse body of literature focusing on newspapers has evolved. It focuses on a very wide range of subjects. Journals and magazines devoted to newspapers and other forms of mass communication have appeared. Research and writing about newspapers are certainly no longer limited to those historical or biographical treatments.

In the mid-1990s, students of the newspaper can find scholarly and professional approaches to the industry in many sources and disciplines. In addition to the structure, organization, and management of the newspaper, upon which this chapter focuses, newspaper literature follows categorical themes similar to those in book publishing and other media industries in the United States.

Major categories of literature have evolved that discuss newspaper law and ethics, advertising, readership and circulation/marketing studies, content studies, economics and management, news decision making, government and regulation issues, international issues, news writing and reporting techniques, relationships of the press and society, the impact of the newspaper on public opinion, production (editing, printing, and distribution) technology, and even special newspaper environments such as urban areas. Clearly, much of the literature on newspapers falls within, and is often a part of, larger concerns for the news media or mass media in general. This orientation seems to apply in literature that addresses media and society issues and literature that presents theoretical perspectives on the role of news media in society or on processes of news communication.

Contemporary research on newspapers is exemplified by studies published in scholarly journals and professional publications. Two of the leading newspaper research periodicals produced by the academy are *Newspaper Research Journal* and *Journalism Quarterly.* In the industry, newspaper-related issues and problems are addressed in the Newspaper Association of America's *Presstime,* in the *Bulletin of the American Society of Newspaper Editors,* and in a more timely manner in the weekly commercial publication *Editor & Publisher.* Popular publications in the area of press criticism include the *Columbia Journalism Review, The Quill,* and the *American Journalism Review.* There are several other regional press reviews available as well.

Many of the professional organizations, press associations, and other organizations serving the individuals and institutions in the newspaper industry produce their own magazines, journals, and newsletters. These also provide a valuable body of literature for students and scholars. Most of these are available to the public and may be found in university, college, and public libraries.

Books about newspapers continue to be more timely and broader in their perspectives. In the past decade, several publishing companies have initiated new journalism series targeting new subjects for inquiry. Among the most popular new subjects added to the literature in the past decade have been newspaper management, news ethics, graphics, research skills for journalists, and computer technology.

The literature, regardless of whether it is in periodical or book form, has a rich tradition of historical, sociological, and psychological perspectives. Books and articles with social-psychological orientations have dominated historical and legal approaches, perhaps a manifestation of the social science traditions of most journalism doctoral programs, which have produced the field's scholars in the past half century.

SOCIAL RESPONSIBILITY OF THE PRESS

For several generations of journalists in this century, one of the most-discussed professional values is the responsibility of newspapers to the public they serve. Newspapers have historically led those individuals and organizations involved in information distribution in creating and defending an independent and socially responsible news media.

Much of this discussion has focused on what is called the "social responsibility theory." The theory professes that the duties of journalists are important social obligations. Mass communications scholars Theodore Peterson, Jay Jensen, and William Rivers (1965) maintained the role of the news media is singularly important to a complex modern American society. "People need the information to serve as good citizens and, because of the busy lives most people lead, they cannot always attend meetings and participate directly. People depend, instead, on their local news media to tell them what they need to know on a day-to-day basis," Garrison (1992, p. 7) wrote. Scholars who have explored the interaction and relationship of the press and government, for example, have long described this independent oversight role as critical in the process of keeping the public informed about government activities.

Responsible newspapers and other mass media have been expected to provide five general categories of information service to the public. The 1947 Commission on Freedom of the Press, directed by Robert M. Hutchins and funded by a grant from *Time,* said news organizations are obligated to (1) provide truth and meaning in the news, (2) serve as a forum for the exchange of ideas and commentary, (3) provide a representative picture of the various groups and activities in society, (4) clarify the goals and values of society, and (5) provide full access to information and news of the day (Peterson, Jensen, & Rivers, 1965).

The work of Peterson, Jensen, and Rivers defined the responsibility of newspapers to include serving the economic system in addition to providing news and information. Newspapers also serve the public by providing entertainment. But they need to do this and still produce a profit to remain independent and financially viable businesses in a capitalistic system.

Newspapers also have the responsibility to serve as watchdogs of government for the public they serve. In doing so, newspapers help protect civil liberties and other freedoms given citizens by the Constitution and serve the democratic political system in which they exist.

Throughout this century, journalists have tried to analyze this responsibility ethic. Many codes of professional performance address it. One of the most widely distributed and visible codes is that of the Society of Professional Journalists. That organization states in its preamble that the primary responsibility of journalists is to serve the truth and the public's right to know about events of public interest. And this responsibility cannot be delegated. Social responsibility of newspapers was developed as an alternative to libertarianism, which endorses freedom of the press without responsibility. Advocates of the social responsibility approach strongly advocate freedom in selecting topics for coverage but argue that it must be exercised with responsible decision making. In being responsible, journalists value duty, accountability, obligation, truth and accuracy, objectivity and fairness, professionalism, balance, and credibility (Garrison, 1992; Black & Barney, 1991; Day, 1991).

EFFECTIVENESS

Newspapers are valuable to their readers because they offer certain advantages over other forms of news media. Newspapers are permanent. But they have other advantages that enhance their effectiveness as vehicles for dissemination of information.

First, newspapers, despite technological advances in the electronic media, remain more portable. Readers can find newspapers in many distribution points and can take them literally anywhere without regard for batteries, electricity, or reception interference.

Second, the specialized, zoned, and segmented content of the contemporary newspaper is still more appealing to readers than the often less organized content of radio and television newscasts. This makes newspapers effective in presenting large amounts of information through their highly sectionalized and indexed content designated for specific audiences.

Third, newspapers are still the leaders among news media in presenting current, in-depth information on news events. Broadcasters cannot provide comparable depth of information, in most cases, because of time constraints.

Scholars have spent millions of dollars and entire research careers studying the effects newspapers have on their audiences. One thing is clear in all of the research: Readers use newspapers for a wide variety of purposes. The effects of the newspaper on society are broad, and still many of these effects are not fully understood. A student perusing the pages of *Newspaper Research Journal* or *Journalism Quarterly* may quickly get the impression that a great deal is known about these effects, when the opposite is probably true.

A wide base of communication theory has evolved over the past half century that addresses many of these known effects. Much of the research has concentrated on readers' use of newspapers. "*Use* is the key to this area of investigation," wrote former *Newspaper Research Journal* editor and newspaper scholar Gerald Stone (1987, p. 127).

Recent research about effects of newspapers on audiences has focused on both the use of the newspaper and the psychological gratifications the use gives readers. Additional research has looked at what has been labeled the "agenda-setting" effects of the news media on audiences. Scholars using this approach argue that newspapers and other news media often set the public agendas by telling the public what to *think* about but not what to *think* (McCombs & Shaw, 1972).

But these are not the only ways social scientists measure the effects of newspapers. There have been numerous other theories and strategies for looking at the process and effects of communication through newspapers. For example, earlier research on the effects of the content of newspapers, conducted by government researchers in the 1920s and 1930s, focused more on the diffusion of information through newspapers when they were still the primary means of distributing public information.

THE FUTURE

As you have seen, the future is uncertain. New technology and changing social and economic conditions have clouded the crystal balls of those who forecast the newspaper industry's direction in the next century. But it is clear that the computer—mainframe, mini-, and personal-size—and other related technological advances will undoubtedly continue to have major impact on the newspaper.

The industry of the mid-1990s is in a dynamic period that will lead to new approaches in newspapering for the twenty-first century. Technology will impact not only on organization but on the content of the newspaper company's products. Faster and more comprehensive news reports will be available. Geographically zoned editions will be more precise and customized for subscribers. Advertising preprint insertions will be more specifically targeted for markets sought by clients. Ultimately, computer- and telecommunications-based technology will permit personal newspapers to be provided to the customer of the twenty-first century. Ordering, by interactive connection such as a telephone line, from a menu the day before, or on a standing basis, customers will be delivered a standard product enhanced by specific interest content.

Much of the discussion in this chapter has focused on how technology has affected newspapers, and not so much on how social and economic matters have had their impact. But, considering the advice of communication consultant Wilson P. Dizard, Jr. (1985), we can expect even more influence by technology in the years ahead: "In little more than a generation, the technology to match this challenge [of the promise of our democratic society] has moved from the laboratories into everyday use. Our applications have been primitive compared to the potential of the new machines" (p. 20).

The social conditions, such as changing life-styles and changing work styles of millions of Americans, also will have a significant impact on newspapers in the years ahead. The industry must monitor and adapt to these changes to be competitive and viable.

What the newspaper industry learned in the early 1990s was that it cannot control economic conditions. But it must be able to adjust to economic conditions as they change, for better or for worse. Donald L. Shaw, professor of journalism at the University of North Carolina, observes that he is optimistic about newspapers in the next decade but says they must continue their evolution "toward a vital and important niche in the marketplace. Never again will they be the jazzy, spicy vehicles of the '20s and '30s. They will be more in-depth, more useful, more like daily magazines, experimenting in all kinds of ways to serve audiences in different ways" (Rockmore, 1992, p. 28). Shaw says that the newspaper, like all other news media, will not return to its previous dominance and that content alone will not attract audiences back after they have left. He feels that the process of change in the news industry is becoming more rapid, and media that are flexible and can adjust will find their profitable segment of the audience. "Newspapers have the potential for highly creative re-engineering if they would just do it," Shaw believes (Rockmore, 1992, p. 28).

Knight-Ridder Inc. executive Roger Fidler also feels optimistic about the future of newspapers. The director of New Media Development does not believe newspapers will disappear. New technology developed in this century, he says, has not wiped out newspapers, only made them stronger. "They cannot survive as they are. They will have to change," he believes (Rockmore, 1992, p. 30). "Survival will demand innovation and a radical change in thinking. They will have to forgo tying their futures to the printing presses. They will have to undergo what I call 'mediamorphosis'—a creative transformation into a new electronic medium. To become relevant to the new age, journalists will have to change their concept of what a newspaper is" (p. 112).

NOTE

The author would like to thank Alan Prince, Michael Salwen, and Paul Steinle, on the journalism faculty at the University of Miami, for reviewing this manuscript and for their helpful comments and suggestions.

BIBLIOGRAPHY

Aumente, Jerome. (1989, April). New PCs revolutionize the newsroom. *Washington Journalism Review, 11*(3), 39–42.

Barnhart, Thomas F. (1952). *Weekly newspaper management.* New York: Appleton-Century-Crofts.

Black, Jay, & Barney, Ralph. (1991, March). *Journalism ethics since Janet Cooke.* Paper presented to the Association for Education in Journalism and Mass Communication, Southeast Colloquium, Orlando, FL.

Blodger, John D. (1990, January). Focus on people. *Presstime, 12*(1), 34.

Carpenter, Edmund. (1960). The new languages. In Edmund Carpenter & Marshall McLuhan (Eds.), *Explorations in communication.* Boston: Beacon Press.

Day, Louis A. (1991). *Ethics in mass communications: Cases and controversies.* Belmont, CA: Wadsworth.

DeFleur, Melvin, & Ball-Rokeach, Sandra. (1975). *Theories of mass communication.* New York: David McKay.

de Sola Pool, Ithiel. (1983). *Technologies of freedom.* Cambridge, MA: Harvard University Press.

Dizard, Wilson P., Jr. (1989). *The coming information age: An overview of technology, economics, and politics* (3rd ed.). New York: Longman.

Fink, Conrad C. (1988). *Strategic newspaper management.* New York: Random House.

Friedheim, Jerry W. (1990, January). Ready for the decade. *Presstime, 12*(1), 19.

Gans, Herbert J. (1979). *Deciding what's news: A study of CBS Evening News, NBC Nightly News,* Newsweek & Time. New York: Pantheon Books.

Garrison, Bruce. (1979). *The video display terminal and the copy editor: A case study of electronic editing at* The Milwaukee Journal. Unpublished doctoral dissertation, Southern Illinois University, Carbondale.

Garrison, Bruce. (1992). *Professional news reporting.* Hillsdale, NJ: Lawrence Erlbaum Associates.

Genovese, Margaret. (1987, January). "Desktop publishing" spurs weeklies. *Presstime, 9*(1), 18–20.

Giles, Robert H. (1988). *Newsroom management: A guide to theory and practice.* Detroit: Media Management Books.

Goltz, Gene. (1989a, November). Management, labor can work together. *Presstime, 11*(11), 28–30.

Goltz, Gene. (1989b, September). The work force reorganization. *Presstime, 11*(9), 18–23.

Hynds, Ernest C. (1980). *American newspapers in the 1980s.* New York: Hastings House.

Innis, Harold. (1972). *Empire and communications.* Toronto: University of Toronto Press.

Lavine, John M., & Wackman, Daniel B. (1988). *Managing media organizations: Effective leadership of the media.* White Plains, NY: Longman.

McCombs, Maxwell, & Shaw, Donald. (1972). The agenda-setting function of the mass media. *Public Opinion Quarterly, 36*(2), 176–187.

McLuhan, Marshall. (1964). *Understanding media.* New York: Signet Books.

Newsom, Clark. (1985a, May). Employee attitudes: Newspapers of all sizes are seeking opinions from their employees about working conditions. *Presstime, 7*(5), 22–23.

Newsom, Clark. (1985b, August). Trading places: A way to learn what others do. *Presstime, 7*(8), 6–7.

Newsom, Clark. (1986, March). The state of the unions. *Presstime, 8*(3), 22–30.

Newsom, Clark. (1987a, March). The changing face of the newspaper work force. *Presstime, 9*(3), 26–34.

Newsom, Clark. (1987b, October). Training takes on a more vital role. *Presstime, 9*(10), 20–27.

Okola, Gina. (1993, May 19). Personal correspondence.

Peterson, Theodore, Jensen, Jay, & Rivers, William. (1965). *The mass media and modern society.* New York: Holt, Rinehart & Winston.

Polansky, Sharon H., & Hughes, Douglas W. W. (1986, Fall). Managerial innovation in newspaper organizations. *Newspaper Research Journal, 8*(1), 1–12.

Powell, Walter W. (1982). From craft to corporation: The impact of outside ownership on book publishing. In James S. Ettema & D. Charles Whitney (Eds.), *Individuals in mass media organizations: Creativity and constraint.* Beverly Hills, CA: Sage Publications.

Renfroe, Patricia P. (1990, January). Building skills. *Presstime, 12*(1), 31.

Rockmore, Milt. (1992, May 2). View from the top: Where will newspapers be in 10 years? *Editor & Publisher, 125*(18), 28, 30, 112.

Rucker, Frank W., & Williams, Herbert Lee. (1969). *Newspaper organization and management* (3rd ed.). Ames: Iowa State University Press.

Rykken, Rolf. (1989, August). Weeklies become a sought-after catch. *Presstime, 11*(8), 20–27.

Smith, Anthony. (1980). *Goodbye Gutenberg: The newspaper revolution of the 1980s.* New York: Oxford University Press.

Sohn, Ardyth, Ogan, Christine, & Polich, John. (1986). *Newspaper leadership.* Englewood Cliffs, NJ: Prentice-Hall.

Stempel, Guido H., III. (1991, Fall). Where people *really* get most of their news. *Newspaper Research Journal, 12*(4), 2–9.

Stone, Gerald. (1987). *Examining newspapers: What research reveals about America's newspapers.* Newbury Park, CA: Sage Publications.

Truitt, Rosalind C. (1989, October). The modern mailroom: Zoning demands spur technological advancements, but some key department links are missing. *Presstime, 11*(10), 10–13.

Veronis, Christine Reid. (1989, November). Research moves to center stage. *Presstime, 11*(11), 20–26.

Professional Periodicals

American Journalism Review (was *Washington Journalism Review*)
The Bulletin (of the American Society of Newspaper Editors)
Columbia Journalism Review
Editor & Publisher
IRE Journal (Investigative Reporters and Editors)
News Inc.
Newspaper Marketing
Presstime (Newspaper Association of America)
Publisher's Auxiliary
The Quill (Society of Professional Journalists)

Academic and Research-Oriented Periodicals

Freedom Forum Media Studies Journal
Journalism Abstracts
Journalism Educator
Journalism Monographs
Journalism Quarterly
Journal of Mass Media Ethics
Mass Comm Review
Newspaper Research Journal
Public Opinion Quarterly

7

PUBLIC RELATIONS

Barbara Bealor Hines

There is no universally agreed upon concise definition of *public relations*. However, in 1967 the editors of *Public Relations News* defined public relations as "the management function which evaluates public attitudes, identifies the policies and procedures of an individual or an organization with the public interest, and plans and executes a program of action to earn public understanding and acceptance" (Griswold, 1982). In 1980, the Task Force on the Stature and Role of Public Relations, chaired by the preeminent Public Relations Society of America (PRSA), determined that "the mission of public relations was two-tiered: helping an organization and its publics adapt mutually to each other and an organization's efforts to win the cooperation of groups of people" (Lesly, 1981).

The unifying element in all of the many definitions offered by various groups and publications is management. And to understand the role that management plays in public relations, it is necessary to look at the evolution and dimension of the profession.

Figures on the number of people employed in the field of public relations are also confusing. The U.S. Bureau of Labor Statistics estimated that more than 161,000 people are employed in the field. Of that number, 8 percent, or 13,000, are minorities. Seitel (1992) notes that there are 9,000 communications workers employed by the U.S. Information Agency alone; another 1,000 communications specialists work in the Department of Defense. Baskin and Aronoff (1988) cite the figures offered by the Office of Personnel Management for those working in public affairs: 3,033 public information specialists, 2,272 writers and editors, 1,722 technical writers and editors, 1,659 visual communication specialists, 1,090 foreign information specialists, 2,199 editorial assistants, and 182 foreign-language broadcasting specialists.

HISTORY

Often considered to be a phenomenon of the twentieth century, public relations dates back to the beginning of human communication.

In 1215, Stephen Langton, archbishop of Canterbury, used public relations tactics to lobby for a political cause. He mobilized an influential group of barons to stand up for their rights against King John and forced the king to agree to the terms of the Magna Carta. That document has been used as a political banner ever since by people fed up with oppression and control (Newsom, Scott, & Turk, 1989). Cutlip, Center, and Broom (1985) point to the inhabitants in 1800 B.C. of present-day Iraq who hammered out messages on stone tablets instructing farmers about the latest techniques of harvesting, sowing, and irrigating. In ancient Rome, Greece, and Babylonia, people were persuaded to accept the authority of government and religion through interpersonal communications, speeches, art, literature, staged events, publicity, and current techniques.

Professionals agree that modern public relations involves press agents, publicity, and counseling.

Press Agents

Press agents promoted and built an aura of mythology around emperors and athletic heroes. In the nineteenth century that translated into promoting circuses and glorifying frontier heroes and theatrical performers. Early press agents often misrepresented their clients, using sensationalism bordering on lies. Perhaps the most famous press agent of this period was Phineas T. Barnum, the master of the special event who used deception and exaggeration to thrill audiences across the United States. His showmanship provided a lesson for those public relations practitioners who would come later.

Publicity

The dissemination of information was another form of early public relations. Signs such as "Vote for Cicero. He is a good man" have been found by archeologists in ruins of ancient civilizations. In 1634, Harvard College solicited funds by issuing a public relations brochure. King's College (now Columbia University) issued the first press release to publicize its 1758 commencement exercise. In colonial times, publicity was used to promote revolution, to influence public opinion, and to stage events. When the American colonists revolted against British taxes by staging the Boston Tea Party, they were reacting to propaganda and showmanship in word, action, and deeds. Influencing public opinion during this revolutionary time was Tom Paine's *Common Sense. The Federalist Papers* by Alexander Hamilton, James Madison, and John Jay influenced public opinion in the colonies and England.

Andrew Jackson, the seventh U.S. president, hired the first presidential press secretary, Amos Kendall, a former newspaper editor credited with demonstrating the relationship between publicity, management, and political policy-making.

Expansion prevailed. Settlers traveled west; newspapers became advertisements for the new, fertile land. Throughout this era, activists demonstrated on behalf of antislavery, women's rights, and prohibition. Industrialization and urbanization led to the development of manufacturing and trade, and in 1889, Westinghouse Corporation established what is said to be the first in-house publicity department. That was followed in 1897 by the use of the term *public relations* by the Association of American Railroads.

Counseling

As industrialization moved forward on a major scale and business expanded, corporations experienced a growing need for help with labor problems, government intrusion, and challenges from activists.

With the expansion of printing, newspaper circulation grew, and muckraking became popular. By 1900, there were at least fifty well-known national publications with circulations of 100,000 or more. The father of public relations, Ivy Ledbetter Lee, left newspapering in 1904 to form the Publicity Bureau with George F. Parker. His pioneer work for the Pennsylvania Railroad gave the company its first favorable publicity in years (Ross, 1959). In 1914, he became a personal adviser to John D. Rockefeller, Jr.

The definitive beginnings of public relations date from the early 1900s and may be divided into a number of periods: the Seedbed, 1900–1917; World War I, 1917–1918; Booming Twenties, 1919–1933; Roosevelt, 1933–1945; Postwar, 1945–1965; and Information Society, 1965 to the present (Cutlip, Center, and Broom, 1985).

During World War I, propaganda was used to rally citizens to patriotism. People were asked to donate food to Herbert Hoover's Food Administration, to buy bonds through the Liberty Loan Drive, and to join the Four Minutemen, a network of volunteers covering the nation's 3,000 counties.

Edward L. Bernays originated the term "public relations counsel" in *Crystallizing Public Opinion* (1917), the first book on public relations. He taught the first course in public relations in 1923 at New York University.

The American Telephone and Telegraph (AT&T) Company became one of the first companies to learn that social responsibility was good for public relations and good for business (Golden, 1968). The AT&T vice-president, Arthur Page, helped shape today's practice of public relations by advocating that public relations should have an active voice in management.

During the Great Depression, the tremendous expansion in social welfare needs and agencies and Franklin D. Roosevelt's New Deal called for the support of an informed public. Roper and Gallup polls won wide respect in the 1936 presidential election and thereafter. Sampling and public opinion polling became a regular tool of public relations, in politics, marketing, and research. Public relations grew rapidly after World War II. Companies established public relations departments or expanded existing ones; government staffs increased. With the emergence of television, public relations found new vistas. Hospitals, schools, and other nonprofit institutions dealing with health and welfare sought experts to get their message to a widening audience.

In 1944, Denny Griswold founded *Public Relations News,* which became the most prestigious professional newsletter in the public relations industry. In 1992, the publication was sold to Phillips Publishing Co., a major newsletter publishing company with a diverse group of publications.

Organization

A typical corporation has a vice-president for communications-advertising, with an assistant public relations director and an advertising manager. Departments include community relations, product publicity, motion pictures and exhibits, employee publications, news bureau, and educational relations.

Development of Minority Enterprise

In 1934, Joseph V. Baker left his job as city editor at the *Philadelphia Tribune* to become public relations consultant for the Pennsylvania Railroad Company, the first black to obtain a major corporation client. During the next forty years, Baker and Associates was retained by RCA, Procter & Gamble, the National Broadcasting Company, Scott Paper Co., Hamilton Watch, Chrysler, Gillette, and the Association of American Railroads.

The first black woman to handle major corporate accounts, Barbara Harris, began her career with Baker and Associates in Philadelphia in 1949. She traveled from New York to California, representing corporations and entertainers and, in 1958, became president of Baker and Associates until 1973, when she joined the Sun Oil Company to become manager of community relations and urban affairs (Hill & Farrell, 1988, p. 23).

D. Parke Gibson founded D. Parke Gibson Associates, Inc., in New York in 1960. The minority-owned consulting firm provided management, marketing, and public affairs counsel and services to domestic and international firms. Gibson began publishing *The Gibson Report* and, in 1966, *Race Relations and Industry,* which had a major impact on minorities in the public relations work force (Lesly, 1983, p. 94).

Social and political concerns highlighted the 1960s, 1970s, and 1980s. The Vietnam War caused major divisions in society. The environment became a major concern. The assassination of a U.S. president, civil rights leaders, and political heroes caused Americans to look for answers to all that was wrong with society. It was time for people to talk. Diverse interest groups—consumers, women, minorities, environmentalists, senior citizens, and other social activists—began to mobilize. Social responsibility became the buzzword for industry.

There was renewed interest in community relations because corporations realized the importance of nurturing and protecting their reputation in the marketplace. Publics became more segmented, specialized, and sophisticated.

Realizing the value of this specialized market, D. Parke Gibson published, in 1978, *$70 Billion in the Black: America's Black Consumers,* a follow-up to his earlier effort, *The $30 Billion Negro* (1968).

Companies realize they must reach all the racial and ethnic groups, which has led to greater opportunities for minority-owned advertising and public relations firms. Black, Hispanic, Asian American, and Native American professionals are recruited heavily (Gloster & Cherrie, 1987).

Asian Americans control many of the available consumer dollars and are becoming one of the country's fastest-growing consumer markets. In fact, it is approaching $35 billion annually, according to the Los Angeles firm of Muse, Cordero and Chen (Westerman, 1989).

African Americans compose more than 12 percent of the population, compared with about 8 percent for Hispanics. By the year 2010, Hispanics will be the largest American minority group (see Figure 7.1). This affords great opportunities for diversity in the public relations work force. Major corporations have allied themselves with community efforts and have sought to build strong links with the Hispanic market.

One businessman believes more must be done. Wesley Poriotis (1989), a New York executive recruiter, says the recruitment of blacks for public relations posts has become almost nonexistent, based on his experience with clients in that city. He feels that the pressure must come from the companies who pay the bills of the public relations firms that counsel them.

A 1988 survey of black public relations practitioners in Atlanta, Georgia, revealed that they have more trouble getting jobs and promotions than do whites; they are underrepresented in the field, and they can better handle minority-targeted projects than whites (Lapierre, 1989).

However, the largest U.S. corporations are devoting a significant percentage of their total marketing budgets toward minorities. Most notably, Hispanic public relations is booming, with ad dollars spent on the Hispanic market more than doubling in the past five years, while the black market is also experiencing an upsurge in interest, and many predict that Asian Americans will be the next group targeted for expansion (Holmes, 1989a, p. 16).

According to the Population Reference Bureau, the number of Asian Americans increased by an estimated 50 percent between 1980 and 1985, and if present trends continue, the Asian population in the United States will double over the next ten years.

In October 1989, the Census Bureau announced that the U.S. Hispanic population had officially passed 20 million, meaning that Hispanics now compose more than 8 percent of the population (Wellman, 1989).

And those groups spend money. Johnson Publishing Company estimates that in 1988 blacks were a $218 billion market; Hispanics were worth $134 billion.

Figure 7.1
Projection of U.S. Minority Populations, 1980–2010 (in millions)

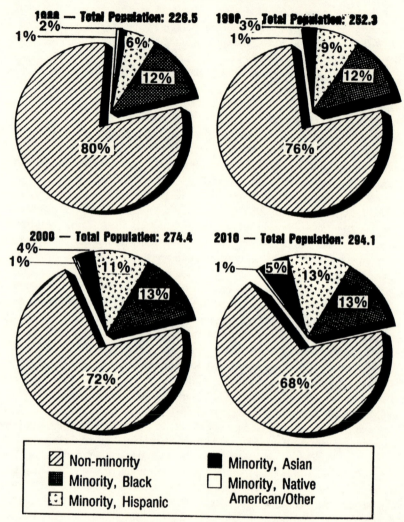

Source: Task Force on Minorities in the Newspaper Business. (1980). *Cornerstone for Growth,* p. 7.

The Los Angeles media firm of Muse, Cordero and Chen valued the Asian market at about $35 billion (Westerman, 1989).

Public relations today is big business. The Public Relations Society of America, organized by a merger of the American Council of Public Relations and the National Association of Public Relations Counsel in 1948, has a growing membership of 16,000 in more than one hundred chapters in the nation. The Public Relations Student Society of America, formed in 1968, has more than 5,500 student members at 177 colleges and universities. The International Public Relations Association has 1,300 members and is increasing by about 20 percent annually. More than 3,000 U.S. companies have public relations departments, and more than 1,400 public relations agencies exist in the United States, some billing millions of dollars per year. More than 500 trade associations have public relations departments.

Boston University's Graduate School of Public Communication is devoted primarily to instruction in public relations activities. The University of Florida's public relations program has passed the half-century mark.

With upwards of 550,000 people in the United States practicing public relations in some form, the field has solidly entrenched itself as an important, influential, and professional component of our society (Kendall, 1984).

PUBLICS AND THEIR RESPONSIBILITIES

Public relations is a profession in constant flux; the publics that are served by the industry change constantly; and industry practices must be altered and refined regularly. The most notable publics include media, communities, employees, consumers, financial institutions, and government.

Media

Today there are 1,570 daily and 6,500 weekly newspapers in the United States, over 50,000 magazines, 10,332 radio stations, and 1,403 television stations. While they attempt to explain and interpret what is happening in our world, they are defined.

Journalists collect the information that is dispersed through the various media. From the public relations practitioner's viewpoint, the journalist is a public. Public relations experts work to ensure that their clients' viewpoints are heard.

Public relations consultants build positive relationships with reporters and editors; report, write, and edit press releases and other written communication; research and plan publicity and special events; develop media kits; plan interviews with employees and management; host news conferences; and deal with all written and verbal communication.

Communities

Urban problems demand that corporations, organizations, and business come to the forefront to work out effective community relationships. Issues like drug abuse, substandard housing, employment of the disadvantaged, and opportunities for minority business enterprises cause companies to become more involved in the communities they serve.

Community relations is an all-embracing activity related to local government and political action, corporate philanthropy, and special publics and problems. It is as diverse as the community it serves. The public relations specialists obtain what the organization needs from the community, organize special events, conduct research on the community, assist the local economy by purchasing local supplies and services, and provide special assistance to all types of groups represented in the community.

Employees

Organizations require a positive organizational climate to give employees trust, confidence, support, security, satisfaction, and high expectations toward the company they serve. Employee communication programs require a strong network or link to thrive. Public relations practitioners provide support and programs to strengthen the link in communication through letters, periodicals, bulletin boards, exhibits, annual reports, advertising, handbooks and manuals, telephone hot lines, and training films, to name just a few. Effective programs can increase employee productivity, enhance an organization's image, build loyalty to the organization, improve cooperation and coordination, and reduce expense and waste.

The responsibilities of workers are to gather information; write; edit; plan, implement, and evaluate programs; establish policy; and conduct training and development programs.

Consumers

Public relations practitioners often respond to consumers, so the relationship between these two publics is a natural one. Two-way communication is crucial; public relations must respond to consumers, and consumer concerns must be translated to management and/or service personnel.

The unrest of the 1960s has provided an impetus for the development of new consumer programs. No longer do calls for reform come from government; today's consumers know how the American business climate works and how to appeal to that climate.

The responsibilities of workers are to research, write, design programs, implement and evaluate, lobby, and perform management tasks.

Financial Institutions

Investor confidence is the hallmark of financial relations. Responsiveness, openness, and regular communication are necessary in this field. Prompt disclosure of corporate news that will affect the financial community is necessary.

Practitioners must be knowledgeable about the Securities and Exchange Commission (SEC), the various stock exchanges, stockholders or shareholders, financial analysts, and the financial press.

Government

Public affairs units help organizations respond to issues affecting their activities. Businesses have become aggressive in increasing their public affairs activities.

Increasingly in the 1990s, state and local governments are handling concerns that were once the domain of the federal government.

Political activities fall into three general categories: electoral, legislative, and regulatory. Fostering understanding, generating public support, and initiating political action through access to opinion leaders and establishing priorities call for mutual understanding.

NATURE OF RELATIONSHIPS

While public relations practitioners respond to many publics, they must maintain a structure for their own system or subsystem they manage, whether it is a department or work unit. As part of that management function, they must choose both a vertical and horizontal structure for the public relations program.

Nature of Vertical Relationships

Grunig and Hunt (1984) believes complex environments require flexible vertical structures, while rigid, vertical structures work best in a static environment. The public relations department using the press agent, publicity, or public information model can be managed with a structured vertical hierarchy.

Hage (1980) defines four attributes of an organization's hierarchy: centralization, formalization, stratification, and complexity. Centralization represents the extent to which power to make decisions is concentrated at the top of the organization. Formalization means that an organization has rules and regulations and follows a strict chart. Stratification means that some roles are more important, and some employees have greater prestige, more pay, and better working conditions. Complex organizations have more specialized roles, more professional employees, and more specialized departments. They tend to operate in more dispersed locations.

Thus, the press agent or publicity or public information office can operate in a structured vertical hierarchy. In this system, communication technicians, rather than professional practitioners, perform routine tasks for an organization. In some instances, public relations departments continue to function in a structured hierarchy under a manager who oversees the work of the communication technicians.

Nature of Horizontal Structures

Horizontal structures define the roles and tasks of the subunits in a department. Grunig and Hunt (1984) cite seven common horizontal structures in public relations: by publics, by management process, by communication technique, by geographic region, by account executive system, by organizational subsystem, and by combination.

Middle-level managers usually serve major groups of publics. In the department, the components may include media relations, employee relations, community affairs, governmental relations, public affairs, financial relations, educational relations, and relations with activist publics.

Planning, evaluation, communication, and research are the components of the management process and require more people in decision making.

In organizations that function as press agents or publicists, there are units or subgroups that perform services based on function: press services, audiovisual, and publications. This is a common structure for a governmental press office, trade associations, and nonprofit organizations.

Geographically diverse businesses often require various units at each site. There is usually another structure present.

A counseling firm serves many masters. In this environment, an individual practitioner serves each client. The structure can vary to fit many situations.

The organizational subsystem is a variation of the account executive system. Different practitioners serve as account executives for different subsystems of the organization. This often occurs in educational organizations and government.

The World Future Society (WFS) has predicted that the year 2000 will bring changes in science, technology, and social developments. These changes have an impact on the role that public relations plays in business, government, and society. Among the trends the society cited:

- Mandatory retirement age will rise to age seventy.

- Approximately 63 percent of the new labor force will be women, and their salaries will be comparable to men's.

- Specialization will increase.

- Every taxpayer will be paying $500 a year to care for AIDS patients.

- Education in the United States will be designed to improve coping with technological advances and with the increasingly competitive and global economy.

- Child care facilities provided by business will grow rapidly.

- Consumers will be more sophisticated, and their purchasing and consumption powers will change.

- Big business will get bigger.

- Information will be the primary commodity in more and more industries (Luckins, 1988).

All of these have major implications for the public relations industry including corporate, nonprofit (including health care and education), and government affairs.

THE FUTURE OF PUBLIC RELATIONS

As public relations continues to expand as a profession into the twenty-first century, it will be affected by many changes: political, global, governmental, technological, and educational.

The United States has had to shift its focus to the Pacific Basin, particularly Japan, Taiwan, and South Korea. With the democratization of Eastern bloc nations and the development of the 1992 European Economic Community, new alliances will be formed that will require public relations practitioners to be increasingly knowledgeable of foreign languages, business culture, management, and economics.

Political reality means understanding changing demographics. Today, minorities make up more than 21 percent of the U.S. work force. By the year 2000, that number will grow to about 30 percent. More significantly, the influx of new workers will be primarily immigrants, women, blacks, Hispanics, and Asian Americans. Twenty-one percent of *all* workers are from minority groups. Among public relations professionals, however, only 7 percent are minorities (Paluszek, 1989).

Business must become more global—competitive, efficient, and quality oriented. The public agenda will continue to focus on those areas that are internationalized: health and safety, and the environment.

The profession must promote the highest standards in American business. To become more competitive, efficient, and quality oriented, public relations will have to deal with its own credibility. Burger (1988) cites public distrust of all the institutions in society. The public relations executive of the future will have to confront this issue competently and honestly.

James Dowling (1990), chief executive officer of Burson-Marsteller, the nation's second largest public relations agency, believes there will be increased governmental intervention in the United States at the federal, state, and local levels.

During the 1970s, twenty-two new regulatory agencies were created, and a total of 120 major regulatory laws were passed during the decade.

Additional direction will come from the president; other action will come from activist groups and popular movements. For every anti-group, there will be a pro-group with a message. Between 1984 and 1989, the number of federally registered political action groups nearly tripled, with the largest increase coming from corporations. In 1989, the political action group that raised the most money was the Democratic Republican Independent Voter Education Committee, followed by the American Medical Association. A continued strong economic base will give individuals and citizen groups increasing voice and purchasing clout.

New technology also forces change in society, and nowhere is that more evident than with the business and practice of public relations where fast, effective communication is the key. The publishing revolution in the field of public relations—desktop publishing on personal computers and high-quality laser printers—now make it easy and inexpensive to produce a newspaper, magazine, newsletter, or directory. Computers make it possible to access data banks worldwide; people will use and store more information than ever before. Computer hardware and software will require less office and storage space and maintenance. Words like *facsimile, satellites,* and *fiber optics* in a public relations practitioner's vocabulary reflect the level of technology that is being used today.

Education remains the key to building a stronger, more effective, multicultural public relations community. According to Gerald Kosicki and Lee Becker, who compile annual statistics on journalism enrollment for the Dow Jones Newspaper Fund, public relations and advertising students made up 31 percent of the total undergraduates in the nation's journalism and mass communications programs in 1991 (Kosicki & Becker, 1992).

A report entitled "Challenges and Opportunities in Journalism and Mass Communication Education" (Murphy, 1989) urges future public relations practitioners to obtain a firm foundation in the liberal arts and sciences, including English, foreign languages, mathematics, natural sciences, and the social sciences. The report also states that because public relations is a management function, where it is possible, public relations students should pursue studies in marketing, business, economics, and finance to complement their liberal arts and professional studies.

Where the opportunity for a minor or second area of concentration exists, many public relations educators and practitioners suggest business. The committee also recommended other minors like sociology (for students pursuing careers in nonprofit public relations), ROTC (Reserve Officers' Training Corps) (for students pursuing military affairs), or a specific area (education or government) for students planning careers in a specific practice (Murphy, 1989).

Professional organizations like the Public Relations Society of America, the International Association of Business Communicators, the Black Public Relations Society, the Asian American Alliance, and the Hispanic Public Relations Society must continue to press for change in the nation's boardrooms, corporate communications offices, and public relations agencies. Through active participation at the local level, minority affairs committees of these organizations must continue to develop programs to ensure the multicultural diversity of the practice of public relations.

BIBLIOGRAPHY

Baskin, Otis, & Aronoff, Craig. (1988). *Public relations: The profession and the practice* (2nd ed.). Dubuque, IA: William C. Brown.

Bernays, Edward L. *Crystallizing public opinion.* 1917. Reprint. New York: Liveright, 1961.

Burger, Chester. (1988). Management's challenges for the '90s. *Public Relations Journal,* 44(3), 34–41.

Burger, Chester. (1990). Public relations in the twenty-first century. In Bill Cantor (Ed.), *Experts in action* (2nd ed.). New York: Longman.

Cantor, William. (1988, January). Sixth annual review and forecast of public relations trends.

Cutlip, Scott M., Center, Allen H., & Broom, Glen M. (1985). *Effective public relations* (6th ed.). Englewood Cliffs, NJ: Prentice-Hall.

Dowling, James H. (1990). Public relations in the year 2000. *Public Relations Journal, 46*(1), 6, 36.

Fry, Susan L. (1991, February). Reaching Hispanic publics with special events. *Public Relations Journal, 47*(2), 12–14.

Gibson, D. Parke. (1978). *$70 billion in the black: America's black consumers.* New York: Macmillan.

Gibson, D. Parke. (1968). *The $30 billion Negro.* New York: Macmillan.

Gloster, D., & Cherrie, J. (1987, Spring). Communication careers: Advertising or public relations may mean opportunities. *Equal Opportunity,* pp. 36–39.

Golden, L. L. L. (1968). *Only by public consent: American corporations search for favorable opinion.* New York: Hawthorn.

Griswold, Denny. (1967). *Public relations news.* New York: International Public Relations Weekly for Executives.

Grunig, James E., & Hunt, Todd. (1984). *Managing public relations.* New York: CBS College Publishing.

Hage, Jerald. (1980). *Theories of organizations: Form, process and transformation.* New York: Wiley.

Hansen, Marcus Lee. (1961). *The Atlantic migration, 1607–1860.* New York: Harper & Row.

Hill, George H., & Farrell, Robert C. (1988). *Blacks in public relations.* Los Angeles, CA: Daystar.

Holmes, Paul. (1989a, October). Melting pot market. *Relate,* pp. 16–18.

Holmes, Paul. (1989b, December). Pride and prejudice. *Relate,* pp. 11–13.

Kendall, Robert. (1984). Public relations employment: Huge growth projected. *Public Relations Review, 10*(3), 23.

Kern-Foxworth, Marilyn. (1989). Status and roles of minority practitioners. *Public Relations Review, 15*(3), 39–47.

Kosicki, Gerald, & Becker, Lee. (1992). Annual census and analysis of enrollment and graduation. *Journalism Educator, 47*(3), 61–70.

Koten, John A. (1986). Moving toward higher standards for American business. *Public Relations Review, 12*(3), 3–11.

Lapierre, Regina. (1989, April 10). How can PR reflect society's composition? *PR Reporter: Tips and Tactics,* pp. 1–2.

Lesly, Philip. (1983). *Public relations handbook.* Englewood Cliffs, NJ: Prentice-Hall.

Lesly, Philip. (1981). Report and recommendation: Task Force on the Stature and Role of Public Relations. *Public Relations Journal, 3,* 32.

Luckins, Rebecca. (1988, December 12). Big changes affecting long-term trends. *Public Relations News,* p. 2.

McElreath, Mark P. (1993). *Managing systematic and ethical public relations.* Dubuque, IA: William C. Brown.

Murphy, Sharon M. (1989). *Challenges and opportunities in journalism and mass communication education.* Report of the Task Force on the Future of Journalism and Mass Communication Education, Association for Education in Journalism and Mass Communication, Columbia, SC.

Newsom, Doug, Scott, Alan H., & Turk, Judy VanSlyke. (1993). *This is PR: The realities of public relations* (5th ed.). Belmont, CA: Wadsworth.

Newsom, Doug, Scott, Alan H., & Turk, Judy. (1989). *This is PR: The realities of public relations* (4th ed.). Belmont, CA: Wadsworth.

Paluszek, John. (1989, May). Speech: *It's time sisters and brothers, it's time.* The Black Public Relations Society, Los Angeles, CA.

Peterson, Paul. (1987). Enrollment up 7 percent in '86, outstripping university growth. *Journalism Educator, 42*(1), 4–10.

Poriotis, Wesley. (1989, September 6). Blacks get run around at companies. *O'Dwyer's Newsletter,* p. 2.

Ross, Irwin. (1959). *The image merchants.* Garden City, NY: Doubleday.

Seitel, Fraser P. (1992). *The practice of public relations* (5th ed.). Columbus, OH: Merrill.

Task force on minorities in the newspaper business. (1980). *Cornerstone for Growth,* American Newspaper Publishers Association, p. 7.

Wellman, David. (1989, December). The growth of Hispanic income. *Food and Beverage Marketing,* pp. S3–S6.

Westerman, Marty. (1989, March). The death of the Frito Bandito. *American Demographics,* pp. 28–32.

The white face of PR today. (1993, March). *Inside PR,* p. 249.

Wilcox, Dennis, Ault, Phillip H., & Agee, Warren K. (1992). *Public relations strategies and tactics* (3rd ed.). New York: Harper & Row.

FOR FURTHER READING

Abramms-Mezoff, Bob, & Johns, Diane. (1989, May). Success strategies: Managing a culturally diverse workforce. *Supervision, 50.*

Almquist, Elizabeth M. (1979). *Minorities, gender and work.* Lexington, MA: Lexington Books.

Awad, Joseph. (1985). *The power of public relations.* Westport, CT: Greenwood Press.

Brody, E. W. (1987). *The business of public relations.* Westport, CT: Greenwood Press.

Brody, E. W. (1988). *Public relations programming and production.* New York: Praeger.

Brody, E. W. (1992). *New technology and public relations: On to the future.* Sarasota, FL: Institute for Public Relations Research and Education.

Brody E. W., & Stone, Gerald. (1989). *Public relations research.* Westport, CT: Greenwood Press.

Broom, Glen M., & Dozier, David. (1990). *Using research in public relations.* Englewood Cliffs, NJ: Prentice-Hall.

Brough, Bruce. (1986). *Publicity and public relations guide for business.* PSI Research.

Cantor, Bill. (1989, July). Minority hiring shows problems in corporate America. *IABC Communication World.*

Cantor, Bill, & Burger, Chester. (1989). *Experts in action: Inside public relations* (2nd ed.). Westport, CT: Greenwood Press.

Gray, Denise. (1990). A curious unpreparedness. *Public Relations Journal, 46* (1).

Haberman, David A. & Dolphin, Harry A. (1988). *Public relations: The necessary art.* Ames: Iowa State University Press.

Hanamura, Steve. (1989). Working with people who are different (diverse workforce). *Training & Development Journal, 43.*

Hiebert, Ray E. (Ed.). (1988). *Precision public relations.* New York: Longman.

International Association of Business Communicators. (1989). *IABC profile 89*. San Francisco: IABC.

Johnson, Willis L. (1986). *Directory of special programs for minority group members: Career information services, employment skills banks, financial aid sources* (4th ed.). Garrett Park, MD: Garrett Park Press.

Johnston, William B. (1987). *Workforce 2000: Work and workers for the 21st century.* Indianapolis, IN: Hudson Institute.

Kern-Foxworth, Marilyn. (1989). Minorities: The shape of things to come. *Public Relations Journal, 45* (8).

Kitano, Harry H. K., & Daniels, Roger. (1988). *Asian Americans: Emerging minorities.* Englewood Cliffs, NJ: Prentice-Hall.

Leaf, Robert S. (1988). Communicating in China. *International Public Relations Review, 12* (1).

Lesly, Philip. (1990). *Lesly's handbook of public relations and communications.* Chicago: Probus.

Lyons, Peter L. (1988). The global village—myth of reality? *International Public Relations Review, 12*(1).

McLuhan, Marshall. (1964). *Understanding media: The extensions of man.* New York: McGraw-Hill.

McLuhan, Marshall, Fiore, Quentin, & Angel, Jerome. (1968). *War and peace in the global village.* New York: Bantam Books.

Minority organization: A national directory (3rd ed.). (1987). Garrett Park, MD: Garrett Park Press.

Morgan, Gordon D. (1985). *America without ethnicity.* Port Washington, NY: Kennikat Press.

Public Relations Society of America. (1989, December). Strengthening the grass-roots foundation. *Public Relations Journal, 45* (12).

U.S. Census Bureau. (1989). *Statistical abstract of the United States: 1989* (109th ed.). Washington, DC: GPO.

U.S. Commission on Civil Rights. (1988, October). *The economic status of Americans of Asian descent: An exploratory investigation.* Washington, DC: Clearinghouse Publication.

Will, George F. (1989, July–August). Prejudice against excellence. *Conservative Digest, 15.*

Wilson, Clint C., & Gutierrez, Felix. (1985). *Minorities and media.* Beverly Hills, CA: Sage Publications.

Zinsmeister, Karl. (1987, July–August). Asians: Prejudice from top and bottom. *Public Opinion, 10* (2).

INDUSTRY PUBLICATIONS

Case Currents. CASE, 11 Dupont Circle NW, Washington, DC 20036. Monthly.

Channels. P. O. Box 600 Dudley House, Exeter, NH 03833. Monthly.

Community Relations Report. P. O. Box 924, Bartlesville, OK 74005. Monthly.

Corporate Annual Report Newsletter. 407 South Dearborn, Chicago, IL 60605. Monthly.

Corporate Public Issues. 219 South Street SE, Leesburg, VA 22075. Twice monthly.

Inside PR. Editorial Media Marketing International, Inc., 235 West 48th Street, Suite 34A, New York, NY 10036. Monthly.

Investor Relations Newsletter. 20 North Wacker Drive, Chicago, IL 60606. Monthly.
Jack O'Dwyer's Newsletter. 271 Madison Avenue, New York, NY 10016. Weekly.
Le Publicitaire. 1010 St. Catherine Street West #735, Montreal, PQ H3B 3R3.
Managing the Human Climate. Philip Lesly Co., 155 Harbor Drive, Chicago, IL 60601.
   Bimonthly.
Newsletter on Newsletters. 44 West Market Street, P. O. Box 311, Rhinebeck, NY 12572.
   Semiweekly.
O'Dwyer's PR Marketplace. 271 Madison Avenue, New York, NY 10016. Biweekly.
O'Dwyer's PR Services Report. 271 Madison Avenue, New York, NY 10016. Monthly.
O'Dwyer's Washington Report. 271 Madison Avenue, New York, NY 10016. Monthly.
PR News. 127 East 80th Street, New York, NY 10021. Weekly.
PR Reporter. P. O. Box 600, Exeter, NH 03833. Weekly.
Public Relations Journal. Public Relations Society of America, 33 Irving Place, New
   York, NY 10003–2376. Monthly.
Public Relations Quarterly. Public Relations Quarterly, 44 West Market Street, Rhine-
   beck, NY 12527. Quarterly.
Public Relations Review. 10606 Mantz Road, Silver Spring, MD 20903. Quarterly.
Ragan Reports. 407 South Dearborn, Chicago, IL 60605. Weekly.
Special Events Report. 213 W. Institute Place, Chicago, IL 60610. Twice monthly.
Speechwriter's Newsletter. 407 South Dearborn, Chicago, IL 60605. Twice monthly.
Sports Marketing News. 1460 Post Road E., Westport, CT 06880. Biweekly.

PROFESSIONAL ASSOCIATIONS

American Society for Hospital Marketing and Public Relations (AMA), 840 North Lake
   Shore Drive, Chicago, IL 60611.
Canadian Public Relations Society, Inc., 220 Laurier Avenue West #720, Ottawa, On-
   tario, K1P KZ9.
Council for the Advancement and Support of Education (CASE), 11 Dupont Circle NW,
   Suite 400, Washington, DC 20036.
International Association of Business Communicators (IABC), 1 Hallidie Plaza, Suite
   600, San Francisco, CA 94102.
International Communication Association, P. O. Box 9589, Austin, TX 78766.
National Association of Government Communicators, 80 South Early Street, Alexandria,
   VA 22304.
National Investor Relations Institute, 2000 L Street NW, Suite 701, Washington, DC
   20036.
National School Public Relations Association, 1501 Lee Highway, Suite 201, Arlington,
   VA 22209.
Public Affairs Council, 1019 19th Street NW, Suite 200, Washington, DC 20037.
Public Relations Society of America (PRSA), 33 Irving Place, New York, NY 10003.
Public Relations Student Society of America (PRSSA), 33 Irving Place, New York, NY
   10003.
Women Executives in Public Relations, P. O. Box 781, Murray Hill Road, New York,
   NY 10156.
Women in Communications, Inc. (WICI), 2101 Wilson Boulevard, Suite 417, Arlington,
   VA 22201.

8

RADIO

M. Kent Sidel

Radio is a complex industry with a fascinating history and an exciting future. This chapter examines radio and shows how it fits into the larger picture of mass media. Radio is both elementary and extremely complex. A radio receiver can be as simple as some wire, a crystal, and a headphone; the simplest form of transmitter has one transistor, is powered by a small battery, and can be heard halfway around the world. At the other end of the equipment scale, audiophiles spend tens of thousands of dollars on speaker, amplifier, and receiver combinations that can fill a room with enough power to be heard in the top rafter seats of the Superdome. Radio transmitters can be so huge that they require cranes to lift the tubes and separate electrical substations just to power them.

For the human mind, radio doesn't take much effort. People can do other things and still listen to the radio. In fact, few *only* listen to the radio and do nothing else. Most do something else at the same time as listening to the radio, which is one of the beautiful elements of radio. Radio also has a magical quality about it, too. It allows the imagination to form pictures of people and places never seen. Also, it's much cheaper to build radio studios than newspaper plants or television stations. Simple radio receiving sets are getting so inexpensive that in many parts of the world the most expensive thing about using a radio is not the cost of the set but the cost of the batteries. Radio is an incredibly complex yet simple form of communication that is an indispensible part of the lives of most Americans.

HISTORY

Radio's story begins decades before broadcasting. Radio was born in the last century during a time when technical developments took it from crude scientific theories and experiments to a usable communication medium. Radio's history is linked to the experimentation and development of electricity in the 1800s when experiments and theories dealing with "wireless" electricity became the foundations of modern radio broadcasting.

Joseph Henry of the United States and Michael Faraday of Great Britain worked with electricity and magnetism. James Clerk Maxwell of Scotland speculated on the existence of radio waves in 1873, and Heinrich Hertz of Germany proved their existence in 1886. But an Italian, Guglielmo Marconi, first packaged early wireless waves using telegraphy (dots and dashes) rather than voice. Marconi was as much a marketer as an inventor. He persuaded the British that his wireless had commercial and military potential and was issued a patent in 1896. Marconi began building an industry and a company that exploited the full potential of wireless as he knew it. The key to the development of wireless was its ability to travel over distances without the need of land lines. Wired telegraphy was already well established in Europe and America, but it was over water where wireless would prove its worth. It was perfectly suited for communication between the shore and ships at sea. Both commercial and military ships were quick to take advantage of this new communication technology. Before the invention of wireless communication, when a ship sailed over the horizon and out in to the open sea, it was literally on its own until it sighted land again. But with wireless telegraphy, navies and businesses could keep track of, and better manage, their ships. The desire to maximize human and business potential was at the core of societal development as well.

Paralleling the development of wireless was the Industrial Revolution with its massive societal changes. People moved off the land and migrated to work in factories. To better centralize control and efficiency, factories funneled labor from rural to urban settings. People were grouped together in higher concentrations than most had ever known. Group public education was easier to conduct than in isolated, geographically disparate one-room schools. Literacy levels increased. Work hours, while not short, were at least standardized, something few farmers could experience throughout a year working the land. Time off and leisure time became more the norm. The setting was perfect for the development of mass media—communication designed for consumption by hundreds and thousands rather than just a privileged few.

By 1920, radio wireless technology had progressed beyond the simple dots and dashes of the Morse code to the voice transmission necessary to appeal to a general audience. The progression to voice was tied to several developers, some of whom were linked to major corporations. Charles Steinmetz and Ernst Alexanderson of General Electric produced a massive alternator that was used by Reginald Fessenden in 1906 to achieve successful voice transmission. The alternator perfected by Alexanderson became a crucial link in America's World War I wireless effort. After the war, the U.S. Navy was concerned about the strategic value of the alternator and fearful the British Marconi interests would gain control of it; thus, General Electric and other wireless patent holders were encouraged to form the Radio Corporation of America in 1919.

Wireless up to then had concentrated mainly on point-to-point communication between sender and receiver. After World War I, several technical, legal, and societal factors combined to push wireless toward broadcasting to groups of listeners. Vacuum tubes had been perfected from the early work of Lee De Forest and John Ambrose Fleming. Not only were the tubes capable of producing more power, but they became available to the general public. Also in large supply were the returning radio operators, many of whom had been amateur wireless operators before the war and were ready to resume their experimentation in 1919. This fueled the development of voice transmission as hundreds and then quickly thousands of young men tried their hand at sending and receiving speech and music.

Prior to World War I, commercial wireless was founded on charging for messages sent over the air to a particular person or company. Little thought was given by either the government or big wireless corporations to sending information over the air by large numbers of listeners. As amateur operators experimented with voice and music transmissions, several companies realized money could be made by selling receiving sets to the general public eager to get in on the wireless craze sweeping the nation. An early proponent of this new marketing thrust was the Westinghouse Electric Company of Pittsburgh, Pennsylvania, which encouraged an engineer (and an avid amateur operator), Frank Conrad, to begin a regular broadcasting schedule in 1920. Westinghouse saw a potential profit in selling receivers through local retail outlets.

Radio broadcasting station KDKA went on the air in late 1920 with news and entertainment programming. Although the first receiving audiences were primarily amateurs, the general public became fascinated with the new technology, and broadcasting was born. Other electrical companies such as General Electric and American Telephone and Telegraph, and newspapers and universities as well, obtained licenses to broadcast and set up transmitters. Curiosity about distant locations, combined with the excitement of receiving intelligence through the air, encouraged radio's march across the country (Douglas, 1987).

The number of radio broadcasting stations and receiver sales skyrocketed. Program techniques were perfected, chain broadcasting networks were formed, and radio established itself as an indispensible part of American life. Those were the golden days of radio when families gathered around their receivers for general entertainment. Broadcasting companies also realized then that additional revenue could be extracted by charging commercial concerns for advertising time on their stations. Commercial advertising quickly became the main economic support for the new radio broadcasting industry.

Programming prior to World War II was primarily entertainment fare. During the early years, corporations would buy blocks of fifteen or thirty minutes and program their own material laced with good words about the sponsoring organization. Music was provided by studio orchestras and live entertainers. Although crude recording and preproduction technology existed, there was a general feeling that the audience wanted live material, adding to the immediacy and excitement of radio, and the networks refused to use recorded material until World

War II. The early networks, National Broadcasting Company, Columbia Broadcasting System, and Mutual Broadcasting System, provided advertisers with hundreds of local stations grouped together across the country. Performers became nationally known and included names such as Bob Hope, Fred Allen, and Edgar Bergen with Charlie McCarthy. Local stations were eager to become network affiliates and offer their audiences such high-caliber performers. In addition, the 1930s were depression years. Few families had the resources to attend concerts or buy records. Radio was cheap, it was reliable, and it provided glimmers of a better life. Radio became part of the fabric of American life. No event better illustrated this than the famous "War of the Worlds" broadcast by Orson Welles's Mercury Theatre on Halloween night, 1938. The program dramatized a fictional invasion of the earth by aliens from another planet. Although clearly labeled as a fantasy before, during, and after its presentation, it panicked many in a nation already tense because of the increasing militarism of Germany and Japan. Sociologically, the event showed how important radio had become nationally in just eighteen years.

From 1939 to 1945, radio grew to maturity. World War II shifted the emphasis of programming from entertainment to information. Radio brought live reports of Hitler's aggression in Europe to a nation struggling with the concept of isolationism. Vivid accounts of broadcast journalists such as Edward R. Murrow helped persuade the American public that it was in the best long-term interests of the United States to assist its World War I European allies. After America entered the war following Pearl Harbor in late 1941, radio served double war duty—bringing word on the battles in Europe and the Pacific home to anxious families and providing soldiers overseas with encouraging words from home.

After World War II, radio's transition to a peacetime medium was shaken by the spread of television. Radio had been a general entertainment medium for three decades. It offered the country an array of programming that ran from high-brow opera to working-class humor and mixed in a good portion of educational and religious programming. Television changed all that. Not only did it assume dominance in the early 1950s, but more important, it exploited radio's biggest weakness (and its strength): Television added pictures. Listeners became viewers, and the imaginative level of programming dropped. No longer was the audience required to become a part of the program and supply its own vision of the talent and setting. Television demanded the audience accept its—and only its—image of what was taking place. Gone was the delightful effort and involvement radio required to create mind pictures to fit the story and its sounds. This meant the end for many successful radio performers and programs.

Radio faltered for several years as it sought a new role. As America's broadcast tastes turned to the more technically complex medium of television, the nation's musical tastes simplified to the basic sounds of rock and roll. The new music swept the country and provided radio with the perfect opportunity for a new niche with a new audience. Teenagers of the 1950s heard radio change from the all-purpose "infotainment" provider to today's portable specialized music box. Format radio arrived with its tight play lists, upbeat delivery, and short program lengths. A new alliance grew up between radio and the recording industry. Radio provided the mass medium to publicize the latest record releases, and the recording industry supplied radio an endless stream of cheap (if not free) programming material.

Distribution of national entertainment material shifted from a few network cities to thousands of local stations across the country. No longer did networks supply the bulk of a local station's air material, and their contributions shrank to national news and public affairs programming. Stations sought more local advertising support and programmed locally spun records. During this period, better-sounding FM (frequency modulation) stations surpassed the original AM (amplitude modulation) stations in popularity.

Today, FM and AM stations are about equal in number, with approximately 5,000 stations for each. Station coverage areas vary, but generally most cover the towns and cities to which they are licensed, although some AM stations reach far beyond their primary coverage area at night. Generally speaking, most Americans turn to FM for music programming and to AM for information-oriented news, sports, and talk programs.

ORGANIZATIONAL STRUCTURE AND SIZE

America has over half a billion radio receivers, almost one-third of all the sets in the world. That's about ten times the number of sets in all of Africa or in India, the world's second-most populous country. U.S. radio station transmitters exceed 11,000, each with its own brand of programming for selected audience segment. These figures are just for radio broadcasting and don't take into account the millions of other radio devices for taxicabs, fire engines, or radios talking to space shuttles. Until recently, it was common for countries like Britain, Germany, or France to have only a half dozen radio services for the entire nation. Many countries in Africa and Asia would usually have just two or three radio services. Of course, small private radio stations are springing up in many countries, and radio is becoming more localized all around the world.

However, some governments are not comfortable with independent private radio stations playing and saying what they want, when they want. In many parts of the world the entertainment function of radio is not nearly as important as the political function. Radio reaches people directly (no reading is necessary), and it tells them what is happening currently. Thus, some governments will not permit open and free broadcasting such as we have in the United States, even if they allow opposition political parties to run newspapers. In many countries, radio broadcasting is government owned and operated.

There is one other role radio can play in addition to its functions as an entertainment and political medium. More and more countries turn to radio to assist in development and public health education. In some poorer countries, radio informs farmers about better ways to plant their crops, or health workers about the latest developments. Some nations use radio to educate students who live at great distances from cities and to teach people about family planning practices to control population growth. In the United States public service announcements (PSAs) discuss current issues.

The philosophy behind American broadcast regulation rests on about a hundred years of history and the development of new inventions. Early ship-to-shore wireless was hampered by commercial communication competition. Part of the exclusive Marconi contract with shipping companies said that they could communicate only with other Marconi stations and ships, not with competing systems. Standard business practice before World War I equipped ships with Marconi wireless equipment for communication only with Marconi shore stations; ships with German wireless could use only German land stations. Under normal circumstances, this was acceptable, but would it be right for business interests to override the saving of human life if a ship was sinking? It took the sinking of the *Titanic* in 1912 for the notion of public good over private gain to become a regulatory cornerstone for the new invention called wireless.

The passage of the Radio Act of 1912 dealt with the regulation of maritime wireless and served as the basis for American radio regulation through the mid-1920s. When officials recognized that the tremendous growth of radio called for a more comprehensive set of rules by which to govern broadcasting, the Radio Act of 1927 set up the Federal Radio Commission (FRC). The FRC later became the Federal Communications Commission (FCC) with the passage of the Communications Act of 1934. Now every country in the world has some government organization comparable to the FCC to regulate its broadcast radio waves. Moreover, these countries formed the International Telecommunications Union (ITU). Part of the United Nations, and headquartered in Geneva, Switzerland, the ITU coordinates worldwide radio spectrum use and sets technical standards. Almost every country is a member. These countries gather in large planning sessions called World Administrative Radio Conferences (WARCs) to determine the specific frequencies for radio and television broadcasting and to define the hundreds of other technical requirements for telecommunications. The ITU has no actual enforcement power other than collective pressure from fellow member states, but without the ITU and international cooperation, successful broadcasting would not be possible.

The Communications Act of 1934 established technical standards for licensing broadcast stations and stated that broadcasting should operate in the public interest. Radio broadcasters in America were required to abide by all FCC technical and other regulations and to have a higher responsibility to the general public in order to obtain and retain their seven-year license. This philosophy was based on the concept of a public trust. In the mid-1920s a great deal of interference occurred when each broadcaster put on the air what he wanted, when he wanted it, and where on the dial he wanted it. The government had to step in and used the Radio Act of 1927 to regulate the stations. The notion of public trust has been the foundation of American radio.

The federal government—and not state governments—controls broadcasting in America, which avoids the confusion of states regulating radio stations within their borders. The legal basis for federal control over broadcasting is the U.S. Constitution, which gave Congress the power to regulate transactions that cross state lines and to deal with foreign governments. This prevents compacts that benefit individual states but that might harm the nation as a whole. Broadcasting has been defined by the courts to be interstate commerce because broadcasting signals do not recognize political boundaries. Because radio waves cross state lines and carry commerce in the form of commercials, they are governed by the federal government, specifically the FCC—which gets its power and financing from Congress. If a station doesn't agree with an FCC ruling, it may take the matter to the federal court system. The final arbiter of broadcast policy is the Supreme Court. While several cases have reached this level, most issues are resolved between the stations and the FCC.

The Communications Act of 1934 concentrates primarily on technical considerations and leaves most programming decisions in the hands of the local stations. But there are some specific prohibitions. Radio stations cannot broadcast obscenities. Court rulings on what constitutes obscenities become more and more specific, but questions usually center on sexual language. Lotteries and gambling cannot be publicized over the radio with the recent exceptions of state lotteries. Deceptive advertising is controlled principally by the Federal Trade Commission (FTC). For many years the radio stations had a gentleman's agreement about what not to advertise and broadcast. This non–legally binding compact was part of the National Association of Broadcasters (NAB) Radio Code. The NAB is the principal broadcast lobbying organization in Washington, and the code was developed because it was felt that an industry active in self-regulation would be less likely to be the target of federal intervention from the FCC. Unfortunately, the NAB Radio Code was officially abandoned by 1983 when the Department of Justice expressed concern over possible antitrust violations. However, many broadcasters still abide unofficially by the Radio Code.

The 1934 Communications Act has governed American broadcasting for almost six decades because it is flexible and may be changed when needed. It has been altered hundreds of times. Its name is really the Communications Act of 1934 As Amended. Devices like television, cellular phones, and satellites have created the need for new regulations. Why didn't Congress simply scrap the old act and start from scratch and create a new Communications Act? Vested interests got in the way. The FCC regulates not only radio stations but also broadcast and cable television stations, space satellites, and telephone companies. It issues licenses for taxicab companies and sets technical standards of equipment like microwave ovens and radar detectors. With all these diverse interests governed by the FCC, any change for one group creates problems for other groups. Everybody is afraid that a total rewrite of the act of 1934 would take away something they already have. Everybody wants more, but no one is willing to give up anything to get it. So the act of 1934 continues to be amended as technology develops.

Most broadcasting in America is a business designed to make money for those who own it and organized along fairly common business lines. Owners may be large corporations, small partnerships, or individuals, but whatever the owner- ship structure, radio stations are much the same across America. They are ar- ranged according to departmental functions. General managers are the real powers with the primary responsibility to protect the license issued by the FCC for the station to broadcast. They serve multiple masters, reporting to the owners (if not the owner), making a profit if the station is to pay its bills and wages and stay on the air, keeping the license safe, managing the staff, and most important, listening to the community. The community is more than just the listeners or the advertisers. The license issued by the FCC requires the station manager to serve the public good, to be attuned to broad issues in the area, to be responsive to public service groups, to relate to the concerns of minorities and women, and to be aware if the city council is considering major changes in laws that might affect the business climate of the city. General managers must have their fingers on the pulse of the area that a radio station serves.

Sales managers are responsible for bringing money into the station from ad- vertisers, selling time on the station between the programming segments to busi- nesses who want their products and services mentioned, and constantly looking for new advertisers and new ways to motivate them to buy more advertising time. Sales managers work with national advertisers such as major beverage companies, automobile manufacturers, and national supermarket chains, local retailers who sell their products, and hundreds of small businesses in the com- munity. In the early days, salespeople just sold radio airtime; now more sales- people have business degrees and special marketing skills.

The chief engineer is responsible for making sure the station stays on the air, checking the electronic equipment in the station to ensure the purest signal possible. They supervise thousands of details like cleaning the heads on the tape players and making sure the antenna tower has warning lights to keep airplanes from crashing into them. Engineers have usually attended technical schools or have university degrees in electronic engineering.

The position at a radio station that probably most affects the listeners is the music programmer, who decides what goes on the air. Usually the owner and his consultants select the music type (or format) for the station. This selection may be based on the wishes of the owners but more likely on market research to determine which musical type is not played currently in the station's coverage area. Program directors put together an on-air staff of disc jockeys who can best present the music format to the listener, remaining abreast of change in the music field to keep the station's sound current.

In the early days of radio broadcasting after the networks were established, the idea of playing a phonograph record on the radio was considered a violation of the public trust. This need for live rather than recorded music was why many of the large stations had full orchestras in the 1920s and 1930s. After World War II, when radio was trying to find its place in the American media scene after television's sudden rise, playing recorded music on the radio became the accepted form of entertainment. Now it is unusual to hear live music coming from a radio station.

The music industry and radio broadcasting are inextricably intertwined. Music recording companies make sure that radio stations receive copies of their latest releases since without air-play new songs could not do well.

Music licensing organizations are also critically important in station/music industry arrangements. They look out for the interests of the songwriters and performers. Radio stations have free material that they use to attract listeners, who will eventually bring them money through their advertisers. The music industry makes money selling records, tapes, and discs to the public, who want the latest songs they have heard on the radio. Songs are copyrighted, giving their creators a share of the profits generated from the music. The two main music licensing groups are the American Society of Composers, Authors and Publishers (ASCAP) and Broadcast Music Incorporated (BMI). They act as the agents of the thousands of songwriters and other artists in the country and collect a portion of the profits from radio stations and other organizations that play their clients' music for a profit. Radio stations usually pay these organizations what is called a "blanket license" fee that allows the stations to play any of the musical selections listed in the BMI or ASCAP catalogs. This amounts to most of the copyrighted music in America.

Promotion directors at radio stations advertise them to their communities in various ways—on the air or off the air. On-air promotion can be the disc jockey reminding you that he or she is on every day at two o'clock, a giveaway contest in which listeners call in at a certain time, or just about anything that encourages the listener to continue listening to that station. Off-air promotion is advertising the station in other media—on bumper stickers or billboards, key rings, sunvisors, coffee cups, or memo pads with the station's call letters and frequency prominently displayed; or at grand openings (called *remotes*), with broadcasts from gasoline stations, automobile dealerships, shopping malls, or other local business.

Consumers should be aware of the power they possess in shaping the direction of this medium. Radio stations survive because they persuade businesses to give them money in exchange for minutes of airtime. This "selling time" on radio is the basis of the American commercial radio industry. Radio salespeople persuade businesses to buy advertising time by using a rating book based on surveys determining who is listening to a radio station. Firms such as ARBITRON specialize in radio surveys several times a year in most major cities in the country. The surveying method may be through direct questioning or, more frequently, by leaving a diary with family or by telephone. The results are compiled in a book form and sold to subscribing radio stations, where staff pore over the data to locate groups of listeners who might appeal to potential advertisers.

The data are broken down primarily by age and sex and are listed by specific daytime listening segments. However, many advertisers also want to have information about listener buying habits, education levels, and other qualitative data. Salespeople tailor their presentations to clients in terms of survey data to persuade advertisers to pay the price the station charges for air minutes based on how many listeners it has and where the minute is located during the broadcast day. The best and most expensive radio advertising "drive" times are in the mornings from 6 A.M. to 8 A.M. and in the afternoons from 4 P.M. to 6 P.M. Number-one-rated stations can charge more per minute than a number-four-rated station. Rates on top-ranked stations can reach over $1,000 a minute.

Up to this point the discussion has been on commercial radio in America, but many other types of radio are available. On the lower end of the FM radio dial, around 88 to 92 MHz, there are stations that do not rely on the selling of commercial time to survive; they are prohibited by the FCC from using commercials. This portion of the FM band is reserved for educational, public, alternative, or religious stations, and sometimes a combination of all four. Some cities and states use this portion of the radio spectrum to broadcast instructional programs to schools in their areas. The number of public radio stations is growing, and many are owned by colleges, boards of education, foundations, or municipalities and are affiliated with National Public Radio (NPR) in Washington. NPR is the radio arm of the partially publicly financed Corporation for Public Broadcasting. NPR programs are usually news or fine arts. Its two well-known news magazine shows are "Morning Edition" and "All Things Considered." Many religious groups maintain FM stations in the noncommercial portion, as do stations owned by listener-supported groups such as Pacifica.

International shortwave broadcasting is another medium. The biggest problem with this service is that standard AM/FM radios will not pick up the stations. It takes a set that can reach from 3 to 30 MHz; this is between standard AM, which stretches from 535 to 1,605 kHz, and FM, which is allocated 88 to 108 MHz. There is a growing interest in shortwave broadcasting, and receiver availability is increasing, because shortwave offers the big broadcasting opportunities to major players. Governments talk to governments with powerful transmitters that put out millions of watts, or hundreds of times the power of some local broadcasters. International broadcasters send country news and views to listeners in other countries often halfway around the world. It is easy to pick up Radio Moscow, Radio Beijing, or the British Broadcasting Corporation with just a simple wire antenna and the proper receiver. The U.S. government service has been the "Voice of America" (VOA), located in Washington, D.C., with huge shortwave transmitters at various remote locations around the country and overseas. VOA has broadcast in over thirty languages to people around the world, telling them about the United States.

RESPONSIBILITY AND CRITICISM

Radio in America bears a major responsibility to its listeners to provide not only appropriate entertainment but reliable news and information. While radio has long been replaced as the primary source of news for most Americans, it still serves as an important medium by which many first hear about stories breaking. Radio may only provide basic information: Is my world safe? Are there traffic problems to avoid? Will I need to take my umbrella? Or it may be the link with major news events that could dramatically affect listeners' lives. In either case, radio should always be responsible to the broad public it serves. Has it lived up to its goal of maintaining the public's trust and furthering public interest? These are hard questions to answer, and there are those who would not give American radio high marks.

It is primarily in the area of news programming that radio attracts many critics. There are those who say news on radio is nothing more than a mouthpiece for major corporations and government agencies. They feel radio has "sold out" its journalistic responsibility as an advocate for the people and has instead become a part of the establishment about which it is to report. Others are more critical, saying that local radio news simply has ceased to exist. Many owners are so interested in profits and so shortsighted that they have simply done away with their station's news department, concentrating instead on playing music. The age of the "wireless music box" predicted almost eight decades ago is upon us. Some contend that the local news that does remain is so trivialized that it insults the intelligence of even the most dedicated listener. The "Morning Zoo News Team" and its spin-offs tend to prefer show business gossip in twenty-second bites to meaningful analysis of events shaping our world. Others say that when there is news of substance on radio, it is so clouded by reporter opinions that it becomes meaningless as a source of information by which intelligent people may form their own understanding of the story. Can broadcasters remain detached from important events taking place or not? Critics say that news coverage over radio has been reduced in some cases to a person crying "Fire" in a crowded theater.

On the programming side, radio is often mentioned as part of the drug problem infecting the country. Critics say that contemporary song lyrics promote substance abuse or violence. On a simpler level, they say radio is the conduit for obscenity. Radio has come under fire for engaging in conduct unbecoming a federal licensee, and the Federal Communications Commission has begun to take an increasingly activist role in policing the airwaves for material considered to violate the public trust concept. For example, for many years, radio stations could program more adult fare late at night when children would probably not be listening. The FCC has said there will no longer be such a "safe harbor" for this programming.

One of the most difficult criticisms to counter about American radio is the charge of "sameness"—that wherever in the country one travels, one finds radio programming boringly similar, except for the local weather and news. The music is the same, the disc jockeys sound the same, the formats are the same. One radio station blends embarrassingly into another as one traverses the nation. Such criticism is the product of market-driven programming. The industry is so finely tuned to giving the public what it wants that it has paralyzed possible change.

Even the "alternative" public radio stations cannot escape this criticism. They have been chided for losing their counterprogramming ambition. Whether commercial or public, radio stations simply stick with what works, and given the increasing emphasis on market programming research, it becomes less likely that totally new programming concepts will emerge.

FUTURE

Most station owners have adopted a "Why rock the boat?" attitude about programming innovation, so little change is likely in programming per se. Radio has always been a technology-driven medium, and the future of radio broadcasting in America centers instead on technological developments. Records are being relegated to archives as compact discs replace them. Programmers take advantage of creative new possibilities through electronic developments. Satellites are having a tremendous impact on radio programming. More stations replace locally played music with satellite-delivered formats with up-to-date material, and technical quality allows the announcer in Los Angeles to sound like he or she is at the local station. Satellite music services will lead to a further refinement of the myriad music formats, but unfortunately, this will contribute also to an increasingly homogeneous sound in American radio. Cable radio is another small but growing area in radio programming. American homes are connected by wire to outside programming and information sources for television, telephone, and now radio.

But no wires have ever connected the family automobile radio with music, weather, and news. Local station signals will soon compete with satellite-delivered programming direct from space to the car to supplement current cassette and compact disc players. In the wings is another technical enhancement, digital audio broadcasting (DAB). DAB dramatically increases technical quality and can be broadcast from local stations or delivered directly from satellites. This innovation will mean hundreds of millions of dollars in equipment changeover costs for listeners.

America's obsession with improved technical quality continues to spell trouble for AM broadcasting. The original service of American radio has fallen on very hard times. Listenership is down dramatically and continues to fall. Programming has shifted from music to information and talk because the AM signal isn't capable of handling as much fidelity as FM. A much-publicized attempt of AM stereo to boost frequency response of the signal and to recover music lovers failed because the FCC refused until 1993 to set a technical standard and stick by it.

BIBLIOGRAPHY

Educational/Public Radio

Communication Media in Higher Education: A Directory. Murray, KY: Association for
    Communication Administration.
Community Radio News. Washington, DC: National Federation of Community Broad-
    casters.
Corporation for Public Broadcasting. (1987). *A report to the people: 20 years of your
    national commitment to public broadcasting 1967–1987.* Washington, DC: Cor-
    poration for Public Broadcasting.
Current. New York: Educational Broadcasting Corporation.
Journal of College Radio. Cherry Hill, NJ: Inside Radio.
Lewis, Peter M. (1990). *The invisible medium: Public, commercial, and community radio.*
    Washington, DC: Howard University Press.
Media in Education and Development. Stevenage, Eng: Peter Peregrinus Ltd.
Witherspoon, John. (1987). *The history of public broadcasting.* Washington, DC: Current
    Newspaper.

Employment in Radio

National Association of Broadcasters. (1986). *Careers in radio.* Washington, DC: NAB.

History

Bannerman, LeRoy. (1986). *Norman Corwin and radio: The golden years.* Tuscaloosa:
    University of Alabama Press.
Carothers, Diane Foxhill. (1991). *Radio broadcasting from 1926 to 1990: An annotated
    bibliography.* New York: Garland.
Douglas, Susan J. (1987). *Inventing American broadcasting, 1899–1922.* Baltimore:
    Johns Hopkins University Press.
Garay, Ronald. (1992). *Gordon McLendon: The maverick of radio.* Westport, CT: Green-
    wood Press.
Head, Sydney W., & Sterling, Christopher H. (1982). *Broadcasting in America: A survey
    of television, radio, and new technologies* (4th ed.). Boston: Houghton Mifflin.
Hilmes, Michele. (1990). *Hollywood and broadcasting: From radio to cable.* Urbana:
    University of Illinois Press.
Historical Journal of Film, Radio, and Television. Dorchester-in-Thames, Oxford, ENG:
    Carfax Publishing Co. in association with the International Assn. for Audio-Visual
    Media in Historical Research and Education.
Kaid, Lynda Lee. (1991). *Political commercial archive: A catalog and guide to the
    collection.* Norman, OK: Political Communication Center.
Lewis, Thomas S. (1991). *Empire of the air: The men who made radio.* New York:
    Edward Burlingame Books.
Schiffer, Michael. (1991). *The portable radio in American life.* Tucson: University of
    Arizona Press.
Skretvedt, Randy, & Young, Jordan R. (Eds.). (1991). *The nostalgia entertainment sour-*

cebook: The complete resource guide to classic movies, vintage music, and old time radio and theatre. Beverly Hills, CA: Moonstone Press.

Smith, Wes. (1989). *The pied pipers of rock 'n' roll: Radio deejays of the 50's and 60's.* Marietta, GA: Longstreet.

International Radio

Browne, Donald. (1989). *Comparing broadcast systems: The experience of six industrialized nations.* Ames: Iowa State University Press.

Education Broadcasting International. Stevenage, ENG: Peter Peregrinus Ltd.

Review of International Broadcasting. Enid, OK: Glen Hauser.

Rosen, Philip T. (Ed.). (1988). *International handbook of broadcasting systems.* Westport, CT: Greenwood Press.

Voice of America. (1992). *Broadcasting to the world.* Washington, DC: VOA.

World radio TV handbook. (Annual). New York: Billboard Publications.

Radio Criticism

Critical Studies in Mass Communication. Annandale, VA: Speech Communication Association.

Journal of Broadcasting and Electronic Media. Washington, DC: Broadcast Education Association.

Radio Diversity

Cantor, Louis. (1992). *Wheelin' on Beale: How WDIA-Memphis became the nation's first all-black radio station and created the sound that changed America.* New York: Pharos Books.

Newman, Mark. (1988). *Entrepreneurs of profit and pride: From black-appeal to radio soul.* New York: Praeger.

Radio Journalism

Biagi, Shirley. (1987). *NewsTalk II: State-of-the-art conversations with today's broadcast journalists.* Belmont, CA: Wadsworth.

Bliss, Edward. (1991). *Now the news: The story of broadcast journalism.* New York: Columbia University Press.

Gannett Center Journal. New York: Gannett Center for Media Studies.

Scannell, Pady. (Ed.). (1991). *Broadcast talk.* Newbury Park, CA: Sage Publications.

Radio Management

Abel, John. (1988). *Radioutlook: Forces shaping the radio industry.* Washington, DC: National Association of Broadcasters.

Bacon's radio-TV directory. (Annual). Chicago: Bacon's.

Broadcaster's Promotion Association Newsletter. Lancaster, PA: Broadcast Promotion Association.

Broadcasting. Washington, DC: Broadcasting Magazine.

Broadcasting and the Law. Miami: Broadcasting and the Law.

Broadcasting Yearbook. (Annual). Washington, DC: Broadcasting Magazine.

Business Radio. Alexandria, VA: National Association of Business and Educational Radio.

Buzzard, Karen. (1990). *Chains of gold: Marketing the ratings and rating the markets.* Metuchen, NJ: Scarecrow Press.

Channels: The Business of Communications. New York: Act III.

Communication Daily. Washington, DC: Warren.

Electronic Media. Chicago: Crain's Communications.

Greenfield, Thomas. (1989). *Radio: A reference guide.* Westport, CT: Greenwood Press.

Inside Radio. Cherry Hill, NJ: Inside Radio.

O'Donnell, Lewis. (1989). *Radio station operations: Management and employee perspectives.* Belmont, CA: Wadsworth.

Powell, Jon, & Gair, Wally. (1988). *Public interest and the business of broadcasting: The broadcast industry looks at itself.* Westport, CT: Quorum Books.

Radio Active. Washington, DC: National Association of Broadcasters.

Radio Marketing Kit. New York: Radio Advertising Bureau.

Radio Week. Washington, DC: National Association of Broadcasters.

Ray, William. (1990). *FCC: The ups and downs of radio-TV regulation.* Ames: Iowa State University Press.

TV-Radio Age. New York: Television Editorial Corporation.

Radio Programming

Billboard. New York: Billboard Publications.

Eastman, Susan. (1989). *Broadcast/cable programming: Strategies and practices.* Belmont, CA: Wadsworth.

Halper, Donna. (1991a). *Full-service radio: Programming for the community.* Boston: Focal Press.

Halper, Donna. (1991b). *Radio music directing.* Boston: Focal Press.

Keith, Michael. (1987). *Radio programming: Consultancy and formatics.* Boston: Focal Press.

MacFarland, David. (1990). *Contemporary radio programming strategies.* Hillsdale, NJ: L. Erlbaum Associates.

McSpadden, Roger. (1987). *Broadcasting and cable: An elementary historical programming structure sourcebook.* New York: Vantage Press.

Radio and Records. Los Angeles: Radio and Records.

Radio Technology

DBS News. Potomac, MD: Phillips.

Satellite Audio Report. Binghamton, NY: Waters Information Service.

Religious Radio

Directory of Religious Broadcasting. Parsippany, NJ: National Religious Broadcasters.
Doerter, David M. (1988). *Full-time Christian radio stations in metropolitan America.*
    Unpublished master's thesis, University of South Carolina, Columbia.

9

RECORDINGS

Lawrence N. Redd

INTRODUCTION

The recording industry dazzles the public with a kaleidoscope of live concerts, singers and musicians, disc jockeys, retail store displays, music videos, popular magazines, and industry award shows. The formidable promotion campaigns, however, have not generated the recording industry widespread recognition as a major mass communication medium in the United States.

Admittedly, music plays a pivotal role in the omnipresence of records, audiotapes, and compact discs (CDs). It is the chief software of professional recordings and may obfuscate the industry's legitimacy as a bona fide member of the mass communication family. However, the recording industry stands on its own as a mass communication medium. Recorded music is mass-produced by a host of composers, arrangers, sound technicians, musicians, equipment suppliers, singers, record manufacturers, and publishers.

The recording industry is a multibillion-dollar business. Major record companies gross over $9 billion in annual record sales, including cassettes and compact discs. Approximately 2,000 record companies produce and distribute recorded performances to more than 70,000 music store outlets. Publishing rights organizations—Broadcast Music, Inc. (BMI), the American Society of Composers, Authors and Publishers (ASCAP), and the Society of European Stage Authors and Composers (SESAC)—supervise music licensing arrangements that extend around the world. Successful money-raising events such as "We Are the World," "Live Aid," and "Farm Aid" reinforce the recording industry as a major world player in mass communication.

The recording industry's structure ranges across several fields or professions, and its major components include not only music and record manufacturing but radio, television, cable, theaters, and professional associations. The total interrelated organizational structure was formed through a series of legal interpretations.

HISTORY

The growth and development of the recording industry is interwoven with the history of the American music business. The latter is based on a European model and developed from print, musical notes written on sheets of paper. This sheet music industry began to expand in America about the time of the Revolutionary War, and a period of sustained growth and development was spurred by minstrel music, beginning in the early 1800s.

The blackface minstrel show, America's first major entertainment form, was derived from African music, dance, and caricatures. Thomas Rice's dance and song "I Jump Jim Crow," stolen from an enslaved African, became America's first international hit song in 1832. In the early 1800s, enslaved Africans had no rights, and in essence, as a songwriter, Rice had few himself. Nonetheless, the phenomenal hit became the foundation to minstrel show music that fed a growing sheet music publishing industry for nearly one hundred years.

The rise to power and influence of minstrel show music coincided with songwriters gaining intellectual property rights through the passage of copyright laws. This economic foundation of the music publishing industry developed substantially during the period that America became fascinated with whites performing blackface song and dance.

Intellectual Property Rights

Intellectual property rights that specifically safeguarded songwriters were slow to be recognized in the United States. Not until the early 1800s did federal legislation pass legally permitting only a song's copyright owner to approve its sale and to earn money on it.

Historically, the concept of intellectual property can be traced to Europe where scholars produced written works or were commissioned to write or draw specific work. A letter carrying a custom seal from the owner permitted a craftsman to make additional copies. After the invention of Johannes Gutenberg's press in 1451, sponsors and authors found that they could earn money by selling copies of the original work. However, the reproduction process of printed works became difficult to control.

Financial investments paid to scholars for intellectual labor were often invisible to those who handled finished products. Unscrupulous printers or agents could reproduce an author's work without fee or investment toward the intellectual creation. Over time, authors and financial sponsors decided that anyone who reproduced printed copies and sold them without consent infringed on their rights. The concept of intellectual property rights evolved and became a factor in England in 1710.

The Statute of Anne, the basis for copyright law in the West, originally did not include music among its provisions. Music seemed less tangible than books, charts, and maps. The U.S. Copyright Act of 1790 was amended to include musical compositions in 1831. Only then was a songwriter or his assignees assured copyright protection for fourteen years and the renewal of an additional fourteen years, as stated in the Statute of Anne.

Initially, the recognition of intellectual property rights for music did not resolve the songwriter's financial problems because there was no efficient way to monitor pirates who infringed on intellectual property by reprinting copyrighted works. Even after 1831, performers, theater owners, and others could use copyrighted music and make a profit without sharing it with the writers or publishers. Many authors were forced to sell their songs and music outright to publishers at meager prices.

From the publisher's perspective, no proven formula existed to predict the sale of sheet music. An expenditure of funds to purchase an unproven song printed on paper meant taking a chance in an uncertain economic environment. These conditions resulted in inadequate earnings by many early songwriters. Even a short list of financially poor composers of great music is shocking: Samuel Coleridge-Taylor, Ludwig van Beethoven, Franz Schubert, Wolfgang Amadeus Mozart, Frederick Chopin, and in America, John Howard Payne and James A. Bland.

Sheet publishers controlled the music business, and to enhance sheet music sales, they traditionally hired pluggers to travel on site to demonstrate and promote a song's popularity. The best situation was to hire a popular minstrel show or well-known vaudevillian singer to add a publisher's song to his or her act. Sheet music publishers finally reached the million-seller mark with "After the Ball" in 1892. The success was made possible in part by the piano industry. In 1870, 1 in 1,500 Americans owned a piano, and by 1890, the ratio was 1 to 900.

A second amendment to the Copyright Act of 1790 was made in 1897 to give songwriters control of the public performance of their music. Unfortunately, the language did not adequately clarify "public performance."

Recorded Music

The invention of music machines and their public exhibitions exacerbated the copyright problem and helped spur an entirely new act. Entrepreneurs of the late 1800s established companies such as Regina, the Victor Talking Machine Company, and the Columbia Phonograph Company to both record and play back music on machines. The new independent companies developed fresh consumer markets and manufactured and sold automatic reed organs, player pianos, and a variety of phonograph players triggered by Thomas Edison's 1877 talking machine. A music-hungry public purchased perforated paper rolls to play on the reed organs, player pianos, recorded cylinders, and discs for the phonograph machines.

Music machines were the main attractions at public exhibitions, penny arcades, and listening parlors around the turn of the century. Sears, Roebuck &

Company advertised phonograph kits as a means of making a financial profit by holding public exhibitions of recorded music. At least one article appeared in print describing how to conduct public exhibitions of recorded music. Copyrighted music was used publicly for profit.

Publishers felt recorded music manufacturers and public entertainment parlors competed unfairly in the same lucrative market. Although publishers held copyrights to the music used by the new machine entrepreneurs, they did not receive any royalty payments from exhibition hall profits.

The Copyright Act of 1909 clearly specified the term *public performance for profit*. Companies that recorded music, including piano rolls and phonograph firms, were required to pay royalties to authors and publishers of copyrighted music. Entrepreneurs or operators of music exhibition parlors were also required legally to pay royalties to copyright holders of songs played on their machines. The Copyright Act of 1909 attempted also to protect songwriters in their relationships with publishers. Under the new law, authors were protected even if they signed away their rights to a publisher. After twenty-eight years, rights and future royalties to a particular song reverted to the author or heirs for another twenty-eight years. Twentieth-century copyright law provides a legal framework behind a system that yields maximum financial returns for music writers and publishers.

Songwriters, led by Victor Herbert, enhanced their financial position in 1914 by organizing ASCAP. This organization made systematic efforts to collect fees for music used by theaters, player piano roll producers, record companies, reed organs, penny arcades, and restaurants, among others. ASCAP surveyed the marketplace and directed members to legally challenge public performances of copyrighted music except for charitable purposes. In 1915 Victor Herbert sued the Shanley Company in New York City, claiming that its restaurant used his song "Sweetheart" to attract customers, which amounted to "public performance for profit." A 1917 U.S. Supreme Court decision upheld the ASCAP position, and conditions for determining royalty payments to copyright holders for public performance for profit became better defined.

Radio and Music Publishers

Radio broadcasts of music represented a new challenge. On Christmas Eve in 1906, Reginald Fessenden first transmitted human voice over the air and became the first "disc jockey." From a ship at sea, he delivered a hopeful message, entertained with his violin, and hooked up a phonograph to his equipment and played music. Early radio experimenters programmed a lot of light opera and classical music, the core of the young phonograph industry.

The commercial radio station developed slowly, but as it did, phonographs and live music were important programming resources, and ASCAP members were vigilant about collecting royalties. But when radio executives used music programs sponsored by advertising clients, they did not pay the copyright holders for the radio music. Thus, in early 1923 ASCAP set royalty payments in motion among radio stations when WEAF Radio in New York City voluntarily agreed to pay an annual fee of $500 to use ASCAP-copyrighted music. Refusal by other stations to follow suit resulted in M. Witmark and Sons, a music publisher, taking to court the Bamberger Department Store of Newark, New Jersey. Bamberger owned and operated station WOR and used a Witmark song, "Mother Machree," without permission under the public performance for profit copyright clause. In August 1923 the courts concluded that the performance or use of the music was not charitable, and Bamberger had to pay royalties to Witmark. Since that time, commercial radio stations have paid royalties to ASCAP.

In the next decade, live and recorded music was used regularly in motion pictures and on radio. Songwriters and publishers became keenly aware of the importance of music to radio programming and the money made by radio broadcasters from advertisers. Actually, music played on radio truncated the economic life of records and sheet sales, but broadcast networks and large city commercial stations earned large profits during the Great Depression.

When ASCAP notified radio in 1937 of a royalty payment increase after the 1935–1939 contract period, radio broadcasters resisted. Their organization, the National Association of Broadcasters (NAB), formed to protect broadcasters against the music industry, was well organized to repel external financial pressures. In 1941, ASCAP blocked broadcasters from playing its music, and radio programmed a limited amount of songs, mainly noncopyrighted—or public domain—music.

The broadcasters, through the NAB, established Broadcast Music, Inc., a nonprofit performance rights company similar to ASCAP. The U.S. Justice Department pressured the groups to sort out their feuds, work out agreements on music licensing and performance rights, and return to normal programming.

Disgruntled ASCAP members, mainly younger writers, joined BMI, along with some unhappy publishers. Although African Americans such as Harry T. Burleigh and Rosamond and James Weldon Johnson were among the early members of ASCAP, they were educated in the written language of status quo popular music. A vast number of "Negro songwriters" practiced oral skills and were not always able to write their blues, jazz, and gospel songs down on paper. Many of these writers, some literary composers and publishers of "race music," were not members of ASCAP. BMI opened its membership to "less conventional" songwriters and publishers, including "hillbilly" musicians, publishers, and songwriters.

Music, Africans, and Records

After the Civil War, some freed Africans formed their own music shows, such as Hicks Georgia Minstrels. Others were hired by white-owned companies, and the black American presence was increased in music and show business generally through variety acts, the circus, and theater. Many of these great performers deliberately cultivated cross-cultural bridges, and collectively they gave America, aided by recordings, its musical signature.

Music written in 1896 by Ernest Hogan, a literate African American, helped popularize the syncopated music genre. The style revolutionized show business and developed into the signature of popular American music. It also saved a failing record industry.

Learning syncopation from his musically illiterate African brothers in and around Chicago, Hogan then wrote and had published "All Coons Look Alike to Me." The lyrics were cowritten by Isidore Witmark whose father had been a Confederate officer. "All Coons" equaled the popularity of "After the Ball," the 1892 white popular song that became the first 1 million seller in sheet music.

Black performance companies in the late 1890s proliferated to meet the public demand for "All Coons" and became profitable on the basis of showcasing the song. The success of black performers forced white minstrels and vaudeville variety acts to adopt the song and a "coon song" craze mushroomed. Blacks and whites began writing all kinds of songs in the same syncopated music style (African virtuoso treatment of tearing a song apart or ragging it), and ragtime music developed.

African Americans created and dominated ragtime, led eventually by composer Scott Joplin. By 1900, however, ragtime also became the rage among white publishers and writers in Tin Pan Alley, the music publishing mecca in New York City, which supplied vaudeville, a network of traveling performers and theaters across the United States. From East European Jews who largely influenced the establishment of Tin Pan Alley came Irving Berlin's "Alexander's Ragtime Band," which added to the national popularity of ragtime. In the early 1900s, John Phillip Sousa won the Paris Exposition music competition with "My Ragtime Baby," written by Fred Stone, an African American from Detroit.

The ragtime experience led to the popularity of jazz. When Freddie Keppard, an African American, could not come to terms with Victor Records to record jazz music, the company contracted the Original Dixieland Jazz Band whose 1917 recordings sold millions. Ragtime began to fade, the jazz era commenced, and the phonograph companies had a gold mine.

The vast majority of music on phonographs consisted of opera, marches, waltzes, classical music, or light versions of those genres. The calm and easy style of music was also the primary type of performance played by inventors and engineers experimenting with radio broadcasting upon their return home from World War I. As the number of radio stations increased, listenership grew, and phonograph sales dropped dramatically.

By 1920, Perry Bradford, an African-American publisher and songwriter educated on the Negro vaudeville circuit, had spent several years trying to persuade white record companies to record an African-American female singing the blues accompanied by a jazz band. Finally, Fred Hager of Okeh Records signed Bradford to a contract and rescued Okeh from bankruptcy with Bradford's recording of "Crazy Blues" by Mamie Smith and The Jazz Hounds, which sold 3 million copies. Major record companies then began to cut records of African Americans singing blues and jazz to increase their sales and escaped financial ruin.

Bradford's breakthrough developed opportunities for Bessie Smith, Ida Cox, Ethel Waters, Alberta Hunter, Sippie Wallace, and others. Blues recordings featuring men accompanying themselves on guitar, the country blues style, became even more popular than the combination female and jazz band. Blind Lemon Jefferson, Robert Johnson, Leroy Carr, Blind Boy Fuller, and Tampa Red became legendary figures, and jazz bands flourished.

As radio grew rapidly in the 1920s, the programming of jazz and blues on the airwaves was minimal due to a preference for opera and classical music. Not until the early 1930s did jazz and spirituals with Duke Ellington, Louis Armstrong, the Wings Over Jordan, the Southernaires, and Golden Gate Quartet gain regular national exposure on live radio playing jazz and singing spirituals.

Broadcasters turned to live and recorded black music to help radio survive during the Great Depression. Extensive access was relatively short-lived, however. The development of radio drama became a successful entertainment format, and use of the electric organ led to a decline of the use of live musicians on radio.

An increased use of recorded music in the 1930s by radio stations also reduced the presence of live musicians working in radio. The pattern gathered momentum as disc jockey programs evolved and gained more popularity going into World War II. The musicians strike protesting the increasing firings of musicians in the early 1940s was aimed more at broadcasters than at record companies. Musicians were caught in the vortex of the record industry's developing structure and could not win. Phonograph-based programming in radio was the wave of the future, and recording companies were not going to disappear. Major record companies such as Decca, RCA Victor, and Columbia set up an assistance fund for musicians, and music returned to the airwaves.

By the end of World War II, the basic elements of the recording industry consisted of phonographs, music, broadcasting, and their related associations. Music publishers had successfully challenged and won the right to control the use of copyrighted music through legislation and legal rulings. Songwriters, in the process of protecting their intellectual property rights, established relationships with record companies and broadcasters. Last, BMI was helping to diversify America's recording industry by admitting a broader range of cultural representatives including African-American and country and western writers and publishers.

ORGANIZATIONAL STRUCTURE OF THE RECORD INDUSTRY

The complex structure of the record industry can be divided into five general areas: (1) invention and copyright, (2) publishing and licensing, (3) associations, (4) production and distribution, and (5) and media. Each area comprises smaller units that interconnect the various parts into an organizational whole. An overview of the general structure is represented in Figure 9.1 (also see Table 9.1 for related associations).

Copyright and licensing are critical economical factors that must be understood clearly. They are also the processes by which songwriters, publishing companies, producers, performance rights organizations, and record companies receive and control invention rights and become protected by the U.S. government.

Joining a professional music association or guild is indispensable to understanding the structure and functions of the recording industry. The information that associations disseminate is aimed at benefiting professional and potential members of the record industry. Since the purpose of information is to reduce uncertainty, knowledge made available from association data bases can serve as guideposts in the complex structure and functions of the record industry (see Table 9.1).

Production and distribution are directed by recording companies and related firms, including those that produce music videos. Until recording firms activate the system with productions, the fruits from copyright and licensing tend to remain largely dormant. Record companies cannot do business without mechanical licenses. Lastly, broadcast, film, and cable companies cannot function efficiently without securing music performance licenses.

Invention

Songs are created in factories, core of the copyright and licensing area and control center of the recording industry. Without the production of songs, the recording industry would not function. There would be no Rhythm and Blues, Top 40, or Country Western radio; no Grammy awards, American Music Award programs, or motion picture musical sound tracks. Song factories produce music, the world's most universal language. In reality, song factories are the minds of human beings such as James Bland, W. C. Handy, Jessie Mae Robinson, Hank Williams, Michael Jackson, and teams such as Jimmy Jam and Terry Lewis or Kenny Gamble and Leon Huff. Their minds creatively bring together keen social observation and musical technology. Songwriters give life and leadership to the recording industry music—not the recording facilities, pressing plants, or tape duplicating companies.

The U.S. government protects the manufacturer, for whoever uses the product thereafter must pay the inventor. So once a song is created, it becomes a potentially valuable commodity or investment. Foremost, "the form of the song is not important, only that it exists."

The songwriter can vocalize his or her song onto cassette tape and then employ a trained musician to transcribe the melody and words into a written lyric sheet. The writer also has the option of hiring a pianist to accompany a demonstration of the song and capture it on audiotape. Anyone can aspire to become

Figure 9.1
The Structure of the Record Industry*

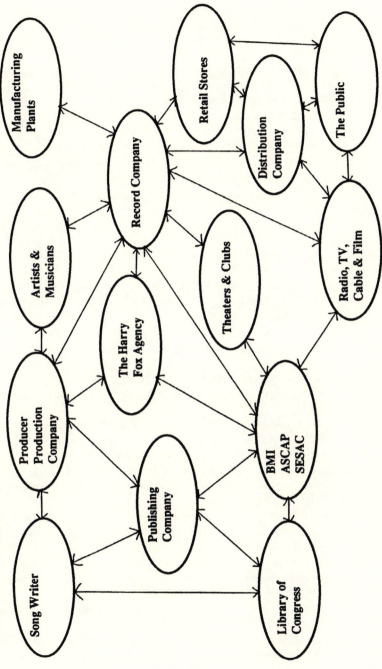

Source: Composed by the author, 1990.
*See Table 9.1 for related associations.

Table 9.1
Record Industry Associations

1. American Composers Alliance (ACA), New York. Represents American composers of concert music and acts as a creative force in public relations and lobbying for the rights of its members.

2. American Federation of Musicians (AFM), New York. A union of professional musicians with members in Canada and the United States. Negotiates, administers, and protects the contractual rights of its members. Is affiliated with the AFL-CIO.

3. American Federation of Television & Radio Artists (AFTRA), New York. Represents professional performers and broadcasters. Negotiates and administers for live and taped broadcast performances, phonograph recordings, and audiovisual productions.

4. American Music Center (AMC), New York. Promotes the creation, performance, publication, and recording of all forms of contemporary American music.

5. American Society of Composers, Authors and Publishers (ASCAP), New York. ASCAP licenses and collects fees for public performance of its members' copyrighted music and distributes the income.

6. Audio Engineering Society (AES), New York. Promotes the common interest of member engineers, technicians, administrators, and educators from the areas of broadcasting, film, and recording.

7. Black Music Association (BMA), Philadelphia, PA. The BMA's membership includes performers, producers, and record company executives. Its objective is to promote, perpetuate, and preserve black music domestically and internationally.

8. Broadcast Music, Inc. (BMI), New York. BMI is a licensing organization for domestic writers, publishers, and international affiliates. It collects and distributes royalty fees for its members.

9. Country Music Association (CMA), Nashville, TN. The CMA promotes the development of country music internationally through seminars, publications, and presentations.

10. Creative Audio & Musical Electronics Organization (CAMEO), Farmington, MA. The membership is composed of electronic audio equipment distributors and manufacturers. It is dedicated to the advancement of the retail audio industry.

11. National Association of Independent Record Distributors & Manufacturers (NAIRM), Pennsauken, NJ. Its members work to solve the problems of independent record distributors and manufacturers.

12. National Music Publishers Association (NMPA), New York. An association of publishers reflecting a cross section of American music. Works in conjunction with the Harry Fox Agency to collect royalties.

13. Recording Industry Association of America, New York. Members are creators and producers of recorded music sold in America. It promotes the mutual interests of recording companies and improvement of the industry.

14. SESAC Inc., Nashville, TN. A rights organization that licenses and collects fees for its songwriters and publishers.

15. The Songwriters Guild (TSG), New York. An organization to protect its membership in dealings with publishers and keep them informed on copyright law changes.

a songwriter, for surely, as Barry Sadler encouraged, "there is a song inside of everyone."

Imperatively, the songwriter must claim his or her legal creation rights. Lack of basic knowledge of copyright and licensing policies in the recording industry has caused fortunes to be forever lost, stolen, or given away. Without copyright ownership, someone else could claim or use the creator's song without ever paying the creator. Copyright ownership of songs is the economic foundation to the recording industry because the owner of the copyright is paid a fee, sometimes called a *royalty* or *residual,* by companies or other persons that use the music.

Copyright

The U.S. Copyright Office is located in the Library of Congress in Washington, D.C. It maintains a twenty-four-hour telephone service to receive requests for copyright forms, which are mailed without direct cost. All songwriters, professional and amateur, access the same system and file the completed forms to protect their creations. Under the Copyright Act of 1976, ownership is given to the author for life plus fifty years to his or her estate.

Another copyright is given to the producer or record company that owns the technical or completed sound production of a song. A copyright can be obtained also on the arrangement of a particular song. The appropriate form must be filed with the Copyright Office along with a copy of the sheet music, finished cassette, record, or CD. The intent of Congress is to make the copyright process an easy and simple one. Once the song or production is protected by copyright, the author is ready to license it in the marketplace and to find a publisher.

Publishing and Licensing

The publishing company is the oldest part of the recording industry structure and most lucrative, operated properly. The publisher earns money from several important sources through licensing agreements involving songs to which it holds copyright. Public performance sites, radio and television stations, motion picture and video companies, sheet music sales, and record companies pay royalties to publishers. Earnings accrue each time a song is used.

The publishing company's relationship with the songwriter is one of representation. The publisher tries to place the songs and music of its writers with an artist or company for recording and distribution. The publisher is responsible for committing the financial resources necessary to develop basic songs into a more complex musical demonstration in the form of demonstration tapes or records. It then promotes a sample recording of songs to producers, artists, and record company executives. The publisher purposefully establishes and maintains contacts throughout the industry in order to give a songwriter high visibility. The publisher strives to build and maintain an attractive and productive catalog of songs. Companies maintain a network throughout the nation's night-clubs and other entertainment spots to listen to new songwriters.

The publisher may offer a songwriter a flat fee contract for a song, a percentage usually no more than 50 percent, or put the writer on salary. Ownership or financial interest in songs enables a publishing company to earn money from the sale of sheet music and royalties through licensing from record sales, radio airplay, television commercials, or motion picture sound track use.

Of course, songwriters can publish their own works, setting up a corporation or company to do so. The easiest method is to obtain a DBA (doing business under an assumed name) by registering the name of the company with the local county clerk's office. The selected performing rights company will require submission of at least three possible names when applying for membership; an alternative will be selected if the first choice is already in existence. The process can start with a simple telephone call placed to ASCAP, BMI, or SESAC.

Publishing means to print and distribute sheet music or to manufacture and distribute a song on record, cassette, video, or compact disc. The name of the song, publishing company, and performing rights organizations must be printed on the label, accompanied by a copyright date and insignia and the author's name. Publishing opportunities are open to all citizens, not just performing artists, songwriters, or record producers.

It is common practice for companies or individuals to own and operate both a record company and a publishing company, which is one reason recording industry executives prefer to dual sign artists who are also songwriters. In fact, the songwriting contract may be offered first. The corporation obtains additional economical benefits in potential hit songs if it owns both the record and publishing company.

Complexities in entertainment industries in the United States and internationally create problems for publishers in monitoring the use of their songs. It is not always possible to know who is using a record, video, or compact disc. Thus, licensing and other associations play a momentous role in the recording industry. A number of associations issue and protect three types of licenses: (1) public performance, (2) mechanical, and (3) synchronous.

Public Performance License Associations. Songwriters and publishers are encouraged to join one of three performance rights associations: Broadcast Music, Inc.; American Society of Composers, Authors and Publishers; or SESAC ("see-sack"). These organizations issue licenses to theaters, auditoriums, colleges and universities, clubs, and radio and television stations. An estimated 75,000 performance sites exist in the United States that use copyrighted music.

It is impossible for publishers individually to monitor all performances throughout the United States. Consequently, publishing firms contract with BMI, ASCAP, or SESAC to issue performance licenses to clients on their behalf. Indeed, performance rights associations send representatives into the field to survey entertainment sites on behalf of writers and publishers. They collect license fees for music used and distribute the funds to publishers and songwriters. When a theater does not carry a performance license, a show's promoter must pay the fee. Under U.S. law, theaters or promoters booking performers must be licensed.

Performance Licenses: Radio, Television, and Cable. Performance fees are not paid to record companies by radio, television, and cable stations for the use of their recorded productions. Stations must, however, pay performance license fees to publishers and songwriters for the use of their creations (an extension of the sheet music concept). BMI, ASCAP, and SESAC issue licenses to radio and television stations on behalf of publishers and writers and collect fees from broadcast stations and cable companies. For example, in the early 1990s, BMI charged radio stations 1.39 percent of their annual revenue for playing copyrighted music by its members; the ASCAP rate was 1.59 percent. Songwriters and publishers are paid from those collected fees.

Distribution of funds to publishers and writers is done mathematically. BMI, ASCAP, and SESAC take random samples quarterly of programming on the nation's more than 9,000 radio stations to determine the airplay frequency of all songs. Computer mathematical models project the songs played by stations nationally. The writer and publisher split between six and twelve cents, depending on station size or earnings, each time a record has aired.

Each label on CDs, cassettes, and albums names the performer, producer, song, songwriter, publishing company, and performance rights organization to which the publishing company is a member: BMI, ASCAP, or SESAC. Sometimes separate publishers belonging to BMI and ASCAP, respectively, will have purchased interest in the same song, and both organizations will appear. Surveys identify the respective performance rights organization, song title, artists, and publishing company through the label information.

Television stations and networks also pay license fees to BMI, ASCAP, and SESAC to use music. The performance license rates for cable companies are handled collectively through the Copyright Royalty Tribunal (CRT). The CRT pays fees to the performance organizations on behalf of the cable industry.

Mechanical and Synchronous Licenses. Mechanical and synchronous licenses, another important resource, are different from performance licenses. Mechanical licenses are issued to record companies to produce songs on cassettes, CDs, and records. Synchronous licenses go to producers or companies for motion picture and/or video use. Mechanical and synchronous clearinghouses issue licenses and collect fees for their members.

When the public hears a song (new, old, or one with a varied arrangement) on the radio or in a movie, a license to use the song has been issued and/or coordinated through a mechanical/synchronous clearinghouse. Licensing often is administered by the Harry Fox Agency. Other smaller clearinghouses include MCA/Universal, BEG (RCA), CBS, and EMI. The public is most likely to recognize these companies as record labels, but they own huge song publishing catalogs and control their own mechanical and synchronous licenses for reproduction.

The Harry Fox Agency, a subsidiary of the National Music Publishers Association, also lists BMI and ASCAP among its members. Consequently, the entire catalogs of more than 4,900 publishing companies, all members of BMI and ASCAP, are accessible through the Harry Fox Agency. Millions of song titles are available in one resource for record, movie, or video companies. The licensing rates are set by the Harry Fox Agency and, in some cases, supported by legal rulings.

Another function of the clearinghouse is to monitor record company sales. The Harry Fox Agency may audit the financial records of a record company to protect the license holder. The publisher is then assured of the accuracy of the number of records reproduced and distributed and for which that company must pay mechanical rights in accord with the license issued for the works involved. The same monitoring policy holds true for film use and motion picture company receipts.

The mechanical and synchronous fees collected by the Harry Fox Agency and other license clearinghouses are paid to publishers, so songwriters receive mechanical and synchronous fee payments through the publisher. The songwriter's contract language with a publisher regarding percentage of interest in a song and payment rate is therefore very important.

The acute importance of licenses became evident in the career of Michael Jackson. Following the success of his 1980s "Thriller" album, Jackson purchased ATV Music, a large international publishing company, for $47.5 million. Jackson's newly acquired publishing company was then grossing $15 million annually from licensing and rights fees issued to various users of songs from the corporation's catalog. Nearly 50 percent of ATV's earnings came from licenses to use or record old Beatles songs.

When legendary record company executive Berry Gordy sold Motown Records, he kept control of Jobete Music, his publishing firm. Although he no longer owns Motown Records, the record company pays licensing fees to Jobete Music, directly or via Harry Fox, for records, compact discs, or tapes produced and distributed that used classic Motown songs. Any company that records and distributes a classic Motown song will pay mechanical fees to Jobete Music.

The Record Company

Record companies are the center of the production-distribution area in the recording industry. They are responsible for transforming ideas into complete musical products. Their functions interconnect directly with more components than any other part of the structure. For those reasons alone, record companies often project a highly visible image to the public.

The major record company owned by U.S. interests is Warner Communications, Inc. Polygram Records is owned by Phillips, a Dutch-controlled firm; MCA was purchased by Matsushita of Japan; and Capitol Records is owned by Thorn EMI of England. Sony of Japan bought CBS Records, and RCA Records and Arista Records were acquired by Bertlesmann, a German company. The majors account for about 90 percent of the $6 billion that the recording industry is grossing annually in sales in the 1990s. The remaining 10 percent in recording sales is controlled by independent record firms.

Independent record companies are those not part of large conglomerates or corporate structures and do not generally own their national distribution companies. Solar Records, Island Records, and Malaco Records are independent corporations. Many independent recording companies exist in practice but appear as production firms because their productions are released on a conglomerate's record label.

Regardless of size or complexity, the recording company has four main goals: (1) to obtain a song license from a publisher, (2) to record the song, (3) to distribute the product, and (4) to make a profit. Company strategies implemented to achieve those objectives may vary among companies, but their concepts are similar. A producer for the record company is responsible for coordinating the singers, musicians, arranger, and studio facility to develop the song on audiotape. There are literally hundreds of recording studios in cities and hamlets throughout the United States. They can be found in any telephone directory. Recording sessions and subsequent editing time are paid for by the hour.

Technology has recently made the home studio possible. Professionals and novices using synthesizers, digital technology, and computer programs are changing the manner in which music is being produced. Large, expensively equipped recording studios are no longer essential to produce professional audio sounds.

Once the completed recording session is edited on audiotape called a *master*, it is sent to a record pressing, cassette duplicating, or CD plant. When companies reach this manufacturing stage, they are likely to have interacted directly with at least eight of the basic industry components: (1) songwriter, (2) publishing company, (3) Library of Congress, (4) performance organizations, (5) license clearinghouses, (6) producer/production company, (7) artists, and (8) manufacturing plants. Each is essential to transforming a song into a full musical production ready for public life where the execution of strategies in media marketing, promotion, and sales dovetail with the distribution process.

Distribution

Completed music productions need distributors just as simple songs need to be assigned to publishers who can promote them among artists, producers, and record companies. It is vitally important for a record company to develop a well-structured distribution system, the most difficult and complex aspect of the recording industry.

Distribution is the gateway to the public and where cash flow commences. Rewards from copyright and licensing remain largely dormant until the public takes an interest in the songwriter/artist/producer's recorded work. The record company can invest thousands of dollars in a project and never see a return unless people buy the recording.

Major record companies such as CBS, MCA, and RCA own and operate their own distribution companies. They divide the country into regions and staff branch offices. Regional personnel in Atlanta, Cleveland, Chicago, and other large cities coordinate with their headquarters to supply radio stations with records and/or compact discs. They wholesale to major retail chain stores, one-stop record stores, and rackjobbers.

Independent distribution firms handle releases from smaller record companies or those not distributed by the majors. In some cases, independent distributors will contact area radio stations, just as major distributors do. By dividing the nation into regions and identifying a series of regional distribution firms, a small record company can establish a national independent distribution delivery system.

One-stop record stores are wholesale distribution operations that also double as retail outlets and are smaller than independent distributors. One-stops purchase wholesale from major and independent distributors and then wholesale to small "mom and pop" retail record shops.

Corporations known as rackjobbers serve as outside buyers for discount stores such as K-Mart and department store chains. Store space is often rented by rackjobbers who purchase recordings from major and independent wholesale distributors. Known for their colorful display racks, rackjobbers provide the store with a full marketing service, sales personnel, fixtures or decorations, weekly product replenishment, and inventory.

Promoters and Radio

Promotion of CDs, records, and tapes by recording companies and their distributors is of paramount importance. In some cases, an artist's management firm may hire an independent promoter to push a record, and special public relations campaigns are directed toward radio, television, and cable operations. A network of promotion people make personal visits to radio stations regularly in an effort to influence or gain airplay for their music. Often, a promoter is responsible for radio station contacts in several states or a region.

Record promotion jobs are coveted, and many professionals begin their careers with record companies while attending college and work up from "campus reps." Campus radio station reps for major companies such as Warner, MCA, or CBS promote their labels. Promoters for independents may operate with smaller marketing budgets and handle many unrelated labels.

The competition for air space on radio stations in major large cities has forced some radio stations to designate special days during the week for promoters to make their pitch. The promoter may point out the advantages and value of a company's new releases, lyric relevance, innovative techniques, or the sales position of a record in given markets, or list other radio stations playing the record, particularly the local competition.

Since the inception of Music Television (MTV) as a cable channel, music videos have played an increasingly important role in the promotion and sale of records. Nearly every major record release has been accompanied by a music video since the mid-1980s. Music videos are now promoted by record companies to local, regional, and national programmers, just as records are to radio stations.

EFFECTIVENESS

For nearly a century the recording industry and music have functioned effectively as a mass communication medium. Economically, music and phonographs are an inextricable part of radio programming, television, and motion picture sound tracks. Culturally, and socially, the recording industry has helped America heal itself from African enslavement and the Civil War.

The popularity of minstrel shows, vaudeville, ragtime, jazz, and blues gave black band directors a preeminent status and led to white-owned phonograph companies hiring many African Americans to supervise their recording sessions. Others became music directors of successful white companies such as Atlantic, Mercury, and Chess Records. Black-owned record companies, such as the Pace Phonograph Company, Black Swann Records, the Black and White Record Company, DooTone Records, and Duke Records, were pioneers in the field and helped construct the foundation for Vee Jay Records of Chicago, Motown Records, in Detroit, and Philadelphia International. Their success stimulated the establishment of hundreds of black-owned record companies.

Harry Pace, founder of Black Swann Records, insurance executive, and business partner of W. C. Handy, became the mentor of John H. Johnson, who later built a mass communication empire of magazines, radio, and television. Vee Jay Records was first to sign the Beatles to a recording contract and release their music in America. Berry Gordy, the founder of Motown, became one of the nation's wealthiest individuals and created opportunities for thousands of talented artists and business professionals in the entertainment world.

The world's airwaves never cease vibrating with recordings from African Americans, and the music's value to building cross-cultural and racial relationships cannot be overstated. A legacy of struggle for human dignity by black minstrels, the Fisk Jubilee Singers, white supporters, and other entertainment pioneers is present in both the history and structure of the recording industry. Yet more needs to be written on the cooperative role between blacks and whites in this important mass medium.

CRITICISM

Recently, the record industry was challenged by human rights leader Jesse Jackson who charged Warner Communications with practicing racism. Included among his charges were (1) unfair treatment of its black music marketing division—e.g., allocation of smaller advertising and promotion budgets to black acts; (2) lower black executive salaries compared with white executive salaries for similar positions; (3) a low number of blacks in management positions; (4) not extending credit to black retailers as it does to white firms; (5) raiding small black record companies for artists; and (6) investments in South Africa.

In separate actions, the National Association for the Advancement of Colored People (NAACP) condemned all major recording companies in its five-year study of "The Discordant Sound of Music," which described overwhelming segregation, rampant discrimination, and pressure on African-American artists not to target blacks as their primary audience (George, 1987).

The two major recording firms owned by the Japanese, MCA and CBS Records, were the first to work out agreements with the NAACP. They agreed to improve trade with black firms, develop a minority job skills bank, and open avenues for job opportunities and career advancement. Warner Communications divested its financial holdings in South Africa but denied Jackson's charge of racial discrimination in hiring.

Citations about unscrupulous practices in many components of the record industry are legendary. Little Richard and the late Arthur "Big Boy" Crudup are among many who have protested the loss of millions in royalties and payments to publishing companies, club owners, promoters, managers, or recording firms. Even broadcasters have been criticized.

The Federal Communications Commission (FCC) requires that radio stations protect themselves from other recording industry practices. Payola, the practice by some promoters to pay disc jockeys money under the table to play certain songs over the air, plunged broadcasting into controversy several times. In 1980 the FCC issued a public notice that clearly held radio station license holders responsible for controlling the conditions that attracted payola from record and/ or publishing companies.

Black owners of black music–programmed radio stations often claim discrimination from advertisers including record companies. They complain of grossing less money than white stations in the same market even when black stations achieve higher listening ratings. Under such conditions, black stations are locked into a lower economic bracket, which reduces royalty payments to publishing companies and songwriters.

THE FUTURE

The struggle to protect human intellectual property rights continues in the face of advancing technology. The compact disc, introduced by Japanese and Dutch scientists, has made it an instant technological player in the recording industry. Digital technology has also made it possible for producers to copy such small portions of another's work, protection of creativity is more difficult, and hardware advancements will endure.

The recording industry developed slowly, taking almost one hundred years to work out basic legal rulings. Each segment of the recording industry is composed of hundreds of financially wealthy corporations. Subinstitutions are generally unregulated and largely closed operational systems. They are not easily challenged from the outside, and dramatic and quick change is unlikely.

BIBLIOGRAPHY

Dykstra, Ron (1990, February 6). Personal interview.

Fletcher, T. (1954). *100 years of the Negro in show business.* New York: Burdge.

Franklin, Randy. (1990, February 6). Personal interview.

George, N. (1987, January). NAACP report socks it to the music biz. *Billboard,* p. 3.

Handy, W. C. (1941). *Father of the blues.* New York: Macmillan.

Herbert v. Shanley, 242 US 591 (1917).

Hurst, W. E. (1977). *Copyright: How to register your copyright, an introduction to new and historical copyright law.* Hollywood: Seven Arts Press.

Latman, A. (1979). *The copyright law* (5th ed.). Washington, DC: Bureau of National Affairs.

Morgan, Andre. (1990, March 12). Personal interview.

Roth, E. (1969). *The business of music.* New York: Oxford University Press.

Sadler, B. (1978). *Everything you want to know about the record industry in Nashville, Tennessee: Country music capital of the world.* Nashville, TN: Aurora.

The Smithsonian Institute. (1975). *History of music machines.* New York: Drake.

10

TELEVISION

Robert G. Finney

Television is credited with having a tremendous impact on our culture, both positive and negative. Virtually everyone from public figures and media critics to the lay public has both lauded and villified television for its alleged role in affecting our perceptions of ourselves and perceptions of America by other nations throughout the world.

Television needs to be defined because it has different meanings to different people. To the average American viewer, the generic term refers to any pictures and sound that appear on the video screen. To broadcasters, television is a traditional over-the-air broadcast technology that uses the frequency spectrum the same way radio does by sending an electromagnetic signal at the speed of light from a transmitter to an antenna in your home.

Television has the capability of receiving a variety of video signals. A few are television broadcast signals; others, like Home Box Office (HBO) and Music Television (MTV), are signals sent via cable or satellite. The discussion of television here focuses on over-the-air broadcast television.

A television signal consists of FM sound and four video pulses: horizontal, vertical, synchronization, and color burst. The combined signal is relayed from a nearby television station to the home via powerful transmitters (100 to 1,000 kilowatts, depending on channel assignment). Many local television stations are affiliated with broadcast networks (ABC, CBS, NBC, Fox, Public Broadcasting Service [PBS]) that provide programming to them via microwave or satellite.

HISTORY

Experimentation with television technology began almost as early as radio in the early part of the twentieth century. Unlike radio, sole credit for its development cannot be traced to one or two inventors. Two individuals credited with contributing major advances during the 1920s were Vladimir Zworykin and

Philo Farnsworth. Zworykin, a Westinghouse engineer, invented the iconoscope, the first electronic camera image tube in 1923. Farnsworth, a self-educated inventor, invented the image dissector, which could break down pictures into tiny parts for transmission. By 1930, David Sarnoff, head of the Radio Corporation of America (RCA), put together the RCA Laboratories in Camden, New Jersey, and hired Zworykin to head a group of research scientists to make television available to the public by the end of that decade. Sarnoff unveiled RCA's television technology to the public at the New York World's Fair in 1939 (Head & Sterling, 1990, pp. 47–49). Introducing television service in the home was delayed for several years, however, due to World War II.

Refinements During the War

The television signal is not a solid picture but the compilation of bits of information into horizontal lines. The greater the number of horizontal lines, the finer the detail of the picture. The picture quality introduced at the 1939 World's Fair contained only 441 horizontal lines of resolution, a relatively crude image. RCA refined its electronic system, eventually achieving 525 lines of resolution at thirty picture frames per second, the system adopted for use nationwide by the National Television Systems Committee (NTSC) in 1941. This was black and white television, or monochrome, and the precursor of the color system in use today. Color television did not debut until the 1950s. Advanced television systems of more than 1,000 lines of resolution that promise to provide the viewing public with image quality comparable with current feature films are likely to be adopted by the government and the industry before the turn of the century.

World War II brought manufacture and marketing of most consumer electronic products to a complete standstill. From 1942 to 1945, research scientists and engineers devoted most of their energies toward perfecting radar and other electronic technologies with military applications. Research and development on video technology for civilian applicability followed the war. During World War II, there were only six experimental television stations in existence and only about 10,000 television sets in homes, half of them in New York City where two of the six stations were located. The other four were in Chicago, Los Angeles, Philadelphia, and Schenectady, New York.

Television did not become popular immediately after the war primarily because there were few stations, and most of those were on the air less than four hours per day. Television receivers were very expensive, and radio remained the primary family information and entertainment medium until the end of the decade.

Postwar Growth

In 1948, RCA introduced the Image Orthicon camera pickup tube, which improved the television image dramatically, and the first network interconnection began via cable between New York and Washington, D.C. New television stations were licensed and began broadcasting between 1946 and 1948. By summer 1948, there were forty-eight television stations in twenty-three cities broadcasting, and the audience had grown by 4,000 percent (Head & Sterling, 1990, p. 50).

Government Oversight

The Federal Communications Commission (FCC), the government agency charged with overseeing the broadcasting industry, was established by the Communications Act of 1934, which made no mention of television because it did not exist then. The act was an outgrowth of the Radio Act of 1927 and part of President Franklin D. Roosevelt's "New Deal" legislation. It combined sections of the 1927 Radio Act with parts of public utility law concerning regulation of telegraph and telephone and mandated the formation of the FCC to regulate radio and to interpret provisions of the Communications Act (Head & Sterling, 1990, p. 41).

Prior to World War II, the FCC was concerned with radio, primarily. Thereafter, it became much more interested in television. Fearful that television broadcasting would grow in the same haphazard and uncontrolled way that radio stations did in the early 1920s, resulting in electronic chaos, the FCC instituted what is known today as the "Famous Freeze" in September 1948. The freeze lasted until spring 1952. Only 108 previously authorized stations were permitted to go on the air during the freeze.

The FCC held public hearings to resolve concerns regarding policy, regulation, and technology. The reason there is no channel 1, for example, is that the regulators reassigned part of the frequency spectrum to the government for military communications at the beginning of World War II and chose not to re-number all the channels following the lifting of the freeze because of the negative impact this would have on the consumer television market. In 1951, American Telephone and Telegraph linked New York and San Francisco together with telephone long lines designed to relay television signals, providing networking capability.

In April 1952 the FCC lifted the freeze by issuing its Sixth Report and Order, which is the foundation for television broadcasting in the United States today. The Sixth Report and Order set out a plan of channel assignments for over 2,000 television stations to almost 1,300 communities throughout the nation. It established VHF channels 2 through 13, UHF channels 14 through 83, and reserved 242 specific channel assignments nationally for educational television, which later became the cornerstone for the development of public television (Head & Sterling, 1990, p. 50).

Development of UHF

Two technical problems not addressed by the Sixth Report and Order were inherent weaknesses in UHF signal transmission and color television. Because a UHF channel assignment is higher than a VHF channel assignment in the frequency spectrum, it requires a transmitter with more power output to send a signal comparable with that of a VHF signal. During the 1950s, transmitters capable of providing a comparable signal did not exist. Progress of UHF television broadcasting was impeded also by the fact that UHF tuners were an extra option on TV receivers. In 1962 Congress amended the Communications Act, requiring manufacturers to include UHF tuners in television receivers sold in 1964 and thereafter. This helped, but early all-channel receivers had separate tuners for VHF and UHF; not until single and digital tuners were introduced in the late 1970s did UHF channels begin to compete with VHF channels effectively.

Color Television

The color television issue was under consideration during the freeze but was not settled until 1953. In 1950 Congress selected a mechanical noncompatible color system developed by CBS as the national color television standard. The CBS system used a mechanical device in the receiver, not unlike a pinwheel or kaleidoscope, to generate its color picture and required viewers to have two separate television receivers, one for color programming and another one for monochrome. RCA developed a compatible system that produced color images electronically and permitted viewers to watch programming transmitted in color on their monochrome receivers in black and white. In 1950 the RCA system was more expensive, and color images simply were not as good as CBS's system. Congress reversed itself in 1953 and adopted a compatible electronic color system proposed by the NTSC that was patterned closely after the RCA system.

Color Programming

Color programming was slow to develop. NBC, a wholly owned subsidiary of RCA, was the only color network in 1958. Total color prime-time network programming was achieved when CBS, the last holdout, finally joined ABC and NBC with prime-time programming exclusively in color in 1966 (Head & Sterling, 1990, p. 53).

Television gradually blanketed the country with new stations and live television programming during the early 1950s. The "golden age" of television programming is generally considered to have lasted from 1948 to 1957 when networks allowed programming to take priority over everything else in order to sell more TV sets. Most of it was done live, sometimes twice, once for the Eastern and Central time zones and again for the Mountain and Pacific zones. Almost two-thirds of the programs originated in New York. Hollywood provided some programs on film during this period; most were feature films produced for theater distribution prior to 1948. Film production techniques were not adapted easily to producing television programs quickly and inexpensively, and the film industry resisted television until the 1960s when ABC merged with Paramount. One notable exception to film-produced programming was the "I Love Lucy" show, which pioneered the three-camera production technique used in most studio video production today.

Videotape

The invention of videotape by Ampex in 1956 brought the golden age of television programming to an end. Videotape made it possible to stockpile programs and to produce programming rapidly using film production techniques without the delays or costs of film production. Live television programming, except for news and news events, was totally eclipsed by programs produced on film or videotape.

Television replaced radio as the primary entertainment medium for the American home by 1956. Its predominant role as an information medium was not realized until 1963 when the nation watched the events following President John F. Kennedy's assassination on television. Television turned that tragedy into a media event that established its primacy as an information medium.

Another factor contributing to the immediacy of television as a news medium was the invention of the portable videocamera in the mid-1960s, which demonstrated that television can sway public opinion. Television brought the Vietnam War into American living rooms and is credited with swinging public opinion away from the policy of President Lyndon B. Johnson.

Public television had its roots in educational television of the early 1950s, but from its inception, noncommercial television has suffered from a lack of consistent revenue. In spite of federal government efforts to aid noncommercial television with the Educational Television Facilities Act of 1962, which provided matching dollars for building noncommercial television stations, and the Public Broadcasting Act of 1967, which provided an omnibus amendment to the Communications Act, public television remains an economically poor stepchild to commercial television today.

The Public Broadcasting Act of 1967 established the Corporation for Public Broadcasting (CPB), an independent, nonprofit corporation designed to funnel federal dollars appropriated by Congress to television stations. It did so through the Public Broadcasting Service, which developed a station cooperative for producing television programs and funding them with government money. Unlike the commercial networks, PBS has no central production house. Its member stations seek grants and contracts for producing noncommercial programming along with independent producers. These programs and series are then bid upon by member stations; the most popular programs are the ones selected for network relay via PBS. WGBH in Boston, for example, is the producer of "Nova," and the Children's Television Workshop in New York is the producer of "Sesame Street."

Because a major source of funding for public television is the federal government, revenue requests go through congressional budget hearings. Historically, CPB and PBS have not received long-term government appropriations. A commercial television station can seek higher advertising dollars to cover increased production costs if the higher-quality productions draw larger audiences, whereas the public television station must seek viewer donations through pledge drives or corporate underwriting of its program costs. The growth of cable and cable services, such as the Arts and Entertainment Network (A&E), that provide programming that was once considered PBS's sole responsibility portends more difficulties for noncommercial television in the years ahead.

Traditional over-the-air broadcast television is really a young industry that owes a great deal of its technical success to America's involvement in armed combat, during which video technology was perfected for military use and then later applied to consumer electronics. The coverage of the war in the Persian Gulf was one step further in the evolution of reporting armed combat with viewers sitting in their homes watching live or "instant replays" of air strikes, missile attacks, and troop movements.

Development of Cable

During the famous freeze, broadcast television provided commercial services primarily to larger metropolitan areas. Smaller markets received few television signals, if any. In order to receive distant signals from the larger markets, small communities subscribed to CATV (community antenna television) services. The forerunner of cable television today, CATV began in the late 1940s. The earliest systems consisted of a master antenna installed at a high elevation that would receive distant line-of-sight television signals and relay these to television receivers in homes via coaxial cable that was strung throughout the community on utility poles. CATV had no origination programs and merely relayed the Big Three network signals, an independent station or two, and perhaps a public station. Subscribers paid a minimal fee of $4 or $5 per month to get five or six stations and better images with less "snow." During these early years, cable was a local concern regulated by the municipal government, which issued a franchise to the cable operator to install and operate the community's system for fifteen years or so.

Cable system operators expanded their services by adding local origination programming and access channels that the public could appear on or produce programs for by using video recording equipment provided by the cable company.

FCC Involvement in Cable Regulation

By the 1960s, cable began to expand into larger markets because of the concentrated populations and became a threat to broadcast television. This prompted broadcasters to appeal to the FCC for protection from cable's intrusion into their local markets. The FCC responded with an omnibus law regulating cable in 1972.

Within five years, however, a U.S. Court of Appeals limited the FCC's jurisdiction over cable, and cable technology began to develop toward the multichannel service it is today, with over 11,000 local cable systems and nearly 60 million subscribers nationally.

The emergence of "superstations" like Ted Turner's WTBS contributed to this growth. Turner owned a small UHF channel in Atlanta that broadcast Atlanta Braves baseball games. By renting space on a communications satellite, he provided WTBS's signal to cable system operators throughout the United States free of charge. Cable operators gladly accepted the signal and relayed to homes in their own communities. Turner made a profit by charging higher advertising rates because of the larger, cable-enhanced audience.

Pay cable services began in 1972 when Home Box Office offered cable operators a high-quality program service of movies and concerts that cable subscribers would pay a premium for.

Cable Technology

Many people refer to cable as cable television. This is a misnomer. Television is an over-the-air signal that sends electromagnetic waves through the spectrum on assigned frequencies, whereas cable is a closed-circuit system of coaxial cable that does not use broadcasting frequency assignments.

Theoretically, a cable system's channel capacity is limitless. To add more channels, one merely must add another coaxial cable, and with fiber optic technology on the horizon, cable will be replaced with a miniature fiber with even greater capacity. The only part of the frequency spectrum used by cable systems are satellite and microwave frequencies that are shared with other telecommunications technologies. Cable is not a rural medium because the population is too dispersed. Cable system operators must have a population density that passes enough homes per mile to make the cost of stringing cable profitable. The alternative for rural residents is a satellite dish called a TVRO (television receive only.) With proper positioning, the rural resident can receive any transmissions being relayed via satellite, even network feeds from one coast to the other. Program providers have had to scramble their signals to prevent unauthorized "pirating" of programs by TVRO owners.

In the years ahead, we can anticipate the introduction of other technological innovations like direct broadcast satellite (DBS), which could eliminate the local television station. High-definition television (HDTV) is coming also and will provide images with much higher resolution in a 3 by 5 aspect ratio, as opposed to the 3 by 4 ratio that television has used since its inception.

Television is evolving continually, adding to this medium's history and role in our society. Not only is its technology changing, but economics, government policy, and social pressures are impacting on its evolution as well.

TELEVISION FREQUENCIES, CHANNELS, AND REGULATIONS

Picture the frequency spectrum as a highway with many lanes of varying width for accommodating traffic. Each lane is dedicated to a particular type of "vehicle." The vehicles consist of a wide variety of wireless electromagnetic wave services. Marine mobile, citizens' band, military, commercial radio, and television are several examples. In order to prevent one signal or service from "crashing" or interfering with another, a station is licensed by the Federal Communications Commission to be the exclusive operator on a particular frequency in a particular area for a specified time. For example, a local television station may receive an exclusive license to broadcast on Channel 2 (the 54 to 60 MHz frequency band "lane") for five years. The license protects that local TV station from interference, giving it a monopoly on that particular frequency in that population center, or market, for five years. Other regulations specify minimum geographical distances between transmitters so that another Channel 2 is far enough away that it cannot interfere with the local Channel 2's signal.

This exclusivity inflates the value of television station properties when they are sold. A typical television station's assets (e.g., land, buildings, equipment, vehicles), if liquidated, may be worth only $3 to $5 million, yet television stations bring multimillion-dollar prices. Disney Enterprises paid over $500 million for an independent VHF station in the Los Angeles market. Given the potential impact of television, a licensee is able to charge incredibly high rates to advertisers who want to reach the local audience via television. Like most domestic communications media in the United States, the television industry is a profit-oriented private enterprise. It differs in this respect from newspapers only in that it is licensed and regulated by the federal government. The government has a two-part rationale for regulating television: (1) to prevent signal interference between frequency assignments and (2) to ensure that those licensed to broadcast programs via television do so in the public interest. The federal government views the frequency spectrum as a national resource, not unlike our rivers or our railroads, to be monitored so that those privileged to use it do not abuse it. The station owner is a public trustee who must ensure a responsible use of the channel assignment for the public good. Broadcasters must provide programming that meets the needs of their communities, and they are held accountable for indiscretions in programming content by the FCC.

This concept, sometimes called the *public trustee model,* raises First Amendment issues. Print media are basically unregulated, except for obscenity, which is covered under the U.S. Criminal Code. There are no special regulations for newspapers and magazines. Common carriers, like telephone and postal service, are awarded monopoly control in specific areas in return for providing universal service to all and have no jurisdiction over or responsibility for the content of what they send. Radio and television broadcasting are the only major media in our country subject to extensive content regulation.

The fundamental premise for privately owned companies being regulated by the federal government is the scarcity rationale, an argument that the frequency spectrum is finite and a scarce national resource. Owing to technological advances and economic realities, that rationale no longer exists, according to many media experts. Some critics of the current regulatory system argue that the trustee model approach itself is what restricts the effectiveness of television, and that it ought to be replaced with a free market approach like that used in the newspaper business.

The FCC and the Congress have yet to settle this issue. The position on a free market model versus the current trustee model has swung back and forth like a pendulum over the years. During the 1970s, there was pervasive government control over program content. The policy during the 1980s was to deregulate broadcasters and allow them much more autonomy with respect to programming. The decade of the 1990s began with a swing back toward closer content controls, especially with respect to decency and children.

A number of other laws and regulations place limits on the television industry and, to a lesser degree, on radio but not on other mass media. The FCC also enforces a multiple-ownership rule that, until recently, limited any individual or company from owning more than twelve AM radio, twelve FM radio, and twelve television stations nationwide (Carter, Franklin, & Wright, 1989, pp. 171–175). In 1992, however, the FCC voted to raise the limits on radio station ownership to twenty AM and twenty FM nationally, with a provision to increase that to twenty-five AM and twenty-five FM over several years. There is also a restriction on the size of the audience that one company can reach with all its stations. The total geographic area covered by all television stations owned by the same company may not reach more than 25 percent of the potential national audience. This is why the largest television station group owner, Capital Cities/ABC, does not own twelve stations. It owns eight stations, one each in New York; Los Angeles; Chicago; Philadelphia; Houston; San Francisco; Fresno, California; and Durham, North Carolina. These reach close to 25 percent of the national audience because all eight are in large metropolitan areas.

One exception to the multiple-ownership rule is designed to encourage further investment in UHF television. When computing the size of the audience in a local television market, a UHF licensee receives a 50 percent discount. In other words, Home Shopping Network's Los Angeles UHF station, Channel 46, although located in the nation's second-largest television market is considered to reach only 2.7 percent of the potential national audience even though it actually reaches 5.4 percent, as does Capital Cities/ABC's Channel 7.

Another exception is designed to encourage greater minority representation in station ownership. If a television group can document minority control ownership in at least two of the stations belonging to the company, that company may own up to fourteen stations, providing that their signals do not cover more than 30 percent of the potential national audience.

Another rule places limits on how many stations an individual or company can own of the same service in any one local area. Known as the *duopoly rule,* until recently it forbade the same owner from having two AM stations, two FM stations, or two TV stations when their transmitted signals overlap (Carter, Franklin, & Wright, 1989, p. 157). However, the 1992 FCC ruling raising the limits on radio ownership nationally effectively removed the duopoly rule for radio also by allowing overlap of radio signals owned by the same company. It remains for television station ownership.

Another rule called the *one-to-a-market rule* has restricted ownership to only one station in a single broadcast market. Still, ownership of AM-FM-TV combos is common owing to grandfather clauses or FCC waivers, which are granted freely in larger markets. The 1992 FCC ruling on radio ownership limits also modified this rule and allows the same company to own several stations, depending on the size of the market.

Cross-ownership rules prevent daily newspapers and television stations located in the same market from ownership by the same company. Similarly, TV stations, TV networks, and telephone companies are not permitted to own cable companies. These rules, extensions of antitrust law, are designed to prevent monopoly of mass media by special interests either locally or nationally. Just as radio ownership limits were liberalized, there is a groundswell among media owners and others to liberalize or eliminate certain cross-ownership rules, allowing for more free market competition across media lines, since virtually all markets have a diversity of media owned by a variety of companies.

The nation is blanketed by radio and television stations and their signals. There are more than 11,600 radio stations and about 1,500 television stations nationwide, over 350 of which are noncommercial educational television broadcasters.

Most television stations become affiliated with a network, which is a national distributor of programs from afternoon soap operas to national evening newscasts. The Big Three commercial national television networks, ABC, CBS, and NBC, once commanded over 90 percent of the national television audience during prime time. Because of a number of factors—economics, the growth of cable, new transmission technologies—this audience share has eroded to approximately 50 percent today.

There have been a number of abortive attempts to establish a fourth commercial network in the past. In 1988, Fox Television began to offer network prime-time programming on weekend evenings only and gradually expanded its schedule during prime-time programming in the evenings. Fox continues to garner a large share of the prime-time audience each season and appears to be the most successful effort to date to establish a viable fourth commercial television network.

Along with the establishment of Fox, the introduction of specialized cable networks such as Cable News Network (CNN), ESPN, HBO, and MTV plus the proliferation of videocassette recorders (VCRs) and movie rentals in the American home have gradually drawn viewers away from the Big Three commercial television networks. ABC, CBS, and NBC's share of the audience has dwindled from over 90 percent in the 1980s to less than 50 percent today.

Although the networks are certain to remain a dominant force in prime-time programming, their influence is no longer as pervasive, and corporate executives must rethink their objectives. Instead of attempting to garner as many viewers as possible, the major networks must plan carefully what they program on the basis of who they want to reach, focusing on categories of viewers and developing strategies to draw those particular viewers to specific programs. This is not unlike what happened to radio in the 1950s when it was replaced as "the family medium" by television.

This is accomplished by studying TV market research results and modifying programming to appeal to particular categories of viewers called *target audiences*. Research data are gathered by the station, network, and the major research services (e.g., Arbitron and Nielsen) and analyzed by management, which then develops programming to appeal to those target audiences. The intended audience for a particular program is easily identified by the types of products and services advertised in the program's commercials.

Organization

A typical television station is usually organized into five major divisions: engineering, news, programming, sales, and administration. The engineering division's primary function is to ensure that the station transmits a quality signal on its assigned frequency at its authorized power. This requires monitoring, maintenance, and record keeping. The station may be subjected to a surprise technical inspection by an FCC field representative at any time it is on the air to ensure that the station's signal does not interfere with those competitors assigned to adjacent channels in the same market or with stations in distant markets assigned to the same channel.

The news division is responsible for the same things as the city desk or any other news department at a daily newspaper. Generally, the news director has a staff of several reporters and a couple of anchors who may double as reporters, informing the public about what is going on of importance in the station's local market. Except in very small markets, news is separate from programming, and the news director reports directly to the station's general manager. When a controversial issue arises that may impact on the station's revenue (e.g., an industry that buys a lot of commercial time on the station is involved in polluting the local environment), decisions regarding the station's approach to the story are thus made jointly by the news director and the general manager.

Programming is in charge of all other noncommercial airtime and is intimately involved in producing local programs and purchasing entertainment programs from syndicators. Program syndicators are independent companies that specialize in selling program packages of either old network reruns, called *off-network programs,* or packages of programs designed to be sold directly to stations, called *original syndication.* Most game shows are original syndication programs. Network-affiliated television stations usually offer little original production other than news and commercials; the bulk of their programs come from the network or program syndicators.

Stations not affiliated with a network, or independents, must fill their weekly program schedules with more hours of either local or syndicated programs since they receive no network programming. Therefore, independents normally produce more original local productions than network-affiliated competitors, although the largest portion of their programming budgets still go into purchasing syndicated programming.

Only one of the five divisions in a typical television station brings in revenue; the others spend it. Sales sells an intangible commodity that cannot be seen, heard, felt, smelled, or banked for future use—time. Time slots, or *availabilities,* are usually bought in bulk by an advertiser who takes advantage of what are called *frequency discounts.* Buying one hundred spots during prime-time evening programming over several weeks means paying less per spot than buying only ten.

There are three levels of sales in a network-affiliated television station: local, network, and national spot. Local availabilities are sold by the station's own personnel to local advertisers. Network availabilities are sold by network sales personnel to ad agency time buyers who represent national clients. And network commercials are included on the tape when the network relays the program to the local station for broadcast. National spot availabilities are sold by "middlemen," or station representatives, who work for a "station rep" firm and represent the station to a national advertiser. For example, if Nissan wants to introduce a new model car nationwide during the National Football League's (NFL) Super Bowl, it would probably buy network time through its advertising agency so the ad for the new car would appear simultaneously on all stations carrying the Super Bowl telecast. On the other hand, if Goodyear wanted to introduce a new snow tire, it would be a waste of money to buy network availabilities because the snow tire ad would appear not only in Chicago and Buffalo, New York, but in Miami and San Diego. Obviously, residents of the Sunbelt are not interested in buying snow tires. By buying through station reps, however, Goodyear purchases time only on stations in the Frostbelt and reaches only residents of those markets where Goodyear wants to sell its new snow tire.

Another type of sale that is growing in popularity is called "co-op," where a national advertiser pays for part of the commercial and a local merchant pays the rest. For example, the Nissan commercial has a tag at the end of the commercial that advertises the local Nissan dealer.

A major consideration after the sale is where to place the commercial in the station's broadcast schedule. Within the sales division is a "traffic and continuity department," which ensures that the content of the commercials, and the products or services that they market, is appropriate for broadcasting in the program and at the time of day that they are scheduled. Airline commercials are scheduled carefully. If the newscast reports an air disaster, the station or network avoids running an airline ad during the next commercial break. Traffic and continuity also keeps track of whether a commercial actually aired as scheduled or if it was preempted or interrupted and why so that advertisers reach the audiences that they have paid to reach. If a commercial is cut off because of a news bulletin or a technical problem, the station must compensate the advertiser by running it later in a comparable time slot. This is known as a *make good.* Nissan's Super Bowl commercial could cost over $1 million per minute; if somebody at the network made a mistake, it could cost the network over $2 million because the minute originally scheduled is wasted, and the commercial must be run at another comparable time. Understandably, general managers of television stations often rise from the ranks of the sales division.

The administration division is in charge of general management, billing, promotion of the station's image and reputation in the community, and community relations. The station's image and relationship with its community are important for the station's economic success.

Television networks are organized similarly, but they also maintain a station affiliate division that is responsible for fostering relationships between the network and its station affiliates. Since a network cannot own more than twelve television stations, it signs a renewable contractual agreement, normally for two years, with stations in those television markets where the network does not own a station. The local affiliate station agrees to carry both the network programs and the network commercials in that market.

Because the FCC holds the local broadcaster accountable at license renewal time, the local station affiliate is not required to carry either all of the network's programs or all episodes of a network program series. The local station manager has the authority to refuse to air a program or series or to censor part of a program. If the station refuses to carry a particular program or series, the network may offer that show or series to another station in that local market, even to an affiliate of a different network.

The network pays the local station to carry its programs. Network compensation is based on the size of the audience, the time the program appears, and the type of program it is. How does the network make its profit? Its revenue comes from the advertiser who has bought a network time availability and whose commercial is included in the program tape that the network sends via microwave or satellite from its transmission facility in New York. Each of the Big Three networks has over 200 affiliates, including the stations it owns and operates itself. In 1993, ABC owned and operated eight stations; NBC, six; and CBS, five. Fox, the fledgling fourth network, reported a little over 100 affiliates and seven owned and operated stations in 1993. PBS, the public television network, is not a true network because it does not produce its own programs but is primarily an electronic interconnection or delivery system for programs produced by individual public television stations. That is why public television viewers frequently see call letters of stations from all over the United States at the beginning and ending of almost all PBS programs.

A network is also limited in terms of ownership over the programs it airs. Because of the financial interest and syndication rules, networks cannot own the prime-time programs that they broadcast other than news, documentaries, and informational programs. They may own programs broadcast during hours other than prime time. Prime-time entertainment shows (those broadcast in the evenings from 7 to 10 P.M. or 8 to 11 P.M., depending on the local market) are actually owned by the production companies that film or tape them. The network signs an agreement with the production company to produce episodes of a series at a certain average cost to the network per episode. In return for its financial investment in production, the network obtains the exclusive right to broadcast each episode twice. This is really a licensee fee whereby the network rents the show for airing ahead of anyone else. For example, Carsey Werner Productions, a New York–based production company, owns the "Bill Cosby" show. During NBC's prime-time broadcasting of "Cosby," the network paid Carsey Werner a license fee for each episode, which covered part of the production costs. Carsey Werner leased the exclusive rights to NBC to air the program twice— the original airing and one rerun—before syndicating episodes to other stations independently. Popular programs that last several seasons bring in very high license fees. For example, in 1992, "Cheers" was in its tenth season and received a license fee of $65 million from NBC for twenty-six new episodes, or $2.5 million per episode, the highest license fee in television history to date.

Independent television stations are major consumers of off-network syndicated series, often scheduling them opposite network newscasts or local network affiliate station newscasts. These, along with programs produced directly for original syndication, are the bread and butter of the production and program distribution industry. Royalties to producers and performers are figured into the costs of syndication, and revenues are considerable; the production company is lucky to break even financially with its network licensing arrangements.

Game shows are a common example of programs produced originally for syndication rather than for network distribution. A show like "Jeopardy" is produced by a production company and without a network license fee and sold individually to as many local markets nationally as possible but to only one station in each market.

Financial interest and syndication rules are only one example of government regulation of television content that has had considerable economic impact on the television industry. Recently, the FIN–SYN rules have been relaxed by the FCC, and networks are permitted to own some types of primetime programs.

Ratings and Audience Behavior

Although the decision to cancel a favorite television show may seem arbitrary to the audience, network decisions regarding which series to cancel (or to schedule in the first place) are a result of careful market and audience research. The A. C. Nielsen Company and the American Research Bureau (ARBITRON) are the two largest ratings services that provide audience data for the television industry.

Nielsen provides two measures for television broadcasters: the National Television Index (NTI) and the National Station Index (NSI). The NTI is a weekly estimate of how many people with certain demographic characteristics view which programs. The estimate is provided by selecting a random sample of American homes where a special measuring instrument called a ''people meter'' is attached to all the TV receivers in each sample home. This meter records automatically which channels each television receiver in that home is tuned to. Demographic information regarding who in the family is watching is entered by the viewer(s) pushing certain buttons on the meter at the time. Audience ratings overall have gone down since implementation of the ''people meter'' data-gathering system, and the broadcast industry has criticized this technique, claiming that active participation by the viewer when entering demographic data results in distorted results. Media critics attribute the drop in audience sizes to the proliferation of alternative programming via cable and satellite. The NTI also provides overnight ratings by measuring viewership in selected large markets, again using the people meter.

The NSI is a measurement of each local television station in each television market nationwide and occurs quarterly, usually during February, May, August, and November. Separate samples of viewers are selected in what Nielsen calls *designated market areas* (DMAs), and these people fill in diaries chronicling their viewing habits for one to three weeks. NSI results assist a local television station in establishing the rates it will charge prospective advertisers for time availabilities during the next fiscal quarter.

The American Research Bureau, known better as ARBITRON, indicated it was getting out of the TV ratings business in 1993, but recently announced it planned to reenter the competition with Nielsen. ARBITRON also uses a diary gathering technique. Because each ratings service determines television market boundaries differently, DMAs and ADIs (areas of dominant interest) for the same market do not necessarily agree with each other. Obviously, this can affect the results of each estimate to some degree. Local television stations that subscribe to both ratings services generally promote the audience estimate that puts them in the more favorable position.

The role of television ratings in buy-and-sell programming decisions has been studied for years. We know that ratings estimates are accurate. They measure the size of an audience and its demographic characteristics very well. What they do not do well is tell us much about qualitative factors involved in program viewing decisions.

For qualitative measures, program developers and television managers do other types of research. Two common methods are program pretesting and focus group interviews.

New ideas for programs and commercials are frequently tested on audiences prior to appearing on television. Preview House in Hollywood, California, is one such testing facility. People are selected randomly to view a series of programs and/or commercials and attend Preview House screenings. They are asked to react to the programs by pressing buttons on installed electronic equipment, which tallies the results. These are provided to the stations or networks by Preview House and affect programming and scheduling decisions made later by the network or station.

Focus group interviews are conducted both before and after a show appears in a schedule. In these situations, a selective group of individuals with very specific demographic and sociographic characteristics is interviewed in depth about its reaction to a program. For instance, if the network is considering a new medical series on prime-time television, it is likely to form a focus group of medical personnel, including doctors, nurses, hospital administrators, and paramedics, and have them view a pilot episode. They are interviewed in depth about their reactions to the program.

REVIEW OF THE LITERATURE

The National Association of Broadcasters' (NAB) Library and Information Center (Washington, DC) published its third edition of a selected *Broadcasting Bibliography* in 1989. It lists 520 books, bibliographies, compendiums, dictionaries, directories, histories, indexes, primers, and program guides covering everything from advertising and promotion to careers, economics, engineering, history, the law, management, performing, production, programming, and new electronic media technologies in addition to looking at the cable, radio, and television media.

There are a number of guides to television programming, most of which specialize in a particular program genre (e.g., Eisner & Krinsky, 1984) or a certain period of time (e.g., Einstein, 1987). Most books on advertising, promotion, programming, and management are not television specific either, except a few on economics and media investment (e.g., *Investing in Television* by Broadcast Investment Analysts, annual.)

There is growth in the publication of texts on electronic media law and policy, new technologies, and the impact of television on various audiences, including an ongoing interest in the influence of television on children. Publishing in the television field is influenced by industry and government interest in various issues that appear on television or are affected by it.

A selected list of 110 trade periodicals appear in the NAB bibliography. Among these, the most important weekly publications that provide general information about television are *Broadcasting, Electronic Media, Television Digest, TV Today, Variety,* and *Video Week.* The calendar and entertainment sections of major newspapers regularly contain information about television economics, policy, and programming.

Another valuable source for learning about new publications in the field is *Communication Booknotes,* an annotated bibliography published bimonthly by the Center for Advanced Study of Telecommunications at Ohio State University. This is a popular source that college professors use in finding new texts for college-level media courses.

RESPONSIBILITY

Television stations are regulated by the FCC, and they must maintain public files subject to public inspection during normal business hours. Any viewer may inspect television stations' public file. This occurs frequently just prior to license renewal when special interest groups pressure local stations to provide better programming for their audiences.

Contrary to popular opinion, most stations are responsive to their audiences. The stations' operating licenses require them to determine what their audiences want and need in programming, and they must schedule programming that attempts to meet those wants and needs. Stations vary considerably in the ways that they fulfill this requirement because the FCC leaves it to the discretion of each licensee, preferring to review the station's overall record, including its public service programming, every fifth year at license renewal time. The most successful television stations realize that providing their local community with what it wants and needs will virtually ensure a profitable business. If viewers get what they want, the audience will grow, and the station can then charge higher rates for its commercial time availabilities.

There are few federal laws restricting television advertising and programming. Instead, stations and networks regulate themselves. The only products specifically banned by the government from TV advertising are cigarettes, little cigars, and smokeless tobacco. There are no federal laws specifically forbidding the advertising of firearms or alcoholic beverages, although the alcoholic content in a beverage cannot be mentioned over the air. Viewers do not see commercials for handguns or hard liquor, and they do not see an actor in a beer commercial actually drink because broadcasters are responsible for safeguarding the public interest. They follow self-imposed guidelines regarding program and commercial content. The NAB, the industry's largest and most influential lobby organization, promulgated the NAB Codes of Good Practice, which included self-imposed restrictions on both advertising and programming content. These codes were ruled unconstitutional by the federal courts several years ago, but NAB member networks and stations continue to follow most of their provisions. The NAB published a new statement of principles about programming in 1990 that reinforces the industry's desire to regulate itself, discouraging more government regulation. NAB member stations and networks follow those principles today.

There are no specific laws dealing with violence in television programming and very few laws pertaining to obscenity, indecency, or profanity. The few existing laws apply only to time periods when children are likely to be in the audience. Which time periods those are, as well as the definition of "children," are issues themselves. The FCC has tried to prevent indecent material from being broadcast at any time, or a twenty-four-hour ban on such programming, but the federal courts have ruled that the FCC must provide a "safe harbor" for airing adult programming. What those hours will be has yet to be decided, but they are likely to be late at night.

Another area of responsibility concerns news information and political programming. Television broadcasters are not required to be objective or balanced in reporting controversial issues. Agreeing with broadcasters' long-advanced argument that the balanced coverage requirement, known as the "fairness doctrine," has a chilling effect on news coverage of controversial issues, the FCC abolished it in 1987.

This decision did not eliminate two other legal requirements, however. Broadcasters are still required to notify a person who, in the context of a political message, is attacked verbally over the air by anyone appearing on the station, and to provide that person with an opportunity to reply. Stations and networks are also required to provide equal opportunity for comparable airtime to candidates for elective office. If one candidate for governor, for example, is given free airtime and sold $10,000 of commercial time, then every other gubernatorial candidate must have the opportunity to receive a like amount of free airtime and to buy up to $10,000 of comparable commercial time. Furthermore, candidates for political office are entitled to the lowest unit cost when purchasing time at frequency or other discounts given to the station's most favored advertiser.

EFFECTIVENESS AND CRITICISM

There is almost universal agreement that television is the most pervasive communication medium our society has ever known. It reaches millions of people simultaneously and immediately with on-the-air news events. The vividness of its images has a strong impact on our perceptions and opinions. In many respects, television has made the world smaller. Marshall McLuhan (1964), a noted media theorist, talked of the world's becoming a "global village" because of television, and in many respects, that has occurred. Certainly, the television coverage of the Persian Gulf war was like nothing the world has ever seen before.

However, some experts believe that over-the-air broadcast television has peaked in terms of influence. Since viewers have many options available to them, reliance on ABC, CBS, and NBC as their source of news is waning. But the average citizen also reads less, including newspapers. An annual survey conducted by the Roper organization shows that over 50 percent of our adult population today depends on television as its only source for news of the day. Ten years ago, it was 40 percent, and twenty years ago, it was 30 percent. Readership figures for newspapers have remained constant for over thirty years.

Thus, television has a special responsibility to provide accurate and comprehensive coverage of news events and to inform the public about issues of concern to them. Most TV critics agree that television could do much better in this regard. To date, television's greatest moments have been its coverage of live news events like President John F. Kennedy's funeral, the Apollo mission to the moon, international summit meetings, sports programs like the Olympics, and more recently, CNN's coverage of the war in the Persian Gulf. These dramatic moments when the impact of television is fully realized require tremendous financial and technical resources and a willingness by the networks and stations to forego profit in order to broadcast in the public interest. Most of the time, the medium has not lived up to its promise. Other than an increasing dependence on television as its only source of news, the public has relied on the medium primarily for entertainment, much of which is pure escapism. Soap operas, situation comedies, and formula action-adventure series continue to be the most popular programs, although many series try to deal with significant social issues responsibly.

Most social science research on the effects of television on children, the elderly, students, or any other demographic group has been inconsequential. Often, cause-and-effect research offers confusing evidence of a correlation between heavy television viewing and antisocial behavior.

THE FUTURE

Some critics have predicted the demise of the current system of broadcast television because of an explosion in cable and satellite technologies. New technologies are likely to have the opposite effect. The telephone industry is eager to enter the cable television field and would employ fiber optic technology, multiplying the capacity of video transmissions immeasureably and allowing for two-way interactive television. Portable satellite and microwave transmitters and new high-definition television transmission capable of providing photographic-quality pictures will make access to locations easier and more instantaneous. Some new high-definition video technologies have the potential to revolutionize the film industry, replacing celluloid with high-definition videotape, which is less costly and easier to work with in editing and postproduction. The Big Three networks, along with other broadcasting conglomerates, are investing in these technologies for a time when home information and entertainment centers become a reality. They have tremendous libraries of programming ''software'' as a bargaining chip.

Television is flourishing and embracing new video technologies as they become perfected. It is seen as an essential component to our culture in this information age. The movement marrying the computer and the television monitor, predicted by futurists less than a decade ago, is already beginning. This portends a fundamental change in how we live and work as we approach the twenty-first century.

BIBLIOGRAPHY

Bibliographies, Compendiums, Dictionaries, Directories

Broadcasting and cable marketplace. (Annual). Washington, DC: Broadcasting Publications.

Brown, Les. (1982). *Les Brown's encyclopedia of television.* New York: New York Zoetrope.

Cassata, Mary, & Skill, Thomas. (1985). *Television: A guide to the literature.* Phoenix, AZ: Oryx Press.

Kittross, John M. (1978). *A bibliography of theses & dissertations in broadcasting: 1920–1973.* Washington, DC: Broadcast Education Association.

Steinberg, Cobbett. (1985). *TV facts* (2nd ed.). New York: Facts on File.

Sterling, Christopher H. (1984). *Electronic media guide: A guide to trends in broadcasting and newer technologies—1920–1983.* New York: Praeger.

Sterling, Christopher H. (1989). *Mass communication and electronic media: A survey bibliography* (12th ed.). Columbus: Center for Advanced Study in Telecommunications, Ohio State University.

Television & cable factbook: The authoritative reference for the television & electronics industries (Annual). (2 vols.). Washington, DC: Warren.

Histories, Primers, Program Guides

Abramson, Albert. (1987). *The history of television, 1880–1941.* Jefferson, NC: McFarland.

Barnouw, Erik. (1982). *Tube of plenty: The evolution of American television* (rev. ed.). New York: Harper & Row.

Bliss, Edward. (1991). *Now the news: The story of broadcast journalism.* New York: Columbia University Press.

A broadcasting primer: With notes on the new technologies. (1985). (rev. ed.). New York: Television Information Office.

Broadcasting: The first sixty years—supplement to December 9 issue. (1991). Washington, DC: Broadcasting Publications.

Brooks, Tim, & Marsh, Earl. (1985). *The complete directory to prime time network TV shows, 1946–present* (3rd ed.). New York: Ballantine Books.

Dominick, Joseph, Sherman, Barry L., & Copeland, Gary. (1990). *Broadcasting/cable and beyond: An introduction to modern electronic media.* New York: McGraw-Hill.

Einstein, Daniel. (1987). *Special edition: A guide to network television documentary series and special news reports, 1955–1979.* Metuchen, NJ: Scarecrow Press.

Eisner, Joel, & Krinsky, David. (1984). *Television comedy series: An episodic guide to 153 TV sitcoms and syndications.* Jefferson, NC: McFarland.

The first fifty years of broadcasting. (1982). Washington, DC: Broadcasting Publications.

Gianakos, Larry James. (1978–1987). *Television drama series programming* (5 vols.). Metuchen, NJ: Scarecrow Press. Vol. 1, *A Comprehensive Chronicle, 1947–59.* Vol. 2, *1959–75.* Vol. 3, *1975–80.* Vol. 4, *1980–82.* Vol. 5, *1982–84.*

Head, Sydney W., & Sterling, Christopher H. (1990). *Broadcasting in America: A survey of electronic media* (6th ed.). Boston: Houghton Mifflin.

Lewis, Tom. (1991). *Empire of the air: The men who made radio*. New York: HarperCollins.

Marill, Alvin H. (1987). *Movies made for television: The telefeature and the mini-series, 1964–1986*. New York: New York Zoetrope.

McLuhan, Marshall. (1964). *Understanding media: The extensions of man*. New York: McGraw-Hill.

McNeil, Alex. (1984). *Total television: A comprehensive guide to programming from 1948 to present* (2nd ed.). New York: Viking/Penguin Books.

Schemering, Christopher. (1985). *The soap opera encyclopedia*. New York: Ballantine Books.

Schiffer, Michael. (1991). *The portable radio in American life*. Tucson: University of Arizona Press.

Schwartz, David, Ryan, Steve, & Wostbrock, Fred (Eds.). (1987). *The encyclopedia of TV game shows*. New York: New York Zoetrope.

TV Guide 25 year index. (1983). *1978–1982 Cumulative supplement*. (1988). *1983–1987 Cumulative supplement*. Radnor, PA: Triangle Publications.

Economics, Policy, and Law Impact

Arlen Communications. (1987). *Tomorrow's TVs: A review of new TV set technology, related video equipment and potential market impacts, 1987–1995*. Washington, DC: National Association of Broadcasters.

Auletta, Ken. (1991). *Three blind mice: How the TV networks lost their way*. New York: Random House.

Beville, Hugh Malcolm, Jr. (1988). *Audience ratings: Radio, television, and cable* (rev. ed.). Hillsdale, NJ: Erlbaum.

Broadcast Investment Analysts. (Annual). *Investing in television*. Washington, DC.

Campbell, Richard. (1991). *60 Minutes and the news: A mythology for Middle America*. Urbana: University of Illinois Press.

Carter, T. Barton, Franklin, Marc A., & Wright, Jay B. (1989). *The First Amendment and the Fifth Estate: Regulation of electronic mass media* (2nd ed.). Westbury, NY: Foundation Press.

Cooper, Thomas W., Sullivan, Robert, Weir, Christopher, & Medaglia, Peter. (1988). *Television & ethics: A bibliography*. Boston: G. K. Hall.

Emord, Jonathan. (1991). *Freedom, technology, and the First Amendment*. San Francisco: Pacific Research Institute for Public Policy.

Gerbner, George et al. (Eds.). (1986). *Television's mean world: Violence profile no. 14–15*. Philadelphia: University of Pennsylvania Annenberg School of Communications.

Gross, Lynne Schafer. (1986). *The new television technologies* (2nd ed.). Dubuque, IA: William C. Brown.

Krasnow, Erwin, Longley, James, & Terry, Herbert. (1982). *The politics of broadcast regulation* (3rd ed.). New York: St. Martin's Press.

Le Duc, Don R. (1987). *Beyond broadcasting: Patterns in policy and law*. New York: Longman.

Legal guide to broadcast law and regulation. (1988). (3rd ed.). (1991). *1991 Supplement*. Washington, DC: National Association of Broadcasters.

Meyrowitz, Joshua. (1985). *No sense of place: The impact of electronic media on social behavior.* New York: Oxford University Press.

Newcomb, Horace (Ed.). (1987). *Television: The critical view* (4th ed.). New York: Oxford University Press.

Shanks, Bob. (1976). *The cool fire: How to make it in television.* New York: W. W. Norton.

Tichi, Cecelia. (1991). *Electronic hearth: Creating an American television culture.* New York: Oxford University Press.

U.S. Department of Commerce. National Telecommunications and Information Administration. (1988). *NTIA Telecom 2000: Charting the course for a new century.* Washington, DC: Government Printing Office.

Van Petten, Vance Scott. (1987). *Television syndication: A practical guide to business and legal issues.* Los Angeles: Los Angeles County Bar Association.

Vogel, Harold L. (1986). *Entertainment industry economics: A guide for financial analysis.* New York: Cambridge University Press.

Webster, James, & Lichty, Lawrence. (1991). *Ratings analysis: Theory and practice.* Hillsdale, NJ: Lawrence Erlbaum.

Periodicals

Advertising Age. Chicago: Crain Communications. Weekly.

BM/E. New York: Broadband Information Services. Monthly.

BPME Image Magazine. Los Angeles: Broadcast Promotion & Marketing Executives. Ten times yearly.

Broadcast Engineering. Overland Park, KS: Intertec Publishing. Monthly.

Broadcast Financial Journal. Des Plaines, IL: Broadcast Financial Management Association. Six times yearly.

Broadcasting & Cable. Washington, DC: Broadcasting Publications. Weekly.

Channels: The Business of Communications. New York: C. C. Publishing. Monthly.

Communication Booknotes. Columbus, OH: Center for Advanced Study of Telecommunications. Bimonthly.

Daily Variety. Hollywood, CA: Daily Variety Ltd. Daily.

Electronic Media. Chicago: Crain Communications. Weekly.

Entertainment Law Reporter. Santa Monica, CA: Entertainment Law Reporter Publishing. Monthly.

The Hollywood Reporter. Hollywood, CA: Hollywood Reporter. Daily.

Journal of Broadcasting & Electronic Media. Washington, DC: Broadcast Education Association. Quarterly.

Television Digest. Washington, DC: Warren Publishing. Weekly.

TV Guide. Radnor, PA: Triangle Publications. Weekly.

TV Today. Washington, DC: National Association of Broadcasters. Weekly.

Variety. New York: Variety, Inc. Weekly.

Videography. New York: Media Horizons. Monthly.

Video Week. Washington, DC: Warren Publishing. Weekly.

View. New York: View Communications. Semimonthly.

Part II

ITS AUDIENCES

11

MINORITIES

Katherine C. McAdams

This chapter discusses the stubborn prevalence of scarce, negative media portrayals of minorities.

The 1990 U.S. Census indicates that of 250 million Americans more than 50 million are classified as members of minority groups, including African Americans, Hispanics, and Asian Americans, and this number increases daily (Prodigy Interactive Personal Service, 1993). Minorities now account for at least 20 percent of the U.S. population, and this percentage may climb throughout the 1990s to more than 50 percent.

One in five Americans is a member of a minority group, and these Americans are consumers of American media; Steinberg (1985) reported that television penetration in the United States was at least 98 percent and that Americans spent about one-third of their free time watching TV. About 8 percent of leisure time was spent reading newspapers, Steinberg found, while another 6 percent of non-working hours was divided among other media. Altogether, then, the average American in the late 1980s spent well over 40 percent of leisure time with media, more than with any other single activity—including interaction with family and friends, which accounted for only 27 percent of leisure hours. With the proliferation of cable and other new media, time spent with media may have increased.

Minorities tend to spend more time with television than these averages indicate because Nielsen statistics show that households headed by people with less than one year of college watch television more than other groups at a rate that has been increasing steadily since the mid-1970s (Steinberg, 1985). Because more minority Americans have less education, they may be more affected by television than other groups.

A review of the literature indicates that as frequent consumers of American media minorities may be particularly at risk. Many media messages contain negative and false stereotypes of minorities and underrepresent minorities. Such scarcity and stereotypes stubbornly remain, despite public perceptions that newer media offer more diversity. A 1993 study by Gerbner indicated that little or no change has occurred in media portrayals over the last ten years. Gerbner told the *Washington Post* that African Americans compose about 11 percent of prime-time dramatic characters. Out of 355 characters presented on prime-time network television each week, Gerbner reported, only 4 are African Americans. Even more surprising is Gerbner's finding that viewers may see only one Hispanic character every two weeks on prime-time TV (*Carmady,* 1993).

Media content often has a dramatic effect on both minority and majority perceptions and behaviors. Unfortunately, few changes in these media patterns seem likely in the near future.

BEYOND KERNER: MEDIA BIAS PERSISTS

"The media report and write from the standpoint of a white man's world" (Kerner, 1968, p. 203), according to the 1968 report of the Kerner Commission, appointed by President Lyndon Johnson to study the causes of urban unrest in cities across the nation in 1967. More than twenty-five years have passed since the commission concluded that media content contributes to interracial problems in the United States. This indictment still rings true, despite census projections that by the year 2000 Hispanics, Asians, and African Americans may constitute more than half of all Americans (Ellis, 1989).

Stroman, Merritt, and Matabane (1989), in a content analysis of 1987–1988 television, found that more than half of all African-American characters in prime time were in only four shows and that a disquieting number were poor and in comic, all-black settings, evidence of what MacDonald (1983) calls "the new minstrelry." Other minorities, according to Greenberg (1986), are virtually invisible on television, and he noted that attempts to place shows about minorities have failed.

One would expect increased minority presence in media over the past decade, but recent studies indicate little change (Gerbner, 1993). During the 1980s, African Americans were underrepresented in newspapers; and when coverage increased slightly in the 1970s, so did stereotypical portrayal of African Americans involved in crime and entertainment (Martindale, 1986).

Chaudhary (1980) studied coverage of African-American officials in nineteen different newspapers and found them to be less favorably displayed and less positive than officials from other groups. Lieb (1988) found that African Americans were underrepresented in initial issues of the *Washington Post Magazine,* the Sunday magazine of a city with an African-American majority; he also found that after protests, coverage of African Americans increased, but ad and photo content remained white oriented.

Although music is a traditional forum for African-American achievement, minority performers stay in the background on music television. Brown and Campbell (1986) found that African Americans were underrepresented on Music

Television (MTV), where in videos they were most often found dancing, singing, or playing musical instruments in the background. (Brown and Campbell also determined that on both MTV and its African-American equivalent, Black Entertainment TV [BET], women were underrepresented and given passive roles, even if the video featured a song by a woman artist.)

Twenty-five years after Kerner, media stereotypes remain. Evidence of these stereotypes contradicts the view of America in the 1980s and 1990s as a "kinder, gentler nation" and a model for diverse, heterogeneous societies throughout the world.

What do audiences, minority and nonminority, learn about themselves and one another from media content? Research has established that (1) media content is an influential source of cultural learning and that (2) inaccurate portrayals of dominant minority groups—African Americans, Asian Americans, and Hispanic Americans—abound. Media content of all kinds over the past twenty years continually has underrepresented minorities and has depicted them primarily in outdated stereotypes hindered by numerous subtle limitations.

LEARNING FROM MEDIA

Maccoby and Markle (1973) propose that much of learning stems from "incidental" rather than purposeful characteristics of messages. Tannenbaum (1985) cites a new emphasis in media research on "secondary, incidental byproducts of the main purpose of the production" and notes that studies of latent content require sharper theories and methodologies to tease out values that are transmitted in encoding and decoding, which are not "value free" (p. 45).

The study of media portrayals of minorities has been an ideal forum for studying transmission of values by incidental characteristics of media. Researchers have found a preponderance of evidence that communication about minorities is subtly value laden and that audiences internalize these values in a number of ways (Greenberg, 1986; Matabane, 1988; Stroman, Merritt, & Matabane 1989). Research in this area is ongoing; Atwater (1988) cites the Kerner Commission's concern with media noncoverage of "latent" problems of race relations and encourages continued work in this still-problematic area.

Mass media audiences do a great deal of cultural learning from media, forming ideas about unfamiliar topics and revising ideas about more familiar ones. In addition, audiences use their preexisting cultural knowledge, much of which originated with media messages, to understand and organize new messages.

MEDIA LEARNING: THEORETICAL BACKGROUND

Several widely supported theories help explain how ideas about minorities are transmitted by subtle characteristics of media. Perhaps the first to come to mind is the theory of agenda setting described by McCombs and Shaw (1972). These researchers found that, over time, saliences of particular issues in the news quietly become public priorities. In this way, media *topics* can influence public perceptions, regardless of media *content.* The mass media do not tell us what to think but, rather, what to think about (Cohen, 1963), and this telling is indirect; few audience members are aware that they adopt media views about public issues.

The lack of portrayals of minorities—and the lack of variety among available portrayals—suggests that minority concerns are not likely to be represented on public agendas that affect future media priorities, public policy, and even political and social behavior. The white homogeneity of media content may have a powerful influence on audiences and may help explain the persistence of stereotypes in our culture.

Agenda setting is grounded in Festinger's (1957) theory of cognitive dissonance. Festinger explains attitude change with the concept of dissonance, which is roughly defined as a state that occurs when an individual is confronted with information that conflicts with an established mind-set. This new, conflicting information is termed *dissonant,* and it leads to discomfort. Most people seek relief in one of two ways: (1) by ignoring the dissonant information and seeking facts to support the existing mind-set or (2) by altering existing views to be more consistent with a new view that is perceived as a majority view.

The power of majority values is explained by a related and widely supported theory, Noelle-Neumann's "spiral of silence" theory. Noelle-Neumann (1974) suggests that a spiral of silence is created when a widely held public opinion is publicized. People who hold the opposing, or minority, view become increasingly silent, and some in the minority eventually join the majority. As a result, the majority view seems even more all-encompassing than it really is and continues to grow in numbers and in force as the minority fades from public notice.

The majority view, sometimes called the *dominant paradigm,* of the world clearly is what television represents. Kerner (1968) noted, "The ills of the ghetto, the difficulties of life there, the negro's burning sense of grievance, are seldom conveyed" (p. 203). Twenty years later, Stroman, Merritt, and Matabane (1989) concluded that there still is little media emphasis on issues of importance in the lives of African Americans. Perhaps the minority view has been minimized over the years through a spiraling process—so that now, even though minorities are strong in numbers, they and their concerns are absent or underrepresented. The spiral of silence theory suggests that because they were once a true minority, they now are ignored; and because they have been ignored, they now are silent.

Visual "silences"—that is, the lack of televised images of minority characters in realistic settings—may have been underestimated as a negative influence on audience perceptions. Graber (1990) found in a study of news that most learning from television results from visual material. She found that a vast majority of verbal material failed to capture audience attention, while almost half of visual themes were retained on some news stories. Graber concludes, "We cannot afford to ignore the major ways in which learning is shaped by the vistas gleaned by the human eye and the cognitions, emotions and memories that these vistas produce'' (p. 154). Media representations of minorities, and the lack of such representations, are in and of themselves a visual theme from which audiences may learn.

What are the effects of media's obscuring or silencing all but a white, middle-class world? Stroman, Merritt, and Matabane (1989) suggest that such unbalanced media portrayals deny a source of strength in our culture: "When one considers the working class origins of African American notables such as Jesse Jackson, Rosa Parks, Althea Gibson, Coleman Young, and others, it becomes clearer that television fiction has not captured the positive potential that exists in non-middle-class environments" (p. 53). Stroman and colleagues take issue with newer media approaches that portray minorities in upscale settings, believing that these portrayals "further devalue the ghetto and . . . equate human value with income and social class" (p. 54). Perhaps, through media models, an entire value system—a productive and hopeful one—has been silenced.

A study by Lieb (1988) suggests that breaking the spiral of silence through vocal action on the part of minority audiences can have a marked effect on media content. Heated protests in 1986 over the content of the then-new *Washington Post Magazine*—showing a white, and even antiblack, bias in a city that has an African-American majority—led to marked changes in the magazine's editorial content. Lieb's content analysis showed that the ratio of coverage of whites to African Americans before the protest was 5.7 column inches for whites to every 1 column inch for African Americans; after the protest, the ratio changed to 2.5 to 1, a figure that still underrepresents the black-white ratio in the city but that accurately reflects the ratio in the metropolitan area. Lieb mentions, however, that advertising content was largely unaffected by the protest except in the months of active protests. African Americans were "noticeably absent" from ads, he notes, adding that photos and illustrations also did not reflect the changes made in editorial coverage. Lieb concludes, "Editorial coverage can be changed with the efforts of those who hold the media's purse strings" (p. 66).

A "purse strings" approach, considering economic factors as determinants of media content, may also help to explain the lack of ethnic diversity in U.S. media. Advertising is the tail that wags the media dog; print and broadcast media serve advertisers by attracting audiences with buying power. This appeal to the economically advantaged may have, over time, perpetuated another kind of spiral—that of buying power. Could it be that as minorities are portrayed as absent from most markets that they are increasingly unlikely to accumulate buying power? If minorities are perceived by the public as nonparticipants in the world of commerce, they may lose out on business opportunities and indeed may grow increasingly disadvantaged.

CULTIVATION OF PERCEPTIONS

Gerbner and others have found support for their "cultivation" hypothesis: the idea that media cultivate images of, and beliefs about, the world in the minds of audiences, particularly where little personal experience is involved (Gerbner et al., 1977; Gerbner et al., 1980; Gerbner et al., 1982). Greenberg and Atkin (1978, 1982) found that viewers who had little personal contact with African Americans tended to get their information about African Americans from television.

Matabane (1988) found evidence of cultivation theory when she studied audience perceptions of minorities in Washington, D.C. In her study, heavy viewers of television more often than nonviewers (1) overestimated the incidence of racial integration, (2) judged that African Americans and white Americans were more similar than different, and (3) overestimated percentages of African Americans in the U.S. middle class. The optimism gained from watching television may at first appear to be a positive influence, but Matabane warns that perceptions of viewers indicate that television "overestimates how well African Americans are integrating into society" (p. 30).

Matabane's work also revealed two disturbing trends about heavy television viewing by two groups who have long been assumed less susceptible to media influence—(1) those with higher levels of education and (2) those with real-life experience with minorities. She found that heavy television viewers, regardless of education or real-life social experience, gave inflated estimates of racial integration, inflated to levels similar to those of less educated people. She explains: "Heavy television viewing appears to mold the ideas of the best educated to those of the less educated. From the standpoint of cultural and political hegemony that is a startling observation" (p. 29).

In their study of television news about unemployment, Barkin and Gurevitch (1987) found that African Americans and women were unemployed in far greater numbers than broadcast representations indicated. Unemployment for African Americans, they found, was double that of whites, yet only 4.7 percent of sampled news stories dealt with minority issues. Women were even less visible: Half of all unemployed workers were women, but less than 1 percent of sampled stories dealt with women. Clearly, the plight of women and minorities was ignored in coverage that, researchers found, was patterned on an outdated stereotype of breadwinners in breadlines.

Media professionals use stereotypes frequently, usually in order to communicate a great deal of information quickly; audience members who see a breadline are given instant context for a news story—without costly time, words, and use of attention span. Efficient use of stereotypes involves the audience in the message because, as Dates and Barlow (1990b) explain, "a stereotype must be anticipated by the conditioned perceptions of the beholder as well as existent in the imagination of the image-maker" (p. 2). This sharing of perceptions makes for a message that is easily sent and received, but one that perhaps "imposes a certain character on the data of our senses" (Lippman, 1922, pp. 88–89).

In their book *Split Image* (1990b), Dates and Barlow argue that in its early days mass media followed the lead of popular theater and literature, pointing to today's comic African American as a descendant of early twentieth-century minstrel shows, which were actually created by whites for white audiences. Repeated use of such stereotypes has resulted in a lack of change in media content. Dates and Barlow note, "Stereotyped black images often are frozen, incapable of growth, change, innovation or transformation" (p. 4). The danger of dealing in fixed stereotypes is that the world in which they exist *does* change, so that stereotypical media portrayals communicate not a shorthand of reality but a distorted reality. Dates and Barlow (1990a) conclude that these distortions "help to mold white public opinion patterns and set the agenda for public discourse on the race issue, thus broadening the cultural gap between African American and white Americans" (p. 456).

Stereotypes in media presentations today may cultivate perceptions in minority and majority audiences that African Americans are faring better than they actually are. Matabane (1988) warns that misconceptions from heavy viewing may curtail activism and concern in the African-American community that are needed to make life for minorities better—life that evidence indicates has been worsening in the past several years. Matabane suggests that "we consider the role television plays in the cultivation of an overall picture of growing racial equality that conceals unequal social relationships" (p. 30). This is consistent with earlier work by Gandy (1982) that argues that the media preference for the upper middle class decreases understanding and actually increases distance between the races.

The theoretical perspectives described here support ideas that media may influence audience ideas about minorities and even determine behaviors. They also suggest that changes in existing audience models of minorities would require some dramatic—and unlikely—changes in media, including (1) portraying cultural change in existing media, breaking the spiral of silence where minority coverage is concerned; (2) placing minority issues on media agendas; and (3) helping audiences resolve dissonance by gradually changing, rather than reinforcing, popular stereotypes.

But such changes in media are unlikely. Audiences are comfortable with particular ideas, or models, that media are reluctant to challenge.

MEDIA USE OF CULTURAL MODELS

Media professionals know that audiences will identify with familiar themes and verbal cues—and that audience members will use this existing cultural knowledge to decode and organize new information. Graber (1989) acknowledges that broadcasters make use of cues and stereotypes that prompt quick understanding among audiences and cites an example of this kind of communicator shorthand: "[C]haracterizing a brutal dictator as 'another Hitler' immediately evokes images of persecution, racial discrimination and genocide in many audiences" (p. 148). Such invoking of familiar themes is common in media messages. When available models of reality are applied to new situations, the new becomes organized—and perhaps tainted—by old knowledge. Environmental problems that are referred to as "a second Love Canal" or a politician labeled as "no Jack Kennedy" are inextricably, and perhaps inaccurately, linked to old models of reality.

Holland and Davidson (1985) suggest that cultural knowledge is organized in complex cognitive models and that when any part of the model is elicited, the whole model is brought forth to apply to a new situation. Such models often have a semantic foundation, and semantic cues such as "Hitler," "Love Canal," and "Jack Kennedy" call forth complex models of knowledge, attitude, and behavior. Media writers of all kinds, aware only of the increased comprehension and emotional impact that such cues provide, need to consider problems that may occur from invoking outdated, negative models of minorities.

Perhaps the dominant paradigm for understanding minorities also is revealed in narrative content of media. First, the very term *minorities* implies that these groups are few in numbers and insignificant in power in a country where the majority rules. This image of insignificance is exaggerated in media through underrepresentation. But soon the composite of minorities in the United States may compose the majority, defying this paradigm for minorities that still dominates media. Such an inaccurate view of the world will hardly prepare audiences for imminent changes and challenges in our society that will come with changes in racial composition; the old paradigm, therefore, already may be dysfunctional.

This traditional media paradigm for minorities involves many separate themes that also may be dysfunctional, causing distorted audience perspectives of self and others. What are the dominant themes through which media messages define minorities? And are these themes used by audiences in organizing and understanding media messages about minorities? Research indicates that they are.

Matabane (1988), in an extensive review of content analyses of media, found that media presentations make the following "statements" about black social reality: that African Americans (1) tend to be cast either in all-black settings or as lone African-American persons in otherwise all-white settings; (2) tend to be low income and feature few socially productive persons concerned about social problems; (3) when in white settings, tend to be upscale and productive; and (4) tend to use black English in low-income, all-black settings. Matabane also found that racism is rarely discussed or portrayed in media presentations.

Greenberg (1986) suggests that these statements apply to other minority groups as well *when they are represented in media.* He notes underrepresentation of all minority groups and the virtual invisibility of Hispanic Americans on television as a particular case in point, saying that this fast-growing segment of our population is notably absent from all shows.

Graber (1989) suggests that audiences interpret such messages "in ways that go beyond manifest content," but she cautions against a simplistic "hypodermic" view of what audiences learn from media content (pp. 144–146). Latent meanings, she says, depend on a number of highly individual factors, including (1) background information, (2) the symbols and connotations embedded in the message, and (3) the experiences of the audience. No one fully understands how audiences reconcile what they know about the world with the inaccuracies they perceive in media.

Gerbner and others (1977; 1980; 1982) provide some answers for these questions with their work on cultivation and media dependency, suggesting that media become important sources of knowledge in areas where little experience exists. This suggests that media may provide much information on race relations in a society that still is largely segregated by race and ethnicity.

Reep and Dambrot (1989) found that individual, personal characteristics were the greatest determinant of stereotyping in their sample audience, but they also found support for media dependency and cultivation of stereotypes. After individual differences, the most potent predictor of stereotyping was frequency of television viewing. Reep and Dambrot urge that more research be done on particularly strong or powerful minority characterizations: "Perhaps television's portrayal of a few, high-impact, non-stereotypical characters is more important for reducing stereotypical perceptions than sheer numbers of characters which make little or no impact" (p. 556).

SOCIAL EFFECTS OF MEDIA PORTRAYALS

No one is sure of exactly how the sparse, inaccurate portrayal of minorities in popular media affects audiences. Existing theories of media effects suggest that media approaches to minorities may contribute to the formation of negative images and self-images of minorities. Such a perpetuation of negative effect may help explain why, in the years since the Kerner Commission study, many "urban pathologies" have actually gotten worse (Stroman, Merritt, & Matabane 1989).

Prevalent media images of minorities are sadly inaccurate in terms of numbers and content. Old shows, with their old stereotypes, continue to be broadcast; meanwhile, content of newer shows appears to have changed little. It is little wonder that, with these negative stereotypes in mind, the present majority may, in fact, *prefer* to ignore impending demographic changes, reducing dissonance through inaccurate media content.

The Kerner Commission report (Kerner, 1968) charged that news representations of urban rioters were woefully inaccurate, and gave this factual profile of the 1967 activist:

The typical rioter in the summer of 1967 was a Negro, unmarried male between the ages of 15 and 24. He was in many ways very different from the stereotype. He was not a migrant. He was born in the state and was a lifelong resident of the city in which the riot took place. Economically his position was about the same as his Negro neighbors who did not actively participate in the riot.

Although he had not, usually, graduated from high school, he was somewhat better educated than the average inner city Negro, having at least attended high school for a time.

Nevertheless, he was more likely to be working in a menial or low status job as an unskilled laborer. If he was employed, he was not working full time and his employment was frequently interrupted by periods of unemployment.

He feels strongly that he deserves a better job and that he is barred from achieving it, not because of lack of training, ability, or ambition, but because of discrimination by employers.

He rejects the white bigot's stereotype of the Negro as ignorant and shiftless. He takes great pride in his race and believes that in some respects Negroes are superior to whites. He is extremely hostile to whites, but his hostility is more apt to be a product of social and economic class than of race; he is almost equally hostile toward middle class Negroes.

He is substantially better informed about politics than Negroes who were not involved in the riots. He is more likely to be actively engaged in civil rights efforts, but is extremely distrustful of the political system and of political leaders. (pp. 73–74)

Where in the media is this serious, respectable character? He is unfamiliar to audiences whose ideas about African Americans are based on Buckwheat and Cosby. As the Kerner report suggests, he is altogether unlike the comfortable stereotypes that are preferred in media content. White discomfort with serious African Americans and with serious black issues may be a driving force in maintaining the media status quo. The Kerner Commission in 1968 cited white fear as "another factor" that explains poor media performance on racial issues.

Now, twenty-five years later, it seems that those who determine media content of all kinds may be superaware of a "background of anxieties" about race and deal with it by masking disturbing issues and promoting an optimistic sense of well-being and a reinforcement of existing social values—white, middle-class values. The trend to "optimism" found by Barkin and Gurevitch (1987) and the "new minstrelsy" cited by MacDonald (1983) were evident in the popular "Cosby Show" of the upper-middle-class Huxtable family. Dates and Barlow (1990a) describe Cliff Huxtable as a remake of an old stereotype, "the noble Negro, living in an upper middle class utopia" (p. v). This image appeals to both African-American and white audiences, suggesting a more subtle function of such stereotypical entertainment—that of reducing cognitive dissonance induced by direct information on minority issues, thereby appealing to the broad economic power of the middle class.

Lazarsfeld (1940), in the early days of broadcasting, suggested that the need for a vast audience would make media tend toward conflict avoidance and mediocrity: "A program must be entertaining and so it avoids anything depressing enough to call for social criticism; it must not alienate its listeners, and hence caters to the prejudices of the audience; it avoids specialisation, so that as large an audience as possible will be assured; in order to please everyone it tries to steer clear of controversial issues" (p. 6). Both minority and majority audiences benefit only in the short term from such comforting content; in the long term, injustice and tragic urban conditions go unaddressed, and so they worsen and spread.

Figure 11.1
How Media May Perpetuate Minority Stereotypes

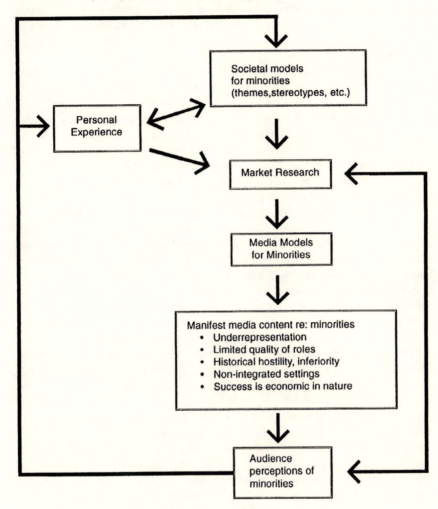

MAINTENANCE OF MEDIA STEREOTYPES

The model illustrated in Figure 11.1 provides some understanding of processes that may result in distorted media presentations about minorities and of
possible effects of these patterns of misrepresentation. The model also defines

the tangle of relationships among minorities, media, and audiences, pointing the way to further research on media transmission—and perpetuation—of stereotypes. The model represents relationships that are suggested by previous research and discussed in the previous research; and with some modifications, this model could apply to media effects on other audience-held stereotypes that may be inaccurate or outdated.

This figure shows that existing cultural models shape media content, which in turn shapes cultural models. This cycle is not likely to be interrupted so long as the need for mass appeal requires, and is governed by, market research. And dependence on ratings, readership studies, and other forms of audience surveillance appears to be a secure element in the media mix. In discussing the shortcomings of all methods of analyzing broadcast audiences, Wimmer and Dominick (1990) note that "one basic fact remains: until further refinements are made, ratings as they currently exist, will remain the primary decision-making tool in programming and advertising" (p. 283).

Determining media content by ratings and similar techniques in analysis of both print and broadcast audiences ensures that majority tastes and values will dominate media content and that such views are likely to remain unchallenged. Wimmer and Dominick also note that minority groups are generally underrepresented in audience surveys, so that companies need to use special techniques to increase responses among minorities and statistically to adjust results for fairer representation of minorities in survey results. Market research paints, for advertisers and program creators, a generalized picture of what people *want* to see and think they *should* see—and this composite determines media content.

In this process, the majority rules because the majority forms the largest media market. In calculations of average audience interests, minority concerns lose out, and media models are determined based on a majority view.

This determination of majority needs and desires then affects the manifest content of media presentations, resulting in the documented characteristics of media news and fiction about minorities: Minorities typically are underrepresented overall; their roles are stereotypical and limited; a backdrop of historical conflict governs presentation; most settings are all minority, or white with a single minority; and only their economic success can provide escape from minority limitations. A steady diet of these attributes in media presentation then leads to distorted audience perceptions of minorities.

The process is ongoing and self-perpetuating, so that inaccurate perceptions may continue to dominate both cultural models and media presentation indefinitely. The process begins anew each time distorted audience perceptions are captured by audience research and shape the market accordingly, stereotypes and all. At the same time, media influence becomes part of personal experience by determining what kinds of social contacts are deemed desirable. And social and media inputs combine to create audience perceptions of minorities that have little resemblance to reality.

FUTURE TRENDS

Many hope that an increasingly diverse system of media outlets, accompanied by increasing diversity of ethnic and racial groups in the U.S. population, will provide greater diversity of media presentations of all kinds. But economic and psychological forces resist and offer few prospects for change. Perhaps demographic changes in the next century will provide a sufficient force for change and overcome tradition and current indications that minorities are too fragmented to act as a majority.

Lieb (1988) points to the efficacy of social action and pressure from minority groups. Vocal consumerism on the part of minorities may yet have marked effects. But Matabane's proposal that inaccurate media content makes for a complacent audience suggests that strong enough social action is less and less likely as the cycle of media stereotyping continues.

Perhaps the cycle of negative portrayals of minorities may only be interrupted by a change in one of its component parts—that is, in audiences, or in audience research, or in media content. But given the trend to deregulation in recent years, change in any of these areas also is unlikely. A more promising source of change appears to be the avenue suggested strongly by the Kerner Commission (1968)—that is, to integrate media personnel, placing people with firsthand minority points of view at the very source of inaccurate media content. This would interrupt the cycle depicted in Figure 11.1 by breaking the links between media research and planning; conceivably, minority planners would have different approaches even to conducting research about what audiences want and need from media content.

Efforts to integrate media professions have been only moderately successful thus far. Despite affirmative action efforts over the past two decades, journalism and related fields still are dominated by white males. Stone (1988) found that all minorities accounted for less than 15 percent of all broadcast jobs. He notes the particular absence of African-American men in management, or even in jobs that may lead to upper-level positions: No minority group constituted more than 2.5 percent of broadcast managers. Stone also notes that only 64 percent of commercial TV stations employ any minorities; the same is true of an amazing 15 percent of radio stations, a figure "essentially unchanged from 1972" when Stone conducted a similar survey (1988, p. 12).

Taylor and Jeffrey (1989) note an even more discouraging *decline* in minority employment in broadcasting, and they describe a similar lack of progress in print media: "For example, while blacks, Hispanics and other minorities constitute upwards of 25 percent of the American population, they still only constitute approximately 7.5 percent of editorial staffs of the nation's newsrooms. Moreover, more than 55 percent of all American newspapers hire no minorities whatsoever" (p. v). Taylor and Jeffrey attribute some of this decline to minorities' decreasing ability to participate in programs of higher education, noting that African-American college student enrollment peaked in 1980 and has been declining since then. They note that in the period 1980 to 1986, African-American enrollment declined by some 26,000 students (p. vi).

As long as minority media professionals are unavailable to correct inaccurate stereotypes, to report without historical fear and misunderstanding, current stereotypes are likely to thrive. Present economic trends—concentration of wealth among the already-wealthy, with decreasing government service to disadvantaged groups—suggest that enlightenment and change in the cycle of negative portrayals that could be provided by an integrated media profession is another unrealized dream of the 1960s.

Taylor and Jeffrey close by saying that "there is now a greater urgency to increase the representation of minorities in the communications industry than there has ever been before in our nation's history" (p. iv), urging fast affirmative action as the globe shrinks through new and numerous technologies that extend the reach of negative stereotypes.

No change is likely as long as the public, including media professionals, continues to be blissfully unaware of the cycle of negative sameness of minority portrayals in news and fiction. Programs of consciousness raising need to be constructed to break the cycle. Our present self-satisfaction with race relations as they are represented in media is based on false information. In the area of minority representation, media service to audiences has not advanced—and may even have declined—in the last decade. Economic, political and cultural factors, rather than individuals, are perhaps to blame, but media disservice to minority audiences must be faced honestly if all audiences are to meet the human challenges of the next century.

BIBLIOGRAPHY

Atwater, T. (1988). Editorial note on Kerner plus 20. *Mass Comm Review, 15* (2, 3), 2.

Barkin, S. M., & Gurevitch, M. (1987). Out of work and on the air: Television news of unemployment. *Critical Studies in Mass Communication, 4* (1), 1–20.

Brown, J. D., & Campbell, K. (1986). Race and gender in music videos: The same beat but a different drummer. *Journal of Communication, 36* (1), 94–106.

Carmady, John. (1993, June 10). Women, minorities still shut out, survey reports. *Washington Post*, p. B1.

Chaudhary, A. G. (1980). Press portrayal of black officials. *Journalism Quarterly, 57,* 636–646.

Cohen, B. C. (1963). *The press and foreign policy.* Princeton, NJ: Princeton University Press.

Dates, J. L., & Barlow, W. (1990a). Conclusion: Split images and double binds. In J. L. Dates & W. Barlow (Eds.), *Split image: African Americans in the mass media* (pp. 455–460). Washington, DC: Howard University Press.

Dates, J. L., & Barlow, W. (1990b). Introduction: A war of images. In J. L. Dates & W. Barlow (Eds.), *Split image: African Americans in the mass media* (pp. 1–21). Washington, DC: Howard University Press.

Eason, D., & Fogo, F. (1988). The cultural turn in media studies. *Mass Comm Review, 15* (1), 2–5.

Ellis, D. M. (1989). Communication at the crossroads: Parity and perceptions of minority participation. In C. A. Stroman & M. A. Williams (Eds.), *Minorities and communications* (pp. 11–20). Washington, DC: Howard University Center for Communication Research.

Festinger, L. (1957). *A theory of cognitive dissonance.* Stanford, CA: Stanford University Press.

Gandy, O. H., Jr. (1982). *Beyond agenda setting: Information subsidies and public policy.* Norwood, NJ: Ablex.

Gerbner, G. (1993). *Report of the Cultural Indicators Research Team.* Philadelphia: University of Pennsylvania Annenberg School of Communications.

Gerbner, G., Gross, L., Eleey, M. F., Jackson-Beeck, M., Jeffries-Fox, S., & Signorielli, N. (1977). TV violence profile no. 8: The highlights. *Journal of Communication, 27* (2), 177–180.

Gerbner, G., Gross, L., Morgan, M., & Signorielli, N. (1982). Charting the mainstream: Television's contribution to political orientations. *Journal of Communication, 32* (2), 100–126.

Gerbner, G., Gross, L., Signorielli, N., & Morgan, M. (1980). The mainstreaming of America: Violence profile no. 11. *Journal of Communication, 30* (3), 11–29.

Graber, D. A. (1989). Content and meaning. *American Behavioral Scientist, 33* (2), 144–152.

Graber, D. A. (1990). Seeing is remembering: How visuals contribute to learning from television news. *Journal of Communication, 40* (3), 134–155.

Greenberg, B. S. (1986). Minorities and the mass media. In J. Bryant & D. Zillman (Eds.), *Perspectives on media effects* (pp. 165–188). Hillsdale, NJ: Lawrence Erlbaum Associates.

Greenberg, B. S., & Atkin, C. (1978). *Learning about minorities from television: A research agenda.* Paper presented at a conference on Television and the Minority Child, Center for Afro-American Studies, University of California, Los Angeles.

Greenberg, B. S., & Atkin, C. (1982). Learning about minorities from television: A research agenda. In G. Berry & C. Mitchell-Kernan (Eds.), *Television and the socialization of the minority child* (pp. 215–243). New York: Academic Press.

Holland, D. C., & Davidson, D. (1985). Prestige and intimacy: The folk model behind talk and gender types. In N. Quinn & D. C. Holland (Eds.), *Cultural models in language and thought.* Cambridge: Cambridge University Press.

Kerner, O. (1968). *Report of the National Advisory Commission on Civil Disorders.* Washington, DC: U.S. Kerner Commission, GPO.

Lazarsfeld, P. (1940). *Radio and the printed page: An introduction to the study of radio and its role in the communication of ideas.* New York: Duell, Sloan & Pearce.

Lieb, T. (1988). Protest at the *Post:* Coverage of blacks in the *Washington Post Magazine. Mass Comm Review, 15* (2), 61–67.

Lippman, Walter. (1922). *Public opinion.* New York: Harcourt, Brace.

Maccoby, E., & Markle, D. G. (1973). Communication and learning. In I. D. Pool (Ed.), *Handbook of communications.* Chicago: Rand McNally.

McCombs, M. E., & Shaw, D. L. (1972). The agenda-setting function of mass media. *Public Opinion Quarterly, 36,* 176–187.

MacDonald, J. (1983). *Blacks and white TV: Afro-Americans in television since 1948.* Chicago: Nelson Hall.

Martindale, C. (1986). *The white press and black America*. Westport, CT: Greenwood Press.

Matabane, P. W. (1988). Television and the black audience: Cultivating moderate perspectives on racial integration. *Journal of Communication, 38* (4), 21–31.

Noelle-Neumann, E. (1974). The spiral of silence: A theory of public opinion. *Journal of Communication, 24,* 43–51.

Prodigy Interactive Personal Service. (1993). *Academic American encyclopedia*. Danbury, CT: Grolier.

Reep, D. C., & Dambrot, F. H. (1989). Effects of frequent television viewing on stereotypes: 'Drip, drip' or 'drench'? *Journalism Quarterly, 66* (3), 542–580.

Steinberg, C. S. (1985). *TV facts: Revised and updated*. New York: Facts on File Publications.

Stone, V. A. (1988). Pipelines and dead ends: Jobs held by minorities and women in broadcast news. *Mass Comm Review, 15* (2, 3), 10–19.

Stroman, C. A., Merritt, B. D., & Matabane, P. W. (1989). Twenty years after Kerner: The portrayal of African Americans on prime-time television. *Howard Journal of Communications, 2* (1), 44–56.

Tannenbaum, P. H. (1985). To each his/her own: A personal research agenda. In M. Gurevitch & and M. R. Levy (Eds.), *Mass Communication Yearbook* (Vol. 5). Beverly Hills, CA: Sage Publications.

Taylor, O., & Jeffrey, R. C. (1989). Preface. In C. A. Stroman & M. A. Williams (Eds.), *Minorities and communication*. Washington, DC: Howard University Center for Communication Research.

Wilson, C. C., II, & Gutierrez, F. (1985). *Minorities and media: Diversity and the end of mass communication*. Beverly Hills, CA: Sage Publications.

Wimmer, K. A. (1988). Deregulation and the future of pluralism in the mass media: The prospects for policy reform. *Mass Comm Review, 15* (2, 3), 20–31.

Wimmer, R. D., & Dominick, J. R. (1990). *Mass media research* (3rd ed.). Belmont, CA: Wadsworth.

12

WOMEN AUDIENCES

Maurine H. Beasley

NATURE AND SCOPE OF AUDIENCE

The importance of women as an audience for mass communication cannot be overlooked. Although women often are considered a minority group, they really constitute a majority of the U.S. population. In part, this is because women live longer than men. According to the Bureau of the Census, the U.S. population totaled 254,922,000 in 1992, with females numbering 130,564,000 compared with 124,358,000 males. Women constituted 51.2 percent of the total (see Table 12.1).

Life expectancy at birth is 78.5 years for women, compared with 71.8 years for men (Bureau of the Census, 1991). The annual population rate of growth has been around 1 percent through the last decade. But the population category of 65 years old and over, where women markedly outnumber men, has continued to increase at a rate of more than 2 percent (Bureau of the Census, 1990).

Women are an important group for advertisers to reach. In recent years, women have been moving into the labor force in record numbers. From 1989 to 1990 alone, the numbers of adults with jobs in the U.S. labor force rose by 710,000 for women, compared with 361,000 for men. Overall, the employment of women increased by 27 percent from 1980 to 1990, while the employment of men rose only 12.7 percent. Women increasingly are maintaining families without the presence of a male in the household (Bureau of the Census, 1991) (see Tables 12.2 and 12.3).

Yet women, as a group, have less money to spend than men. Women do not earn as much as men, making sixty-eight cents to every dollar made by men, based on median earnings of year-round, full-time workers. More than half (51.7 percent) of all poor families are maintained by a woman with no husband present. In contrast, only 12.5 percent of nonpoor families are maintained by women (Bureau of the Census, 1991) (see Table 12.4).

Table 12.1
Projections of the Population, by Age, Sex, and Race, 1992

[Numbers in thousands. Resident population. Consistent with the 1990 Census, as enumerated.]

Date and age	Total			Race												
				White			Black			American Indian, Eskimo, and Aleut			Asian and Pacific Islander		
	Total	Male	Female	Total	Male	Female	Total	Male	Female	Total	Male	Female	Total	Male	Female
JULY 1, 1992															
All ages ·········	254 922	124 358	130 564	212 648	104 169	108 478	31 673	15 000	16 674	2 150	1 066	1 084	8 451	4 123	4 328

Source: Bureau of the Census, 1992a.

Table 12.2
Percentage of Women in the Civilian Labor Force, 1990

> *Civilian labor force, 1990:* **124.8 million**
> *Numerical increase, 1989–90:* **918,000**
> *Civilian unemployment rate, 1990:* **5.5%**
> *Civilian labor force participation rate, 1990:*
>
> | *Total:* | **66.4%** |
> |---|---|
> | *Male:* | **76.1%** |
> | *Female:* | **57.5%** |

Source: Bureau of the Census, 1991.

Still women's earnings are rising compared with men's, a fact that helps make women a consumer group of vital interest to the mass media. In addition, many women who do not work outside the home exercise a considerable voice in making purchases. For years advertisers have recognized the buying power of women consumers and targeted messages to them via the mass media. The movement of women into the labor market has enhanced advertiser interest in reaching a female audience.

According to census data made available in 1991, the real median earnings of year-round, full-time women workers stood at $18,780 in 1989, an increase of 1.8 percent from the previous year. Comparable earnings of men declined by 1.8 percent to $27,430. (Comparable information has not been released based on the 1990 census.) The sixty-eight cents to a dollar ratio of women's to men's earnings represented an all-time high. In 1982, for example, the ratio was sixty-two cents, and in 1980, it was sixty cents (Bureau of the Census, 1991) (see Table 12.5).

There is no doubt that men and women audiences use mass media differently. Women have their own preferences and interests, based on different socialization and gender roles. Table 12.6 shows their consumption of mass media compared with men's.

Television

In terms of usage, television clearly stands out as the most inclusive media. According to the *Statistical Abstract of the United States* (Bureau of the Census, 1992b), of an adult population of 183,814,000, a total of 93.3 percent of males and 92.4 percent of females watch network and local television. Numerically, more women than men watch, since there are more adult females than males in the United States (96,158,000 women compared with 87,656,000 men) (see Table 12.6).

In recent years, daytime television viewing, once considered almost solely a woman's domain, has declined as more women have entered the labor force. According to researchers, the 4:30 to 7:30 late afternoon and early evening time

Table 12.3

Percentage of Families with Employed Mother and/or Father, by Type of Family and Age of Children, 1990

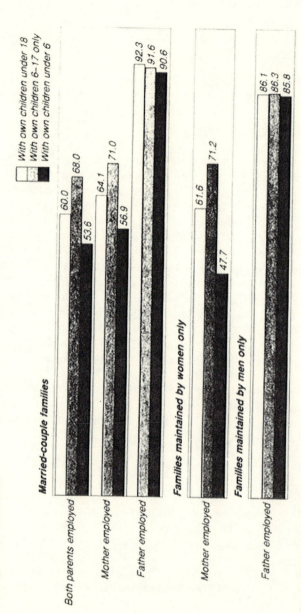

Source: Bureau of the Census, 1991.

Table 12.4
Median Income Comparison, 1989

- All families: $34,210
- Married-couple families: $38,550
- Married-couple families,
    wives in paid labor force: $45,270
- Families with a male householder,
    no wife present: $27,850
- Families with a female householder,
    no husband present: $16,440

Source: Bureau of the Census, 1991.

period is the only one in which women viewers are growing. Black and Hispanic women have been found more likely than white women to be television viewers (Marketing to Women, 1989).

By contrast, cable television reaches a far smaller proportion of the adult audience—58.6 percent of males and 53.8 percent of females (see Table 12.6). Still in relative infancy, cable has had phenomenal growth in recent years and can be expected to attract an increased number of women viewers in the years ahead with its ability to reach highly differentiated segments of the audience. Different cable formats appeal differently to men and women.

In 1991, for instance, in an average week, more women than men watched cable's Lifetime (61 percent versus 39 percent) and the Family Channel (58 percent versus 42 percent). An equal number of men and women watched BET (Black Entertainment TV) and the Weather Channel. The majority of subscribers of the Disney Channel (53 percent) were women ("Media," 1992).

Research findings vary, however, as to how much women audiences prefer television to other leisure-time pursuits, including reading in general. One study found 36 percent of women overall selecting television compared with 32 percent who cited reading as their first choice (Miller, 1989). Another study, conducted by *Family Circle* magazine, asked women what they would most like to do if they had one hour alone. Researchers discovered that 61 percent chose reading compared with 29 percent who picked watching television (Miller, 1989).

Older women make greater use of television than women in the middle stage of life, according to research. On the average, women aged fifty-five to sixty-four watch television 199.4 minutes a day, while women aged forty-five to fifty-four watch it 171.6 minutes a day. The average amount of viewing of all women eighteen years and older is 182.8 minutes a day ("Media," 1992).

Newspapers

Daily newspaper reading is not necessarily a popular choice for women. Although more than 115 million American adults read a daily newspaper, accord-

Table 12.5
Median Earnings of Year-Round, Full-Time Workers, by Sex, 1967–1989

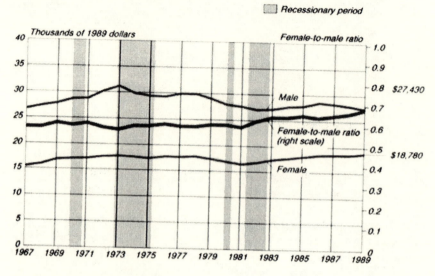

Source: Bureau of the Census, 1991.

ing to the Newspaper Association of America, 1992b), newspaper reading has not kept pace with population growth in the United States since World War II. The percentage of the total adult population who read daily newspapers has declined from 78 percent in 1970 to 62.6 percent in 1992 (see Table 12.7).

While the number of women readers exceeds the number of male readers, this simply reflects the greater number of women than men in the population as a whole, rather than a preference of women for newspapers. In terms of percentages, men continue to outpace women in daily newspaper readership with 64 percent (versus 60 percent of women) reading a newspaper on the average weekday (Newspaper Association of America, 1992a). Older women read both weekday and weekend newspapers more thoroughly than younger women (an average of 44.1 minutes a day during the week and 53.4 minutes on Sunday). This compares with the average time of 40.2 minutes daily and 48.4 minutes on Sunday spent reading the newspaper by all women eighteen years and older ("Media," 1992).

Women's readership has remained relatively stagnant since 1982, whereas readership among men has increased. For both men and women, however, daily newspaper reading is becoming a less frequent habit. Sunday newspaper circulation, on the other hand, is showing some increase (see Table 12.7).

A 1991 study showed that men and women read different parts of the newspaper. Women liked general news, entertainment content (movies, theater, etc.),

Table 12.6
Multimedia Audiences: Summary, 1991

[In percent, except as indicated. As of spring. For persons 18 years old and over. Based on sample and subject to sampling error; see source for details]

ITEM	Total population (1,000)	Television viewing/ coverage	Television prime time viewing/ coverage	Cable viewing/ coverage	Radio listening/ coverage	Newspaper reading/ coverage
Total	183,814	92.8	79.4	56.1	84.7	83.9
18 to 24 years old	25,866	91.7	74.9	56.3	93.8	78.5
25 to 34 years old	44,367	92.0	79.0	57.1	91.9	84.2
35 to 44 years old	36,739	92.3	79.0	59.2	89.6	88.7
45 to 54 years old	25,123	91.5	77.9	59.0	85.6	86.9
55 to 64 years old	21,937	95.2	82.0	57.9	76.6	84.7
65 years old and over	29,782	94.9	83.6	46.9	65.0	81.4
Male	87,656	93.3	78.0	58.6	86.8	84.6
Female	96,158	92.4	80.6	53.8	82.7	83.2
White	158,153	92.4	78.6	58.1	84.8	85.5
Black	20,734	95.8	85.2	44.9	84.5	76.3
Other	4,926	92.5	79.6	41.0	80.1	64.4
Spanish speaking	13,949	94.8	82.9	39.4	87.9	72.4
Not high school graduate	41,614	93.5	81.0	40.3	75.5	65.4
High school graduate	71,872	93.1	80.9	58.5	85.2	86.2
Attended college	34,878	93.2	77.7	62.9	89.5	89.9
College graduate	35,449	91.1	76.1	63.1	89.6	95.1
Employed:						
Full-time	101,332	92.2	77.7	59.8	90.8	87.8
Part-time	14,797	91.4	77.9	58.4	88.3	86.2
Not employed	67,685	94.0	82.3	50.1	74.6	77.5
Household income:						
Less than $10,000	21,383	93.3	80.3	35.0	73.2	60.9
$10,000 to $19,999	30,690	94.0	82.2	44.2	78.7	76.5
$20,000 to $29,999	30,248	93.4	80.2	52.3	83.3	84.3
$30,000 to $34,999	15,122	92.6	78.9	60.6	85.2	85.8
$35,000 to $39,999	13,333	94.5	90.4	61.1	67.9	87.9
$40,000 to $49,999	21,970	92.6	78.3	64.6	90.3	90.1
$50,000 or more	51,070	91.2	77.2	68.1	90.4	93.3

Source: Cited in Bureau of the Census, 1992b.

food or cooking material, editorial opinion, home improvement articles (furnishings, gardening, etc.), comics and television/radio listings, classified advertising, business/financial news, and sports, in that order.

Men, on the other hand, liked general news, sports, business/financial news, entertainment content, editorial opinion, comics, classified advertising, and television/radio listings, in that order, with food or cooking and home improvement material at the bottom of their list. A total of 85 percent of the men usually read sports pages compared with 64 percent of the women, while 82 percent of the women read food or cooking pages compared with 67 percent of the men (Newspaper Advertising Bureau, 1992).

The women's media audience can be understood only in relation to women's changing demographics. As more women work, they face competing demands on their time, which make them less likely to view television or read newspapers. As more women become heads of households, they face economic problems that make it difficult for them to subscribe to newspapers even if they would like to. This means that mass media must change to meet the needs of its contemporary female audience if it wishes to hold the group's attention. Newspapers, in particular, need to attract younger women to remain a competitive force in the mass media.

Table 12.7
Daily Newspaper Reading Audience

Year	Weekday Readers				Sunday/ Weekend Readers	
	% of Total Adult Population	Adult Readers (thousands)	Male (thousands)	Female (thousands)	% of Total Adult Population	Adult Readers (thousands)
1970	78	98,183	46,659	51,524	72	91,642
1973	73	98,803	47,127	50,876	68	90,088
1977	69	103,543	49,968	53,575	68	102,690
1980	67	106,043	52,559	53,484	67	106,740
1982	67	108,366	52,399	55,967	67	107,706
1983	66	109,363	52,933	56,430	66	108,352
1984	65	109,190	52,459	56,731	65	109,661
1985	64	108,812	53,718	55,094	65	110,255
1986	63	107,753	52,597	55,156	64	109,775
1989	63.6	113,337	56,018	57,319	67	119,349
1990	62.4	113,090	55,798	57,292	67	121,622
1991	62.1	113,322	56,114	57,207	66.9	122,045
1992	62.6	115,296	57,499	57,797	68.4	125,940

[1]Age 18 and over
[2]Based on Simmons Market Research Bureau national survey estimates
Source: Newspaper Association of America, 1992b. Reprinted by permission.

Magazines

So far, magazines have been the segment of the mass media that has responded best to the new realities of women's roles. Over half of all magazine buyers are women (54 percent). They constitute an advertiser's dream since they are generally more affluent, better educated, younger, and in pursuit of a more active life-style than nonbuyers ("Media," 1992).

Through market segmentation, publishers have been able to target various audiences of women and offer magazines geared to individual needs. Publications such as *Lear's,* aimed at the mature woman, and *Working Woman,* directed toward the growing number of women employed outside the home, have had phenomenal success. Women account for three out of every four single-copy magazine sales and two out of every three magazine subscriptions ("Media," 1992).

Women read more magazines than men, with 87 million women, or 96 percent of the population, reading at least one issue per month, compared with 77 million men, or 93 percent of the population, who read at least one issue. In recent years, some women have decreased their television viewing in favor of increased magazine readership (Marketing to Women, 1989). A total of 148 different magazines are published in the United States aimed at women, according to the *Gale Directory of Publications & Broadcast Media* (1993). Other authorities estimate the number of titles to be closer to 300 when all types of organizational, regional, and ethnic publications are taken into account (Biagi, 1990).

As women's life-styles have altered, the seven women's magazines that once ruled the magazine world—*Better Homes and Gardens, Family Circle, Good Housekeeping, Ladies' Home Journal, McCall's, Redbook,* and *Woman's Day*— have repackaged their offerings somewhat to modify the heavy emphasis on love, family life, and homemaking that traditionally has dominated their content (Fannin, 1989). These publications continue to appear on lists of the largest-circulation magazines, but they no longer stand at the top. Their slipping circulation reflects basic social changes affecting women in the late twentieth century. These include employment outside the home, sexual liberation based on birth control and access to legal abortion, and the women's movement for equality with men.

Yet these magazines still reach millions of readers. They remain advocates of what has been called a "cult of femininity." This tries to appeal to all women through presentation of "female interest" categories covering such topics as recipes, fashion, celebrity profiles, home decorating, and beauty tips (Ferguson, 1983).

According to the Audit Bureau of Circulation, six of these publications appeared on the list of the top eleven best-selling magazines in the United States in 1991. *Better Homes and Gardens* ranked in sixth place with 8,003,263 readers, followed by *Family Circle* with 5,151,534, *Good Housekeeping* with 5,028,151, *McCall's* with 5,009,358, *Ladies' Home Journal* with 5,002,900, and *Woman's Day* with 4,751,977 in eleventh place. *Redbook* stood in thirteenth place with 3,841,866. *Cosmopolitan,* the first woman's magazine to capitalize on sexual liberation, ranked in twenty-second place on the best-selling list with 2,679,356 circulation (*World Almanac,* 1993).

All the women's magazines were outdistanced by five magazines of interest to both men and women. *Modern Maturity* led the field with 22,450,000 circulation. It was followed by *NRTA/AARP* (National Retired Teachers Association and American Association of Retired Persons) *Bulletin* with 22,174,021 readers, *Reader's Digest* with 16,306,007, *TV Guide* with 15,353,982, and *National Geographic* with 9,921,479 (*World Almanac,* 1993).

Traditional women's magazines consider themselves service publications designed to advise consumers on purchases and the best use to make of what they buy. They also see themselves as self-help manuals for women, giving readers guidance on how to improve their appearances, their homes, and their family life. They offer a mainstream, middle-class view of the world and are sold at supermarket checkout counters. Because advertising revenues have declined in recent years, costs have been passed on to readers in the form of higher prices.

Newer women's magazines are being directed to a culturally and racially diverse population: professional women, women interested in fitness, mothers, and so forth. *Essence,* one of the relatively few publications aimed at minority women, is designed for college-educated black women who work outside the home. With a circulation of 853,297, it stood in ninetieth place on the list of best-selling magazines in 1991. Right behind it came *Working Woman* with 849,772 circulation (*World Almanac,* 1993).

Radio

Like magazines, radio provides an opportunity to reach segmented audiences. Overall, however, it reaches a greater percentage of men than of women (86.8 percent of males compared with 82.7 percent of women) (see Table 12.6). With an average of more than five radios per household, family members can listen in all parts of the house—living room, kitchen, bedroom.

As the number of women working outside the home has soared, the number listening at home has declined, although the number listening in cars has increased. On the average, according to research, half of all women in nearly all age groups and more than half of black women hear the radio from 7 P.M. to midnight. Working women listen to the radio at least twenty-five hours per week, compared with twenty hours for women not employed outside the home. Various formats appeal to different ages and life-styles, with working women preferring adult contemporary, rock, and country programs. Older women who remain at home select nostalgia, news/talk, and religious formats (Marketing to Women, 1989).

Older women spend more time than younger women listening to the radio. For example, women aged fifty-five to sixty-four tune in an average of 145.1 minutes daily. This compares with 140.4 minutes a day for those aged forty-five to fifty-four ("Media," 1992).

IMAGES OF WOMEN

Considerable evidence exists to show that mass media does not represent women carefully, primarily because women are perceived as subordinate to men and not worthy of respect in their own right. In 1989 the Women, Men and Media Conference, cosponsored by the Gannett Foundation and the University of Southern California, released its first study of the images of women as depicted on the front pages of ten major newspapers and on the network nightly newscasts. It found that women are "symbolically annihilated by the media."

The study covered front-page photos, bylines, and story sources of ten leading newspapers for 1989. It showed 27 percent of the bylines were of women. A total of 24 percent of the photos included women, usually pictured as members of families. Only 11 percent of the persons quoted as sources were women. This led to the conclusion that apparently women did not come close to men as far as covering and making news was concerned.

According to the study, a similar situation existed on the network news. Women correspondents filed a relatively low percentage of reports (22.2 percent on CBS, 14.4 percent on NBC, and 10.5 percent on ABC). Women had relatively few chances to file, however, because they constituted a low percentage of correspondents. Their total had risen only six percentage points—from 9.9 percent to 15.8 percent—from 1975 to 1989. Women appeared relatively infrequently as newsmakers or experts providing news background. During the month the study was conducted, women provided the interview focus for only 13.7 percent of the ABC newscasts, 10.2 percent of the CBS newscasts, and 8.9 percent of the NBC newscasts.

This situation stems from the fact that traditional news values represent conflict, controversy, power struggles, political battles, and changes in the status quo—all elements linked to the masculine domination of society (Covert, 1981). Women, as a group, have not been key players in the political, economic, and military developments that make headlines. Women's activities traditionally have been seen as unworthy of prominent news coverage, either on the front pages of important newspapers or on nightly network newscasts.

Women's news generally has fitted into the ''soft news'' category of entertainment or feature material. The rankings of newspapers on coverage of women in the Women, Men and Media study underscored this point. Of the ten newspapers studied in 1989, *USA Today,* which emphasizes short, feature-oriented news articles, ranked at the top of the list in coverage because it did not focus attention exclusively on a male world of public affairs. On the other hand, the *New York Times,* considered the nation's leading newspaper of public record, fell at the bottom in coverage of women, owing to its emphasis on activities of heads of government and other officials who usually are male (see Table 12.8).

A follow-up survey, commissioned in 1990 by the Media Watch Project of the University of Southern California and the American Society of Newspaper Editors, resulted in similar findings. Once again, the *New York Times* stood at the bottom in coverage of women, this time out of twenty newspapers (the same ten surveyed in 1989 plus ten from smaller markets). The survey showed the *Times* used women as sources in 6 percent of its front-page stories in 1990 compared with 5 percent the previous year (American Society of Newspaper Editors, 1990). Commenting on this finding, Max Frankel, executive editor of the *Times,* wrote, ''As soon as Mr. Gorbachev [Soviet leader] lets Mrs. Gorbachev do his deciding or even speaking, we will be quoting or photographing more women on page one'' (American Society of Newspaper Editors, 1990, pp. 11, 12).

An update of the study in 1992 showed front pages of the same twenty newspapers overwhelmingly male dominated. Males made up 87 percent of the individuals referred to or solicited for comment, and females made up only 13 percent. The study contended women fared a little better in television, with the number interviewed on nightly network news programs increasing from one in ten persons featured in 1989 to about two in ten in 1992 (''Front Pages,'' 1992)

Another study released in 1992 found women's position slipping rather than improving in terms of news coverage. Researchers from California State University at Sacramento replicated a study done in 1974 and reported that women

Table 12.8
Rankings of Newspapers on Coverage of Women

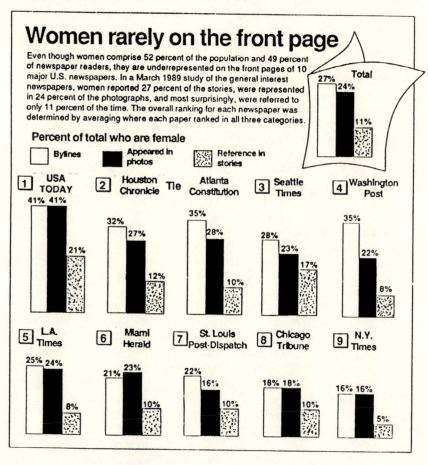

Source: Women, Men and Media Conference, 1989.

actually had lost ground as reported newsmakers over a seventeen-year period. For instance, they found that from 1974 to 1991 network television news stories about women declined from 10 percent to 3 percent, and feature stories from 16 percent to 15 percent. While straight news stories about women almost doubled—from 3 percent to 5.5 percent—in the *New York Times*, straight news stories about women actually decreased—from 9 percent to 5 percent—in the *Sacramento Bee* ("Women Have Lost Ground," 1992).

The organizers of the Women, Men and Media Conference took the position that more images of women would appear in the news if women held more powerful positions in media industries. Data presented by Jean Gaddy Wilson of the University of Missouri at Columbia showed that media women were congregated in lower-level jobs (57 percent of beginning reporters and advertising salespersons and 94 percent of support and clerical staff) and that they failed to climb the ladder as successfully as men (Women, Men and Media Conference, 1989).

Wilson also found that the entry level was the only place where women earned salaries equal to men. Her survey of 1,599 daily newspapers, 1,219 television stations, and 1,091 radio stations revealed that even when experience was equal, "a woman boss earns significantly less than a man in the same job" at the same size media outlet, with an annual cost to the woman of $9,074 in television, $7,793 in newspapers, and $3,323 in radio (Women, Men and Media Conference, 1989). Only 25 percent of the women were in middle management and thus in a position to move up (See Table 12.9).

It will probably require new definitions of news rather than more women entering the media for women to have better representation. Since 1977, the enrollment of journalism schools, a source of entry-level employee, has been predominantly female (Beasley & Theus, 1988). Nationally, female enrollment has stabilized at about two-thirds of total enrollment. Women students, however, are not necessarily being taught new ideas on news or educated to subscribe to values at variance with those of males in the media. Therefore, they may perform the same way as men when employed.

Curiously, the increasing number of women students has not changed women's overall representation in the newsroom. In 1992, women remained at the same percentage as a decade ago—34 percent—according to two professors from Indiana University, who speculate that this is due to poor retention of women as well as to limited job growth in journalism. Their research, however, found that the salary gap between men and women was narrowing with women making 85 percent of what men were being paid (Weaver & Wilhoit, 1992).

A study by the American Society of Newspaper Editors found that "the news values and professionalism of the women currently in the newsroom are the same as that of their male colleagues," although men and women differ somewhat in career plans (Stinnett, 1989, p. 13). More women than men want to remain as reporters and copyeditors rather than to move into management, the study reported.

These findings tended to counter assertions that women's presence has changed the field by leading to more stories on women's issues (Mills, 1988). News values remain based on an ideology of reporting events involving competition, achievement, and independence—all factors associated with male, not female, experience (Rush & Gutierrez-Villalobos, 1990). Yet this may not be commonly recognized by women journalists themselves. When a University of Maryland research study on the impact of the growing number of women in journalism schools questioned whether the nature of news might change if more women entered the newsroom, a group of women editors was outraged. "News

Table 12.9
Female Versus Male Job Mobility in Media

THE POWER GAP: MEN MANAGE THE MESSAGE MACHINES

Only 6% of the top media bosses are female. Women lack control over content, policy, money and direction. Men choose the messages, men determine what is news and what is entertainment. The messages the American people receive pass through a male filter.

At the very top level, women are:

■ 3% of television presidents/vice presidents.
■ 6% of newspaper publishers.
■ 8% of radio presidents/vice presidents.

And even when women have these jobs, their salaries are only 92% of what their male counterparts earn.

Women fill jobs at the bottom of the ladder

The most powerful jobs in newspapers, television and radio still remain the domain of men. Only at the very bottom of the ladder do women outnumber men. Typically, a man's salary is larger than a woman's in the same job.

Rungs on the ladder	Position	All media		Newspapers		Television		Radio	
		Percentage of jobs held by women	Percentage of men's salary earned	Percentage of jobs held by women	Percentage of men's salary earned	Percentage of jobs held by women	Percentage of men's salary earned	Percentage of jobs held by women	Percentage of men's salary earned
Top	Publisher, President/VP	6	92	6	83	3	105	8	81
Second	General manager	8	69	7	52	7	80	10	76
Third	Ad director, Sales mgr.	18	83	18	70	10	88	23	88
	Editor	16	71	14	61	10	76	25	92
Fourth	Local sales mgr.	24	92	23	72	22	95	32	105
	National ad mgr.	33	79	44	54	24	73	16	108
	Managing editor	26	83	27	84	25	84	24	110
Bottom	Long-term sales staff	36	88	41	79	28	90	34	94
	New sales staff	61	92	63	91	60	92	58	94
	Long-term reporter	35	78	36	86	34	67	26	87
	New reporter	53	101	54	95	52	92	48	125

Women hold only about 25% of the mid-management jobs, contradicting the long-held premise that large numbers of women are far enough up the career ladder that they are ready to break through to the top.

Women outnumber men in only two places in the media:

■ On the bottom rung of the ladder, as beginning reporters and on advertising sales staffs — 57%.
■ Beside the ladder and holding it up, as support and clerical staffs — 94%.

Source: Women, Men and Media Conference, 1989.

is news; it has no sex,'' retorted Linda Cunningham, editor of the *Trenton Times* (quoted in Beasley, 1989).

Apart from their relative absence in the news, the images of women in other areas of mass communications have come under attack. Researchers consistently have found the portrayal of women in advertisements at stereotypical levels. A content analysis of men and women depicted in advertising in *Time* and the

Ladies' Home Journal from the 1930s to the 1980s found that 97 percent pictured both men and women as decorative sex objects or as typical "males" or "females" (women shown as wives, mothers, secretaries, elementary school teachers, and men shown in business or sports roles). This leads to socially undesirable results for women, according to researchers. Their conclusion: "Constant bombardment in the media via advertising of images that reinforce the traditional submissive position of women can only weaken efforts for women to receive wages and status equal to men" (Cooper, Rogers, & Jenkins, 1990, p. 20).

European researchers reported in 1991 on a study of twenty years of advertising in *Time* and *Stern,* a German publication. Concluding "nonverbal sex stereotypes still linger on," they called attention to the fact that men tended to be overrepresented in the ads (64 percent male verses 36 percent female in *Time*). Women were more often scantily clad than men (5 percent of women verses less than 2 percent of men in *Time*). Women were consistently pictured more often than men as submissive, with little change over time in either *Time* or *Stern* "Twenty Years of Stereotypes," 1992).

Studies of television's images of women in advertising have drawn similar conclusions. They have pointed out that women are seen mainly in three roles—maternal, domestic, and decorative—and that they are discriminated against by being portrayed as less authoritative, powerful, and intelligent than males (Lazier-Smith, 1989). Similar complaints have been made of the portrayal of women on television in general.

Spurred by dissatisfaction with the image of women presented in the general mass media, feminists have set up their own media. From 1963 to 1983, about 1,300 feminist publications were started (Allen, 1989). They have emphasized a positive portrayal of women as self-reliant, independent beings able both to nurture a new generation and to exist without men. Their messages, however, do not make them attractive to the type of corporate advertisers who subsidize mainstream media.

ACTION TO CHANGE THE ROLE OF WOMEN

Since the future can only be understood in terms of the past, it may be instructive to quickly note the history of women's efforts to influence media content. Feminists have been trying for one hundred years to attack the pervasive stereotypes used in media portrayals of women as well as the frequent absence of women from media coverage, with its implicit message that women are not important (Jolliffe, 1990). Women were discovered as an audience for newspapers and magazines before the Civil War when advertisers first realized they had buying power. Nevertheless, press treatment of women both sentimentalized and ridiculed them. Nineteenth-century feminists protested against biased coverage, demanded increased opportunities to participate in the press, and set up their own alternative publications, which often circulated among a narrow circle of those with similar views. Then, as later, protests met with resistance from male hierarchies, conservative advertisers, and reactionary forces.

During the women's movement era of the 1960s and 1970s, a liberal feminist audience organized in various ways to make the media more responsive. It used a variety of tactics:

- Consciousness raising among women employed in the media
- Demonstrations designed to gain public attention, such as a sit-in at the *Ladies' Home Journal*
- Demands to do away with the traditional women's pages closely tied to department store advertising
- Protests against advertising seen as demeaning to women
- Monitoring of newspapers and television programs to combat sex-role stereotyping
- Challenges to renewals of broadcast station licenses by the Federal Communications Commission, which requires that stations operate in the public interest
- Legal actions under the Title VII of the U.S. Civil Rights Act of 1964 to press for affirmative action plans to make hiring, training, assignments, and promotion opportunities more equitable at media companies
- Pressure for nonsexist language guidelines and use of the term *Ms.* instead of *Miss* or *Mrs.*, which identifies women, unlike men, in terms of marital status
- Establishment of *Ms.* magazine, as the first mass circulation feminist publication (Beasley & Gibbons, 1977

To press these points, women worked both inside and outside of the media. Armed with the protection of federal law, groups of women organized their own caucuses and met with their male employers to demand more opportunities within media companies. They also demanded an end to sexist content. Their supporters included members of women's organizations like the National Organization of Women (NOW), the American Association of University Women (AAUW), and church groups. Banding together, this liberal feminist audience represented a strong voice. Media owners and managers could not help hearing it.

Initially, it appeared that the activism of the liberal feminist audience met with considerable success. The sit-in at the *Ladies' Home Journal,* designed to protest the magazine's emphasis on domesticity, resulted in an eight-page section that appeared in the August 1970 issue of the *Journal.* Written by a collective of thirty writers, it expressed feminist views on education for women, childbirth, homemaking, marriage, love, and sex. But the *Journal* soon returned to its standard fare.

Complaints about the demeaning nature of women's pages led to more far-reaching change. Editors transformed women's pages into life-style sections. Feminists were not totally pleased, however, when they observed that slick entertainment material replaced news of women. Also, placement of serious subjects there—like abortion rights—kept them off the front page (Van Gelder, 1978).

The advertising industry also reacted when feminist groups applied pressure through demonstrations, complaints, and in some cases, boycotts. In 1975, the National Advertising Review Board, an industry group that investigates complaints about advertising, recommended "constructive portrayals" of women. Advertisers and agency personnel were urged to "assume intelligence" on the part of women. But the recommendations were not binding on advertisers or agencies (Beasley & Gibbons, 1977).

Broadcast monitoring projects carried an implied threat—that women's groups would try to block station license renewals. In 1972, NOW filed a petition against the license renewal of WABC-TV in New York, charging the station with deficiencies in ascertainment of women's opinions on community issues, news, and programming about women's concerns and employment of women. After three years, the Federal Communications Commission (FCC) rejected NOW's petition against WABC-TV as well as a similar petition to deny a license renewal to WRC-TV in Washington, D.C. Fear of time-consuming license challenges, however, spurred some stations to agree to negotiate agreements with women's groups. A 1971 FCC ruling helped the women's cause by requiring that women be given equal opportunities in hiring. This opened the way for far greater employment of women on network and local news staffs.

During this period, women working in the media took legal action against sex discrimination. Four days before the *Journal* sit-in, forty-six women at *Newsweek,* which is owned by the *Washington Post,* filed a complaint with the Equal Employment Opportunities Commission on grounds that women were limited to being researchers while men were reporters and writers. In the following years, almost all major news organizations—including the *New York Times,* the Associated Press (AP), *Reader's Digest,* NBC, and others—found themselves targets of class-action sex discrimination complaints and suits.

As a group, the complaints and suits were settled in favor of the women, representing a feminist victory. The Associated Press suit, for example, ended with an out-of-court settlement in 1983 that established an affirmative action plan for women and minorities and $2 million in compensation to more than 800 women who had worked at the AP since 1972. Five years later, the percentage of women at the AP had risen from 22 to 44 percent. Women made similar gains in other news organizations.

Feminists also scored a victory in the use of the term *Ms.* to replace *Mrs.* or *Miss.* By the early 1980s about half of the nation's newspapers and magazines had adopted *Ms.* as part of their effort to eliminate sexist language. Since then the number has dwindled, although an influential proponent remains the *New York Times,* which somewhat belatedly changed to *Ms.* in 1986 (Camire, 1989).

The term *Ms.* made publishing history in 1972 as the title of the first mass circulation feminist magazine. Founded by Gloria Steinem, the publication reached 500,000 subscribers by 1983. But even this huge audience did not keep

Ms. in the black. It died as an advertising-supported magazine in 1990, with Steinem publicizing charges that advertisers had tried to undercut *Ms.*'s feminist message ("Steinem to Detail," 1990). It continues today as an adless publication.

Feminists continue to criticize the mass media for demeaning women by portraying them either as sex objects, on the one hand, or, on the other hand, as symbols of a watered-down "equal opportunity" feminism that teaches women to adopt male marketplace values (Gordon, 1991). According to these critics, women's publications tell their readers either how to be more alluring to men or how to succeed in competition with them. *Cosmopolitan,* a virtual self-help manual on how to get men (or get rid of them) symbolizes publications with the former orientation, while *Working Women, Savvy,* and similar magazines preach a doctrine of economic success. In the process, critics contend, women are being taught by the mass media to relinquish age-old feminine values of compassion and nurturing.

It appears that women today continue to strive for a "fairer" depiction in the mass media. Yet depiction varies widely, depending on what segment of the total women's audience is being addressed. The women's audience is split along age, class, racial, life-style, and cultural lines. Feminists themselves break into separate political groups. Numerous problems arise in attempting to decide what "fair" depiction should be, especially in an advertiser-dominated, male-controlled media structure.

For years critics assumed that the employment of more women in the field would assure a fairer depiction. The current situation, with large numbers of women congregated at the lower levels, shows that this is not necessarily true. Women who achieve in the media frequently subscribe to, or have been conditioned to subscribe to, the same competitive, marketplace values as men. Consequently, although mainstream media has a few women in policy-making positions, it presents a picture of women out of focus with reality, according to its critics. Sex continues to sell to a women's audience. Now, however, it is joined by success in terms of image projected. Critics maintain both are false images since American women as a group are both older and poorer than men.

To give a more representative picture of women, some newspapers are reinstituting women's sections, trying to strike a balance between content aimed at career women and that of interest to women who stay home. One of the leaders of this movement has been the *Chicago Tribune,* which has a colorful, twelve-page section called WOMANEWS. It runs articles on sexual harassment, women's health issues, and international issues pertaining to women, but it also presents news on fashion and cosmetics. Critics contend the section trivializes significant issues by running stories on them next to cosmetic ads (Cox, 1992).

FUTURE TRENDS

The future of women as a media audience is tied to their general political, social, and economic status in society. If women continue to be a submerged

Figure 12.1
Newspaper Readership: Percent Read "Every Day," by Sex, 1972–1991

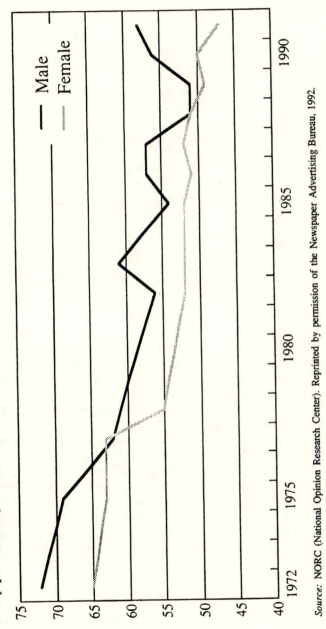

Source: NORC (National Opinion Research Center). Reprinted by permission of the Newspaper Advertising Bureau, 1992.

group economically and politically, in spite of their numerical majority, their role as an audience will remain a segregated one. Advertisers will note, of course, that even though they are poorer than men, women as a group have enormous buying power. By the year 2000 women are expected to make up about 47 percent of the labor force. Without question, working women are here to stay, but will they move up the ladder more rapidly than they have to date?

- Today the average American woman is thirty-two; works in a technical, sales, or administrative job; and makes less than $20,000 a year (Cutler, 1989).
- She is married, has a child, and has more than a 50 percent chance of becoming single again through divorce.
- She is used to media, as least as background noise—televisions or radios are on for eleven hours a day in an average American home.
- She puts in another three and one-half hours of housework and child care when she comes home after driving her eight-year-old car to work and back.
- She is not a sex symbol—indeed, at an average five feet, four inches height, she weighs an average of 143 pounds and considers herself overweight.
- Neither is she a supersuccess in terms of her career.
- No matter how much she might like to "dress for success," as popular books advise, she probably can't afford it. As housing and transportation costs have increased, expenditures on clothing have fallen from 12 percent of the household budget in 1940 to 5 percent over the last half-century (Cutler, 1989).

But she still is making and spending money, and the media wants her attention. Newspapers, in particular, worry that she has deserted their ranks, and they want her back (see Figure 12.1). Whether new women's sections will prove the key to getting her to return is a matter of great concern to the newspaper industry. If these sections reverse declining readership, they will be adopted by every newspaper in the nation.

It is the bottom line that counts in the mass structure of the United States. When women demand changes in the media—as they did during the women's movement of the 1970s—the media responds to make its profits and keep its audience. It seems likely that feminism will be revived as a major social movement in the next decade as the nation confronts a new political-social agenda. Issues of child care and single-parent households demand attention, as do the lagging educational and health care systems. These concerns can be expected to set the stage for new discussions of women's rights. When this happens, one can expect new attacks on, and changes in, the media. Should women's interests unify, as the interests of many women did at the high point of the women's movement, the women's audience will become a potent force.

BIBLIOGRAPHY

The author would like to thank Lee Jolliffe, assistant professor at the University of Missouri-Columbia, whose initial ideas laid the foundation for the chapter.

Allen, Martha. (1988). *The development of communications networks among women, 1963–1983.* Unpublished doctoral dissertation, Howard University, Washington, DC.

American Society of Newspaper Editors. (1990). *About and by women.* Reston, VA: Human Resources Committee, Author.

Beasley, Maurine. (1989). Newspapers: Is there a new majority defining the news? In Pamela J. Creedon (Ed.), *Women in mass communication: Challenging gender values* (pp. 180–194). Newbury Park, CA: Sage Publications.

Beasley, Maurine, & Gibbons, Sheila. (1977). *Women in media: A documentary sourcebook.* Washington, DC: Women's Institute for Freedom of the Press.

Beasley, Maurine, & Theus, Kathryn. (1988). *The new majority: A look at what the preponderance of women in journalism education means to the schools and to the professions.* Lanham, MD: University Press of America.

Biagi, Shirley. (1990). *Media impact.* Belmont, CA: Wadsworth.

Bureau of the Census. (1990). *United States population estimates by age, sex, race, and Hispanic origin: 1980 to 1988.* Washington, DC: U.S. Department of Commerce.

Bureau of the Census. (1991). *Population profile of the United States.* Washington, DC: U.S. Department of Commerce.

Bureau of the Census. (1992a). *Population projections of the United States, by age, sex, race and Hispanic origin: 1992 to 2050.* Washington, DC: U.S. Department of Commerce.

Bureau of the Census. (1992b). *Statistical abstract of the United States.* Washington, DC: U.S. Department of Commerce.

Camire, Dennis. (1989, June 23). Is "Ms." disappearing from the lexicon? Gannett News Service. *Montgomery* (MD) *Journal,* p. 2.

Cooper, Brenda, Rogers, Cathy, & Jenkins, Glenda. (1990, August). *Depictions of men and women in advertising: Time and Ladies' Home Journal, 1930's–1980's.* Paper presented at the annual convention of the Association for Education in Journalism and Mass Communication, Minneapolis, MN.

Covert, Catherine L. (1981). Journalism history and women's experience: A problem in conceptual change. *Journalism History, 8,* 2–6.

Cox, James. (1992, November 23). Newspapers court women. *USA Today,* p. 8B.

Cutler, Blayne. (1989, June). Meet Jane Doe. *American Demographics,* pp. 25–27, 62.

Fannin, Rebecca. (1989, October). The growing sisterhood. *Marketing & Media Decisions, 24,* 38–44.

Ferguson, Marjorie. (1983). *Forever feminine: Women's magazines and the cult of femininity.* Aldershot, England: Gower.

Front pages, network newscasts still overwhelmingly male-dominated. (1992, Summer). *Media Report to Women,* p. 7.

Gale directory of publications & broadcast media. (1993). (Vol. 3). Detroit: Gale Research.

Gordon, Suzanne. (1991). *Prisoners of men's dreams: Striking out for a new feminine future.* Boston: Little, Brown.

Jolliffe, Lee. (1990, August). *Liberal feminism: The strategies of an activist audience.* Paper presented at the annual convention of the Association for Education in Journalism and Mass Communication, Minneapolis, MN.

Lazier-Smith, Linda. (1989). Advertising: Women's place and image. In Pamela J. Creedon (Ed.), *Women in mass communication: Challenging gender values* (pp. 247–260). Newbury Park, CA: Sage Publications.

Lull, J., Mulac, A., & Rosen, S. L. (1983). Feminism as a predictor of mass media use. *Sex Roles, 9,* 165–177.

Marketing to Women, Inc. (1989). *Marketing media to women.* Oneonta, NY: Author.

Media. (1992, December). *Marketing to Women: 1992 Compendium of Trends,* p. 81.

Miller, Susan. (1989). *Women's lifestyles: A special report.* Cincinnati, OH: Scripps Howard Editors Newsletter.

Mills, Kay. (1988). *A place in the news: From the women's pages to the front page.* Reprint, 1990. New York: Columbia University Press.

Newspaper Advertising Bureau. (1992). *1991 Newspaper page and section readership.* New York: Author.

Newspaper Association of America. (1992a). *The daily and Sunday newspaper audience: Major demographic segments.* Annual report. Reston, VA: Author.

Newspaper Association of America. (1992b). *Facts about newspapers '92.* Reston, VA: Author.

Rush, Ramona, & Gutierrez-Villalobos, Sonia. (1990). *From making of myths into hardening of realities: Media images and employment of women—case in point, Latin America.* Paper presented at the annual convention of the Association for Education in Journalism and Mass Communication, Minneapolis, MN.

Steinem to detail Ms. advertiser pressure in re-launch issue in June. (1990, May–June). *Media Report to Women,* p. 1.

Stinnett, Lee (Ed.). (1989). *The changing face of the newsroom.* Reston, VA: American Society of Newspaper Editors.

Twenty years of stereotypes. (1992, December). *Marketing to Women: 1992 Compendium of Trends,* p. 2.

Van Gelder, Lindsay. (1978). As quoted in Gaye Tuchman, *Making news: A study in the construction of reality.* New York: Free Press.

Weaver, David, & Wilhoit, G. Cleveland. (1992). *The American journalist in the 1990's* (preliminary report). Arlington, VA: Freedom Forum.

WOMANEWS. (1990, April). *Chicago Tribune* prototype distributed to members of the American Society of Newspaper Editors.

Women, Men and Media Conference. (1989, April 10). Media releases prepared for program, National Press Club, Washington, DC.

Women have lost ground in TV and newspaper coverage, Cal State study finds. (1992, Summer). *Media Report to Women,* p. 6.

World Almanac and Book of Facts 1993. (1993). New York: Pharos Books.

OTHER WORKS MENTIONED

Bogart, Leo. (1989). *Press and public: Who reads what, when, where, and why in American newspapers* (2nd ed.). Hillsdale, NJ: Lawrence Erlbaum Associates.

Butler, Matilda, & Paisley, William. (1980). *Women and the mass media: Sourcebook for research and action.* New York: Human Sciences Press.

Cantor, Muriel C. (1980). *Prime-time television: Content and control.* Beverly Hill, CA: Sage Publications.

Courtney, Alice E., & Whipple, Thomas E. (1983). *Sex stereotyping in advertising.* Lexington, MA: D. C. Heath.

Friedan, Betty. (1963). *The feminine mystique.* New York: Norton.

Friedman, Leslie J. (1977). *Sex role stereotyping in the mass media: An annotated bibliography.* New York: Garland.

Gelb, Joyce, & Palley, Marian L. (1982). *Women in public politics.* Princeton, NJ: Princeton University Press.

Hartman, Susan M. (1989). *From margin to mainstream: American women and politics since 1960.* New York: Knopf.

Hosley, David H., & Yamada, Gayle K. (1987). *Hard news: Women in broadcast journalism.* Westport, CT: Greenwood Press.

Lengermann, Patricia M., & Wallace, Ruth A. (1985). *Gender in America: Social control and social change.* Englewood Cliffs, NJ: Prentice-Hall.

Marzolf, Marion. (1977). *Up from the footnote: A history of women journalists.* New York: Hastings House.

Poole, Keith T., & Zeigler, L. Harmon. (1985). *Women, public opinion, and politics: The changing political attitudes of American women.* New York: Longman.

Rush, Ramona R., & Allen, Donna. (1989). *Communications at the crossroads: The gender gap connection.* Norwood, NJ: Ablex.

Sanders, Marlene, & Rock, Marcia. (1988). *Waiting for prime time: The women of television news.* Urbana: University of Illinois Press.

PERIODICALS

There are no periodicals devoted entirely to the subject of women as a mass media audience. An excellent periodical source, however, is listed below:

Media Report to Women
Communication Research Associates, Inc.
10606 Mantz Road.
Silver Spring, MD 20903-1228

The *Quill,* a journalism review published by the Society of Professional Journalists, devoted its February 1990 issue to the subject of women and the media. Copies may be obtained from the society at the following address:

Society of Professional Journalists
P. O. Box 77
Greencastle, IN 46135-0077
(317) 653-3333

Other sources of current information are women's organizations pertaining to the media. Names and addresses follow:

American Women in Radio and Television
1101 Connecticut Avenue NW, Suite 700
Washington, DC 20036
(202) 429-5102

National Federation of Press Women
Box 99
Blue Springs, MO 64015
(816) 229-1666
(Publishes *PressWoman* Magazine)

National Organization for Women
Women's Media Project
1000 16th Street NW, Suite 700
Washington, DC 20036
(202) 331-0066

Women in Communications
2101 Wilson Boulevard, Suite 417
Arlington, VA 22201
(703) 528-4200
(Publishes *The Professional Communicator* Magazine)

Women's Institute for Freedom of the Press
c/o Dr. Donna Allen, President
3306 Ross Place NW
Washington, DC 20008
(202) 966-7783

Numerous papers on academic research related to women and audiences are given at the annual conventions of the Association for Education in Journalism and Mass Communication. Information on the association, which includes a Commission on the Status of Women, can be obtained from its headquarters:

Association for Education in Journalism and Mass Communication
1621 College Street
University of South Carolina
Columbia, SC 29208-0251
(803) 777-2005

For research related to women as newspaper readers, contact the following:
Newspaper Association of America

The Newspaper Center
Box 17407 Dulles Airport
Washington, DC 20041
(703) 648-1000

13

CHILDREN AND YOUTH AUDIENCES

Lowndes F. Stephens

NATURE AND SIZE

Television is the first medium used by children, and in some low-income, single-parent families, it is a "constant companion" (Medrich, Roizen, & Buckley, 1981). According to Nielsen Media Research, the typical child age two to five watches about twenty-one hours of television a week, compared with sixteen hours a week for children ages six to eleven and twenty hours a week for all viewers age two or higher. While the amount of time Americans spend watching television is declining modestly, the typical family still has the set on forty-nine hours a week, and viewing is substantially greater in television markets like Dallas where viewers can select from over sixty cable stations (Kritz, 1989).

Today, children not only depend on commercial broadcast stations for entertainment and educational programs, but they increasingly get it from cable TV and videocassettes. There are more than 1,340 television stations today (versus 953 in 1975); 300 of them are independent (versus 79 in 1976). Today, about three out of four television households receive nine or more stations, up from 31 percent in 1974. More than 80 percent of today's television households are located within cable television markets, and over 50 percent of them are actually subscribing to cable. Moreover, more than 62 percent of television households have videocassette recorders (VCRs).

The Cabletelevision Advertising Bureau (CAB) says in 1990 cable television was received by 54.9 million (59 percent) American households. The CAB estimates, based on its KidCume reach and frequency system, that cable reaches about 70 percent of the total kids ages two to eleven living in cable households (Advertising Age, 1991, p. Cable-27). The networks are cognizant of their loss of young viewers to cable programs like Viacom's MTV (Music Television). So in June 1991 NBC launched an eight-week advertising campaign claiming it attracts far more young adult viewers than MTV to prime-time shows such as "Fresh Prince of Bel Air," "Blossom," and "Seinfeld" (Goldman, 1991).

Television is the preferred source of visual stimulation among children, and it is used increasingly by schools as a source of instruction. "Distance-learning" projects, involving two-way hookups between remote teachers and students, are planned or now operative in all fifty states. More than 2,500 secondary schools in the United States are using "CNN Newsroom," a noncommercial news feed started in 1989 from Turner Broadcasting System.

More controversial is Whittle Communications's "Channel One," a commercially sponsored fourteen minute news feed offered to nearly 11,000 high schools (Bishop, 1992).

Whittle includes two minutes of commercials on these feeds, but the schools pay nothing for the service or the $20,000 in free equipment that is part of the deal. Nevertheless, New York and California have banned the service, and North Carolina is embroiled in a battle to determine whether individual schools, rather than school superintendents or the state department of education, have the right to decide on their own if the service is worth it. Whittle, which is 50 percent owned by Time Warner, announced in May 1991 that it plans to operate its own "for-profit" schools, and one hundred education researchers will help it decide what these schools should teach (Putka, 1991b). The school superintendents who object to Whittle's "Channel One" service are concerned about the advertising messages. The superintendents, on the other hand, are no doubt elated at the kind of benevolence demonstrated by Walter Annenberg, who pledged $60 million in 1991 to the Corporation for Public Broadcasting to support instructional television programs in mathematics and science for grades K–12.

The Newspaper Advertising Bureau examined multiple media use in a 1970s national sample study of 817 households with children ages six to seventeen. Readership of newspapers, books, and magazines increases with age, and children of newspaper-reading parents are much more likely to develop the newspaper-reading habit. Children and parents from lower socioeconomic backgrounds (usually poorer, nonwhite, rural, and single-parent homes) are much less likely to be readers. While only one-third of children ages six to eight report "ever" reading newspapers, about 61 percent of the nine- to eleven-year-olds have read them. About one-third of the six- to eight-year-olds also say they listen to radio each day or play records, and about the same number spend "a lot" of time each day with these media. Use of radio and records increases substantially in the teen years; more than 90 percent of fifteen- to seventeen-year-olds report listening to radio or playing records "yesterday." About one in five youngsters six to eight years of age attend movies each week, compared with 48 percent of the fifteen- to seventeen-year-olds.

Several newspapers and magazines are trying new techniques to attract readers. The *Wall Street Journal* launched a Classroom Edition in 1991. The American Newspaper Publishers Association has encouraged the "Newspaper in the Classroom" program for many years, and several metropolitan papers make copies of their newspapers available for use by teachers in the classroom. But the *Journal*'s "Classroom Edition" is a specially edited, twenty-four-page, four-color edition that teachers have an active role in shaping. They help the editors decide what stories from the *Journal* are appropriate, and these stories are then edited in the classroom. The *Chicago Tribune* employs five teenage film reviewers, and *Newsday* publishes a "Student Briefing Page" (Reilly, 1991). Consumers Union publishes a youth version of its *Consumer Reports,* and *Sports Illustrated* does the same with its successful weekly magazine. Other magazines like *The New Yorker* maintain active classroom programs to introduce students at an early age to their products.

EFFECT OF MASS COMMUNICATIONS ON CHILDREN

1920s

Since the 1920s, communication researchers have taken a special interest in children as an audience segment. In fact, the most significant and well-funded research in the public interest on mass communication effects has focused on children. Movies became enormously popular in America in the 1920s. About 40 million movie tickets were sold each week in 1922. By 1929, when more than 90 million movie tickets were being sold each week, there were as many minors buying those tickets as there were total moviegoers in 1922 (Lowery & DeFleur, 1988, pp. 32–33).

The movies produced during the 1920s were hardly wholesome fare. One exhaustive study of the themes of more than 1,500 films of this period showed about three out of four films focused on love, crime, and sex (Dale, 1935, p. 8). The parents and grandparents of 17 million or so children under the age of fourteen who were seeing these movies were raised during the Victorian Age (1819–1901). They were concerned about the impact of these movies on the moral development of their children.

Thus, in the 1920s the Motion Picture Research Council, with funding support from the Payne Fund Foundation, commissioned thirteen studies of the influence of movies on children. These studies by psychologists, sociologists, and educators determined, among other things, that movies bring new ideas to children, influence their attitudes, stimulate their emotions, disturb their sleep, and present children with moral standards different from those of many adults (Lowery & DeFleur, 1988, pp. 51–53). The Payne Fund studies stimulated tighter motion picture industry production standards in the 1930s.

1950s–1960s

When television swept the nation in the 1950s, researchers wanted to know how children use it. Believing children were active, rather than passive, consumers of television content, three Stanford University professors published the results of eleven studies from 1958 to 1960 in *Television in the Lives of Our Children* (Schramm, Lyle, & Parker, 1961). Ten communities in the United

States and Canada, broadly representative in terms of socioeconomic character-istics and local television availability, were selected as study sites. The research-ers collected data from 6,000 students, 2,000 parents, and several hundred teachers and other officials. In 1960 the population of the United States was about 179 million, and 150 million Americans, or 84 percent, owned television sets. The researchers found that by age five 82 percent of the children were watching television about two hours on weekdays and somewhat longer on weekends. By the time a child reached first grade, about 40 percent of their viewing time was devoted to adult programming; almost 80 percent of the view-ing time of sixth graders was devoted to adult programming. Children ages three to sixteen spent more time with television than with any other activity except sleep.

Children three to eight learned the most from television because they saw new things on television not experienced elsewhere. Children viewers started school with larger vocabularies than nonviewers, but these differences disap-peared by the time the children entered sixth grade. Children of moderate to below average intelligence, working-class children, and children with family and peer-group conflicts watched more television. More than half the program op-tions during the "children's hour" (weekday 4 to 9 P.M.) was fantasy program-ming (crime shows, westerns, and cartoons). About 20 percent of the program options during this time were reality programs (news and public affairs, for example). Children mostly preferred fantasy programming until they reached the tenth grade, when many of them became more interested in reality programming and print alternatives such as newspapers, magazines, and books. A movement of preferences toward print and reality-oriented television programs character-ized children who had internalized middle-class norms. The Stanford scholars concluded that while television may lead to "premature aging" and to a world-view that was a "markedly erroneous picture of adult life," children who were loved at home, respected by peers, and active in extracurricular activities were unlikely to be harmed by television.

MEDIA AND VIOLENCE

In the 1960s, Americans were shocked by the assassinations of four prominent political leaders, the civil rights and anti–Vietnam War movements, airplane hijackings, and a bloody Democratic National Convention in Chicago. In June 1968, President Lyndon Johnson issued an executive order creating the National Commission on the Causes and Prevention of Violence. The commission pub-lished evidence linking violence in the media to real-world violence more pro-foundly than the limited-effects conclusions reached by the Stanford researchers (Baker & Ball, 1969). Although the findings in this government report are less directly related to children than either the Stanford study or subsequent reports by the Surgeon General, the results are significant because children do develop a preference for adult programming at an early age.

The news media were chided also for not giving enough access to groups bent on social change. Not only could lack of access to media engender a sense of political impotency among blacks who were seeking redress against institutional discrimination, but stereotypical portrayals of blacks on television could foster personal discrimination and bigotry. The report concluded that the mass media are powerful agencies of socialization. For example, young males, in search of their masculinity, might identify with actors playing violent roles on television, especially if they have no other role models.

Television also teaches the viewer how to perform violent acts and what consequences victims and perpetrators might expect if conflicts were resolved by resorting to violence. Viewers of television violence over long periods of time may be prone to adopt a violent worldview that mirrors the world of television violence. The way violence is portrayed may also influence the extent to which viewers act aggressively in the real world. Inaccurate portrayals of class, ethnic, social, and occupational groups in the mass media can be extremely damaging to communication between groups.

In the early 1970s, the Surgeon General's *Report on Television and Social Behavior* was published as the war in Vietnam raged and just a year after the Kent State massacre of antiwar protesters. The full report showed a strong causal relationship between televised violence and real-world aggression. Watered-down and limited-effects conclusions in an executive summary were insisted upon by the industry representatives of the advisory group, notably Joseph T. Klapper, head of the Office of Social Research at CBS (Lowery & DeFleur, 1988, p. 321).

George Gerbner and his associates at the Annenberg School of Communications at the University of Pennsylvania, location of the Cultural Indicators Project, analyzed the content of prime-time and Saturday-morning programs for one-week periods in 1967, 1968, and 1969. The Cultural Indicators Project defines violence as ''any overt act or threat to hurt or kill a person.'' They found some modest declines in the amount of violence on prime-time programs but a marked increase in the amount of violent acts in children's cartoons. The content analyses revealed that the portrayal of television violence is unrealistic—the people, relationships, settings, places, and times all depart from real life.

Interviews with these television professionals revealed a belief that parents and the television networks, not the scriptwriters and producers, should decide whether children should be excluded from the audience for their violent, action programs. These professionals argued that television violence is unlikely to contribute to real-world violence because their programming allows for a cathartic release of aggression, and because the television ''violents'' are appropriately rewarded or punished.

A famous experimental study by Bandura (1965) involving a ''Bobo doll'' victim demonstrated the importance of reward/punishment to observational or social learning. Children observed a model hitting and kicking a plastic Bobo doll. Those in one group saw the model rewarded for his aggression; a second group of children subjects observed the model being punished for his aggression; and a third group observed no consequences—the model was neither rewarded nor punished. The children were then placed in a play situation with the doll. The children from the group observing the model rewarded for his aggressive behavior directly imitated his aggression in the play situation, as did the children who observed the model neither punished nor rewarded for his aggressive behavior. But the children from the group observing the model punished for his aggressive behavior were much less likely to strike the doll. Later, when all the children were asked to reproduce the aggressive acts performed by the model in the experiment, and were told they'd be rewarded for doing so, children from each of the three treatment groups were just as likely to imitate the model's aggression. Undoubtedly, children are exposed to violence on television, and they actually learn how to perform violent acts. Whether they internalize aggression as a means of resolving conflicts may have to do with the extent to which "violents" are portrayed as rewarded or punished for their aggressive behaviors. They also surely assess the consequences of their intentions to behave violently by evaluating whether "real-world others" have been rewarded or punished.

A panel study of 436 New York third-grade children, interviewed again ten years later, used aggressiveness ratings by self, peers, and parents as the basis for judging television viewing effects over time (Lefkowitz et al., 1977). The researchers found that third-graders who were heavy viewers of violence on television were more aggressive eight-year-olds, and they were more aggressive as eighteen-years-olds than were those boys who watched less television violence. Heavy violence viewing is associated with a more violent worldview. While the correlations between television violence viewing and aggressive behavior are not as strong among girls, the researchers found no differences in the correlations when controlling for school achievement or socioeconomic status.

In the early 1980s the National Institute of Mental Health (NIMH) published the results of a comprehensive review of academic studies of television's effects on human behavior (Pearl, Bouthilet, & Lazar, 1982). The focus was much broader than television violence alone. The reviews looked not just at antisocial behavioral effects but at prosocial behaviors (e.g., altruism, friendly behavior, self-control), cognitive processing, affective aspects of television, health-promoting effects of television, family communication patterns, sex-role stereotyping, and the impact of television on American institutions (e.g., does television viewing alter the public's confidence and trust in American institutions such as the courts, the mass media, the schools, etc.).

CHILDREN AND MEDIA

An extraordinary amount of research on television and human behavior was produced in the 1970s because the government-sponsored research programs and reviews of research had not resolved the causality questions, both the direction and strength of the relationship between viewing of televised violence and subsequent aggressive behavior. The experimental studies in the laboratory showed on a balance a strong causal linkage between viewing and subsequent aggressive behavior. The survey studies, however, showed modest correlations between viewing and aggression. Congress and federal regulatory agencies such as the Federal Communications Commission (FCC) could become no tougher with the networks than to establish "family viewing hours," without stronger evidence that television violence posed a strong threat to citizens because it directly contributes to real-world aggression. The courts supported the First Amendment freedom of expression privilege of the artists even as a defense against the FCC-required "family viewing hours" policy.

Even in the face of more reliable evidence from 1980s studies that television violence was contributing to real-world aggression, President Ronald Reagan's administration deregulated much federal communication policy. Many FCC guidelines established in the 1970s were dropped in the early 1980s because they were judged to violate First Amendment rights.

Groups like Action for Children's Television, the American Pediatrics Association, and the Parents Music Resource Center, however, were concerned with the increasing levels of violence in media, with rising levels of narco-terrorism and drug abuse and declining levels of literacy at a time when more than one-half of married women were entering the labor force to augment family income. *Newsweek* reported in its special edition "The 21st Century Family" that Gallup queried a national sample of 757 American adults in October 1989 and found 49 percent believed the American family was worse off than it was ten years earlier, and 42 percent believed it would be worse off ten years from now than it is today (Footlick, 1990, p. 18). Also disconcerting to many parents was the explosion in new technologies for delivering popular culture (e.g., videocassettes and stores to distribute tapes, cable television and computer games, commercially sponsored school news programs).

Industry officials argued before Congress that advertisers and broadcasters were capable of self-regulation, had implemented special measures such as the Children's Advertising Review Unit (Council of Better Business Bureaus), had financially supported services such as KIDSNET, and had sufficient competitors (e.g., cable and videocassettes) to make a broad range of programming available to children. They also argued against government control on First Amendment grounds and encouraged parents to intervene and counsel with their children.

CONTEMPORARY RESEARCH ON CHILDREN AND MEDIA

Media, Language, and Symbols

Wartella and Reeves (1987) and Greenfield (1984) provide two of the most thoughtful reviews of children and media research studies since the NIMH reports were published in 1982. Wartella and Reeves concluded that there are more research citations of studies about children's processing of media messages than about the effects of media content. The variables of interest among these researchers are message structure, mental representations of symbols, processing of narrative, attention, comprehension, and understanding of messages. Much of the research has focused on the famous "Sesame Street" program produced by the Children's Television Workshop.

EXPLOITATION AND PUBLIC POLICY

Other critics have focused on the language of music recordings and videos, most notably Tipper Gore, wife of the U.S. vice-president from Tennessee (Gore, 1987). The work of her Parents Music Resource Center, and other interest groups listed in her book, has recently influenced the recording industry's decision to voluntarily place "warning" labels on records that contain profane language and explicit images of sex and violence. Other critics have taken a proactive stance by disseminating lists of recommended videos for children of varying ages (Kiernan, 1990).

Children's advertising is also a significant issue. Public interest groups like the Center for Science in the Public Interest and Action for Children's Television (ACT) complain that deregulation of television in the 1980s put children at more risk to exploitation by broadcasters and advertisers. For example, a February 1991 study by the Center for Science in the Public Interest indicated that fewer than one in ten of the food advertisements (60 percent of all ads aired on Saturday morning) focused on "good breakfast" items (i.e., less than 25 percent of caloric intake from refined sugar, less than 30 percent of calories from fat, and fewer than 400 milligrams of salt) (Knight-Ridder, Washington Bureau, 1991).

In hearings before the House Subcommittee on Telecommunications and Finance to reconsider a bill limiting the amount of advertising for children on television, legislation that was vetoed by President Reagan before he left office in 1988, Congressman Edward J. Markey, chair, opened by noting that a fall 1988 survey of stations in the Boston market by ACT showed that television stations were carrying more commercials than the pre-1984 FCC guidelines recommend. For example, children's programs on a representative independent TV station in Boston aired in excess of twelve minutes and as much as fourteen minutes of commercials each hour (twelve minutes per hour FCC guidelines existed prior to 1984). Yet, with regard to adult prime-time programming, commercials did not exceed eight minutes per hour (U.S. Congress, House, 1989).

Prior to 1984, when the FCC enforced commercial guidelines, the television networks were either at or below the 9.5 minute per hour limit. However, in the nine years since the FCC deregulation order, commercial time has been on the rise, with stations at two of the networks now offering as many as 12 minutes of commercials per hour. For example, one recent content analytic study of 604 hours of children's programming in seven U.S. television markets shows an average of 12.09 minutes per hour of nonprogram content on the three major networks, 13.26 minutes per hour of nonprogram content on independent television stations, and 10.38 minutes per hour of nonprogram content on cable networks (Kunkel & Gantz, 1992, p. 142). A recent federal law requires commercial TV broadcast licenses to limit advertising in children's programs to not more than 10 minutes per hour on weekends and not more than 12 minutes per hour on weekdays.

During the Reagan presidency, the FCC was reluctant to interfere with the First Amendment rights of broadcasters, deciding that the guidelines on children's advertising and violent content were too restrictive. Commercial broadcasters have argued that since advertising is their only source of revenue, Congress should not restrict their right to compete with alternative forms of entertainment and content for children (e.g., cable TV and videocassettes). They also claim competition from these alternative sources of children's entertainment has improved the quality of programs available to children and that broadcast stations and the networks have initiated self-regulation, as has the advertising industry itself. For example, industry spokesmen testified at the hearings that the National Advertising Division of the Council of Better Business Bureaus maintains a "Children's Advertising Review Unit," which scrutinizes children's advertising.

At present, public interest groups that called for a return to the pre-1984 FCC standards require stations to provide educational programming for children and to limit the amount of advertising on children's programs. They have succeeded in their insistence that broadcasters regard children as part of their public interest obligations. Indeed, one of these groups, ACT, disbanded in early 1992, saying it had achieved its legislative agenda calling for more responsible television for children.

EFFECTIVENESS

News magazines celebrated the twentieth year of "Sesame Street" in 1989 with mostly flattering "report cards" like this one that appeared in *U.S. News & World Report*. "'Sesame Street,' which revolutionized educational programming with an integrated cast and an entertaining format aimed specifically at disadvantaged kids, turns 20 this year, and 11 million U.S. households still watch it every week. The Emmy-award-winning show has become such a cultural force that the Smithsonian's National Museum of American History is honoring it with a retrospective that will run through October" (Rachlin & Burke, 1989, p. 50).

The article also reported that the commercial TV industry had been slow to emulate the "Sesame Street" approach, but advocates of quality children's TV were hoping President Bush would soon sign legislation forcing networks to devote time to educational programming. "Sesame Street" has been enormously successful with an income of more that $55.7 million in 1988 from products, home videos, software, magazine sales and international TV.

The *New York Times'* story on "Sesame Street's" twentieth anniversary notes that the program has helped scholars recognize that children can make intuitive leaps across time and space, like the ones required when television shifts from a scene outside a building to a scene of the inside (Chira, 1989). While "Sesame Street" is designed to reach three- to five-year-olds, experiments have demonstrated that even fourteen-month-olds are able to assemble a toy after watching it being put together on television. Today, Children's Television Workshop generates more than $90 million in operating income as a sophisticated publishing, licensing, and TV-production conglomerate, one that refuses to exploit kids for material gain (Crossen, 1992).

"Sesame Street" has provided a kind of workshop on language development—at the pragmatic level of semiotics (study of signs). We've been able to see how children use language and symbols to communicate with each other and with the characters on the program. Children learn best from the segments that give them time to respond, clap, or sing along; from animation that is repeated in a show and throughout the season; and from those skits that they find entertaining. They are not glued to the tube during the entire hour, but they look at and away from "Sesame Street" as many as 150 times during each program, selectively viewing segments they understand best (Chira, 1989).

Programs such as "Sesame Street" and "Mister Rogers' Neighborhood" have extended the social and cultural knowledge of children, which contributes to the communicative competencies of children. As early as age two children have acquired important social understanding about communication, about pragmatics of conversations (such as turn taking and question asking), and about people and events (Wartella & Reeves, 1987).

Lemish (1986) explains that two types of "codes" are used by these types of educational programs to facilitate learning. "Perceptually salient" codes, or forms, serve as markers or cues of content to follow. These codes—a quick change or a visual or auditory surprise—elicit children's attention. "Reflective" codes, or forms—dialogue, singing, moderate action levels—maintain attention and aid in rehearsal, reflection, and comprehension. Some critics of the early years of "Sesame Street" argued that too much attention was given to "attention-grabbing" codes, to constant orientation that is detrimental to learning and understanding, and not enough to reflective codes (Singer & Singer, 1983). Others have argued that orientation codes might facilitate learning of materials that immediately follow visual surprises (Zillman, 1982) and that the constant orientation codes, designed to keep children interested in the program, facilitate learning because children actively select content that is comprehensible to them (D. Anderson & Lorch, 1983). For example, one recent study shows that children who hear sound effects immediately prior to a flashback sequence are more

likely to reorient attention to the television program but that sound effects do
not increase selective attention to the flashback segment itself (Calvert, 1988).

While the influential psychologist Jean Piaget may have underestimated the
importance of the social environment in the development of communicative
competence, his theory of age-related differences in cognitive development continues to be confirmed in studies of retention and inference making. Older children (fifth and eighth grade) remember more information central to television
plots than do younger children (second grade), whose retention is unaffected by
whether scenes are presented in a jumbled or logical order. Older children also
demonstrate higher-order inference-making skills (information children assign
to television that goes beyond what is available on the screen) (Collins, 1983).

Children's retention or memory of television narrative can be aided when
story lines are conceptualized as "scripts" or "schemata," hypothetical cognitive structures that represent associations among units of information. Meadowcroft and Reeves (1989) argue that television scriptwriters help children
bridge the gap between mere attention and the more lasting goals of comprehension and memory by minimizing subplots and irrelevant event sequences. In
experimental studies of children ages five to eight, children are more efficient
viewers when they comprehend television narrative as "stories" (with, for example, a setting, beginning, focal problem, and solution) and when they bring
highly developed story schema skills (e.g., ability to distinguish between central
and incidental story content and the ability to put events in correct temporal
order) to a viewing situation. For example, children with highly developed story
schema skills (not before age seven) expend less effort attending to television
stories, recall more central-story than incidental-story content, and attend more
to the main idea when television scripts are written as stories. Greenfield and
Beagles-Roos (1988) have also demonstrated experimentally that television is
more effective than radio in increasing children's recall of central ideas, cued
recall, and reconstruction of story sequence with pictures.

Salomon (1979, 1981, 1983) and his associate (Salomon & Leigh, 1984) agree
that schema theory explains in part why children comprehend more of what they
read in print than what they see on television because "words" (rather than
pictures) cultivate a style of information processing (e.g., conceptualizing content as story schema) that requires more effort in converting word signs into
mental images. Picture-based content is easier than word-based content to interpret, but comprehension is greatest when the mental effort is greatest. Their
research shows that children comprehend more from television than they might
otherwise when they expect television messages will be difficult to process,
when viewing departs from expectations, or when children are instructed to
learn. Of course, the type of program on television or the type of book (Beentzjes, 1989) influences the amount of mental effort expended.

In a recent experiment with elementary school children, grades K–4, Wilson
(1991) takes some scary "dream" scenes from a 1986 version of the movie

Invader from Mars and shows that adding either a prologue or epilogue to the scary scenes helps children understand that the "scary" segment is just a dream, not reality. The prologue, but not the epilogue, was also effective in reducing the children's negative interpretations of and emotional reactions to the scary scene. Wilson argues her research confirms the findings of other scholars who believe that formal features, like the prologue and epilogue conditions manipulated in her experiment, are understood by children and that they can activate schemata.

Parents, siblings, and peers, as coviewers with children, can increase how much and how quickly the child learns from television. Children do more dial switching than parents, but parent-child viewing styles are related (Heeter et al., 1988). Other research indicates that coviewing among parents and children occurs less often from a conscious effort on the parents' part to mediate children's viewing than it does from a similar interest in types of programs. Moreover, coviewing occurs less often with young children who need the most guidance (Dorr, Kovaric, & Doubleday, 1989).

IMPACT OF TV ON READING AND ACADEMIC PERFORMANCE

Neuman (1988) analyzed eight statewide reading assessment studies and a 1984 study by the National Assessment of Education Progress and concluded that children who watch more than four hours of television a day score lower on reading assessment tests than children who watch fewer than four hours a day.

One recently reported three-year panel study of eighth graders in California contrasts the academic performance and media usage of "recreational" computer users (video games) and "intellectual" computer users (word processing and other school-related applications). Recreational users were the heaviest viewers of television and performed the most poorly in school. Intellectual users were the lightest television viewers and performed the best in school; they were also less frequent leisure readers. "Multiusers" (those who used computers for both leisure and work) were the most infrequent readers. "Low users" (seldom or never use computers) were the most frequent leisure readers. The authors conclude that computers may be viewed as a functional equivalent to reading for some children who use them and that computers may be displacing time that may otherwise be spent with print media (Liberman, Chaffee, & Roberts, 1988). Other researchers are looking at how preschoolers relate to media toys (toys with microprocessors that are capable of synthetic speech and humanlike animation) and whether parasocial speech and interaction with these toys improve or retard sociability with real people (Turkle, 1984; Brown, 1989).

Audiovisual media for children are so prevalent that a national data base called KIDSNET was established in 1983 to keep track of it. The founders, sponsored by grants from the Corporation for Public Broadcasting, the National

Endowment for the Arts, and some private foundations, call it the first centralized data base to offer a comprehensive source of information concerning children's television/radio, audio, and video programming. Users include children, parents, teachers, media specialists, doctors, museum curators, school principals, and broadcasters (U.S. Congress, House, 1989). Futurists say the mind-set of Western civilization, for so long (4,000 years) dependent on print media, and left-hemisphere thinking where quantitative reasoning is enthroned, is shifting to an age of "robotism" where visual media dominate, the right hemisphere reins, and qualitative thinking is enthroned (McLuhan & Powers, 1989). Many issues we now highlight focus on these transformations. It is fair to note that most of the observers who see these concerns as issues are adults who are products of a print culture.

BLURRING OF CHILDHOOD AND ADULTHOOD

Today there is more of a blurring of childhood and adulthood. Joshua Meyrowitz, in his widely acclaimed book *No Sense of Place: The Impact of Electronic Media on Social Behavior* (1985), argues that television is revolutionary because it allows the very young child to be "present" at adult interactions. "The widespread use of television is equivalent to a broad social decision to allow young children to be present at wars and funerals, courtships and seductions, criminal plots and cocktail parties. . . . [TV] exposes children to many topics and behaviors that adults have spent several centuries trying to keep hidden from children" (p. 242).

We see the effects of this blurring in television programs like "Doogie Howser, M.D." (ABC prime-time) and the blockbuster movie and video favorite *E.T.,* where children are portrayed as equal to or more mature, sensitive, and intelligent than adults. Children and adults dress alike, watch the same videos and movies, and discuss the same topics. Meyrowitz argues that electronic media have changed the logic of the social order (e.g., parent-child relationships) by restructuring the relationships between physical place and social place and by altering the ways in which we transmit and receive social information.

Many of the traditional distinctions among groups, among people at various stages of socialization, and among superiors and subordinates were based on patterns of information flow that existed in a print society. Some observers note that we are so inundated with visual imagery today that the environment created by language and the printed word has now been moved to the periphery of our culture, and the image is now at the center of the culture (Postman, 1988). Postman believes the critical thinking and reasoning skills based on Aristotelian logic, which Western civilizations developed when the print culture was dominant, are no longer sufficient for judging the truth or falsity of the "images" we consume in the electronic media. We need a different set of defenses for coping with the seductions of eloquence.

Our command of the print culture and general knowledge of American culture apparently is declining at a rate that parallels our dependence on visual imagery. One educator says as many as 60 million Americans, age sixteen or older, are unable to read at a twelfth-grade level of comprehension (Harman, 1989). In a 1975 study of 7,500 adults, University of Texas researchers determined as many as 23 million American adults could not read an aspirin bottle label, understand the directions for cooking a TV dinner, or write a personal check! The economic cost of illiteracy today is measured in tens of billions of dollars. According to a study by the Organization for Economic Cooperation and Development, functional illiteracy is responsible for an annual loss to U.S. companies of $40 billion ("Illiteracy Dogs Industrial World," 1992).

Two best-selling books in the late 1980s by university professors touched a responsive cord among a large segment of the American public with their message that the crisis in American education is that our young people are leaving college without an understanding of their own culture or cultures of other nations. E. D. Hirsch, Jr., author of *Cultural Literacy: What Every American Needs to Know,* believes a truly literate citizen must be able to grasp the meaning of any piece of writing addressed to the general public. He notes, "[A]ll citizens should be able, for instance, to read newspapers of substance" (Hirsch, 1987, p. 12).

Even though television is an instrument of demystification and empowerment, it is also disruptive when its messages conflict with what parents, church, and the schools tell children. It may create unrealistic expectations regarding the resolution of societal problems, and it may create such false views of reality that children are unable to cope with the real world. Consider, for example, the television violence profile of the Cultural Indicators Project for the period 1967 to 1989 (Gerbner & Signorielli, 1990). Figure 13.1 shows that the amount of violence on children's weekend-daytime programs has remained higher than the violence on adult prime-time programs (an average violence index of 234 versus 159). After dismantling the codes pertaining to violence during children's programs due to deregulation in 1980, the rate of violent acts per hour of weekend daytime programming increased from 18.6 to 26.4. In terms of the violence indexes in Figure 13.1, the index averaged 229 before deregulation and 243 after deregulation (weekend). There has been only a modest increase in the average violence index for adult programming (prime-time), from 155 before to 159 after deregulation.

FUTURE

Children have been a significant audience segment for the mass media since the movie industry discovered such a strong following among children in the 1920s. When television matured in the 1950s, children were there to watch, and we wondered what it was doing to them or how children used it. In the 1960s and 1970s, we questioned whether much of the real-world violence was related to too much violence on television. The prevailing view is that television and

Figure 13.1
Violence on Television: Twenty-two-Year Profile: Prime-Time and Children's Programs

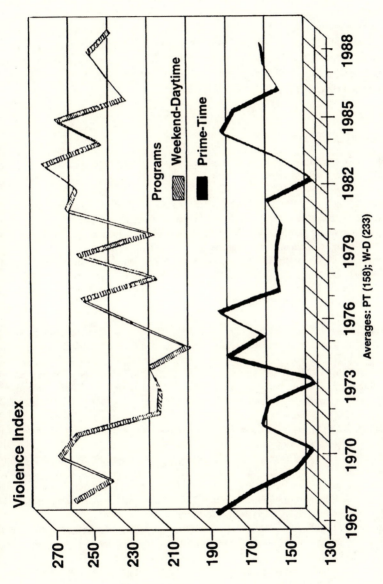

Source: Gerbner and Signorielli, 1990.

related electronic toys are no longer simply toys but rather are powerful tools for learning and socialization. Television violence can contribute to a violent worldview among children. Our concerns in the 1980s have focused on how children learn from television, how television fits into the media-usage mix, whether too much viewing affects reading and literacy skills, and how children are using computers and media toys. These issues will be at the forefront as well in the 1990s, as will the issue of privatization of elementary and secondary education. Whittle Communications L.P., Time Warner Inc., Philips Electronics N.V., and Associated Newspaper Holdings Ltd., for example, hope to open 200 campuses by 1995 and 1,000 by the year 2000.

BIBLIOGRAPHY

The author acknowledges the assistantship support of Kathleen McGuire.

Adelson, A. (1991, February 7). How TV is creating new perceptions about blacks. *New York Times,* p. B1.

Advertising Age. (1991). *1991 Advertiser's guide to cable.* Chicago: Crain.

Anderson, B., Mead, N., & Sullivan, Susan. (1986). *Television: What do national assessment results tell us?* (ERIC, ED. 277 072). Princeton, NJ: National Assessment of Educational Progress, Education Testing Service.

Anderson, D., & Lorch, E. (1983). Looking at television: Action or reaction. In J. Bryant & D. Anderson (Eds.), *Children's understanding of television.* New York: Academic Press.

Baker, Robert, & Ball, Sandra (Eds.). (1969). *Violence in the media.* Washington, DC: GPO.

Bandura, A. (1965). Influence of models: Reinforcement contingencies on the acquisition of imitative responses. *Journal of Personality and Social Psychology, 1,* 589–595.

Bandura, A. (1977). *Social learning theory.* Englewood Cliffs, NJ: Prentice-Hall.

Beentzjes, J. (1989). Learning from television and books: A Dutch replication study based on Salomon's model. *Educational Technology Research and Development, 37*(2), 47–58.

Bishop, Katherine. (1992, June 4). Commercial TV programs for schools faces a test. *New York Times,* p. A16.

Bloom, A. (1987). *The closing of the American mind.* New York: Simon & Schuster.

Brown, B. (1989, August). *Influence of talking media toys on children's perceptions of people and machines.* Paper presented at the annual conference of the Association for Education in Journalism and Mass Communication, Communication Theory and Methodology Division, Washington, DC.

Calvert, S. (1988, July–September). Television production feature effects on children's comprehension of time. *Journal of Applied Developmental Psychology, 9*(3), 263–274.

Chen, M., Ellis, J., & Hoelscher, K. (1988, Fall). Repurposing children's television for the classroom: Teachers' use of "Square One Television" videocassettes. *Educational Communication and Technology, 36*(3), 161–178.

Chira, Susan. (1989, November 15). Taking stock of learning. *New York Times,* p. 26Y.

Chomsky, N. (1957). *Syntactic structures.* The Hague: Mouton.

Chomsky, N. (1965). *Aspects of the theory of syntax.* Cambridge: MIT Press.

Cohen, A., Levy, M., & Golden, K. (1988, December). Children's uses and gratifications of home VCRs: Evolution or revolution? *Communication Research, 15*(6), 772–790.

Collins, W. (1983). Interpretation and inferences in children's television viewing. In J. Bryant & D. Anderson (Eds.), *Children's understanding of television.* New York: Academic Press.

Condry, J., Berme, P., & Scheibe, C. (1988, Summer). Nonprogram content of children's television. *Journal of Broadcasting and Electronic Media, 32*(3), 255–270.

Crossen, Cynthia. (1992, February 21). "Sesame Street," at 23, still teaches children while amusing them. *Wall Street Journal,* p. A1.

Dale, E. (1935). *The content of motion pictures.* New York: Macmillan.

Dorr, A., Kovaric, P., & Doubleday, C. (1989, Winter). Parent-child coviewing of television. *Journal of Broadcasting and Electronic Media, 33*(1), 35–51.

Footlick, J. K. (1990, Winter–Spring). What happened to the family? *Newsweek* (The 21st Century Family), pp. 14–20.

Gadow, K. D., Kelly, E., & Sprafkin, J. (1987, June). Reality perceptions of television: A comparison of school-labeled learning-disabled and nonhandicapped children. *Journal of Developmental and Behavioral Pediatrics, 8*(3), 149–153.

Gerbner, G., & Signorielli, N. (1990, January). *Violence profile 1967 through 1988–89: Enduring patterns.* Paper from the Cultural Indicators Project, Annenberg School for Communication, Philadelphia, PA.

Goldman, K. (1991, June 10). NBC claims it's the place to reach young. *Wall Street Journal,* p. B4.

Gore, P. (1987). *Raising PG kids in an X-rated society.* Nashville, TN: Abingdon Press.

Greenfield, P. (1984). *Mind and media: The effects of television, video games, and computers.* Cambridge, MA: Harvard University Press.

Greenfield, P., & Beagles-Roos, T. (1988, Spring). Radio vs. television: Their cognitive impact on children of different socioeconomic and ethnic groups. *Journal of Communication, 38*(2), 71–92.

Harman, D. (1989). Keeping up in America. In P. Cook, D. Gomery, & L. Lichty (Eds.), *Media: The Wilson Quarterly.* Washington, DC: Woodrow Wilson Center Press.

Heeter, C. (1988). Watching Saturday morning television. In C. Heeter & B. S. Greenberg (Eds.), *Cableviewing.* Norwood, NJ: Ablex.

Heeter, C., Greenberg, B. S., Baldwin, T. F., Paugh, R., & Srigley, R. Atkin. (1988). Parental influence on viewing style. In C. Heeter & B. S. Greenberg (Eds.), *Cableviewing.* Norwood, NJ: Ablex.

Hirsch, E. D., Jr. (1987). *Cultural literacy: What every American needs to know.* Boston: Houghton Mifflin.

Hymes, D. (1974). *Foundations in sociolinguistics: An ethnographic approach.* Philadelphia: University of Pennsylvania Press.

Illiteracy dogs industrial world. (1992, February 24). *Wall Street Journal,* p. A10.

Inglehart, R. (1990). *Culture shift in advanced industrial society.* Princeton, NJ: Princeton University Press.

Johnstone, J., & Ettema, J. (1982). *Positive images: Breaking stereotypes with children's television.* Beverly Hills, CA: Sage Publications.

Karpatkin, R. (1990, January–February). The executive director's annual report. *CU Letter for Consumers Union Associates*, p. 2.

Kiernan, M. (1990, January 22). *U.S. News & World Report*, pp. 66–70.

Knight-Ridder. Washington Bureau. (1991, June 4). TV ads plug lousy diets, survey says [Review of survey by Center for Science in the Public Interest]. *(Columbia, SC) State*, p. A7.

Kritz, Francesca Lunzer. (1989, June 19). Finally a way you and your TV can talk. *U.S. News & World Report*, p. 70.

Kunkel, D., & Gantz, W. (1992, Summer). Children's television advertising in the multichannel environment. *Journal of Communication, 42*(3), 134–152.

Lefkowitz, M.M., Eron, L.D., Walder, L.O., & Huesmann, L.R. (1977). *Growing up to be violent: A longitudinal study of the development of aggression.* New York: Pergamon.

Lemish, D. (1986). The pampered "Sesame Street" viewer. In T. Lindlof (Ed.), *Natural audiences.* Norwood, NJ: Ablex.

Liberman, D., Chaffee, S., & Roberts, D. (1988, Summer). Computers, mass media and schooling: Functional equivalence in uses of new media. *Social Science Computer Review, 6*(3), 224–242.

Lipman, J. (1989, July 31). Enticing teen moviegoers with 900 phone numbers. *Wall Street Journal*, B1.

Lowery, S. A., & DeFleur, Melvin L. (1988). *Milestones in mass communication research.* 2d ed. New York: Longman.

McLuhan, M., & Powers, B. (1989). *The global village: Transformations in world life and media in the 21st century.* New York: Oxford University Press.

Mead, G. (1934). *Mind, self and society.* Chicago: University of Chicago Press.

Meadowcroft, J., & Reeves, B. (1989, June). Influence of story schema development on children's attention to television. *Communication Research, 16*(3), 352–374.

Medrich, E., Roizen, J., & Buckley, S. (1981). *The serious business of growing up: A study of children's lives outside of school.* Berkeley: University of California Press.

Meyrowitz, J. (1985). *No sense of place: The impact of electronic media on social behavior.* New York: Oxford University Press.

Moyers, B. (1989, November 8). *Consuming images, show #1.* In *The Public Mind with Bill Moyers* [Journal Graphics, Inc., transcript]. New York: Public Affairs Television, Inc., and Alvin H. Perlmutter, Inc.

Mundell, L. (1900, March 21). Minnesota's Center for Research on Children's Literature. *Chronicle of Higher Education*, p. B7.

National Geographic Society. (1988). *Geography: An international Gallup survey 1988: Summary of findings.* Washington, DC: National Geographic Society.

Neuman, S.B. (1988). Displacement effect: Assessing the relation between television viewing and reading performance. *Reading Research Quarterly, 23*(4), 414–440.

O'Brien, C. (1981). The big blue marble story. *Television and Children, 4/5*, 18–22.

Papert, S. (1980). *Mindstorms.* New York: Basic Books.

Pearl, David, Bouthilet, Lorraine, & Lazar, Joyce. (1982). *Television & behavior: 10 years of scientific progress. Implications for the eighties.* Washington, DC: GPO.

Peterson, R., & Thurstone, L. (1933). *Motion pictures and the social attitudes of children.* New York: Macmillan.

Piaget, J., & Inhelder, B. (1969). *The psychology of the child.* New York: Basic Books.

Piatelli-Palmarini, M. (1988). *Language and learning: The debate between Jean Piaget and Noam Chomsky.* Cambridge, MA: Harvard University Press.

Postman, Neil. (1988). Critical thinking in the electronic era. In Trundy Govier (Ed.), *Selected issues in logic and communication.* Belmont, CA: Wadsworth.

Putka, G. (1989, December 26). Schools giving TV warmer reception. *Wall Street Journal,* p. B1.

Putka, G. (1991a, June 20). Annenberg pledges $60 million for use in TV education. *Wall Street Journal,* p. C8.

Putka, G. (1991b, May 15). Whittle develops plan to operate schools for profit. *Wall Street Journal,* p. B1.

Rachlin, J., & Burke, S. (1989, July 31). Why can't they clone Big Bird? *U.S. News & World Report,* pp. 50, 51.

Reilly, P. (1990, February 28). Media firms target captive audiences, taking a page out of Whittle's book. *Wall Street Journal,* p. B1.

Reilly, P. M. (1991, May 6). Newspapers are paging young readers. *Wall Street Journal,* p. B1.

Reiser, R., Williamson, N., & Suzuki, K. (1988, Spring). Using "Sesame Street" to Facilitate children's recognition of letters and numbers. *Education Communication and Technology, 36*(1), 15–21.

Roberts, D., & Bachen, C. (1982). Mass communication effects. In D. Whitney & E. Wartella (Eds.), *Mass communication review yearbook* (pp. 29–78). Newbury Park, CA: Sage Publications.

Rosenthal, A. (1990, October 4). Children's-TV bill troubles White House. *New York Times,* p. C18.

Salomon, G. (1979). *Interaction of media, cognition and learning.* San Francisco: Jossey-Bass.

Salomon, G. (1981). Introducing AIME: The assessment of children's mental involvement with television. In H. Gardner & H. Kelly (Eds.), *Children and the worlds of television.* San Francisco: Jossey-Bass.

Salomon, G. (1983). Television watching and mental effort: A social psychological view. In J. Bryant & D. Anderson (Eds.), *Children's understanding of television.* New York: Academic Press.

Salomon, G., & Leigh, J. (1984). Predispositions about learning from print and television. *Journal of Communication, 34,* 119–135.

Saville-Troike, M. (1982). *The ethnography of communication: An introduction.* Baltimore, MD: University Park Press.

Schramm, W., Lyle, J., & Parker, E. (1961). *Television in the lives of our children.* Palo Alto, CA: Stanford University Press.

Schutte, Nicola S., Malouff, John M., Post-Gorden, Joan C., & Rodasta, Annette L. (1988). Effects of playing videogames on children's aggressive behaviors. *Journal of Applied Social Psychology, 18*(5), 454–460.

Scribner, S., & Cole, M. (1981). *The psychology of literacy.* Cambridge, MA: Harvard University Press.

Shrieves, L. (1991, June 20). Taking control: Parents are becoming guardians of TV time [Reprinted from the *Orlando Sentinel*]. *(Columbia, SC) State,* p. D1.

Singer, J., & Singer, D. (1983). Psychologists look at television: Cognitive, developmental, personality and social policy implications. *American Psychologists, 38,* 826–834.

Slesin, S. (1991, July 11). New parental nightmare: An ecology-smart child. *New York Times*, p. B1.

Sprafkin, J., & Gadow, K. (1988, March). The immediate impact of aggressive cartoons on emotionally disturbed and learning disabled children. *Journal of Genetic Psychology, 149*(1), 35–44.

Tan, A. (1986). Social learning of aggression from television. In J. Bryant & D. Zillman (Eds.), *Perspectives on media effects*. Hillsdale, NJ: Erlbaum.

Tangney, J., & Feshbach, S. (1988, March). Children's television-viewing frequency: Individual differences and demographic correlates. *Personality and Social Psychology Bulletin, 14*(1), 145–158.

Times Mirror Center for People and the Press. (1990a, June 28). *The age of indifference: A study of young Americans and how they view the news*. Washington, DC: Times Mirror Center for People and the Press.

Times Mirror Center for People and the Press. (1990b, July 15). *The American media: Who reads, who watches, who listens, who cares*. Washington, DC: Times Mirror Center for People and the Press.

Turkle, S. (1984). *The second self: Computers and the human spirit*. New York: Simon & Schuster.

U.S. Congress. House. (1989, April 6). *Children's television: Hearing before the Subcommittee on Telecommunications and Finance* [Bill in 101st Cong., 1st sess.]. Washington, DC: 101st Congress.

Ward, S., Wackman, D., & Wartella, E. (1977). *How children learn to buy*. Beverly Hills, CA: Sage Publications.

Wartella, E., & Reeves, B. (1985). Historical trends in research on children and media, 1900 to 1960. *Journal of Communication, 35*, 118–133.

Wartella, E., & Reeves, B. (1987). Communication and children. In C. Berger & S. Chaffee (Eds.), *Handbook of communication science* (pp. 619–651). Beverly Hills, CA: Sage Publications.

Watkins, B. (1988, April). Children's representations of television and real-life stories. *Communication Research, 15*(2), 159–184.

Wilson, B. J. (1991, June). Children's reactions to dreams conveyed in mass media programming. *Communication Research, 18*(3), 283–306.

Wyatt, R. O. (1991). *Free expression and the American public: A survey commemorating the 200th anniversary of the First Amendment*. Murfreesboro, TN: American Society of Newspaper Editors and Middle Tennessee State University.

Zillman, D. (1982). Television viewing and arousal. In D. Pearl, L. Bouthilet, & J. Lazar (Eds.), *Television and behavior: Ten years of scientific progress and implications for the 1980s*. Washington, DC: Government Printing Office.

14

DISABLED AUDIENCES

Alice A. Tait

REDEFINING THEMSELVES

Controversy surrounds the appropriate terms for persons with disabilities. *Gifted, physically challenged,* and *exceptional* are generally considered positive terms. *Handicapped, mentally retarded, learning disabled, crippled,* and *emotionally disturbed* are viewed as negative terms.

Longmore (1987) accused movies, television, and print of frequently presenting images reinforcing prejudice against people with disabilities. He lists three common misconceptions about people with handicaps: They are being punished, they are embittered by their fate, and they resent the nondisabled.

PRINT

In 1976, there appeared to be an increased number of television programs and magazine and newspaper articles covering those with disabilities. Byrd, Byrd, and Allen (1980) categorized 256 programs.

In 1978, Wall cited a 1900–1959 survey of the *Reader's Guide to Periodical Literature* that showed an increase in articles related to mental illness, psychology, psychiatry, and related subjects.

In 1977, Byrd selected ten magazines having the greatest circulation to determine the disabilities covered, including *Reader's Digest, National Geographic, Better Homes and Gardens, McCall's, Ladies' Home Journal, Good Housekeeping, Redbook, Time, Newsweek,* and *Senior Scholastic.* Magazines covered drug abuse more than any other disability, followed by alcoholism, heart disease, and mental illness. The two news magazines were leaders in the frequency of articles covering disability. Of 59 articles listed in the 15 magazines surveyed, a mean of 5.9 articles for each magazine covered disabilities.

Thompson (1980) noted a gradual change in coverage of people with disabilities in the book publishing industry. Although books about the disabled increased, Thompson maintained the message was uniform: To succeed in the able-bodied world, a person had to be a genius.

Biklen (1986) described the narrow focus of newspapers in covering the Baby Jane Doe and Elizabeth Bouvia cases. Baby Jane Doe was an infant born with several disabling conditions, including hydrocephalus and spina bifida. Elizabeth Bouvia had severe cerebral palsy and required assistance in order to live. She asked a hospital to administer pain-killing drugs to help her endure her attempted suicide through starvation. In these and similar stories, Biklen accused newspapers of describing handicapped persons in traditional and debilitating terms, rather than focusing on discrimination, civil rights, and political organizing issues. Newspapers characterized both subjects with despair, pain, sorrow, desperation, and defeat. Reporters failed to cover both stories objectively and comprehensively. Disagreements among doctors as to whether Baby Jane Doe should be treated were unpublished. Newspapers incorrectly interpreted a doctor's prognosis and failed to report services available to both individuals and Bouvia's experience with the unavailability of competent aides. Newspapers have failed also to report on the development of national policies affecting severely handicapped persons.

In 1982, Bogdan et al. accused newspapers of subtly linking disability with violence when covering murders and other violent crimes. The researchers cited the following headline examples: "Crippled Man Charged in Bomb Attack," "Police Arrest Amputee in Slaying of Doctor," and "Suspect Has Low IQ, Two Psychologists Testify."

A five-year analysis of the *Des Moines Register* (Arnold, 1986) revealed only thirty-nine news stories about persons with disabilities or disability issues. The study failed to support agenda setting by the press in this area, during a time when key disability rights legislation was approved.

J. Johnson (1986) offered a list of terms journalists should know when referring to persons with disabilities. Orjasaeter (1986) praised the increase since 1976 in the number of picture books relating to handicapped children. Books are important for handicapped children and for the nondisabled to help them understand the problems and daily life of handicapped people. Especially interesting are picture books by authors or artists who are parents or siblings of handicapped children.

In 1988, M. Johnson applauded the print media for coveraging Gallaudet University's shutdown in Washington, D.C. She credited the reporters for covering the protest as straight news, omitting the common soft, human interest approach. However, she expressed little faith that the press would continue coverage of the national campaign to obtain more civil rights and opportunities for the nation's millions of deaf people. Newspapers also ignored presidential candidates who did not sign pledges to have the debates interpreted by sign-language interpreters. A report by the Commission on Education of the Deaf submitted to the Senate Labor and Human Resources Committee's subcommittee on the handicapped did make the news because of its timing with the Gallaudet protest.

Krossel (1988) reinforced Johnson's observation. The press coverage of Rick

Hansen who, injured in an automobile accident, used a wheelchair to circle the globe and Terry Fox, who attempted to run across the country on his one leg and an artificial limb, failed to transcend the hoopla. Some exceptions included a Canadian columnist who documented how little the federal government spent on medical research; the *Region Leader-Post* described the difficulties a person with impaired mobility would find getting into major buildings in that city and highlighted gaps in government services for disabled persons; and both the *Washington Post* and Toronto's *Globe and Mail* argued Hansen and Jim Dickerson, a blind man attempting to navigate the Atlantic, should abandon their heroic endeavors as their efforts would not benefit the disabled.

M. Johnson (1988) criticized the press for careless language usage. Most irritating was the description of an individual as a "victim" of a particular disability. She noted that even though the latest edition of the *Associated Press Stylebook* forbids the use of the term *wheelchair-bound,* she continued to notice repeated use of the term.

Keller et al. (1990) found that newspapers mention disabilities more often than critics have claimed, but not in a positive context. A content of twelve representative U.S. newspapers from one week in 1987 revealed 696 references (an average 8.3 per day) to persons with disabilities or their family members. Most refernces tended to occur in features, most were negative, and most emphasized the possibility for improvement of the person's condition (reinforcing the stereotype of helplessness and pity).

Yoshida, Wasilewski, and Friedman (1990) found that the traditional topics of budget expenditures, housing, and institutionalization were the most prevalent in five metropolitan newspapers. Keller et al. (1990) found that persons with disabilities were noted in feature stories rather than in hard news stories, and that these articles tended to present the negative impact of disability on people's lives. Clogston (1990) examined sixteen prestige and high circulation newspapers and found that while coverage was not overwhelmingly negative, neither was it positive or progressive.

Clogston (1992) analyzed entries in the *New York Times* Index from 1941 to 1991. Results from Clogston's research indicate a trend in the *New York Times* away from traditional coverage of individuals with disabilities as charity recipients and toward a more progressive, civil rights view of disability in news coverage over the last fifty years.

It shows a large decline in entries portraying disability in a traditional economic sense (particularly the image of people with disabilites as dependent on the generosity of charity organizations). The study also found a steady rise, particularly from 1976 to 1991, in entries showing stories portraying disability from a progressive civil rights perspective. With a few exceptions, story entries covering physical disability from a traditional medical viewpoint remained constant during the period.

The *Detroit Free Press* is one of a growing number of newspapers in North America with a regular column on disability. Jim Neubacker, who has multiple sclerosis and uses a wheelchair, writes the column.

Comics also fail the disability portraying test. Disability, physical deformity, and criminal behavior are reflected in Dick Tracy's rogues as "Ugly Christine," "Mumbles," "Bee Bee Eyes," "Shakey," and "Mrs. Prune Face." Comic characters Batman and Robin are accused of the same disregards.

From 1976 to 1991, print media increased coverage of persons with disabilities. However, increased coverage portrayed those persons successful at dealing with disabilities as geniuses. Moreover, coverage of persons with disabilities tended to lack completeness, comprehensiveness, and broadness. The print media tended to use the soft, human interest approach and negate coverage of national campaigns to obtain more civil rights and opportunities for persons with disabilities. The *New York Times* was an exception to these trends.

FILM

Film is both criticized and praised for portraying persons with disabilities. Horror films have disturbed critics the most because they often portray disabled persons as freaks and associate disabilities with murder, violence, and danger.

Critics have credited war films as primary innovators in changing the depictions of disabled persons. Some recent war films are cited for realistically portraying disabled veterans' feelings, casting disabled persons, discussing sex, showing the relationship between the disabled and society, and describing the rehabilitative process. A few earlier war films failed to address social and economic issues. Other films generalized a variety of disabilities including mental illness, alcoholism, and drug addiction. One author criticized a film for denying the value of the lives of people with disabilities.

In 1932, MGM produced the film *Freaks,* using actual disabled characters from the Barnum and Bailey sideshow attractions. The tendency to associate mental disabilities with murder, violence, and danger is depicted in the several versions of the nineteenth-century tale *Dr. Jekyll and Mr. Hyde* and the twentieth-century version, *The Incredible Hulk. Phantom of the Opera, The Hunchback of Notre Dame* (1923), *Frankenstein* (1931), and *The Bride of Frankenstein* (1935) also featured physical disabilities and violence.

Schwartz (1979) and Quart and Auster (1982) heralded the film *Coming Home* as a pivotal point in the movies, changing the portrayal of the handicapped.

Quart and Auster described post–World War II films as the first attempt to deal with the disabled veteran with some honesty. The 1945 *Pride of the Marines* was described as a film that failed to address social and economic issues. The film was praised for addressing realistically the feelings of anger and rage. *The Best Years of Our Lives,* which actually starred a disabled veteran, followed in 1946. Critics praised the film for not covering the trauma at the onset of the disability and the frustration and pain of rehabilitation. However, in 1950, *The Men* did address these stages.

Coming Home (1978) and *Born on the Fourth of July* (1987) initiated a realistic portrayal of Vietnam veterans. The film discussed a normally avoided issue—sex and the disabled. Because of post–World War II films like *Pride of the Marines, The Best Years of Our Lives,* and *The Men,* audiences received a fuller, more sensitive appreciation of the experiences. The films portrayed injury, the rehabilitation process, and the relationship between the disabled persons and society. The post–Vietnam War film, despite its stereotyped veteran as victim or madman, deepened the disabled image to include sexuality, the tendency of rehabilitation to produce infantilism in the patient, and the intricate, symbiotic relationship that society has with disabled persons as well as their own capacity to use their handicaps to manipulate others.

The film *Whose Life Is It, Anyway?* (Maxson, 1982) portrayed a young sculptor who became a quadriplegic as a result of a car accident and decided that suicide was the only rational choice for a severally disabled man. Maxson criticized the film for openly denying the value of disabled persons' lives.

Harold Michael-Smith, president of the American Association on Mental Retardation, praised the film industry in 1987 for its continued positive portrayal of the disabled. *The Best Years of Our Lives* (1946) was a breakthrough, he said, because it used a disabled person in the leading role. In addition, the film instilled an understanding of the anguish of disabled individuals and barriers created by nondisabled individuals. Smith described *Johnny Belinda* (1948) as perpetuating an old stereotype—deafness equals dumbness; however, he also praised the film for introducing the concept of educability. *The Miracle Worker* (1962) is heralded for emphasizing teachers' roles in helping individuals with severe disabilities. *The Elephant Man* (1980) demonstrated that prestigious advocates make a significant difference in how the world views and often treats the disabled. A radical film, *Mask* (1985) did not avoid confronting the dilemmas individuals with disabilities face. The boy's questioning his normalcy, his mother's possible coverings of his freakish appearance, and his problems with schoolmates were all part of the contributing drama reflected in some earlier film.

In general, Smith praised Hollywood for showing understanding, appreciation, and acceptance of disabled persons. Even though they were primarily made in the interest of box office receipts, these films enlightened people who otherwise might perpetuate negative stereotypes of disabled persons.

Longmore (1985) praised *Mask* for shifting the source of the problem from the disabled individual to society and for showing that disability is not primarily a medical condition but rather a stigmatized social identity. The 1988 film *Mac and Me* (about a twelve-year-old young man with spina bifida and scoliosis) showed that people who use wheelchairs can lead productive, active lives. Coles (1988) praised Frederick Wiseman's four film documentaries describing how the blind, the deaf, or those both blind and deaf managed the nationally known and respected Alabama Institute for the Deaf and Blind.

TELEVISION

A review of television films in 1954 indicated a sharp rise in the number of mental illness–related themes. Television contained proportionately more information relevant to mental illness than any other media, averaging about 2.4 programs per day (Wall, 1978).

In 1968, television aired 149 programs covering disabilities, with NBC airing the most programs (Byrd, McDaniel, & Rhoden, 1980). Paraplegia was the most frequent disability portrayed, followed by mental illness, drug addiction, and emotional disability. Critics lambasted television, as they did film and newspapers, for their portrayal of persons with disabilities.

Unfortunately, the increased coverage was negative. In general, the causes, symptoms, methods of treatment, and social effects portrayed by the media were far removed from what the experts advocated. In particular, the media in their overall presentations emphasized the bizarre symptoms of the mentally ill. In television drama, for example, the afflicted person often entered the scene staring glassy-eyed, with his mouth widely open, mumbling incoherent phrases or laughing uncontrollably (Wall, 1978).

Byrd, Byrd, and Allen confirmed in 1977 that networks aired 256 disability-related programs. Most programs depicted mental illness. Fifty of the 64 programs depicting mental illness were presented by the commercial broadcasting networks. Fifty-one of the 64 programs depicting mental illness were police dramas, movies, drama specials, and situation comedies. The greatest portion of programming depicting mental illness involved dramatization, with minimal effort in educating the viewers. Television continued to portray mentally ill persons as strange and different, unemployed, erratic and unreliable, generally without friends and family, morally and psychologically weak and defective, and violent criminals. Television was singled out as the greatest offender in portraying violent mentally ill characters. These portrayals were more offensive as they inaccurately reflected what mental health professionals communicated about psychiatric patients. Research data showed that mental patients are, in fact, less likely to be involved in criminal or violent acts than are members of the general public (Byrd, 1979).

Results from a 1978 study indicated 256 programs were aired depicting disability, with the largest frequency occurring on public broadcasting. Mental illness was the most frequently aired, followed by alcoholism, emotional disability and the physically handicapped (Byrd, McDaniel, & Rhoden, 1980).

In 1979, Donaldson's study (1981) revealed that of all the characters in the sample 3.2 percent appearing in major roles were depicted as handicapped. Although handicapped characters are seen in major roles on television, this does not adequately represent the estimated 15 to 20 percent of the general population who have handicaps. It should be noted, however, that handicapped characters seldom appear in incidental roles. In the entire sample, in fact, not one handicapped character appeared in a minor role except in juxtaposition with other handicapped persons; none was visible in groups of shoppers, spectators, jurors, customers, or workers. Handicapped people were thus invisible among the thousands of people in the background. Their appearance in positive characterization emphasized the handicap as a condition central to the plot. In their negative roles, they were shown as threats to society, and their handicapping conditions were incidental to the plot.

Trinkaus (1984) studied television game shows to determine the number of contestants who appeared to be disabled. Those displaying an inability to walk or stand and those exhibiting a loss of sight or hearing were judged to be handicapped. Over a six-month period, Trinkaus observed one disabled person.

The Silent Network in its fifth year of operation produced an exercise show, a talk show, a dance program, and teen sexuality discussion tailored to hearing-impaired and deaf people. The Silent Network uses sign language and open captions (Higgins, 1985).

Baltimore agency Smith, Burke and Azzam created and donated an advertisement featuring a nondisabled actor portraying a handicapped person to the Maryland Planning Council on Developmental Disabilities. Organizations representing the disabled disapproved of the advertisement despite the agency's 1986 Clio Award–winning spot called "John," starring a mentally retarded man (Erickson, 1988).

Lipman (1989) says advertisers have increased the casting of actors with disabilities. Nike employed Graig Bloochette, a 1988 Olympic bronze medalist. Levi Strauss was one of the first showing a blue jeans–clad paraplegic. McDonald's featured a deaf teenager and a paraplegic girl. Apple Computer aired a commercial showing disabled people using its computers. IBM, Citicorp, DuPont, and AT&T have featured disabled people in their ads. The increased appearance of people with disabilities in advertisements may perhaps be accounted for by marketers' awareness that about 37 million disabled people live in this country, and their estimated combined spending power is $40 billion.

Viewing Behavior

Among five studies of the television viewing habits of the disabled, two were about mentally retarded (MR) children (one residential and one nonresidential), two reported on institutionalized emotionally disturbed (ED) children, and one compared the viewing habits of ED, learning disabled (LD), and educable mentally retarded (EMR) children with nonhandicapped children. Baran and Meyer (1975) interviewed seventy (forty-five males and twenty-five females) TMR (trainable mentally retarded) children (age: X = fourteen years) from five nonresidential schools about their television viewing habits. Almost three-fourths of the youngsters reported they watched "a lot of TV." The most popular viewing times were after school, on Saturday, and at night. About half of all favorite programs mentioned contained frequent instances of aggressive behavior. For example, the most popular series included "Gunsmoke," "The Three Stooges," and "Kung Fu." Clear sex differences were found in program favorites, with the violent programs being named by 70 percent of the males but by only 37 percent of the females. Parallel findings were reported for favorite character choices. The extent to which the youngsters identified with their favorite television characters was assessed with a conflict situation method in which each child was asked what he or she would do, what his or her favorite television character would do, what his or her parents would want each to do, what his or her best friend would do, and what the right thing is to do when faced with each of four potentially aggression-provoking situations (e.g., "Suppose you were playing with your favorite toy, and a person you didn't like came up and took it away."). The study results indicated that for both males and females the strongest relationships existed between the child's report of what he or she would do and what the favorite TV character would do and what the best friend would do. The identification with TV characters and best friends also was found with nonretarded first-, second-, and third-grade children given the same set of conflict situations (Meyer, 1973); however, for the nonretarded children, the relationship between self and what the parents would want done and what is right were both statistically significant, while neither was significant for the TMR children. This suggests that television may influence the social behavior of TMR children to a greater degree than their nonretarded peers because the alternative socializing forces seem to be less effective for the former group.

Ahrens (1977) examined the television viewing habits of 250 six- to eighteen-year-old children from a residential facility in New Zealand, most of whom were moderately or severely mentally retarded. Staff and parents reported most watched television from one to two hours daily, but about half the children under twelve watched from two to three hours daily. The most popular viewing times were between 5:30 P.M. and 7:30 P.M. About half the children were reported to talk about or act out some of the programs. Based on the children's reports, their favorite programs were the "Flintstones" and "Sing" (a locally produced song and dance show). It is interesting to note that a reliability check of the accuracy of caregivers' responses indicated that they were not accurate reporters of child program preferences. The adults thought that the children's favorite series was "Sesame Street."

Rubinstein et al. (1977) surveyed the television viewing habits of a sample of patients in a residential facility for ED children on Long Island, New York. The youngsters (age: X = twelve years) included forty-eight boys and twelve girls. The televisions on the wards were reported to be operating an average of 9.5 hours daily (3.7 hours during the day and 5.8 hours at night), with the typical child actually watching about 1 hour during the day and 2.6 hours in the evening. The five most frequently selected program types included action/adventure shows (especially those with superheroes), cartoons, situation comedies, crime dramas, and monster movies. Ninety-six percent of the ward staff reported having observed behaviors engaged in by patients that seemed related to what they had viewed. The most frequently mentioned types of TV-linked imitation included aggressive acts, superhero behaviors, or dance steps.

Another survey (Donahue, 1978) of six- to ten-year-old institutionalized ED children (forty-seven boys and six girls) revealed even more television use than was reported by Rubinstein et al. (1977). Based on questions about how many hours they watched television, an average of 7.7 hours on weekdays and 4.2 on Saturday mornings was reported. Of all the favorite programs mentioned, 73 percent were violent. The two most popular program types were action/adventure and cartoon shows, and the two most frequently mentioned favorite characters were Bugs Bunny and Steve Austin ("Six Million Dollar Man"). Sixty-nine percent of their favorite characters engaged in aggressive behavior either periodically or regularly. Donahue also administered the confrontive situation measure described earlier in the Baran and Meyer (1975) study. The children were asked to describe how they, their favorite television character, parents, best friend, and favorite adult at the institution would handle each of four conflict situations. These finding suggest that the ED children identify with aggressive television characters, who in turn may serve as role models.

Sprafkin and Gadow (1982) conducted an interview study to compare the television viewing habits of ED, LD, and EMR children with those of nonhandicapped peers. Tests revealed that the special education group watched significantly more television than each of the control groups, which did not significantly differ from one another. Descriptively, the ED group watched the most, followed by the LD group and then the EMR group. The special education group watched both situation comedies and soap operas significantly more than did the control group. Special education children also watched more crime and superhero programs and were more likely to report they frequently pretended to be their favorite television character.

Engstrom and Stricklin (1992) interviewed deaf Nebraskans to determine their mass media usage. Those interviewed were found to be active audience members who understood their communication needs and how to use mass media to meet those needs. Unfortunately, the deaf respondents also indicated that the mass media, especially local media, were not meeting their needs. On topics that they said were important to them, most reported using complex communication links that may or may not be satisfying. They said these links included both mass media and interpersonal communication. The respondents reported bundling their information by reading local newspapers, watching television and television news, and often, as part of the process, calling others using the TDD (Telecommunication Device for the Deaf), or by using telephone relay services for the deaf, or driving to another deaf person's home to pass along news and information gleaned from the media.

Respondents in both groups indicated that the local mass media were not taking care of their news information needs. They said that was one of the main reasons why deaf Nebraskans must depend so heavily upon newspapers.

One of the group respondents expressed "appreciation" for having newspapers and television that offered local news, while also enjoying them for their own purposes. More news and information about the deaf community would be appreciated by this group.

Those in the "improvement-orienated" group voiced strong opinions that deaf people should be interviewed and quoted in news stories about the deaf, interpreters should be present for such interviews, more local news of the deaf community should be published and broadcast, and employment opportunities for deaf people should be offered in both print and television news operations.

Children with disabilities were heavy consumers of television, liked aggressive programs, favored aggressive characters, imitated aggressive characters, comprehended television's visual aspect the most, and perceived television content as real.

Comprehension of Television Content

A study by Grieve and Williamson (1977) investigated the differences between the nondisabled and MR children's comprehension of auditory or visual content. They found that for both groups of children accuracy was greatest on the visual items, next best on the auditory-visual items, and least on the auditory items. The preschoolers performed significantly better than the MR children on the auditory and auditory-visual items, but the groups performed comparably on the visual items. These findings suggest that handicapped children (in this case, MR) comprehend visual television content better than auditory content.

Donahue and Donahue (1977) compared the responses of eleven- to sixteen-year-old ED and gifted children to questions about the reality of television portrayals. There was no significant difference found for the role stereotype items. Unfortunately, this study provided meager details about the characteristics and size of the two groups and failed to include a more typical comparison group; however, the findings seem to suggest that handicapped children perceive television content as more real than their nonhandicapped peers do.

Sprafkin, Gadow, and Grayson (1984) developed the Perception of Reality on Television (PORT) test to measure children's perceptions of television reality. They compared the performance of ED and nondisabled children. The ED children performed comparably to their nonhandicapped peers on the filler items; the students in regular classes outperformed the ED group on all of the items that pertained to reality of TV violence, discriminating the actor from the role played, and cartoon animation. These results strongly suggest that ED children have many more misconceptions than nonhandicapped children about important reality/fantasy aspects of television.

EFFECTS

Walters and Willows (1968) conducted a study in which institutionalized ED and nondisturbed children's aggressive behavior was compared following their exposure to a four-minute aggressive or nonaggressive videotape model. Exposure to the aggressive tape produced more aggressive behavior toward the toys shown in the videotape by both the disturbed and nondisturbed children. The amount of aggression did not differ between the ED and nondisturbed groups.

Mentally retarded children's reactions to an aggressive model was examined by Fechter (1971). Subjects (age: $X =$ eleven years; IQ [intelligence quotient]: $X = 36$) were exposed to a five-minute videotape of a twelve-year-old nonretarded female playing either in an aggressive or friendly manner with an inflatable Donald Duck doll. Based on observations of the children on the ward after the television presentation, Fechter found a significant media effect, with aggressive responses increasing after viewing the aggressive tape and decreasing following the friendly tape.

Talkington and Altman (1973) compared the subsequent playroom behavior of 144 MR males (age: $X =$ fourteen years; IQ: $X = 49$) after exposing them either to (1) a three-minute silent 16 mm film of a model hitting, kicking, and throwing a Bobo doll; (2) an equivalent film of the same model kissing, cuddling, and petting the Bobo doll; or (3) no film. In the three-minute observation period following the film, the subjects who viewed the aggressive model exhibited significantly more aggressive behaviors and significantly less affectionate behaviors toward a Bobo doll than those who viewed either no film or the affectionate film model. The group that watched the affectionate model did not respond less aggressively or more affectionately than the no-film group. Hence, MR individuals are not likely to equally imitate aggressive and affectionate behaviors. Similarly, with normal children it is far easier to demonstrate media-induced aggression than prosocial or caring behaviors.

Hartmann (1969) conducted a laboratory study that examined reactions to filmed aggression in juvenile delinquents (age: median = 15.5 years). Subjects (N = seventy-two) were shown one of three, two-minute 16 mm films, each of which started with a one-minute scene of two boys shooting baskets. For the remaining minute, the subjects in the control film condition saw the two boys play an active but cooperative basketball game, whereas those in the other two conditions watched the boys engaged in a violent fistfight. The latter film focused on the victim's pain as his opponent repeatedly hit and kicked him, and the camera highlighted the aggressor's behaviors. Half the subjects in each film group were put in an anger-producing situation before the film (an experimenter's confederate criticized them). The postviewing measures of aggression were the intensity and duration of electric shocks that the subjects administered to the experimenter's confederate. Both aggressive films produced more punitive behavior than the control film. The adolescents who were provoked before viewing were more punitive than those who were not, and within this group, those who had seen the film featuring aggression were the most punitive. Of the unprovoked subjects, those who were exposed to the instrumental aggression film behaved most punitively. The most aggressive subjects were those who committed the greatest number of criminal offenses, were criticized by the confederate, and watched the film of a victim's responses to pain.

In a series of three ambitious field experiments, Parke et al. (1977) examined the effects of full-length, violent commercial films on the aggressive behaviors of male juvenile delinquents residing in minimum security institutions in the United States and Belgium. In all three studies, media-induced aggression was demonstrated in naturalistic (i.e., not contrived) situations. The first study, which was conducted in the United States, involved thirty adolescents in each of two living unit cottages. For five consecutive evenings, subjects saw an aggressive or neutral film. The results indicated that the adolescents who saw the aggressive films behaved more aggressively on measures of general aggression (defined as the sum of physical threat, physical attack, verbal aggression, noninterpersonal physical and verbal aggression, and physical and verbal self-aggression) and physical aggression (defined as the sum of physical attack, noninterpersonal physical aggression, and physical self-aggression) than those who saw the neutral films. Prior aggression levels did not influence the magnitude of the media effect. Furthermore, the level of aggressive behavior remained stable over the experimental period rather than increasing with repeated exposures to media aggression.

The second study was conducted in the same institution with 120 adolescents who had not previously participated. The two studies were similar except the latter included neutral films that were better equated to interest level, and two additional conditions were added. To determine the effect of repeated exposures, an aggressive and a neutral film group were added, which viewed only one film (either aggressive or neutral). For the single-film exposure conditions, adolescents initially high in aggression became more physically aggressive after exposure to the aggressive film than they did to the neutral film. A similar pattern was found for the repeated exposure groups. Contrary to expectation, the aggression became more intense after exposure to the aggressive film than to the neutral film. A similar pattern was found for the repeated exposure groups. Contrary to expectation, the aggression effects were not greater for the multiple, compared with the single, exposure to film aggression group; in fact, the reverse was true for general and physical aggression.

Their third study was conducted in Belgium and followed essentially the same procedure as their first investigation. As with their previous research, the results showed that the adolescents exposed to the aggressive films became more physically aggressive relative to those who viewed the neutral films. However, unlike the first study, the adolescents who were rated as highly aggressive showed a greater increase in general and verbal aggression after exposure to the aggressive film (than to the neutral film) compared with those who were initially rated as less aggressive. An additional feature of the Belgian study was that it included an assessment of group membership characteristics: The adolescents ranked each other based on dominance and popularity. It was found that the most dominant, popular, and aggressive adolescents were the most reactive to media aggression. The least popular youths were also affected to a large degree.

DISABILITY AND TELETHONS

In 1977, Lattin accused telethons of not revealing the whole story. Telethons fail to talk about the laws that provide for architectural and transportation accessibility, that make education available to all children; they do not discuss employment opportunities, affirmative action, or the capabilities and initiative of handicapped people themselves. They present only a horror story of a "hopeless" life.

Although Lattin criticizes telethons for their disabled portrayals, she lauded them for fostering unity and bringing society together to assist its less fortunate members, something she thinks society does not do often enough.

Lattin (1979) both praised and criticized United Cerebral Palsy (UCP) but reflected her constituents' feelings that telethons can be positive if they follow certain guidelines: using both adults and children in demonstrations of programs and services, accurately reflect the degrees of disabilities and variety of living situations, inform nondisabled talent about appropriate terminology, avoid references encouraging viewers to be thankful for their healthy children, avoid allowing the disabled to attempt to prove their ability to perform activities of the nondisabled, and emphasize UCP's advocacy roles for the disabled.

Sheed (1980) was also negative toward the disabled media events. He suggested the media show the disabled in buildings, inaccessible to them because of swinging doors and other structures that have not been redesigned to accommodate them.

British telethons are more suitable; their images usually are more positive and optimistic. The British disability movement dislikes the twentieth-century version of the beggar in the streets (Karpf, 1988). British Central Television examined the material and social obstacles forced upon people with disabilities who were trying to live independent lives.

USING MEDIA TO CHANGE ATTITUDES TOWARD THE DISABLED

Guldager (1973) assessed the impact of viewing spot television announcements on 390 college students to determine their attitudes toward deaf-blind children. Subjects were assigned to one of three groups in which they viewed a television program inserted with (1) three commercials containing a discussion of deaf-blind children, (2) three commercials showing deaf-blind children, or (3) no commercials (control condition). The results indicated that the students who watched the "discussion" commercials reported a significantly higher positive attitude toward deaf-blind children than subjects in the other two conditions. Analysis of the interactions of 30 students from the control group and 45 students from the combined experimental groups also showed a greater positive attitude toward deaf-blind children in the latter. The relative effectiveness of the two experimental conditions remained unclear, however, because a direct comparison of the interactions of subjects from these two groups was not conducted.

Sadlick and Penta (1975) found attitudes of senior nursing students toward quadriplegics as social and working persons were significantly altered in a positive direction through viewing and discussing a seventeen-minute videotape of a successfully rehabilitated quadriplegic. The significant change persisted (though diminished) over a ten-week period in which the students worked with quadriplegics in a rehabilitation setting. Attitudes toward other nurses working with quadriplegics were not significantly altered by this videotape. Attitudes toward themselves working with quadriplegics were significantly altered following the videotape, but the effect did not persist over time.

Donaldson (1976) examined the effects of different modes of presenting a panel discussion about disability on attitudes toward the disabled. The six-member panel, comprising young adults with visible disabilities (quadriplegia, blindness, cerebral palsy), presented a fifty-minute discussion that centered on the idea that disabled and nondisabled individuals share many common feelings, values, and goals. College students (N = ninety-six) were randomly assigned to either the live (L), video (V), audio (A), or control (C) group. All subjects in the three experimental groups viewed and/or listened to the same discussion. The live presentation was significantly more effective than the other modes in generating favorable attitudes. Video was more effective than the control groups, but differences among A, C, V, and A were nonsignificant. Donaldson concluded that although the live presentation was more effective, there are many practical disadvantages (e.g., management, cost) associated with this approach.

Ardi (1977) evaluated the effects of viewing six "Sesame Street" "Play to Grow" segments on forty-five second-graders. The children viewed the tapes individually and were then given a structured interview. The data revealed that although the children were aware of differences between the MR and normal children, negative attitudes toward the latter did not appear. However, the absence of a control group leaves the impact of the "Play to Grow" series unknown. Baran (1977, 1979) attempted to alter parents' attitudes toward their MR children using four, half-hour educational television (ETV) dramas portraying MR people in everyday situations.

There was a significant increase in favorable attitudes on four of the eighteen "Reactions and Concerns of Parents" items from the Thurston (1959) "sentence completion form" for parents who viewed the programs compared with those who did not. On three of seventeen items measuring parents' ratings of their own children's capabilities, parents who viewed the program rated their children significantly higher than parents who did not view the television shows.

Schanie and Sundel (1978) evaluated the effectiveness of twenty-one public service announcements broadcast over radio and/or television during a sixty-week period. The results indicated that the television announcements had a significant positive impact on adult telephone call activity. No significant effect on adult call activity was observed for radio announcements presented alone or in combination with television spots. Youth call activity was not affected by either mode. Survey data revealed a significant increase in the community's awareness of mental health resources, and a positive change in attitudes toward the cognitive structuring of problem situations. Attitudes concerning the appropriate behavior during a problem situation were not affected. Schanie and Sundel concluded that further research was needed to determine how to reach youths more effectively. They also suggested that media messages should be pretested to prevent an inadvertent increase in negative attitudes.

Potter (1978) found the informal use of television programs portraying the complete experience of the disabled encouraged her sixth-graders to ask questions and develop appreciation, acceptance, and understanding of the disabled life-style. She cited such television programs as "I Can Do It," "Wilma" (a true story about Wilma Rudolph, an Olympic star who had polio), and "The Waltons."

"Khan Du!" is an instructional television series that attempts to (1) "be realistic in the portrayal of disabled children and adults, and in their relationships with others"; (2) "show the similarities between disabled and non-disabled persons, especially with regard to abilities and career"; and (3) "use events modeled to real experiences, plus interaction with adult role models to build self-esteem of disabled youngsters'' (''Khan Du!,'' 1979, p. 3). The effects of viewing this series were evaluated on 1,080 children in grades three through six, 87 of whom were handicapped. None of the latter children were MR; however, the specific handicaps of the children were not identified or analyzed separately. The children were randomly assigned to the experimental (five ''Khan Du!'' programs) condition. Data analysis revealed that both handicapped and nonhandicapped children experienced significant gains in reported attitude toward handicapped people following the viewing of ''Khan Du!'' In addition, the nonhandicapped children showed a significant increase in their knowledge of handicapped people's abilities. (The handicapped children scored high in this area on initial testing.) The one area in which there were no significant increases for handicapped or nonhandicapped children was perception of one's own abilities. Overall, ''Khan Du!'' appears to be most successful in improving attitudes toward the handicapped.

Storey (1979) investigated the effects of viewing six ''Feeling Free'' programs followed by teacher-led discussion on children from twelve mainstreamed classrooms (age: X=9.5 years). ''Feeling Free'' is an ETV series developed as a means of facilitating mainstreaming. Pre- and posttest scores on the Children's Attitudes toward Handicapped People test revealed that only children who viewed the programs and participated in the discussions demonstrated a significant increase in positive attitudes toward handicapped people.

In 1979, Monson and Shurtleff discovered that the media can influence children's attitudes toward people with physical handicaps, particularly when cooperating teachers provide good models and encourage positive attitudes.

Gottlieb (1980) used a two-and-one-fourth-minute investigator-made videotape of an MR boy participating in various activities to stimulate discussion of mental retardation. The study resulted in one significant effect: The children with negative attitudes about MR children reported greater attitude change in the three groups that discussed the treatment videotape than subjects in the control group did. The videotape discussion appeared to be equally effective regardless of initial attitude toward MR (positive or neutral).

In 1980, Westervelt and McKinney studied fourth-grade students to evaluate the effects of a brief film designed to point out how the aspirations and interests of a handicapped child are similar to those of his or her nonhandicapped classmates. It appears the film alone may be useful to show to children immediately before they have a physically handicapped child join their class. However, the film alone does not appear to be sufficient to handle all questions that the nonhandicapped child might have about a handicapped peer, and its effect does not appear to be permanent. Used in conjunction with other experiences, such as listening to handicapped speakers and participating in discussion sessions, the film might help prompt a more receptive and understanding classroom environment for the physically handicapped child.

In 1984, Elliott and Byrd (1984a) conducted a study to investigate the differential effects on attitudes of a nonstereotypical television portrayal of blindness and a film designed specifically to inform viewers about blindness. This study differed from previous ones in that an episode of a popular television program was utilized as one of the treatments. Although the Sadlick and Penta (1975) study referred to the use of television, a videotaped interview with a successfully rehabilitated person who had a spinal cord injury was employed as a treatment, and not an episode from an actual television program. Active discussion after viewing the television episode was incorporated as a part of the treatment—a variable that distinguishes this study from a previous experiment.

Results revealed that both experimental groups experienced positive movement on parallel forms of the ATDP (Attitudes Toward Disabled Persons) Scale. These findings support the effectiveness of the film *What Do You Do When You Meet a Blind Person?* and imply that a potential exists for the mass media to foster more favorable predispositions toward disability.

While television can portray negative stereotypes of persons with disabilities, it can also help reverse stereotypes as indicated by the theories discussed earlier in the chapter. Using television in a combination with discussions and presentation can change attitudes toward persons with disabilities.

DISCUSSION

A review of the research on persons with disabilities and the mass media for the past twenty years supports the following: (1) All media increased their coverage of persons with disabilities: (2) all media tended to negatively portray persons with disabilities: (3) all media showed some improvement in their portrayal of persons with disabilities, no matter how minuscule; (4) all media under certain circumstances can be used to change attitudes toward persons with disabilities; and (5) children with disabilities are heavy television viewers and are influenced by what they see on television.

What do the above observations concerning the mass media and persons with disabilities imply? The potential impact of these observations can only be understood in light of mass media theory.

Traditionally negatively portrayed, persons with disabilities received low-status conferral and were therefore potentially irrelevant or insignificant in the larger society. According to the social comparison theory, persons are likely to compare themselves with persons appearing in the media. Thus, comparisons made by persons with disabilities could result in dissociation from the society that portrayed them negatively.

The meaning theory, which suggests the media play a role in the development of meaning, is significant in analyzing the meaning of phrases descriptive of persons with disabilities. *Disabilities* could be a negative or positive word, depending on how persons with disabilities were presented in the media.

Cultivation analysis suggests that television is representative of the real world. If the media present persons with disabilities negatively, society will view them negatively; conversely, if the media expand the positive portrayal trend, perhaps society may be positively influenced.

The agenda-setting theory suggests that the media determine significant issues for society. Media tended to narrowly cover news related to persons with disabilities. The media focused on persons with disabilities as victims, geniuses, or superheroes. Therefore, because of the media's agenda-setting function, society may view persons with disabilities as victims, geniuses, or superheros. The media failed to introduce society to the full range of issues confronted by persons with disabilities such as civil rights and social and political problems.

BIBLIOGRAPHY

Ahrens, M. G. (1977). Television viewing habits of mentally retarded children. *Australian Journal of Mental Retardation, 4,* 1–3.

Altman, B. M. (1981). Studies of attitudes toward the handicapped: The need for a new direction. *Social Problems, 28,* 321–337.

Ardi, D. B. (1977, April). *New avenues of teaching resources: Sesame Street programs for the mentally retarded child.* Paper presented at the annual meeting of the Council for Exceptional Children, Atlanta, GA (ERIC Document Reproduction Service No. ED 139 197).

Arnold, Richard. (1986). *An examination of The Des Moines Register's coverage of issues affecting persons with physical disabilities.* Unpublished Master's thesis, Iowa State University.

Baran, S. J. (1977). Television programs as socializing agents for mentally retarded children. *Audio Visual Communication Review, 25,* 281–289.

Baran, S. J. (1979). Television programs about retarded children and parental attitudes towards their own retarded children. *Mental Retardation, 17,* 193–194.

Baran, S. J., & Meyer, T. P. (1975). Retarded children's perceptions of favorite television characters as behavioral models. *Mental Retardation, 13*(4), 28–31.

Barth, R. (1984). Electronic mail and rehabilitation. *Journal of Rehabilitation, 50,* 59–61.

Biklen, D. (1986). Framed: Journalism's treatment of disability. *Social Policy,* 45–51.

Bikson, T. H., Bikson, T. K., & Genensky, S. (1982). Television-mediated education for the visually impaired: A longitudinal investigation. *International Journal of Rehabilitation Research, 5*(2), 244–245.

Block, M. H., & Okrand, M. (1983). Real-time closed-captioned television as an educational tool. *American Annals of the Deaf, 128,* 636–641.

Bogdan, R., Biklen, D., Shapiro, A., & Spelkoman, D. (1982). The disabled: Media's monster. *Social Policy, 13,* 32–35.

Byrd, E. K. (1979). Television's portrayal of disability. *Disabled USA,* 3:1:5.

Byrd, E. K., Byrd, P. D., & Allen, C. (1977). Television programming and disability. *Journal of Applied Rehabilitation Counseling, 8*(1), 28–32.

Byrd, E. K., McDaniel, R. S., & Rhoden, R. B. (1980). Television programming and disability: A ten year span. *International Journal of Rehabilitation Research, 3*(3), 321–326.

Byrd, E. K., & Pipes, R. B. (1981). Feature films and disability. *Journal of Rehabilitation, 47,* 51–53.

Canon, G. (1980). Television captioning at the Clarke School for the Deaf. *American Annals of the Deaf, 125,* 643–654.

Carpenter, R. L. (1979). Closed circuit interactive television and in-service training. *Exceptional Children, 45,* 289–290.

Clogston, J. S. (1990). *Disability coverage in 16 newspapers.* Louisville, KY: The Avacado Press.

Clogston, J. S. (1992). Fifty years of disability coverage in the *New York Times. News Computing Journal: A Quarterly Journal on Microcomputer Use in Journalism and Mass Communication,* 8(2).

Cohen, S., & Koehler, N. (1975). *Fostering positive attitudes toward the handicapped: A selected bibliography of multi-media materials* (ERIC Document Reproduction Service No. *ED 140515*). Washington DC: U.S. Department of Health, Education and Welfare, Educational Resources Information Center, National Institute of Education.

Coles, Robert. (1988, August). Senses and sensibility: Frederick Wiseman films the deaf and the blind. *New Republic,* pp. 58–60.

Cornelius, D., & Daniels, S. M. (1977). Prize-winning film: Handle with care. *Rehabilitation WORLD, 3,* 24.

Cronin, B. J. (1980). Closed-caption television: Today and tomorrow. *American Annals of the Deaf, 125,* 726–728.

Davis, D. K., & Baran, S. J. (1981). *Mass communication and everyday life: A perspective on theory and effects.* Belmont, CA: Wadsworth.

DeFleur, M. L., & Ball-Rokeach, S. (1982). *Theories of mass communication* (4th ed.). New York: Longman.

DeFleur, M. L., & Dennis, E. E. (1981). *Understanding mass communication.* Boston: Houghton Mifflin.

Dillon, C., Byrd, E. K., & Byrd, P. D. (1980). Television and disability. *Journal of Rehabilitation, 46,* 67–69.

Donahue, T. R. (1978). Television's impact on emotionally disturbed children's value systems. *Child Study Journal, 8,* 187–201.

Donahue, W. A., & Donahue, T. R. (1977). Black, white, and white gifted, and emotionally disturbed children's perceptions of the reality in television programming. *Human Relations, 30,* 609–621.

Donaldson, J. (1976). Channel variations and effects on attitudes toward disabled persons. *Audio-Visual Communication Review, 24* 135–143.

Donaldson, J. (1981). The visibility and image of handicapped people on television. *Exceptional Children, 47,* 413–416.

Downing, O. J., & Tully, J. E. (1979). Telecad—a television communication aid for the disabled. *Medical & Biological Engineering & Computing, 17,* 476–480.

Elliott, T. R., & Byrd, E. K. (1982). Media and disability. *Rehabilitation Literature, 43,* 348–355.

Elliott, Timothy R., & Byrd, E. Keith. (1984a). Attitude change toward disability through television: Portrayal with male college students. *International Journal of Rehabilitation Research, 7,* 320–322.

Elliott, T. R., & Byrd, E. K. (1984b). Video depictions of blindness and attitudes toward disability. *Journal of Rehabilitation, 50,* 49–52.

Elliott, T. R., Byrd, E. Keith, & Byrd, P. D. (1983). Examination of disability as depicted on prime-time television programming. *Journal of Rehabilitation, 49,* 39–42.

Engstrom, Carla R., & Stricklin, Michael. (1992). Disabled persons and mass media usage: Deaf Nebraskans offer their viewpoints. *News Computing Journal: A Quarterly Journal on Microcomputer Use in Journalism and Mass Communication*, 8(2).

Erickson, Julie Liesse. (1988, April). Disabling move; spots fail to use handicapped actor. *Advertising Age*, p. 36.

Fechter, J. V., Jr. (1971). Modeling and environment generalization by mentally retarded subjects of televised aggressive or friendly behavior. *American Journal of Mental Deficiency, 76*, 266–267.

Gartner, A. (1982). Images of the disabled/disabling images. *Social Policy, 13*, 14–15.

Gerbner, G., & Gross, L. (1976). Living with television, the violent profile. *Journal of Communication, 26*, 173–199.

Gorn, G. J., Goldberg, M. E., & Kanungo, R. N. (1976). The role of educational television in changing the intergroup attitudes of children. *Child Development, 47*, 277–280.

Gourse, L. (1989, January). The amazing Andertons. *McCall's*, pp. 92–99.

Gottlieb, J. (1980). Improving attitudes toward retarded children by using group discussion. *Exceptional Children, 47*, 106–111.

Grieve, R., & Williamson, K. (1977). Aspects of auditory and visual attention to narrative material in normal and mentally handicapped children. *Journal of Child Psychology and Psychiatry, 18*, 251–262.

Gritten, David. (1981, December). Paralyzed by a falling tree, Suzy Gilstrap turned to acting and her career heads skyward. *People Weekly*, pp. 169–172.

Guldager, L. (1973). *The impact of spot television announcements on attitudes towards deaf blind children.* Doctoral dissertation, Boston College.

Haefner, J. E. (1976). Can TV advertising influence employers to hire or train disadvantaged persons? *Journalism Quarterly, 53*, 211–215.

Hartmann, D. P. (1969). Influence of symbolically modeled instrumental aggression and pain cues on aggressive behavior. *Journal of Personality and Social Psychology, 11*, 280–288.

Higgins, Kevin. (1985, March). Silent network reaches untapped market segment. *Marketing News*, pp. 12–14.

Jeffers, Dennis, Ostman, Ronald E., & Skelton, William R. (1979a, August). *An evaluation of the communications climate and performance of communication roles and functions in a mental hospital.* Paper presented to the Magazine Division, Association for Education in Journalism and Mass Communication annual convention, Houston, TX.

Jeffers, Dennis, Ostman, Ronald E., & Skelton, William R. (1979b, May). *The determination of TV viewing patterns in a mental hospital and comment on therapeutic applications.* Paper presented at the International Communications Association annual meeting, Philadelphia, PA.

Jeffers, Dennis, Ostman, Ronald E., & Skelton, William R. (1979c, May). *The importance and perceived reality of TV for normal and deviant adults.* Paper presented at the International Communications Association annual meeting, Philadelphia, PA.

Jensema, C., & Fitzgerald, M. (1981). Background and initial audience characteristics of the closed caption television system. *American Annals of the Deaf, 126*, 32–36.

Johnson, E. W. (1982). Hearing prosthesis and communication aids for the elderly. *Medical Instrumentation, 16,* 93–94.

Johnson, Jim. (1986, February). The press should show more sensitivity to disabled people. *Editor & Publisher,* p. 64.

Johnson, Mary. (1988). The Gallaudet difference. *Columbia Journalism Review, 27,* 21.

Karpf, A. (1988, May). Give us a break, not a begging bowl; T.V. charity. *New Statesmen,* p. 13.

Keller, Clayton E., Hallahan, Daniel P., McShane, Edward A., Crowley, Paula, & Blandford, Barbara J. (1990). The coverage of persons with disabilities in American newspapers. *Journal of Special Education, 24,* 271–282.

KHAN DU! II. (1979). Final Project Performance Report for Grant NO. G007804734 from the Office of Career Education. Austin, TX: KLRN/KLRV-TV (ERIC Document Reproduction Service No. ED 203 082).

Krossel, Martin. (1988). Handicapped heroes and the knee-jerk press. *Columbia Journalism Review, 27,* 46–47.

Kurtz, P. David. (1982). Using mass media and group instruction for preventive mental health in rural communities. *Social Work Research and Abstracts, 18,* 41–48.

Lattin, D. (1977). Telethons—a remnant of America's past. *Disabled USA, 1,* 18–19.

Lattin, D. (1979). United Cerebral Palsy: Communicating a better image. *Disabled USA, 2,* 4–5.

Lattin, D. (1980). The elephant man. *Disabled USA, 3,* 2–5.

Lipman, Joanne. (1989, September 7). Ads featuring disabled people become a little more common. *Wall Street Journal,* p. 6.

Longmore, P. K. (1987, April). Distorted view of disabled. *USA Today,* pp. 6–7.

Longmore, Paul K. (1985, May 5). Mask: A revealing portrayal of disabled. *Los Angeles Times Sunday Calendar,* pp. 22–23.

Mac and Me's Jade Calegory, 12, has spina bifida, but please don't get the idea he's a victim. (1988, September). *People Weekly,* p. 72.

Maxson, Gloria. (1982, October 20). Whose life is it, anyway? Ours, that's whose! *Christian Century,* pp. 1038–1040.

McLoughlin, J. A., & Trammell, N. (1979). Media and the handicapped: Getting the image right. *Pointer, 23,* 60–65.

Meyer, T. P. (1973). Children's perceptions of their favorite TV characters as behavioral models. *Education Broadcasting Review, 7,* 25–33.

Michal-Smith, H. (1987). Presidential address 1987: Hollywood's portrayal of disability. *Mental Retardation, 25,* 259–266.

Monson, D., & Shurtleff, C. (1979). Altering attitudes toward the physically handicapped through print and non-print media. *Language Arts, 56,* 163–170.

Murphy-Berman, V., & Jorgensen, J. (1980). Evaluation of a multi-level linguistic approach to captioning television for hearing-impaired children. *American Annals of the Deaf, 125,* 1072–1081.

Orjasaeter, Tordis. (1986, May–June). Disabled characters in search of an author. *UNESCO Courier,* p. 43.

Parish, Thomas S., Dyck, Norma, & Kappes, Bruno M. (1979). Stereotypes concerning normal and handicapped children. *Journal of Psychology, 102,* 63–70.

Parke, R. D., Berkowitz, L., Leyens, J. P., West, S. G., & Sebastian, R. J. (1977). Some effects of violent and nonviolent movies on the behavior of juvenile delinquents.

In L. Berkowitz (Ed.), *Advances in experimental social psychology* (vol. 10, pp. 136–139). New York: Academic Press.

Pearson, D. E. (1986). Transmitting deaf sign language over the telecommunications network. *British Journal of Audiology, 20,* 299–305.

Potter, Rosemary Lee. (1978). Understanding exceptionality through TV. *Teacher, 96,* 42.

Popovich, Mark, Willis, S. Curt, & Bevens, Fred. (1988, fall). Editing accuracy and speed by handicapped students, nonjournalism and journalism majors. *Newspaper Research Journal, 10*(1), 53.

Quart, L., & Auster, A. (1982). The wounded vet in postwar film. *Social Policy, 13,* 24–31.

Romano, S. (1987). Barrier free in film: Getting the message across. *Journal of Rehabilitation, 53,* 5–7.

Rubinstein, E. A., Fracchia, J. F., Kochnower, J. M., & Sprafkin, J. N. (1977). *Television viewing behaviors of mental patients: A survey of psychiatric centers in New York.* New York: Brookdale International Institute.

Sadlick, M., & Penta, F. B. (1975). Changing nurse attitudes toward quadriplegics through use of television. *Rehabilitation Literature, 36,* 274–288.

Schanie, C. F., & Sundel, M. (1978). A community mental health innovation in mass media preventive education: The alternatives project. *American Journal of Community Psychology, 6,* 573–581.

Schwartz, M. C. (1979). New needs, new heroes. *Disabled USA, 2,* 8–10.

Selwyn, D. (1982). Dealing with handicapped consumers: Added risks and obligations. *Trial, 18,* 64–81.

Sheed, W. (1980, August). On being handicapped. *Newsweek,* p. 13.

Snyder, M. L., Kleck, R., Strenta, A., & Mentzer, S. (1979). Avoidance of the handicapped: An attributional ambiguity analysis. *Journal of Personality and Social Psychology, 37,* 2297–2306.

Sprafkin, J., & Gadow, K. D. (1982). Television viewing habits of children in special education classes. Unpublished manuscript, State University of New York at Stony Brook.

Sprafkin, Joyce N., Gadow, Kenneth D., & Grayson, Patricia. (1984). Television and the emotionally disturbed, learning disabled, and mentally retarded child: A review. *Advances in Learning and Behavioral Disabilities, 3,* 151–213.

Storey, K. S. (1979). The effects of the television series "Feeling Free" on children's attitudes toward handicapped people. Doctoral dissertation, Harvard University.

Talkington, L. W., & Altman, R. (1973). Effects of film-mediated aggressive and affectual models on behavior. *American Journal of Mental Deficiency, 77,* 420–425.

Thomas, Susan, & Wolfensberger, Wolf. (1982). The importance of social imagery in interpreting societally devalued people to the public. *Rehabilitation Literature, 43,* 356–358.

Thompson, W. C. (1980). Media and the myth of mobility. *American Rehabilitation, 5,* 12–14.

Thurston, J. R. (1959). A procedure for evaluating parental attitudes toward the handicapped. *American Journal of Mental Deficiency, 64,* 148–155.

Trinkaus, John W. (1984). Societal activities and the handicapped: An informal look. *Perceptual and Motor Skills, 59,* 526.

Tripp, A. (1988). Comparison of attitudes of regular and adapted physical educators toward disabled individuals. *Perceptual and Motor Skills, 66,* 425–426.

Wall, O. (1978). Mental illness and the media: An unhealthy condition. *Disabled USA,* *2,* 23–24.

Walters, R. H., & Willows, D. C. (1968). Imitative behavior of disturbed and nondisturbed children following exposure to aggressive and nonaggressive models. *Child Development, 39,* 79–89.

Westervelt, V. D., & McKinney, J. D. (1980). Effects of a film on nonhandicapped children's attitudes toward handicapped children. *Exceptional Children, 46,* 294–296.

White, D. A. (1981, May–June). Equality: Step by step. *Canadian Journal of Public Health,* pp. 153–155.

Yoshida, R., Wasilewski, L., & Friedman, D. (1990). Recent newspaper coverage about persons with disabilities. *Exceptional Children, 56,* 5.

15

RELIGIOUS AUDIENCES

Shirley S. Carter

The objective of this chapter is to provide a thorough analysis of the role and scope of the religious audience and its impact on the mass media, examined from both a historical perspective and future projections. Religion has always played a major role in the mass media, most visibly in radio and television, although much of its lasting impact has been felt in the religious press, including newspapers, magazines, and other periodicals.

An examination of this audience would be incomplete without an explication of key terms that have emerged from the 1970s to the 1990s. *Evangelical* refers to those Christians from various denominations or independent churches who emphasize the final authority of sacred scripture, the real historical character of God's saving work recorded in scripture, eternal salvation only through personal trust in Christ, the importance of evangelism (proclaiming the gospel of Christ to the unsaved), and the importance of the spiritually transformed life. *Fundamentalists* are the more militant evangelicals who reject much of modern culture and oppose many of the values, beliefs, and attitudes of modern America. *Mainline Protestants* are members of the large, well-known denominations—Presbyterians, Lutherans, Methodists, and the like—most of which affiliate with the National Council of Churches. And *televangelism* is the use of television by evangelical religious groups.

NATURE AND SIZE OF AUDIENCE

America has witnessed a revival in religious belief and church attendance since the 1980s, which is similar to the increase in religious pluralism that the nation experienced during the Great Religious Awakening of America's mid-1700s. This revival will continue, according to John Naisbitt (1984), for as long as the nation remains in a transitional era because of the need for structure during times of great change.

Actually, the strictest and most demanding denominations grew fastest during this period, as Naisbitt and other religious historians have observed. For instance, this growth was most visible in denominations such as the Southern Baptists, Mormons, Seventh-Day Adventists, the Churches of God in Christ, and the new, native-grown fundamentalist faiths, charismatic Christian movement and the youthful Jesus movement.

Other growth has been noted in the number of independent charismatic and noncharismatic congregations, with California, Florida, Washington, New York, and Alabama with the most adherents among the independent charismatic churches, and Texas, Florida, Ohio, Virginia, Michigan, and Georgia having the most noncharismatic churches.

According to a world religion survey conducted by Gallup's Princeton Religion Research Center in Emerging Trends (1993), the Philippines has the highest percentage of Christians at 97 percent, followed by the United States with 82 percent. The Gallup research center also reports that 70 percent of teenagers consider themselves religious and that low- to moderate-income people are more generous than upper-income people in contributing volunteer time and money to help the needy, and minority groups, often in need themselves, are among the most generous of all people, according to George W. Cornwell (1993), Associated Press.

The growth in the religious revival movement has affected the media industry in tremendous ways. Perhaps least documented is the effect it has had on evangelical publishers. This group accounts for more than a third of the total domestic commercial book sales. The more familiar areas are the *electronic church,* a programming phenomenon that refers to the convergence of media technologies and the gospel, with its more than 1,300 radio stations, television stations, and cable networks devoting all or most of their time to religion. The organization of this section on the nature and size of the religious audience includes an investigation of the religious press, religious radio programming, and religious television and cable programming.

The Religious Press

The impact of the religious press will be analyzed on the basis of the two most common types of religious press. The first type promotes a particular religious belief through a publication sanctioned by church doctrine or denominational influences. The second type of religious press is more mainstream, as it espouses social justice themes, tackles moral and political issues, or provides extensive coverage of world events, while it extols the highest journalistic standards under the aegis of an established church or denomination.

Examples of the first type include the *A.M.É. Church Review,* the longest-surviving African-American journal in the United States, published by the African Methodist Episcopal church (the *A.M.E. Church Review* began as *The Christian Recorder,* originally published in 1843); the *Catholic Worker,* founded in 1933, with an editorialist philosophy of "personalist Christianity" and active pacifism; *Christianity in Crisis* and *Salt,* edited since 1980 for "fair-shake Catholics" by the Claretian fathers and brothers; and *Sojourners,* a Protestant publication with a radical evangelical slant. The 1993 edition of *Bacon's Magazine Directory* cites more than fifty denominational publications including *The Lutheran; Episcopal Life; Catholic Digest; Jewish Monthly; Moody Monthly,* published since 1900 by the Moody Bible Institute; *Christianity Today;* and *World Monitor* (pp. 151–156).

Among the more prominent examples of the second type of religious press, church-sponsored journalistic excellence are *America,* the *Christian Science Monitor, Commentary, Commonweal* (listed under *Bacon's* Political and Social Opinion heading). *America, Insight,* and the *Jewish Press* are cited (in *Bacon* under the News Magazine heading) as the most prominent.

- *America,* founded in 1909, is one of two leading Catholic journals of opinion and focuses on the challenging issues facing modern Catholicism with articles that feature hard core news of crucial topics and prominent individuals as well as book, film, and art reviews. Published in New York, *America's* circulation is 40,000.

- The *Christian Science Monitor* was founded in 1908 by Mary Baker Eddy to promote high journalistic standards and maintain a moderately conservative editorial slant. Although the paper publishes a few religious articles, its mainstay is coverage of world events and publication of positive news. It is a national paper with an international flavor, and according to the 1993 edition of *Bacon's Newspaper Directory,* the Boston daily newspaper's circulation is 125,000.

- *Commentary* was founded in 1945 by the American Jewish Committee of New York as a journal of significant thought and opinion on Jewish affairs and contemporary issues. The New York publication's circulation is 29,000, down from 32,000 in 1992.

- *Commonweal* was founded in 1924, owned by the Commonweal Foundation in New York and is published by Catholic laymen. The publication includes reviews of public affairs, literature, and the arts with emphasis on political and religious issues. Its circulation is 18,000.

- *Insight,* founded in 1986, is a newsweekly of the Unification Church and the Washington Times Corporation. Its editorial focus is to provide a perspective on important issues and information and their implications on the future. Coverage is diverse, including national and international health, business, law, science, education, and entertainment features. The Washington, D.C.–based publication has a circulation of 510,000.

- The *Jewish Press* is published by the Jewish Press, Incorporated, and is written for individuals who follow news and events of the Jewish community in and around New York and throughout the world. It contains extensive coverage of news in Israel, combined with feature topics such as the Bible and the Talmud. The publication has a circulation of 168,000.

Although by the late 1970s the religious press had grown to include 1,700 religious magazines, including 1,100 Protestant, 400 Catholic, and 200 Jewish, and a rise in ecumenical publications, the 1990s has seen a dramatic shift in religious publishing trends, according to *Bacon's* 1993 listing of 83 distinctly religious publications. This change is more perceptible in the number of religious-sanctioned mainstream publications such as *Insight* and *Commentary* and the more than 30 life-style publications cited by *Bacon* with a predominant religious theme, such as *Good Fortune, The Human Quest, Lifestyles, Marriage Partnership, Possibilities,* and *Virtue.* In fact, religion has become a part of the average American reader's editorial environment, as most newspapers regularly devote columns, pages, or entire sections to religious coverage. Some groups, such as Catholics, purchase space in newspapers to provide coverage of religious and moral issues within the context of contemporary affairs.

Religious Radio

Most commentary and observations about the impact of the electronic church have focused on television, primarily because of the emergence and high visibility of the televangelists in the 1980s. However, radio has always been the forerunner to modern-day religious programming, or the electronic church.

Religious broadcasting has changed at an accelerated pace since the 1970s from a role of "sustained religious programming" on noncommercial stations or donated airtime on commercial stations to highly commercialized religious programming. At this time, the phrase *electronic church* became more conspicuous and controversial (Head & Sterling, 1990, p. 340). This evolution from sustained religious broadcasting to commercialized religious programming inevitably changed the nature of religious programming and thus changed the nature of the religious audience.

Evangelical radio is the earliest form of religious programming on radio. It began with the first religious broadcast on KDKA in Pittsburgh in January 1921. As a programming option, evangelical radio is an important but largely unexamined chapter in the history of broadcasting (Schultze, 1988, p. 289). According to Schultze, conservative Protestants took to the airwaves in the 1920s to preach old-fashioned gospel. They learned how to create interesting and attractive messages, cultivate an audience of program supporters, and distribute programming across the country. Radio is credited with helping evangelicals to organize many of their own religious institutions and establish a national identity. This, according to Schultze, has been radio's lasting contribution to the electronic church.

Radio is credited with having made two other significant contributions: (1) locating and promoting symbolic leaders such as Charles Fuller and Paul Rader, who demonstrated the effective use of the audience to support commercial broadcasts, and (2) helping to transform conservative Protestantism into a more acceptable—and more American—style of evangelicism (Schultze, 1988, p. 302).

The *Broadcasting and Cable Marketplace* (1992) survey of top radio formats lists religious programming as the third most popular AM radio station format, when combined with gospel formats, with a total of 818 stations, and fourth most popular FM station format, with a total of 574 stations, or 1,392 stations overall. The religious radio format includes block programming consisting of fundamentalist preaching; news and information talk shows on contemporary issues within a Christian perspective; and religious music that includes traditional gospel, contemporary Christianity, and Christian folk, rock, and country. This shows tremendous growth when one considers the top two station formats are country music, at 2,603, and adult contemporary, at 2,347 total stations.

Religious Television

According to some critics, television itself constitutes a religion.

Television commercials are seen as religious parables organized around a common theology, putting forth concepts of sin, intimations of the way to redemption and a vision of heaven. Technology is seen as an autonomously willful deity. Catholicism uses six main elements to reinforce the Catholic message in the mass media: initial setting of decadence requiring salvation; the arrival of a hero; the trial the hero endures (including danger to his own life); the voyage; the repetition (in which an end of one journey implies that another is needed); and an apotheosis which is the great enthusiastic celebration of the charismatic hero . . . who is going on a sort of pilgrimage to the end of the world, on behalf of, and together with TV audiences. (Wober, 1988, p. 112)

Broadcast religious programming emerged in 1939 as churches began to work exclusively with the Protestant Radio Commission of the Federal Council of Churches. By 1960, according to Judith M. Buddenbaum, independently produced Protestant, Catholic, and Jewish programs hit the airwaves with programming acceptable to a broad cross section of viewers. The themes stressed ethical and social concerns shared by most religions and general audiences (Buddenbaum, 1982, p. 266).

Early religious television programs sought a broad audience by emphasizing the commonality themes, but later, independently produced programs took on a doctrinal approach that attracted audiences based on a blend of entertainment and information with gospel. How has the audience for religious programming changed over the years? According to Buddenbaum (1982), in the 1950s, Parker, Barry, and Smythe found that viewers of regular religious television programming did not differ from nonviewers in social class, income, church attendance, education, age, occupation, or type of household. They also found that the 1950s audience was attracted to different programming on the basis of different demographic characteristics.

By contrast, the 1960s audience viewed religious programming on the basis of church membership and other forms of religious activity and age rather than socioeconomic status as measured by income, education, and occupation. By the 1970s and 1980s, several research studies revealed audience preference for religious programming based on prev'ously held religious beliefs and conservative value orientations. The audiences tended to be attracted to religious television as an alternative to regular television, which was perceived to place too much emphasis on sex and violence. This is consistent with media uses and gratifications theories that people select programming on the basis of content that meets their needs and is more consistent with their values.

A 1981 Gallup poll found that 32 percent of a national sampling watched religious programming. A few years later, a team consisting of Gallup pollsters and the Annenberg School of Communications in Philadelphia, Pennsylvania, conducted a 1984 poll revealing that 25 million people viewed religious programs weekly but that only 13 million people were watching at least fifteen minutes of televangelism each week (Martz & Carroll, 1987, p. 45). Interestingly, the demographics revealed that the television audience for religious programming in the 1980s was downscale, older, less educated, and more conservative than the general population and concentrated in the South and Midwest. Religious programming on television was also found to be preaching to the already converted; 77 percent of those surveyed were church members, and nearly all attended church regularly.

Aside from the television programming provided by ABC, CBS, NBC, and the "superstations," cable has emerged as the network of choice for most televangelists. In its heyday, during the 1980s, televangelism broadcast such programs as the "700 Club," "People That Love" (PTL), and the Christian Broadcasting Network (CBN).

Most religious programmers now refer to themselves as programming for the family. CBN Continental Group, headed by M. G. "Pat" Robertson, has as its principal cable channel the CBN Family Network. The Family Channel, based in Virginia Beach, Virginia, focuses on family entertainment: original and made-for-television films, dramatic and comedy series, classic westerns, specials, and inspirational programs. It's shown on 9,625 cable systems to almost 54 million subscribers.

The New Inspirational Network operates out of Fort Mill, South Carolina. It provides twenty-four-hour multifaith programming on 834 cable systems that serve 6 million subscribers. The Inspirational Network was formed after Tammy Faye and Jim Bakker left PTL.

Other prominent cable network religious programs include the following:

• The Jewish Television Network, Los Angeles, features programs pertaining to the Jewish community in the areas of news, arts, Israel, religion, and other features. Serves 250,000 subscribers.

• ACTS Satellite Network is owned by the Southern Baptist Convention. It reaches 9.8 million homes over 521 cable systems and carries about 25 percent religious and 75 percent family-oriented programming.

• Trinity Broadcasting Network (TBN), a twenty-four-hour nonprofit broadcast and cable service, reaches about 15 million homes over 1,154 cable systems with Christian-oriented health programs, talk shows, and the like. The flagship show is "Praise the Lord."

- Eternal Word Television Network (EWTN) is a nonprofit, Catholic-oriented service from Alabama, carrying twenty-four-hour family programming and reaching about 20 million homes on 756 cable systems.

- The National Jewish Television Network (NJTN) reaches more than 10 million people on 514 cable systems. It offers informational, cultural, and religious programming for the Jewish community.

- VISN Interfaith Satellite Network is based in New York. A full-time cable network, it offers a variety of faith and values programming including music, talk, documentary, worship, situation comedies, and movies.

Religious audiences, like other mass media audiences, have gone high technology. Religious programming is available on audio cable. Moody Broadcasting is the first such network to provide a twenty-four-hour format of religious and educational programming, including music, drama, talk, news, and public affairs. The programming is available on forty-eight cable systems serving 755,179 subscribers, according to *Broadcasting and Cable Marketplace* (1992).

REGULATORY MEASURES

Three significant regulatory events in the history of broadcast regulations have affected religious programming on radio and television. One of the earliest regulatory bodies to govern religious programming on the airwaves was the Federal Radio Commission (FRC), established in 1927. The FRC had the effect of curbing the growth of religious stations by imposing new federal regulations designed to minimize signal interference and establish public standards for issuing and renewing licenses. By 1928, almost all religious and educational stations were reassigned frequencies to be shared with other stations (Schultze, 1988, p. 292).

A second significant period in the history of religious broadcast regulations occurred in the 1960s when the Federal Communications Commission (FCC) ruled that stations could classify paid-time religious programs under *public service,* a category normally limited to "sustaining" programs. The FCC also exempted paid-time religious programs from the prohibition then in effect against program-length commercials. Under the FCC definition, this ruling could have applied to religious programming because of the emphasis on appeals for donations. The FCC also, for the most part, exempted religious programming from the right-of-reply requirements that were formerly imposed on other broadcasts by the Fairness Doctrine (Head & Sterling, 1990, p. 342).

The third critical event in religious broadcast regulations involves a religious broadcasting issue that led to key Supreme Court decisions on the electronic media. Some would argue that *Red Lion* is the touchstone for the people's right of access to the media.

During the 1960s, right-wing radio preachers inundated radio with paid syndicated political commentary. The *Red Lion* case got its name from WGCB, a Southeastern Pennsylvania AM/FM outlet licensed to John M. Norris, a conservative minister, under the
name Red Lion Broadcasting. On November 27, 1964, WGCB carried a fifteen-minute
broadcast by the Rev. Billy James Hargis as part of the minister's "Christian Crusade"
series. In discussing a book written by Fred J. Cook, entitled *Goldwater Extremist on
the Right*, Rev. Hargis accused Cook of working for a communist-affiliated publication
and also leveled other charges. Cook demanded free reply time, which the station refused.
The FCC then declared that the broadcast constituted a personal attack and that the station
had failed to meet its obligation under the Fairness Doctrine by not sending a tape,
transcripts, or summary of the broadcast to Cook and offering him free time to reply.
Such steps were necessary under a FCC decision in 1962 concerning Times Mirror
Broadcasting Company, even though the rules were not formally implemented until 1967.
Red Lion Broadcasting Company lost subsequent appeals. In a nutshell, *Red Lion* allowed
the FCC to impose obligations on licensees to present ideas and information about matters of great public concern without specifically telling the licensee how to do it. (Francois, 1982, p. 599)

RELIGIOUS ISSUES AND THE FIRST AMENDMENT

The overt intrusion of television evangelists in the 1980 political campaign
caused some fervor over First Amendment rights, especially with regard to Pat
Robertson's campaign for the presidency. But the First Amendment protected
Robertson's right to have his say (Head & Sterling, 1990, p. 466).

A related issue is centered on a number of stations owned by religious groups
that have claimed "near immunity" from FCC requirements because they regard
their right of religious freedom as absolute. Nevertheless, according to Head and
Sterling, the FCC has continued to regulate religious broadcasting entities in the
same manner as other licensees.

POLITICAL AND MORAL ISSUES AFFECTING THE
RELIGIOUS AUDIENCE

Many critics believe that the dominant issue affecting the religious audience
centers on whether the electronic church undercuts traditional churches with
televangelists reaching people the traditional churches do not. Another viewpoint
ponders whether, in fact, religious programming provides additional experiences
for people who continue their regular religious affiliations (Becker, 1983, p.
427).

While those are important perspectives that should be part of any discussion
of issues affecting the religious audience, the rise and fall of televangelists in
the 1980s threatened to erode the moral rock upon which even traditional
churches were anchored. These televangelists who had built multimillion-dollar
operations became the focus of "public derision" in 1987 and 1988 with the
disclosure of sex scandals involving Jim Bakker and Jimmy Swaggart, the un-

usual television appeals of Oral Roberts, and reports of more excesses and feud-ing by others. Swaggart, the Baton Rouge, Louisiana–based minister, was defrocked by the Assemblies of God ministries, and his own fall from grace was precipitated as much by his own follies as his reporting Jim Bakker's sexual episode with a church secretary (Wall, 1984, p. 74).

The so-called scandal was subject to satire and caricature by comedians on shows such as "Saturday Night Live," discussion and dissection on "Night-line," and a virtual feast for tabloids and other periodicals. Many a segment of "Saturday Night Live" was devoted to exploiting the scandal, which was often referred to as "Heavengate," "Gospelgate," or "Pearlygate" and prob-ably gave birth to the regular "Saturday Night Live" feature, the "Church Lady."

Wall has provided one of the more provocative views of the effect of the televangelists and "preacher bashing" on the more respected religious com-munity. Did "Heavengate," for instance, result in a reduction of the religious community's role in public policy-making? Wall suggests that de Tocqueville was one of the first to affirm just that in his insight that "the mores of our people do not spring from the soil; they are shaped by the influence of families, voluntary groups and yes, religious communities" (Wall, 1984).

Religious programming has often been criticized for crossing the fine line into the political arena, particularly with the much-publicized presidential campaigns of M. G. "Pat" Robertson and the Reverend Jesse Jackson. The more recent 1992 presidential campaign unleashed a fury of criticism from the Right and Left surrounding the Far Right influence at the Republican National Convention but none as vitriolic as former Vice-President Dan Quayle's "family values" issue with the fictitious television character "Murphy Brown." Quayle lam-basted the so-called Hollywood elite for its Brown story line that had the lead character give birth to a child out of wedlock.

Previous research has isolated four major issues along the religious-political continuum: propriety of on-the-air worship, the exercise of social power, the size and composition of the religious televiewing audience, and the possible erosion of local church attendance and financial contributions (Abelman & Pet-tey, 1988, p. 313). Abelman and Pettey conducted a content analysis of religious programming on television in 1986 to determine its political content and com-pared their findings to a similar study by Abelman and Neuendorf in 1983. Abelman and Pettey found that only 18.8 percent of the topics extracted from their sample had political themes and that they were generally concentrated in a subset of religious programs. They also found that the prevalence of political content in religious programming rose slightly from the 3.8 percent Abelman and Neuendorf reported from the 1983 sample. Their findings also upheld earlier research reports that many viewers watch religious television for information seeking, as an alternative to regular network programming, and for spiritual as well as political enlightenment.

It is interesting to note that between 1983 and 1985 the authors found several new references to political issues and that the incidence of political themes rose slightly among televangelists Swaggart, Bakker, Robertson, Jerry Falwell, and Robert Schuller. Abelman and Pettey identified the following political topics as being most prevalent in religious programming: terrorism, communism, Reaganomics, the Supreme Court, federal spending, armed forces, current wars, relations between the United States and other major powers, and nuclear armament.

On the other hand, there was little or no mention of such topics as the Third World, economic sanctions in South Africa, potential wars, prayer in public schools, welfare, sex education, religious freedom, the environmental movement, the death penalty, busing, gun control, and nuclear power.

These findings suggest that the more conservative issues, or the "politically correct" topics, were those most often treated by the televangelists. Perhaps, too, this emphasis on more conservative political issues has helped to shape the public agenda, as the televangelists' messages have been received by a captive audience.

Since the 1992 presidential campaign, and as a result of a more conservative agenda in national politics, religious programming in the mass media may have taken a different turn. Most of the criticism from religious groups surrounds the so-called liberal agenda of the mass media, particularly a liberal bias in network news and commercial television programming. Other groups have called on more intense lobbying for television that reflects positive family values. The industry responds that its shows are merely reality based. In fact, research has revealed that the effects of television on altering or shaping social values have been minimal.

Another target of anti-Christian bias in the media is film. According to Michael Medved (1990), who served as cohost of the weekly Public Broadcasting Service (PBS) program "Sneak Previews," the film industry's "resounding endorsement of 'The Last Temptation of Christ' and 'The Handmaid's Tale' are examples of Hollywood's overt and pervasive hostility toward religion" (p. 12). Medved cites these two films as examples of the departure of the industry from such classics as *The Ten Commandments, The Robe, Ben Hur,* and *Chariots of Fire* to such films as *Agnes of God* and *Poltergeist II,* which denigrate religious themes and groups but also were resoundingly snubbed at the box office. Medved and others believe that television and film have ignored and overlooked the religious community and that producers and other decision makers are out of touch with mainstream values.

RELIGIOUS AUDIENCES AND THE FUTURE OF RELIGIOUS PROGRAMMING

Religious programming, or the electronic church, will owe its survival in the future to lessons learned from past mistakes and, perhaps most important, its ability to provide spiritual as well as intellectual enlightenment to its audiences.

Religious programming will also survive and hold its own as a media presence, despite the scandals of the late 1980s. As a result of these scandals, religious broadcast entities began to apply strict moral codes on their own, sometimes in the shadows of the National Association of Broadcasters and other organizations. Religious programming will also become less preachy and more family oriented, thus appealing to a wider, more diverse audience. The appeals for donations will become more sophisticated as the audience will become more skeptical of telemarketing appeals of the past.

The religious press will continue in the same vein, using mainstream publications such as *Insight* and the *Christian Science Monitor* as vehicles for discussing social, moral, and political issues with a Christian perspective. Daily newspapers will be used on a continuing basis, as will book publishing, newsletters, and the like.

The religious audience will grow as the population continues to look for spiritual growth during uncertain economic times and the threat of war. The religious audience will also continue to seek alternatives to the more decadent commercial media.

Finally, as the religious audience becomes more exposed to new technologies, traditional churches and religious organizations will be encouraged to continue their early Sunday morning broadcasts of worship services and their diversified radio programming, to experiment with electronic book publishing to keep pace with the changes and variety its audience demands, and to use specialized marketing techniques such as direct mail to promote religion and affect social change whether the cause is television programming that reflects mainstream values or a political candidate that espouses a certain political ideology.

BIBLIOGRAPHY

Abelman, Robert, & Pettey, Gary. (1988). How political is religious television? *Journalism Quarterly, 65* (2), 313–319.

Bacon's Magazine Directory. (1993). Bacon's Information, Chicago, IL, pp. 151–156.

Becker, Samuel L. (1983). *Discovering mass communication.* Glenview, IL: Scott, Foresman.

Broadcasting and Cable Marketplace 1992. (1992). [Formerly Broadcasting Yearbook]. New Providence, NJ: R. R. Bowker, Reed Reference.

Buddenbaum, Judith M. (1982). Characteristics and media related needs of the audience for religious TV. *Journalism Quarterly, 58,* 266–272.

Cornwell, George. (1993, March 13). Poll says change is most enduring value. *Washington Post,* p. B7.

Francois, William E. (1982). *Mass media law and regulation.* 3rd ed. Columbus, OH: Grid.

Frankl, Rozelle. (1987). Televangelism: The marketing of popular religion. Carbondale: Southern Illinois University Press.

Hart, Roderick P., Turner, Kathleen J., & Knupp, Ralph E. (1980). *Review of Religious Research, 21* (3), 256–275.

Head, Sydney W., & Sterling, Christopher H. (1990). *Broadcasting in America.* Boston: Houghton Mifflin.

Lippy, Charles H. (Ed.). (1986). *Religious periodicals of the United States.* Westport, CT: Greenwood Press.

Martz, Larry, with Carroll, Ginny. (1987). *Ministry of greed.* New York: Newsweek Books.

Medved, Michael. (1990). Does Hollywood hate religion? *Focus on the Family Citizen, 4* (4), 12–14.

Naisbitt, John. (1984). *Megatrends.* New York: Warner Books.

Princeton Religion Research Center. (1993, January). *Journal, 15*(1),1-3

Schultze, Quentin J. (1988). Evangelical radio and the rise of the electronic church. *Journal of Broadcasting and Electronic Media, 32* (3), 112, 289, 292, 302.

Wall, James M. (1984). Preacher bashing and the public life. In Warren K. Agee, Phillip H. Ault, & Edwin Emery (Eds.), *Maincurrents in mass communication.* New York: Harper & Row.

Wober, J. Mallory. (1988). *The use and abuse of television, a psychological analysis of the changing screen.* Hillsdale, NJ: Lawrence Erlbaum Associates.

16

SPORTS AUDIENCES

Randy E. Miller

THE SPORTS AUDIENCE

The audience for sports is a large and complex group. About 1 billion people—one-fifth of the world's population—sat before television screens and watched the final match of the 1990 World Cup. The sports fans of the United States did not compose a large portion of that audience, but they did watch the usual American sports festivals such as the Super Bowl, the World Series, the National Collegiate Athletic Association (NCAA) basketball tournament, the National Basketball Association (NBA) championship finals, and the Kentucky Derby in huge numbers. Two million people, the largest parade crowd in Philadelphia history, did not honor victorious American soldiers, astronauts, or politicians but rather the city's professional hockey team. A stunning victory by the U.S. hockey team against the Soviets during the 1980 Olympics led to spontaneous celebrations throughout the country. The nations of Honduras and El Salvador went to war after an emotionally competitive soccer game that decided which team would advance toward the World Cup.

We may consider various categories in examining sports fans: spectators, who attend events, versus viewers and listeners, who follow the event by a medium. Some enthusiastic and zealous members of the sports audience are fans, while others merely attend or watch. The degree to which certain audience members follow sports can be reflected in their attire, their attendance to other sports-related media programs, and even in their self-defined attitude toward life. For example, persons who describe themselves as Chicago Cubs fans may celebrate the value of perseverance and faithfulness (the Cubs rarely win pennants).

A fundamental definition in studying sports requires one to distinguish between sport and play. Huizinga, whose *Homo Ludens* (1938) is considered the classic study in this area, and other writers have philosophized about play and sports in differing definitions and ideological perspectives, but generally *play* refers to a voluntary, spontaneous activity that has no purpose or importance beyond its own reference. *Sports* is an organized, rule-bound activity requiring physical effort and is, in some form, an occupation of athletes.

Financially, the coverage of sports by newspapers is often called tantamount to "free advertising." At one time, journalists were an expense for the sports organization, which paid for their travel, lodging, meals, liquor, and other expenses. Today, news organizations pick up most of the tab, but reporters are still provided with free entrance to games and are often given food and promotional material. Sports organizations provide this support willingly in exchange for free advertising.

Commercial broadcast outlets, however, provide more than free advertising. Networks pay enormous amounts of money for rights to telecast. In 1990, CBS-TV paid more than $1 billion—a 76 percent increase—to continue its package of weekly National Football League (NFL) game telecasts over a four-year period. ABC-TV paid $900 million, an 80 percent increase for a four-year contract of NFL games, thus continuing its popular "Monday Night Football" telecasts. NBC-TV paid $752 million for its four-year NFL package. The NFL, which expanded into cable television during the 1980s, sold a package of forty-seven telecasts over four years to the Turner Broadcasting System for $450 million. For the 1994 season Fox beat out CBS by offering $395 million for that package of profootball games.

The National Collegiate Athletic Association receives more than $1 billion for rights to its football and men's basketball packages. Each National Basketball Association team received $8.1 million a year for a 1990 contract, up from its previous $2.55 million. The National Hockey League (NHL) celebrated when it negotiated an $80 million contract with ESPN. (However, many observers think that the NFL and Major League Baseball [MLB] will receive less lucrative offers when their contracts expire in 1993. ESPN paid $13 million to buy out of a $250 million option of televising MLB in 1994–1995—the cable network is expected to make a less expensive offer for those games.)

Television and cable pay exorbitantly in order to charge advertisers exorbitant rates. Advertisers paid a record $850,000 for thirty seconds of airtime during the 1992 Super Bowl.

Sports events have been among cable television's highest-rated programs and have helped generate the pay-per-view event, in which a viewer pays a sum in order to watch, say, a heavyweight championship fight or a professional wrestling performance. A 1991 fight between Evander Holyfield and George Foreman reportedly earned more than $55 million, almost all of it coming from pay-per-view telecasts. Sports pages have been a staple of the American newspaper since Joseph Pulitzer assembled the first sports staff, and publications specializing in sports, such as *Sports Illustrated* and *Inside Sports,* or the many publications geared toward fans of a particular sport, remain popular.

Clearly, the experience of attending a sports event differs from watching television, listening to radio accounts, or reading about the event later. Sports audiences have a wide variety of media choices available for a particular event.

They might watch an individual player perform during a game telecast over ESPN, a national cable sports channel. During the telecast, an announcer and analyst can focus on the player's performance, compare it with others, provide up-to-the-second statistics, replay earlier highlights of the player's career, and show slow-motion replays. The instant replay has, in recent years, even become part of the experience of viewing a game at the stadium where spectators can watch a huge screen to see a replay and react positively or negatively in such a way that it even seems as if many actually suspend their decisions until shown a slow-motion replay. Immediately at game's end, announcers may interview the player, and the viewer can then tune to a number of news outlets, local and national, to watch highlights. A fan may phone a call-in radio show on an all-sports station such as WFAN-AM in New York. A fan may even reach a sports enthusiasts' bulletin board or subscribe to a sports news service through a personal computer. In the morning, a fan can read the newspaper for game stories, locker-room reports, and the box scores.

A difference often exists between spectators and participants. Some athletes are ill-informed about the history of their sports and often cannot identify key figures in that game's history. Many casual fans, however, soak up historical information and have some degree of knowledge about older, obscure players. In some sports, participation often leads to spectatorship. Golfers and tennis players tend to watch the sports they play, but the same is rarely true for skiers, sailors, and other participants in recreational sports.

Demographically, the audience for sports has been predominantly a male audience, though women have been increasingly involved over the last twenty years. Advertisers attempt to reach a target audience of men from twenty-five to fifty-four years of age. Not surprisingly, the main advertisers for sports are beer companies, automobile manufacturers and suppliers, computer companies, and office products. Even sports that do not draw particularly large segments of viewers, such as golf and tennis, are supported by advertisers who seek a target audience of high-income, high-spending males who follow and play such sports.

Perhaps no greater example of intermingling of sports and advertising can be seen than in the recent popularity of "lite" beer. When brewers planned such a product, it was feared that males would not buy it; machismo would prevent their pride from drinking a "watered-down" beer. The Miller Brewing Company attacked the problem by hiring ex-athletes (still-active athletes are forbidden to advertise alcohol) who espoused the new product. The humorous advertisements featuring the ex-athletes led to a distinctive catchphrase ("Tastes great, less filling"), and low-calorie beer became an accepted alternative in stores and taverns throughout America (see *Miller Lite Report,* 1983).

IMAGES

The sports media focus attention on the importance of individual plays and supply the context to differentiate between levels of competition in all athletic contests. The most famous lead in sportswriting history, written by Grantland

Rice (1954), summoned imagery that went well beyond the simple picture of young athletes running with a football:

Outlined against a blue-gray October sky, the Four Horsemen rode again. In dramatic lore they are known as Famine, Pestilence, Destruction and Death. These are only aliases. Their real names are Stuhldreher, Miller, Crowley and Layden. They formed the crest of the South Bend cyclone before which another fighting Army football team was swept over the precipice at the Polo Grounds yesterday afternoon as 55,000 spectators peered down on the bewildering panorama spread on the green plain below. (P. 177)

African Americans who remember the radio broadcasts of the boxer Joe Louis recall the spirit of community triumph—and the community was present in virtually full force to root for Louis—in his victories and the community agony in his defeat.

It was not just one black man against the ropes, it was our people falling. It was another lynching, yet another black man hanging on a tree. One more woman ambushed and raped. A black boy whipped and maimed. It was hounds on the trail of a man running through slimy swamps. It was a white woman slapping her maid for being forgetful. We didn't breathe. We didn't hope. We waited. (Maya Angelou in Gilmore, 1983, p. 263)

New York sports fans in 1951 can recall where they were and what they were doing when New York Giants batter Bobby Thomson hit a home run off Brooklyn Dodger pitcher Ralph Branca to earn a World Series berth for his team. Giants' broadcaster Russ Hodges screamed repeatedly, "The Giants win the pennant! The Giants win the pennant! The Giants win the pennant!" Dodgers' broadcaster Red Barber was more philosophical: He began a soliloquy by reciting the statistics of the recent war dead in Korea and saying, "It's only a ballgame, folks" (King, 1988).

The media can label a team and receive signals back from its audience on the appropriateness of the label. New York sportswriters in 1962, for example, made the hapless New York Mets a symbol of laughter and struggle against the mighty (the city's other team, the Yankees, was baseball's most dominant). *New York Times* sportswriter Robert Lipsyte recalled how the image of the Amazin' Mets came to stick:

The fans, psychological teenagers all gland and stomach, took their signals from the press. Ahead of their time they "let it all hang out" and "did their thing." The press, in turn, received its signals back, its theories now confirmed and anecdotalized and made newsworthy. We attributed the behavior of the fans to the magical power of the Mets to create love, which I no longer think is the case. Rather, the Mets projected a wounded animal vulnerability that unlatched the repressions that fans normally carry to the ballpark and only let go when they are not awed by the players and the game. (Lipsyte, 1975, p. 34)

The images sent by television are perhaps the most vivid of all. One who watched the remarkable victory by the amateur USA Olympic hockey team against the powerful USSR team in the 1980 Olympics may never forget the exciting third period in which the Americans went ahead and then held for the win. A Boston Red Sox fan can never forget the dismay when his team came within one out of winning the 1986 World Series, only to watch the game get away.

Former *New York Times* sportswriter Leonard Koppett wrote an insightful book about the relationship between sports and journalism titled *Sports Illusion, Sports Reality* (1981) in which his thesis was that sports promoters of the world are selling an illusion—that the outcome of a game matters. These dramatic and poignant images reinforce the illusion by engaging and enthralling a fan's intellect. The illusion is further reinforced by the fan's ability to identify with the home team.

The images of spectators themselves are part of the tableau. The images include the horrible scenes of soccer crowds crushed to death against a fence; the rumbling of hooligans tearing their way to or from a stadium; the destruction of property in downtown Detroit or Pittsburgh or Philadelphia after the home-town team wins a championship; and an outpouring of Cleveland fans during 25-Cent Beer Night onto the baseball diamond in search of confrontations with Texas players, costing their team a forfeit. There are also images of patriotic triumph and spirit, such as the unrestrained joy of the U.S. fans after the hockey upset against the Soviets, or Trinidad and Tobago fans all wearing red while watching their team play the United States in a World Cup qualifying game. There are images of anger. Frustrated Detroit fans pelt St. Louis outfielder Joe Medwick with garbage as their team loses the seventh game of the 1934 World Series. There are the light images of fans singing "Take Me Out to the Ball Game" or of babies snoozing or of college students painted in school colors.

There are also the images that are not seen. In one year, Detroit fans wreak havoc celebrating a championship; in another, earlier, more inflammatory year, 1968, predicted riots did not break out at least in part due to the baseball Tigers' drive toward the World Series. The performance of black baseball player Jackie Robinson is conventionally cited as an important factor in helping to bridge racial differences. There are the cheers and jeers from spectators whose small-college team never receives national media attention.

SPORTS COMMUNICATION

When mass communication researchers consider sports as a subject, they often choose to examine the language used by sports journalists. There is an anecdote that the Associated Press once asked sports editors to provide a list of sports clichés in order to compile a warning list. One wrote back angrily, saying that he had spent a great many years compiling his own sports clichés and that he did not want anyone else using them in sports stories.

One of the earliest studies to look at the language used a coined phrase for the jargon of the sports page: "Sportugese." The authors, Percy Tannenbaum and James Noah (1959), blamed the 1920s, considered by some to be the Golden Age of Sports and of Sportswriting, for the odd jargon sprinkled throughout the sports pages. Sportugese was a collection of adjectives ranging from *aghast* to *zany* and action verbs ranging from *annihilate* to *zoom*. The study tested whether certain action verbs actually reflected a certain score in a ballgame. The authors culled sports sections for game stories and drew a sample of eighty-four verbs used to describe the score of a game. They presented the list to a sample of sportswriters, a sample of frequent sports-page readers, and a sample of infrequent sports-page readers. The sportswriters and frequent readers were able to reasonably estimate the point differential connoted by the action verb, but the infrequent readers were not able to distinguish between *edged* and *trounced*. Tannenbaum and Noah said that the encoding behavior of the professional communicator, the sportswriter, showed a consistency in passing denotative and connotative meaning to his readers. The Sportugese study was conducted when state-of-the-art sports journalism was codified by Stanley Woodward (1949), a noted sports editor of the day. Clichés, he wrote, were being phased out of the sports pages, to be replaced by accurate assessments of the game. The cliché, however, refused to die, started a rally, gave 110 percent, and made a furious comeback, to use four clichés.

Wanta and Leggett (1988) examined sportscasters' clichés during football broadcasts. They argued that clichés are often used in place of more accurate, complex analysis when announcers are calling a closely contested game. Because sports announcers working during an exciting game will undergo more anxiety, they will seek clichés that more comfortably describe the game. Wanta and Leggett used capacity theory as a basis for their study. Capacity theory states that a person can devote only a certain amount of attention to simultaneously performing two or more tasks. If one task calls for an increase in attention, others will decrease. Changes in environmental stimulation can alter the relative efficiency of different processes.

The researchers considered four variables that might lead to increased clichés—the rankings of the teams involved, the experience in years of the sportscaster, the degree to which the underdog upsets the favorite, and the closeness of the score. They examined videotaped college football games during the fourth quarters, since that would be the time in which upsets and the closeness of the score would be most apparent. The most common clichés were *picked off, explosion, heat, daylight, room, unloaded,* and *gunned.* The most important factor in determining the use of clichés was the degree to which the result was an upset, followed in significance by the national rankings of the teams playing. The other factors were insignificant. Wanta and Leggett argued that when a game reaches a climax, announcers tend to divert capacity from communication to processing information and that clichés result. If one were to combine capacity theory with Zillmann, Hay, and Bryant's (1973) drama studies, then it might be argued that games involving highly ranked teams or upsets cause sportscasters to rely on a dramatic angle that heavily employs clichés.

Wenner (1990) has proposed a transactional model to explain the production of sports-related media content. He said the study of the relationship between sports and the media requires understanding of audiences and why they consume sports; critical assessments of mediated sports content; and the interrelationships between sports organizations, news organizations, and individual journalists. These three elements are, in turn, influenced by society (pp. 25–26). In a transactional model, he argues, the audience's perceptions as well as the content consumed are cultural indicators.

HISTORY

Though evidence exists that spectator sports were a part of the ancient Egyptian, Minoan, and Etruscan civilizations, it is with the Greeks that spectators first became known. The Olympic Games were first held in ancient Greece, where at least 126 cities had gymnasia. According to Allen Guttmann (1984), the first Olympic Games probably took place in the eighth century B.C., though the first stadium in Olympia was built in the sixth century B.C. In Greece, men were athletes and women were generally barred from even watching sporting events (except for festivals to Hera, where women competed and men were not permitted to spectate). Despite the demand for amateurism from modern Olympic Games organizers, the original Greek games quickly became dominated by professional athletes.

The spectators apparently behaved with excitement and shouting, and Olympic Games administrators hired assistants to keep both the athletes and the crowd under physical control. The fans were intensely partisan, rarely rooting against Greek competitors.

Anyone who has seen the movies *Ben-Hur* and *Spartacus* has an understanding of spectators during the Roman Empire. Gladiatorial contests and chariot races attracted fans of all classes; imitations of the Olympic Games did not. Spectators attended gladiatorial battles at stone structures like the Colosseum. The seating was strictly controlled, with different "tribes" placed in different "cunei" (wedges.) The front row of stalls was reserved for senators; soldiers were separated from civilians, and women were seated on back rows during Augustus's reign, except for the Vestal Virgins and aristocratic women, who were given their own section. The *plebs frumentaria* (those given welfare grain) were seated at no cost. More often than not, spectators of all classes eschewed the fine points of fighting once blood appeared. Even though the gladiatorial contests were the most violent sport in the empire (and maybe in the annals of history), the crowds were nonviolent. The spectators were much more violent at the Circus Maximus where chariot races were held. Much like modern spectators who identify with a team, spectators at five Roman hippodromes supported either the Reds, Whites, Blues, or Greens.

In medieval times, sports were divided by class. The knights and squires participated in tournaments, the middle-class burghers in crossbow contests, and the lower class in a medieval game that is the root for soccer, football, and rugby. The tournaments began as mock wars in the twelfth century and often seemed to turn into real wars. Many tournaments were held in meadows and fields, though by the fifteenth century, jousting had become urban, and spectators watched from upper-story windows. Spectators, as one would expect in hierarchical medieval times, were segregated by class. The ruling class would sit in elevated pavilions, and eventually some stone structures were constructed for the tournaments. Women, at some time during the Middle Ages, became a part of the crowd, and the sport itself became far less violent and far more of a pageant. Early violence among spectators at tournaments led to rules banning weapons, but the rules were generally ineffective.

Archery tournaments were put on by bowmen's guilds, and the evidence suggests that, like jousts, these quickly became as much a pageant as an athletic contest. Women are known to have been a part of the crowd, which behaved roughly but not, apparently, violently.

Though little historical evidence exists for the lore of medieval football, little spectator violence is known to have occurred. Guttmann (1986) notes that this is because there were almost no spectators to speak of. The game for the common man allowed anyone to participate (p. 49).

In early modern England, the royalty and lower classes favored animal sports such as bearbaiting, cockfighting, and dogbaiting, while the middle class disapproved of such cruelty. During these exhibitions, the crowd behaved wildly and often began wrestling among themselves.

British colonization in later years led to the popularization of British sports around the world. Cricket, rugby, soccer, and field hockey remain popular in former colonial outposts like Australia, India, Zimbabwe, South Africa, and the West Indies. However, Americans refused to support a movement to adopt cricket as the national game and altered the rules for games of rounders and soccer to create baseball and American football.

EFFECTIVENESS

How effective is the catharsis theory in describing the sports audience? How effective is the media at determining sports fans' attitudes? The most prevalent theory involving sports spectators and viewers deals with catharsis, which predicts that the viewing of violence in sports serves as an outlet for the violence within the viewer and that sports may indeed facilitate pleasure and altruism.

Freudian theory and ethologists have each put forth theories of catharsis, but other theories can also be found. Sloan's (Goldstein, 1989) study of sports fans' motives examines several hypotheses: the catharsis theories; frustration-aggression theories; social learning theories; the salubrious effects theories;

stress and stimulation theories; entertainment theories; and achievement theories. His descriptions follow:

Salubrious effect theories predict that after viewing sports, positive feelings should rise and prevail, and some researchers predict enhanced altruism and behavior, whereby feelings like hostility, anger, and other such emotions are minimized or become secondary. Victory and defeat are unimportant in these theories.

Stress- and stimulation-seeking theories call for changes in fan arousal, which may still be high when the game ceases, or may have been dropped in a recovery period. Winning and losing are important factors.

Entertainment theories predict increased pleasure, satisfaction, and happiness regardless of the game's outcome.

Frustration-aggression theories state that though victory has no real effect, a close defeat will trigger frustration and aggression. But social learning theorists would predict viewers emulating the violence seen on the field. If violence is rewarded, as it often is portrayed to be during sporting events, then social learning theory as originally hypothesized by Albert Bandura (1977), predicts that sports viewers would be more apt to imitate the violence.

Two postulates that have received examination, both scholarly and journalistic, are cathartic theories and achievement theories.

Catharsis

In catharsis, the viewer and participant each are said to partake of sports in order to restrain, sublimate, or replace their aggression. If humans do not "let off steam," then the aggression builds to a point where it erupts in inappropriate ways. Aristotle was the first to suggest such a theory. The theory still remains popular among many today, though its critics unflinchingly point out that no one scientific study has ever produced evidence that sports do release catharsis in spectators.

However, almost no empirical studies have shown evidence of catharsis. Instead, empirical researchers point to numerous studies that show no backing for catharsis theory. Viewers of violence are actually more likely to behave aggressively after watching violence than before. Goldstein and Arms (1971) found that male spectators at a football game were more hostile after the game than prior to it, and replication has followed at football, hockey, soccer, and wrestling events in several countries. According to Goldstein (1989), there are certain conditions in which watching violence does not lead to a necessary increase in aggression, particularly when spectators believe that competing athletes harbor no animosity toward each other or when spectators themselves loathe violence.

Nonetheless, the common belief among people, athletes, coaches, and sports journalists is that sports really provide a cathartic effect for fans, spectators, and viewers.

Achievement Theories

Athletes compete in sports to win; a veritable battery of statements and standing orders from athletes and coaches throughout the years lend support to this hypothesis. Gratification studies among sports personnel have found achievement, social approval, and status concern to be vital to sport motives. For those involved in sports either as participants or as spectators, fulfilling achievement needs is most easily identified with victory.

Sloan and his colleagues have argued that fans also fulfill achievement needs by "basking in reflected glory" (Goldstein, 1989, pp. 193–194.) After giving students a sports survey and categorizing them as either successes or failures, the researchers asked if the students knew who had won the last university sports event. Those who had been labeled failures were more likely to identify their university's team if it won than if it lost—thus identifying themselves with success.

The Texas press reported that Texas Christian University, which had been associated with losing football for many years, substantially increased its applications for enrollment after the team had an exciting winning season in 1984. Fans often wear the shirts, caps, and other paraphernalia of winning teams after a victory.

CRITICISM

Sport is the single most influential currency of mass communication in the world. Sport easily hurdles the barriers of age, education, language, gender, and social and economic status that tend to divide a population. Sport has the potential to bring people together, but the evidence suggests that it rarely does. In fact, it often further divides communities by promoting overzealous competition, violence, specialization, professionalization, and an attitude of win at all costs that spills over into other aspects of life (Lipsyte, 1985, p. 111).

Criticism of sports audiences comes pointedly not only from those who purport to admire sport but also from Marxist and neo-Marxist scholars, Guttmann (1986) said. Marxist critics have criticized capitalistic sports—too racist, commercial, militaristic, nationalistic, and imperialistic—while praising the role of sports in Communist countries. Countries such as the former Soviet Union, the former East Germany, and Cuba have achieved a high degree of success in sports, and such success is attributed as an ideological creator of community.

Guttmann also summarizes the neo-Marxist indictment of sports: (1) Capitalist society is characterized by a division of labor in sports as well as in other sectors; (2) both active and passive sports participation stabilizes the capitalist system; and (3) spectator sports function cathartically in such a way that drains hostility toward the capitalist system, preventing fans from becoming interested in political action. Guttmann deflects each criticism.

Sports spectators certainly have shown a propensity to react with violence at times. From the hooligans who ravage the other team's fans and town to wanton looting during victory celebrations in some cities, sports can sometimes erupt in violence. One of the earliest cases in this century was the reaction to the flamboyant black boxing champion Jack Johnson, who handily defeated the original Great White Hope, Jim Jeffries, in a 1910 match. When the news spread by telegraph, white supporters of Jeffries rioted and attacked blacks, especially those who dared to openly cheer Johnson. Of course, spectator violence was present during gladiatorial contests and jousting tournaments as well.

Soccer has led to more spectator deaths than any other modern sport. Fans have been crushed against steel-link fences in stadiums, stampeded on ramps, and trampled on stairways, and players and referees have been attacked. The British hooligans, a group of young, lower-class men who verbally and physically attack fans of opposing teams, have been responsible for the banning of British teams from some European tournaments.

For all this, the press has sometimes failed to bring this side of sports spectatorship into focus. The grim pictures of spectators crushed against fences and of wanton violence are remembered by viewers. And, sometimes, sports organizations and sports media work to erase those remembrances.

Detroit Mayor Coleman Young, among other city leaders, had little trouble placing the blame after a celebration turned into a riot after the Tigers' 1984 World Series victory. Young blamed the media, especially the two local daily newspapers, for negative publicity. During the riot, "[o]ne man was shot to death, dozens were injured and at least 34 were arrested when World Series celebrators turned violent, torching cars, battling with riot-ready police and leaving streets littered with burnt-out vehicles and broken glass" (Salwen & Bernstein, 1986, p. 385). Salwen and Bernstein found that the Detroit press, including the *News* and the *Free Press,* instead tended to support the city by deemphasizing the size of the riot and the involvement of the locals as well as by printing more favorable assertions about Detroit fans than did the national media. The Detroit media, naturally, were more active than the national media in criticizing the manner in which the city of Detroit and the police handled the riot.

Reports of violence have brought dissatisfaction from organizations that run sports. When Puerto Ricans rioted at Madison Square Garden after an unfavorable boxing decision and writer Jerry Izenberg described the fans throwing chairs, beer bottles, and even the Garden pipe organ, a Garden official sniffed that the coverage had been too sensational (Izenberg, 1972). Cleveland baseball fans in 1974, during the ninth inning of a 25-Cent Beer Night promotion, began throwing fireworks and racing onto the field to harass Texas outfielders to the point that both teams had to grab bats and fend off unruly fans. The next day, a Cleveland management spokesman said that he did not think the forfeiture of the game was warranted—that the situation at the ballpark had not been out of control.

American television networks that cover sporting events have agreed on a policy in which spectators who disrupt games by running onto a field or a court are not shown. Broadcasters argue that by ignoring such people they do not foster the desire for others to follow suit in order to be shown on television. Unwarranted behavior, of course, also keeps the camera away from protesters who make statements against the interests of the sports establishment.

Fans, like other persons, compete mightily to focus camera attention on themselves. At games, it is common for spectators to hold up signs praising the broadcasters, the station, and the team, in that order, in hopes of being captured by the camera. Some fans wave placards with biblical references; others scream loudly after a shot during relatively placid golf tournaments; yet others paint their faces in school colors or wear basketball remnants on their heads or dress like sports media celebrities in order to appear before a camera for a few seconds.

Other critics who have expressed a love-hate relationship with sports and their spectators can be counted in a group of American sportswriters whose analyses fall almost into a genre of their own. Robert Lipsyte's *SportsWorld: An American Dreamland* (1975), Jerry Izenberg's *How Many Miles to Camelot?* (1972), Leonard Shecter's *The Jocks* (1969), and John Underwood's *The Death of an American Game* (1980) and *Spoiled Sport* (1984) are books critical of the sports establishment and, in some cases, critical of fans for passively accepting and tolerating the problems besetting sports. Shecter's acerbic book—by a sports journalist who professes to hate sports—denigrates athletes, coaches, owners, sportswriters, and fans, who are portrayed as crass, uninformed, and all too willing to accept this flawed product called sports. It is one of the strongest of the Vietnam era books that debunk America's sports industry along with two other books by sports representatives—Jack Scott's *The Athletic Revolution* (1971) and Dave Meggyesy's *Out of Their League* (1970). Scott, a counterculture figure of the 1970s, wrote about athletes revolting against the authoritarian athletic programs in American colleges. Meggyesy, a former St. Louis linebacker, wrote about the evils inherent in the authoritarian system of football. Neither book focuses directly on the audience for sport but rather provides indirect criticism of those who accept the product of authority and ignorance.

Underwood (1984), who wrote for *Sports Illustrated,* described the 1980s sports fan as "alienated." The fan pays too much for tickets, sees violence instead of grace, watches athletes who make far more than the fan will ever see in his paycheck, and senses that the athletes no longer represent an area but are nationally marketed products set to leave at the drop of a slightly higher contract in a higher–media profile city. Underwood talked to the psychoanalyst Rollo May about sports and its fans. May said that sports had become a symbol replacing other symbols such as marriage or religion that had lost their meanings: "Without the old symbols to rely on, we walk around with all this emotion and no place to put it. So we put it in sports. To building gladiators, and not teams. The Phillies are not really Philadelphia, but as the symbol of 'our place' they become 'us.' We are frustrated because it doesn't really get us anywhere" (May, in Underwood, 1984, p. 61).

Underwood also criticized the sports establishment for not trying to keep individual sports from damaging themselves. He preached against the increase of unnecessary violence in football, saying the sport could be damaged by litigation on behalf of injured players, and warned against the corruption rampant throughout sports, saying it would eventually cause fans to forsake the industry.

His predictions have not held up as of yet, but a best-selling book purporting to trace trends in the 1990s has predicted a decline in the emphasis on sports and an increase in the popularity of the arts, since twice as many people attend arts activities as attend sporting events, and that once corporations understand that trend, they will flock to sponsor operas, plays, art exhibits, and the like (Naisbitt & Aburdene, 1990). Twenty years ago, people spent twice as much on sports as the arts. A 1988 report by the National Endowment for the Arts estimated Americans spent $3.7 billion attending arts events and $2.8 billion attending sports events (Naisbitt & Aburdene, 1990). Other figures, however, show that as of 1992, corporations still placed $2.2 billion of their $3.3 billion sponsorship into sports. Motor sports received the most corporate sponsorship, followed by golf and tennis.

One should note that sports events are held far less frequently than arts events and that the media expand the audience for sports beyond actual attendance. But some predict that as new business executives, those forty-five and under, gain control of corporate spending, the relationship between sports and business will decrease as the relationship between sports and the arts increases.

Lipsyte's (1975) criticism was of a more traditional sort, though its publication was framed as an attack on the sports establishment. His book consists of the notes of a journalist who watched the changes in sports mirror the changes in American society in the 1960s. Lipsyte had learned early in his writing career that images of athletes were false, and his book seems an indictment of the myth created by those who make a profit from the games. The promoters of sport were evil creatures, enticing people to squander their precious leisure time as spectators, rather than bolting from the couch and participating in the concept that Huizinga called play.

I have watched more games than most people, and enjoyed them. I begrudge no one entertainment, only oblivion. Turn down the volume for a moment and think: Why should you be sitting there, where an M. Donald Grant [a New York Mets' executive] wants you, flesh sodden, head filled with gibberish and numbers, past anger, past moving, past caring, when there is still light in the sky and time left in the day to hear the pounding of your heart and taste salt in your mouth and feel cool air caress the dampness of your skin? (Lipsyte, 1975, p. 282)

A similar argument decrying the evil of nonparticipation was made much earlier in the century, when critics of spectator sports claimed that playing sports—at least, amateur sports—was a worthwhile pastime but that watching those sports was slothful and sinful behavior, sure to lead people away from a straight and narrow path.

Howard (1912) described participation as bad and partisanship as evil. Participation, in contrast, is good. Involvement in play is said to excite joyous emotions, and these pleasurable emotions are seen by Howard as building up energy and as restoring the "capacity for straight thinking" and, ultimately, for work. "The mob-mind of the athletic struggle-instinct of the human animal" produced unnecessary, harmful emotions and these emotions are said to tear down and diminish energy.... "Let the apostle of social righteousness break into Satan's monopoly!" (Zillmann, Bryant, & Sapolsky, 1989, p. 247)

In the early twentieth century, pursuing a career as a professional athlete was not approved according to the norms of Christian America. Professionals did not value the Sabbath, and spectating was a worse sin, especially for professional sports like baseball and boxing. A public protest forced California authorities to force promoter Tex Rickard to move the 1910 Johnson-Jeffries fight from San Francisco across the state line to Reno.

Lipsyte's criticism implied that sports had become, to borrow a famous phrase, an opiate of the people. Another writer who examined the relationship of sports and spectatorship in a philosophic manner, Michael Novak, also compared sports to religion—not a Catholicism or a Judaism but its own form of religion—but did so in a favorable way. Novak said "In the study of civil religions, our thinkers have too much neglected sports . . . [which] are an almost universal language binding our diverse nation, especially its men, together" (1976, p. 3). While sports ought not to replace religion in society, he argued, neither should those journalists who cover it resort to criticizing the game. "The main business of a sportswriter is to describe what happened in athletic events. The contests themselves are the forms of his craft. Everything else is secondary, instrumental, and to be judged in that light" (p. 264).

THE FUTURE

Some sports journalists have already wondered at what point Americans will stop caring about athletes who make "outrageously" high salaries. Star outfielder Barry Bonds signed a $43.75 million contract over six years with the San Francisco Giants shortly after the franchise had been sold for $100 million. Even average ballplayers like .243 career hitter Spike Owen signed a 1993 contract for $7 million. National Football League players reaped the benefit of a federal court ruling granting them free agency. Some players increased their paychecks twelvefold between the 1992 and 1993 seasons.

Others wondered when networks would cease to pay high contracts for broadcast rights to sporting events and when sports organizations like the NFL, NBA, and Major League Baseball would begin to charge subscribers a pay-per-fee view in order to watch regular-season games and, eventually, championship events like the Super Bowl. American sports commissioners have stated that such events would remain on network television through the end of the twentieth century, but the balance sheet and ballooning contract prices may bring about the advent of pay-per-view more quickly. Even the leadership of the pristinely imaged Olympic Games have considered making some events available on cable broadcasts only.

If or when the pay-per-view system becomes prevalent in American sports, an interesting phenomenon may occur. Sports traditionally have been one route for the poor to escape the ghettoes, isolated farms, coal mines, and other such locations of despair. In the 1930s, sportswriter Paul Gallico (1938) saw Jews living in poor sections of New York City excelling on basketball courts and described the game as one best suited for the Jewish temperament. The dominance of blacks, a number of whom learned the game on inner-city courts, at all levels of basketball may indicate the game is better suited for athletes trying to escape poverty.

Since cable television capability generally escapes the poor, a switch to pay-per-view might well limit the exposure of poor children to the games. Athletic advertising icons like Michael Jordan, Bo Jackson, and others could conceivably lose their popularity among an audience segment that could be prevented from seeing them on television.

Fiber optic technology is expected to enhance sports viewing. Viewers in Montreal who are included on a new fiber optic system are able to choose which camera shots appear on their screen. Some cable executives have said that fiber optic technology may eventually allow television viewers to create their own versions of programming. For sports, which have no predetermined, scripted endings, fans may order copious instant replays or other angles to create their own dramatic story.

Are Naisbitt and Aburdene (1990) correct in their assessment that corporate sponsorship of sports will decline in the 1990s? Between 1983 and 1987, spending on the arts increased 21 percent, while sports spending decreased 2 percent. Artists rarely carry the baggage of sports heroes, who are expected to perform without mistakes on the field while maintaining status as role models for youths.

Klatell and Marcus (1988), however, predict that as television rights fees paid to teams and leagues enter decline, the fans will have to absorb more and more of the cost of player salaries, which seem to rise to new heights every year. They also forecast that corporate sponsorship will continue to grow until it controls much of what is seen on television sports. One can argue that the NFL is already under a form of corporate uniformity—the players, according to a 1991 rule, cannot celebrate after scoring touchdowns. The players, by rule, must wear socks up the calves with no skin showing or be subject to a fine. They are also forced to wear jersey numbers that affix their positions on the field. For example, receivers must wear a number between eighty and eighty-nine.

Whatever happens in the future realm of sports, one would expect a growth in research from mass communication scholars. Sportswriters' stories are often distinguishable in style from those who write for other sections in the newspaper. If sports journalists have been typecast as workers in the "toy department" and if they have, as Garrison (1985) suggested, been hidden away in the corner to protect the rest of the staff, then does a difference in style and socialization have effects on the journalists' content and their audiences? Clearly, the Michael Novaks of this world expect one set of standards from investigative reporters and another from sports journalists.

The dearth of scholarship in major mass communication journals may either indicate a lack of study in sports journalism and its effects, or a bias among journal editors. Some critics have claimed that until the 1970s and 1980s academicians in all social sciences have ignored sports because of the popularity of campus sports teams and the supposed lack of serious matter to be considered. The argument: Attention and financial rewards are given to athletes who may or may not attend classes and participate in an academic debate. Some athletes may not possess the academic qualifications necessary for admittance to a university. Coaches and athletic directors have, in some cases, supported antiintellectualism. Some studies indicate that money given to athletic programs does not result in gains for the academic programs.

But also, perhaps, researchers just do not consider sports journalism an important enough subject to warrant the time and expense of conducting studies.

Our purpose here is not to evaluate or to pass judgment on contemporary sports language. Good, bad, or otherwise, such a language has evolved . . . nurtured by such reporters as Damon Runyon, Heywood Broun, Ring Lardner and Grantland Rice—great writers all, most of whom went on to bigger and better things in journalism after their sports writing performance. (Tannenbaum & Noah, 1959, p. 164)

Passing judgment on sports journalism, however, was perfectly acceptable and appears, with some exceptions, to remain so.

Researchers who choose to investigate the area can consider seven categories that have been studied in some depth, as noted by the bibliographer Melnick (1989): Sports spectating in sociohistorical perspective, modern-day sport consumption patterns, sports spectating in popular culture, economics of sports spectating, psychology of the sports fan, cultural studies of the sports spectator, and fan violence. Mass media critics might choose to examine the damage caused by the mesmerizing imagery of sport.

As many prominent sociologists have pointed out, however, the lasting effect may be done to a segment of that audience which grows to maturity believing that excellence on the athletic field or gym floor is the easiest and most successful route to achieving the glamour, status, and respect seemingly enjoyed by those televised athletes. The image of success is often highlighted on television sports. Few people wish to watch failure, despair, and pain, and even fewer television producers wish to broadcast it, or advertisers sponsor it. Failure is often treated by the athlete or team simply disappearing from future broadcast schedules. And yet, disappointment is statistically many times more common than success. (Klatell & Marcus, 1988, p. 13)

REVIEW OF THE LITERATURE

Despite the widespread popularity and emotion-packed nature of spectator sports, mass communication researchers have, with few exceptions, avoided the subject altogether. A literature search in the mass communication journals reveals few articles concerning sports journalism, much less the sports audience. Mass communication researchers have provided numerous studies about media organizations, their employees, and how the mass media and government correlate, but only a handful of media researchers have looked at the phenomenon of sports spectatorship.

Perhaps mass communication researchers ignored sports journalism and audience studies because many of them have worked in the mass media. And in many mass media organizations, sports journalists are often segregated from the rest of the newsroom. As *Los Angeles Times* sports editor Bill Dwyre once noted: "The field of sportswriting has evolved from the back corners of thousands of newspapers for hundreds of years. Many of those newspapers were a great deal worse than their sports sections, but you'd never know it by the front-of-the-room attitudes toward the cigar-smoking, sports-loving people back in the corner. Sportswriting has always been the illegitimate child of journalism and will likely continue to be so to some degree" (Garrison, 1985, p. vii).

Wenner (1990), for one, has compiled studies that deal with sports and media in his book *Media, Sports, & Society*. Its chapters examine sports from several different theoretical viewpoints including Real's (1990) critique of the Super Bowl compared with the World Cup, VandeBerg and Trujillo's (1990) rhetorical analysis of how sportswriters define teams and Jhally's (1990) cultural studies of sports.

Instead, the bulk of studies concerning sports audiences can be found in the areas of sports psychology and sports history. Certainly one of the most important sources available about the sports audience is Allen Guttmann's historical and cultural examination *Sports Spectators* (1986). Guttmann, who has examined several sports topics from historical approaches, traces the history of sports spectatorship from before the Greeks through modern times.

The American Psychological Association has created a new division of sports psychology, and publications are growing in that area. One of the most noteworthy publications concerning the sports audience is Jeffrey H. Goldstein's *Sports, Games, and Play: Social and Psychological Viewpoints* (1989), which includes two keystone chapters. The first, psychologist Lloyd Reynolds Sloan's "The Motives of Sports Fans" (1989), examines and weighs theories of sports and theories of the impact and function of sport. The second chapter was co-written by Dolf Zillmann and Jennings Bryant of the University of Alabama and Barry Sapolsky (1989) of Florida State University's Communication Research Center. Zillmann and Bryant examined a theory of affective disposition that states (1) that enjoyment derived from witnessing the success and victory of a competing party increases with positive sentiments and decreases with negative sentiments toward that party and (2) that enjoyment derived from witnessing the failure and defeat of a competing party increases with negative sentiments and decreases with positive sentiments toward that party.

Sapolsky also examined dispositional theory and race when he showed Florida college students a basketball game between Indiana high school teams, one of which fielded five black players and one of which fielded five white players. Black male students showed a much higher propensity (89.6 percent) to enjoy successful plays by the all-black team and, of course, to root for that team. White students were somewhat less likely to enjoy successful plays and far less likely (45.7 percent) to admit rooting for the all-white team.

Zillmann and Bryant also found that arousal was indeed more likely to be found in subjects who viewed the tape describing the players as bitter enemies rather than the neutral or friendly versions. Their experiment focused on a key finding of their research: The sportscaster "serves not only to fill in the knowledge gaps left by the limitations of the visual dimensions of television, but to add histrionics to the 'human drama of athletic competition' " (Bryant, Comisky, and Zillmann, 1977, p. 149).

The sports broadcaster assumes the role of embellisher; the commentary follows a generally established dramatic theme, endeavors to create suspense, and tries to bring the viewer into the game as a participant in the spectacle. Within the broadcasts, Zillmann's and Bryant's content analysis shows that announcers use only a few dramatic themes and that those themes vary somewhat by network. In so doing, the announcers often focus on intrapersonal competition rather than team competition.

Other researchers have found that sportscasters create more than drama. Prisuta (1979) tested whether conservative values were a function of exposure to televised sports and found that sports television seemed to impart the values of authoritarianism, nationalism, and conservatism. The research of Rainville and McCormick (1977) also sought hidden values in the comments of sportscasters. Rainville and his colleagues (1978) analyzed the words of NFL broadcasters in an attempt to find covert racism and found that the white athlete in a matched black/white pair received more praise, more positive comments about education, and fewer negative non-football-related comments than did the black athlete. At the time, all men serving as pro football announcers were white (that has since changed in network and cable football telecasts).

Other researchers have investigated the area of gender inequity in sports content. Wanta and Leggett (1989) studied the content of wire service tennis photographs and found that photographers did not tend to reinforce gender stereotypes but that editors tended to choose those photographs that portrayed male players as dominant and female players as dominated. Two studies sponsored by the Amateur Athletic Foundation of Los Angeles examined content of sports news programs and newspaper sections. Among the findings: Televised sports gave 92 percent of airtime to men's sports and only 5 percent to women's sports; women were more likely to be portrayed as comical targets of sportscasters or as sex objects; quality of production was distinctly higher for men's sports events; and sportscasters tended to infantilize women athletes (and black men athletes) by markedly more references to them by first names only (Duncan et al., 1990).

In four daily newspapers, the researchers found men's sports stories outnumbered women's sports stories by a twenty-three-to-one ratio, 92.3 percent of all sports photographs were pictures of men, and women's sports stories comprised only 3.2 percent of front-page sports stories (Duncan, Messner, & Williams, 1991).

One of the earliest mass communications studies to study sports spectators was Hastorf and Cantril's (1954) study of how Princeton and Dartmouth students regarded a controversial football game that included an on-field brawl. After a fight-marred game in which the Princeton star was injured, Hastorf and Cantril arranged to test students at both campuses. They showed films of the game to student groups at Dartmouth and Princeton and, not surprisingly, found that each university's groups blamed the other team for the trouble. However, they also found that each person appeared to see the game somewhat differently. They concluded that no objective "game" exists but rather spectators each see a different "game."

Not only do spectators from different areas look on an event differently, but also the location of viewing a game apparently makes some difference. Hocking (1982) considered theoretical perspectives for measuring intraaudience effects at sports events and argued that television is designed to cover the game event but fares poorly in covering the stadium event.

Rothenbuhler's (1988) research on how people watch the every-fourth-year spectacle known as the Olympic Games, however, finds that the media may do an excellent job in providing a festival event for viewers. His studies show that Olympics fans differ demographically from regular sports viewers and are more likely to be in a group, to play host to visitors at holidays or other celebrations, to have food and drink during the Games broadcasts, and to plan their viewing around the Olympic schedule. One's race, gender, socioeconomic status, and education play little part in determining viewership, which cuts about equally across all groups mentioned.

BIBLIOGRAPHY

Arms, R. L., Russell, G. W., & Sandilands, M. L. (1979). Effects on the hostility of spectators of viewing aggressive sports. *Social Psychology Quarterly, 45,* 275–279.

Axthelm, P. (1970). *The city game.* New York: Harper's Magazine Press.

Babad, E. (1988). Wishful thinking and objectivity among sports fans. *Sociological Quarterly, 2* (4), 231–240.

Ball, D. W., & Loy, J. W. (1975). *Sport and social order: Contributions to the sociology of sport.* Reading, MA: Addison-Wesley.

Bandura, A. (1977). *Social learning theory.* Englewood Cliffs, NJ: Prentice-Hall.

Beisser, A. R. (1967). *The madness in sports: Psychosocial observations on sports.* New York: Appleton-Century-Crofts.

Bennett, M. J. (1976). Sports and fans and others. A comparison of personality characteristics of sports fans who attend professional games with persons with religious attendance and persons who indicate no formal social affiliations. *Dissertation Abstracts International, 36,* 4221, B.

Birrell, S., & Loy, J. (1975). Media sport: Hot and cool. *International Review of Sport Sociology, 14* (1), 5–19.

Bryant, J., Comisky, P., & Zillmann, D. (1977). Drama in sports commentary. *Journal of Communication, 27* (3), 140–149.

Coakley, J. J. (1982). *Sport in society* (2nd ed.). St. Louis: C. V. Mosby.

Curry T. J., & Jiobu, R. M. (1983). *Sports: A social perspective.* Englewood Cliffs, NJ: Prentice-Hall.

Demmert, H. G. (1971). *The economics of professional team sports.* Lexington, MA: D. C. Heath.

Duncan, M. C., Messner, M. A., & Williams, L. (1991). *Coverage of women's sports in four daily newspapers.* Los Angeles: Amateur Athletic Foundation.

Duncan, M. C., Messner, M. A., & Williams, L., & Jensen, K. (1990). *Gender stereotyping in televised sports.* Los Angeles: Amateur Athletic Foundation.

Dunning, E. (Ed.). (1971). *The sociology of sport.* London: Frank Cass.

Dunning, E., & Elias, N. (1970). The quest for excitement in unexciting societies. In G. Lueschen, (Ed.), *The cross-cultural analysis of sport and games.* Champaign, IL: Stipes.

Edwards, H. (1973). *Sociology of sports.* Homewood, IL: Dorsey.

Farrell, T. B. (1989). Media rhetoric as social drama: The Winter Olympics of 1984. *Critical Studies in Mass Communication, 6,* 158–161.

Gallico, P. (1938). *Farewell to sport.* New York: Knopf.

Gantz, W. (1981). An exploration of viewing motives and behaviors associated with television sports. *Journal of Broadcasting, 15,* 263–275.

Garrison, B. (1985). *Sports reporting.* Ames: Iowa State University Press.

Gilmore, A. (1983). The myth, legend and folklore of Joe Louis. *South Atlantic Quarterly, 82* (3), 256–268.

Godbey, G., & Robinson, J. (1979). The American sports fan. *Review of Sport and Leisure, 4,* 6.

Goldstein, J. H. (Ed.). (1989). *Sports, games, and play: Social and psychological viewpoints* (2nd ed.). Hillsdale, NJ: Erlbaum Associates.

Goldstein, J. H., & Arms, R. L. (1971). Effects of observing athletic contests on hostility. *Sociometry, 34* (1), 83–90.

Guttmann, A. (1978). *From ritual to record: The nature of modern sports.* New York: Columbia University Press.

Guttmann, A. (1984). *The games must go on: Avery Brundage and the Olympic movement.* New York: Columbia University Press.

Guttmann, A. (1986). *Sports spectators.* New York: Columbia University Press.

Harrell, W. A. (1981). Verbal aggressiveness in spectators at professional hockey games: The effects of tolerance of violence and amount of exposure to hockey. *Human Relations, 34* (8), 643–655.

Hastorf, A. H., & Cantril, H. (1954). They saw a game: A case study. *Journal of Abnormal and Social Psychology, 49,* 129–134.

Hoberman, J. M. (1984). *Sport and political ideology.* Austin: University of Texas Press.

Hocking, J. E. (1982). Sports and spectators: Intra-audience effects. *Journal of Communication, 32* (1), 100–107.

Holtzman, J. (1974). *No cheering in the press box.* San Francisco: Holt, Rinehart & Winston.

Horowitz, I. (1977). Sports telecasts. *Journal of Communication, 27,* 160.

Howard, G. E. (1912). Social psychology of the spectator. *American Journal of Sociology, 18,* 33–50.

Huizinga, J. (1938). *Homo ludens: A study of the play-element in culture.* Boston: Beacon Press.

Izenberg, J. (1972). *How many miles to Camelot? The all-American sport myth.* New York: Holt, Rinehart & Winston.

Jhally, S. (1990). Cultural studies and the sports-media complex. In L. A. Wenner (Ed.), *Media, sports, & society.* Newbury Park, CA: Sage Publications.

Johnson, W. O., Jr. (1971). *Super spectator and the electronic lilliputians.* Boston: Little, Brown.

King, Larry. (1988). *Tell it to the King.* New York: Putnam.

Klatell, D. A., & Marcus, N. (1988). *Sports for sale: Television, money, and the fans.* New York: Oxford University Press.

Koppett, L. (1981). *Sports illusion, sports reality.* Boston: Houghton Mifflin.

Lapchick, R. E. (Ed.). (1986). *Fractured focus.* Boston: D. C. Heath.

Lipsky, R. (1981). *How we play the game.* Boston: Beacon Press.

Lipsyte, R. (1985). Varsity syndrome: The unkindest cut. In W. L. Umphlett (Ed.), *American sport culture: The humanistic dimensions.* Cranbury, NJ: Associated University Presses.

Lipsyte, R. (1975). *Sportsworld: An American dreamland.* New York: Quadrangle.

Loy, J. W., & Kenyon, G. S. (1969). *Sport, culture, and society.* New York: Macmillan.

Mann, L. (1974). On being a sore loser: How fans react to their team's failure. *Australian Journal of Psychology, 26* (1), 37–48.

Meier, K. V. (1979). We don't want to set the world on fire: We just want to finish ninth. *Journal of Popular Culture, 13,* 289–301.

Meggyesy, D. (1970). *Out of their league.* Berkeley, CA: Ramparts.

Melnick, M. S. (1989). The sports fan: A teaching guide and bibliography. *Sociology of Sport Journal, 6* (2), 167–175.

Merchant, L. (1971). *And everyday you take another bite.* New York: Doubleday.

Michener, J. (1976). *Sports in America.* New York: Random House.

Miller Lite report on American attitudes toward sports. (1983). Milwaukee: Miller Brewing Co.

Miller, P., & Hall, E. R. (1990). *Television news coverage of women's sports.* Paper presented at the meeting of the Association for Education in Journalism and Mass Communication, Minneapolis, MN.

Miller, R. E. (1984). *Women's sports coverage in six Texas daily newspapers.* Unpublished master's thesis, Texas Tech University, Lubbock.

Naisbitt, J., & Aburdene, P. (1990). *Megatrends 2000: Ten new directions for the 1990s.* New York: William Morrow.

Novak, M. (1976). *The joy of sports.* New York: Basic Books.

Patton, P. (1984). *Razzle-dazzle.* Garden City, NJ: Dial.

Phillips, D. P. (1983). Mass media violence and U.S. homicides. *American Sociological Review, 48,* 560–568.

Phillips, D. P., & Hensley, D. E. (1984). When violence is rewarded or punished: The impact of mass media stories on homicide. *Journal of Communication, 34* (3), 101–116.

Powers, R. (1984). *Super tube.* New York: Coward-McCann.

Prisuta, R. H. (1979). Televised sports and political values. *Journal of Communication, 29* (1), 94–101.

Rader, B. G. (1984). *American sports.* Englewood Cliffs, NJ: Prentice-Hall.

Rainville, R. E., & McCormick, E. (1977). Extent of covert racial prejudice in pro football announcers' speech. *Journalism Quarterly, 54,* 20–26.

Rainville, R. E., Roberts, A., & Sweet, A. (1978). Recognition of covert racial prejudice. *Journalism Quarterly, 55,* 256–259.

Real, M. R. (1990). Super Bowl football versus World Cup soccer: A cultural-structural comparison. In L. A. Wenner (Ed.), *Media, sports, & society.* Newbury Park, CA: Sage Publications.

Rice, G. L. (1954). *The tumult and the shouting.* New York: A. S. Barnes.

Rogosin, D. (1985). *Invisible men: Life in baseball's Negro Leagues.* New York: Atheneum.

Rothenbuhler, E. W. (1988). The living room celebration of the Olympic Games. *Journal of Communication, 38* (4), 61–62.

Rothenbuhler, E. W. (1989). Values and symbols in orientations to the Olympics. *Critical Studies in Mass Communication, 6,* 138–157.

Russell, G. W. (1981). Spectator moods at an aggressive sports event. *Journal of Sport Psychology, 3,* 217–227.

Russell, G. W., & Drewry, B. R. (1976). Crowd size and competitive aspects of aggression in ice hockey: An archival study. *Human Relations, 29,* 723–735.

Sage, G. H. (Ed.). (1970). *Sport and American society.* Menlo Park, CA: Addison-Wesley.

Salwen, M. B., & Bernstein, J. M. (1986). Coverage of aftermath of 1984 World Series. *Journalism Quarterly, 63* (2), 383–385.

Salwen, M. B., & Garrison, B. (1987). Sports and politics: Los Angeles Times' coverage of the 1984 Summer Olympic Games. *Newspaper Research Journal, 8* (2), 43–51.

Sapolsky, B. (1980). The effect of spectator disposition and suspense on the enjoyment of sport contests. *International Journal of Sport Psychology, 11* (1), 1–10.

Schoellaert, P. T., & Smith, D. H. (1987). Team racial composition and sport attendance. *Sociological Quarterly, 28* (1), 71–87.

Scott, J. (1971). *The athletic revolution.* New York: Free Press.

Sewart, J. L. (1986). The commodification of sport. In S. J. Ball-Rokeach & M. G. Cantor (Eds.), *Media, audience and social structure.* Beverly Hills, CA: Sage Publications.

Shecter, L. (1969). *The jocks*. New York: Bobbs-Merrill.

Sloan, L. (1989). The motives of sports fans. In J. H. Goldstein (Ed.), *Sports, games, and play: Social and psychological viewpoints* (2nd ed.). Hillsdale, NJ: Erlbaum Associates.

Smith, G. J., Patterson, B., Williams, T., & Hogg, J. (1981). A profile of the deeply committed sports fan. *Arena Review, 5* (2), 26–44.

Stone, G. P. (Ed.). (1971). *Games, sports and power*. Chicago: Aldine.

Tannenbaum, P. H., & Noah, J. E. (1959). Sportugese: A study of sports page communication. *Journalism Quarterly, 36* (2), 163–170.

Telander, R. (1989). *The hundred yard lie: The corruption of college football and what we can do to stop it*. New York: Simon & Schuster.

Umphlett, W. L. (Ed.). (1985). *American sport culture: The humanistic dimensions*. Cranbury, NJ: Associated University Presses.

Underwood, J. (1980). *The death of an American game*. Boston: Little, Brown.

Underwood, J. (1984). *Spoiled sport*. Boston: Little Brown.

VandeBerg, L. R., & Trujillo, D. (1990). The rhetoric of winning and losing: The American dream and American team. In L. A. Wenner (Ed.), *Media, sports, & society*. Newbury Park, CA: Sage Publications.

Wanta, W., & Leggett, D. (1988). Hitting paydirt: Capacity theory and sports announcers' use of cliches. *Journal of Communication, 38* (4), 82–89.

Wanta, W., & Leggett, D. (1989). Gender stereotypes in wire service sports photographs. *Newspaper Research Journal, 10* (3), 105–114.

Wenner, L. A. (Ed.). (1990). *Media, sports, & society*. Newbury Park, CA: Sage Publications.

Williams, B. R. (1977). The structure of televised football. *Journal of Communication, 27* (3), 133–140.

Wojciechowski, G. (1990). *Pond scum & vultures: American's sportswriters talk about their glamorous profession*. New York: Macmillan.

Woodward, S. (1949). *Sports page*. New York: Simon & Schuster.

Yeargin, M. L. (1985). Who goes to the ball game? *American Demographics, 8* 12.

Zillmann, D., & Bryant, J. (1975). Viewers moral sanction of retribution in the appreciation of dramatic presentation. *Journal of Experimental Social Psychology, 11*, 572–582.

Zillmann, D., Bryant, J., & Sapolsky, B. (1989). Enjoyment from sports spectators. In J. H. Goldstein (Ed.), *Sports, games, and play: Social and psychological viewpoints* (2nd ed.). Hillsdale, NJ: Erlbaum Associates.

Zillmann, D., Hay, T.A., & Bryant, T. (1973). The effect of suspense and its resolution on the appreciation of dramatic presentation. *Journal of Experimental Social Psychology, 9*, 307–323.

SELECTED BIBLIOGRAPHY

Alder, Richard (Ed.). (1975). *Television as a social force: New approaches to television criticism*. New York: Praeger.

Agee, Warren K., Ault, Phillip H., & Emery, Edwin. (1988). *Introduction to mass communications* (9th ed.). New York: Harper & Row.

Agee, Warren K., Ault, Phillip H., & Emery, Edwin. (1982). *Perspectives on mass communications*. New York: Harper & Row.

Bagdikian, Ben H. (1971). *The information machines*. New York: Harper & Row.

Bagdikian, Ben H. (1983). *The media monopoly*. Boston: Beacon Press.

Barret, Mervin (Ed.). (1982) *Broadcast journalism*. New York: Everest House.

Becker, Samuel L. (1983). *Discovering mass communication*. Glenview, IL: Scott, Foresman.

Benjaminson, Peter. (1984). *Death in the afternoon*. Kansas City: Andrews, McMeel & Parker.

Berelson, Bernard, & Janowitz, Morris. (1966). *Reader in public opinion and communication*. New York: Free Press.

Berlo, David K. (1960). *Process of communication*. New York: Holt, Rinehart & Winston.

Bernards, Neal (Ed.). (1988). *The mass media opposing viewpoints*. St. Paul, MN: Greenhaven Press.

Bernstein, Carl, & Woodrow, Bob. (1974). *All the president's men*. New York: Simon & Schuster.

Boller, Paul F., Jr. (1984). *Presidential campaigns*. New York: Oxford University Press.

Bozell, L. Brent, III, & Baker, Brent H. (Eds.). (1990). *And that's the way it is(n't): A reference guide to mass media bias*. Alexandria, VA: Media Research Center.

Brown, J. A. (1963). *Techniques of persuasion*. New York: Penguin.

Brown, Les. (1971). *Television: The business behind the box*. New York: Harcourt Brace Jovanovich.

Carey, James W. (1989). *Communication as culture: Essays on media and society*. Boston: Unwin Hyman.

Carter, T. Barton, Franklin, Marc A., & Wright, Jay B. (1988). *The First Amendment and the Fourth Estate: The law of mass media* (4th ed.). Westbury, NY: Foundation Press.

Chafee, Zechariah. (1947). *Government and mass communication* (2 vols.). Chicago: University of Chicago Press.

Cirino, Robert. (1971). *Don't blame the people: How the news media use bias, distortion and censorship to manipulate public opinion.* New York: Random House.

Cole, Barry (Ed.). (1981). *Television today.* New York: Oxford University Press.

Comstock, George. (1975). *Television and human behavior: The key studies.* Santa Monica, CA: Rand.

Conner, Jeff. (1987). *Stephen King goes to Hollywood.* New York: New American Library.

Cross, Donna Woolfolk. (1983). *Media speak.* New York: Coward-McCann.

Daly, Charles. (1968). *The media and the cities.* Chicago: University of Chicago Press.

DeFleur, Melvin, & Dennis, Everette E. (1985). *Understanding mass communication* (2nd ed.). Boston: Houghton Mifflin.

Dennis, Everette E., & Merrill, John C. (1984). *Basic issues in mass communication.* New York: Macmillan.

Dijk Van, Tien A. (Ed.). (1985). *Discourse and communication.* Berlin: Walter de Gruyter.

Dizard, Wilson P., Jr. (1982). *The coming information age: An overview of technology, economics, and politics.* New York: Longman.

Dominick, Joseph R. (1987). *The dynamics of mass communication* (2nd ed.). New York: Random House.

Donaldson, Sam. (1987). *Hold on, Mr. President.* New York: Random House.

Doob, Leonard. (1966). *Public opinion and propaganda.* Hamden, CT: Archon.

Ellerbee, Linda. (1986). *"And so it goes."* New York: G. P. Putnam's Sons.

Emery, Edwin, & Emery, Michael. (1984). *The press and America* (5th ed.). Englewood Cliffs, NJ: Prentice-Hall.

Emery, Michael, & Smythe, Ted C. (1986). *Readings in mass communication* (6th ed.). Dubuque, IA: William C. Brown.

Epstein, Edward Jay. (1973). *News from nowhere: Television and the news.* New York: Random House.

Ettema, James, & Whitney, Charles D. (Eds.). *Individuals in mass media organizations.* Beverly Hills, CA: Sage Publications.

Evans, Harold. (1984). *Good times, bad times.* New York: Atheneum.

Ewen, Stuart, & Ewen, Elizabeth. (1982). *Channels of desire.* New York: McGraw-Hill.

Fisher, Paul L., & Lowenstein, Ralph L. (Eds.). (1967). *Race and the news media.* New York: Praeger.

Friendly, Fred W. (1967). *Due to circumstances beyond our control.* New York: Random House.

Gamble, Michael W., & Gamble, Teri Kwal. (1989). *Introducing mass communication* (2nd ed.). New York: McGraw-Hill.

Greenfield, Jeff. (1982). *The real campaign.* New York: Summit Books.

Gross, Gerald. (1966). *The responsibility of the press.* New York: Fleet.

Gross, Lynne Schafer. (1986). *The new television technologies* (2nd ed.). Dubuque, IA: William C. Brown.

Hall, Carolyn. *Forties in vogue.* New York: Crown.

Hall, Edward T. (1959). *The silent language.* Garden City, NY: Doubleday.

Hamilton, John Maxwell. (1986). *Main street America and the Third World.* Cabin John, MD: Seven Locks.

Harris, Jay S. (Ed.). (1980). *TV Guide: The first 25 years.* New York: New American Library.

Hess, Stephen. (1986). *Ultimate insiders: U.S. senators in the national media.* Washington, DC: Brookings Institution.

Hiebert, Ray Eldon, & Reuss, Carol. (1988). *Impact of mass media* (2nd ed.). New York & London: Longman.

Holmes, Deborah. (1986). *Governing the press.* Boulder, CO: Westview Press.

Isaacs, Norman F. (1986). *Untended gates: The mismanaged press.* New York: Columbia University Press.

Jacobs, Norman (Ed.). (1964). *Culture for the millions: Mass media in modern society.* Boston: Beacon.

Johnson, Nicholas. (1970). *How to talk back to your television set.* Boston: Little, Brown.

Kahn, Frank (Ed.). (1978). *Documents in American broadcasting* (3rd ed.). New York: Appleton-Century-Crofts.

Kaid, Lynda Lee. (1985). *Political campaign communication: A bibliography and guide to the literature, 1979–1982.* Metuchen, NJ: Scarecrow Press.

Karolevitz, Bob. (1985). *From quill to computer: The story of America's community newspapers.* Freeman, SD: Pine Hill.

Klapper, Joseph T. (1960). *The effects of mass communication.* New York: Free Press.

Kline, F. Gerald, & Tichenor, Phillip J. (Eds.). (1972). *Current perspectives in mass communication research.* Beverly Hills, CA: Sage Publications.

Krasnow, Erwin G., & Longley, Lawrence D. (1972). *Pressures on the press.* New York: Crowell.

Kuralt, Charles. (1985). *On the road with Charles Kuralt.* New York: Putnam.

Larsen, Otto. (1968). *Violence and the mass media.* New York: Harper & Row.

Lee, John. (1968). *Diplomatic persuaders: The new role of the news media in international relations.* New York: Wiley.

Lee, Richard W. (1970). *Politics and the press.* Washington, DC: Acropolis.

Leonard, Thomas C. (1986). *Power of the press: The birth of American political reporting.* New York: Oxford University Press.

Liebling, A. J. (1964). *The press.* New York: Ballantine.

Matuson, Barbara. (1983). *The evening stars.* Boston: Houghton Mifflin.

Mayer, Martin. (1987). *Making news.* Garden City, NY: Doubleday.

McGinniss, Joe. (1969). *The selling of the president 1968.* New York: Trident.

McKerns, Joseph P. (1985). *News media and public policy: An annotated bibliography.* New York: Garland.

McLean, Roderick. (1968). *Television in education.* New York: Macmillan.

McLuhan, Marshall. (1964). *Understanding media: The extensions of man.* New York: McGraw-Hill.

McLuhan, Marshall. (1967). *The medium is the message.* New York: Bantam.

McNeal, James V. (1987). *Children as consumers.* Lexington: Lexington Books.

McQuail, Denis. (1969). *Towards a sociology of mass communication.* London: Collier-Macmillan.

Mendelsohn, Harold. (1966). *Mass entertainment.* New Haven, CT: College & University Press.

Mott, Frank Luther. (1964). *American journalism.* New York: Macmillan.

Peck, Abe. (1985). *Uncovering the sixties: The life and time of the underground press.* New York: Pantheon Books.

Pember, Don R. (1987). *Mass media in America* (5th ed.). Chicago: Science Research Associates.

Phelan, John (Ed.). (1969). *Communications control.* Mission, KS: Sheed & Ward.

Potter, Jan, & Speziale, Bob. (1987). *Dear Ann, dear Abby.* New York: Dodd, Mead.

Reston, James. (1967). *The artillery of the press: Its influence on American foreign policy.* New York: Harper & Row.

Rivers, William. (1965). *The opinion makers: The Washington press.* Boston: Beacon.

Rivers, William L. (1970). *The adversaries: Politics and the press.* Boston: Beacon.

Rivers, William, & Schramm, Wilbur. (1969). *Responsibility in mass communication.* New York: Harper & Row.

Rosenberg, Bernard, & White, David (Eds.). (1971). *Mass culture revisited.* New York: Van Nostrand Reinhold.

Salisbury, Harrison E. (1980). *Without fear or favor.* New York: Times Books.

Schwed, Peter. (1984). *Turning the pages.* New York: Simon & Schuster.

Seldes, Gilbert. (1968). *The new mass media challenge to a free society.* Washington, DC: Public Affairs Press.

Shanks, Bob. (1976). *The cool fire: How to make it in television.* New York: W. W. Norton.

Shaw, David. (1984). *Press watch.* New York: Macmillan.

Shiller, Herbert I. (1971). *Mass communications and American empire.* Boston: Beacon.

Shirer, William L. (1984). *The nightmare years.* Boston: Little, Brown.

Sklar, Robert. (1980). *Prime time America.* New York: Oxford University Press.

Small, William. (1970). *To kill a messenger: Television news and the real world.* New York: Hastings House.

Smith, Alfred (Ed.). *Communication and culture.* New York: Holt, Rinehart & Winston.

Snorgrass, J. William. (1985). *Blacks and media: A selected annotated bibliography, 1962–1982.* Gainesville: University Presses of Florida.

Snow, Robert P. (1983). *Creating media culture.* Beverly Hills, CA: Sage Publications.

Sorenson, Thomas. (1968). *The word war.* New York: Harper & Row.

Starker, Steven. (1989). *Evil influences: Crusades against the mass media.* New Brunswick: Transaction Press.

Steele, Richard W. (1985). *Propaganda in an open society: The Roosevelt administration and the media, 1933–1941.* Westport, CT: Greenwood Press.

Steinberg, Charles S. (1980). *The information establishment.* New York: Hastings House.

Sterling, Christopher H., & Haight, Timothy R. (Eds.). (1978). *The mass media: Aspen Institute guide to communication industry trends.* New York: Praeger.

Tebbel, John William. (1985). *Press and the presidency: From George Washington to Ronald Reagan.* New York: Oxford University Press.

Thomas, Erwin Kenneth. (1991). *Make better videos with your camcorder.* Blue Ridge Summit, PA: TAB Books.

Tunstall, Jeremy. (1970). *Media sociology: A reader.* Urbana: University of Illinois Press.

Twentieth Century Fund. (1972). *Press freedoms under pressure.* New York: Twentieth Century Fund.

Ulloth, Dana R. (1983). *Mass media, past, present, future.* St. Paul, MN: West.

Warner, Charles. (1986). *Broadcast and cable.* Belmont, CA: Wadsworth.

Weaver, David. (1982). *Videotex journalism: Teletext, viewdata and the news.* Hillsdale, NJ: Lawrence Erlbaum Associates.

Whitmore, Edward Jay. (1985). *Mediamerica* (3rd ed.). Belmont, CA: Wadsworth.

Williams, Christian. (1982). *Lead, follow or get out of the way: The story of Ted Turner.* New York: Times Books.

Williams, Francis. (1969). *The right to know.* London: Longmans, Green.

Winfield, Betty H., & DeFleur, Louis B. (1986). *Edward R. Murrow heritage: Challenge for the future.* Ames: Iowa State University Press.

Winston, Brian. (1986). *Misunderstanding media.* Cambridge, MA: Harvard University Press.

Withey, Stephen B., & Abeles, Ronald P. (1980). *Television and social behavior: Beyond violence and children.* Hillsdale, NJ: Lawrence Erlbaum Associates.

Wood, Donald N. (1983). *Mass media and the individual.* St. Paul, MN: West.

Woodruff, Judy. (1982). *"This is Judy Woodruff at the White House."* Reading, MA: Addison-Wesley.

Wright, Charles R. (1975). *Mass communication: A sociological perspective* (2nd ed.). New York: Random House.

Yu, Frederick T. C. (1968). *Behavorial sciences and the mass media.* New York: Russell Sage Foundation.

Zettl, Herbert. (1976). *Television production handbook* (3rd ed.). Belmont, CA: Wadsworth.

Ziesel, William (Ed.). (1984). *Censorship.* New York: Oxford University Press.

INDEX

ABOUT THE EDITORS AND CONTRIBUTORS

MAURINE H. BEASLEY is a professor of journalism at the University of Maryland, College Park, where she has been a full-time faculty member since 1975. She holds bachelor's degrees in journalism and history from the University of Missouri, Columbia, a master's degree in journalism from Columbia University, and a Ph.D. in American civilization from George Washington University. Her professional experience includes about thirteen years of newspaper reporting, three at the *Kansas City* (Missouri) *Star,* where she was education editor, and ten at the *Washington Post.* She is the author/coauthor or editor of seven books, dealing mainly with women and the media. Beasley is a past president of the American Journalism Historians Association and the Washington chapter of the Society of Professional Journalists. She is president-elect of the Association for Education in Journalism and Mass Communication, the largest professional association in its field.

BROWN H. CARPENTER has been a reporter and editor for the Norfolk *Virginian-Pilot* and the *Ledger-Star* for twenty-five years. He has covered news beats ranging from the police station to the state capital. He also contributes book reviews to the newspaper's Sunday Commentary section. He has a bachelor's degree in English from Dartmouth College and has studied German at Old Dominion University since his undergraduate years.

SHIRLEY S. CARTER is professor and chairperson of the Department of Mass Communications and Journalism at Norfolk State University, Norfolk, Virginia. Prior to that, she served as associate professor and founding chairperson of the Department of Communications and Visual Arts at the University of North Florida and assistant professor of journalism at Louisiana State University. Carter has also served as a journalist, educator, and administrator in Alabama, Ohio, and Texas. She recieved her Ph.D. in Journalism at the University of Missouri-Columbia, an M.A. in Journalism at Ohio State University, and a B.S. in English at Tuskegee University. Carter's research interests include audience analysis, consumer behavior, Southern journalism, and advertising values. Other works will be published in upcoming texts on news writing and reporting, and mass media and society. She is active in the Association for Education in Journalism and Mass Communication (AEJMC), Association for Schools of Journalism and Mass Communication (ASJMC), and several other civic and professional organizations.

ROBERT G. FINNEY is a professor and former chair of the Radio, Television, and Film Department at California State University, Long Beach, since 1977. In 1991, he was named CSULB Outstanding Professor and was runner-up in the CSU systemwide award ceremony. Prior to coming to CSULB, he administered or taught in university communication programs for fifteen years at the following universities, respectively: James Madison, Memphis State, Shaw, Ohio State, and Cincinnati. He also was a personnel administrator at the Radio Corporation of America and served in the U.S. Navy and Naval Reserve, retiring from the navy in 1988 at the rank of captain with thirty years' federal service. A 1956 graduate of Marietta College in Ohio, he earned his M.A. in 1957 and Ph.D. in 1971 from Ohio State University. He is a nationally recognized authority on electronic media policy and regulation.

BRUCE GARRISON is a professor of journalism in the Journalism and Photography Program of the School of Communication at the University of Miami in Coral Gables, Florida. Garrison is author of *Sports Reporting* (1993; first edition, 1985), *Professional News Reporting* (1992), *Advanced Reporting: Skills for the Professional* (1992), *Latin American Journalism* (1991), *Professional News Writing* (1990), and *Professional Feature Writing* (1989). He has also written chapters about journalism and newspapers in several other books. He has published numerous articles and papers on mass communication topics, especially newspapers and news reporting, in journals such as *Journalism Quarterly, Newspaper Research Journal, Journalism History, Mass Comm Review,* and *Editor & Publisher.* Garrison earned his Ph.D. degree in journalism from Southern Illinois University at Carbondale and M.S. in journalism at the University of Tennessee at Knoxville.

BARBARA BEALOR HINES is an associate professor in the Department of Journalism at Howard University's School of Communications where she serves as coordinator of the public relations and advertising sequences. Prior to joining the Howard faculty, Dr. Hines was executive director of the Maryland Scholastic Press Advisers Association, a faculty member and assistant dean at the College of Journalism at the University of Maryland, a high school journalism teacher, and press secretary to U.S. Senator Ralph W. Yarborough of Texas. She is chair of the Council of Divisions of the Association for Education in Journalism and

Mass Communication (AEJMC) and cochair of its Task Force on Curriculum. A member of the national Multicultural Affairs Committee of the Public Relations Society of America, she is the editor of the *National Directory of Public Relations Practitioners* (1993). She is the author, with Robert Ruggles and Diane Hall of Florida A&M University, of *Recruiting and Retaining Black Students for Journalism and Mass Communication Education,* published by the Association of Schools of Journalism and Mass Communication (1989). Dr. Hines received her bachelor's degree from the University of Texas at Austin, her master's degree from the American University, and her Ph.D. from the University of Maryland at College Park.

JAMES PHILLIP JETER is an associate professor of journalism and director of University Broadcast Services at Florida A&M University. He has research and teaching interests in audio and video production, media management, minority ownership, and telecommunications policy. A native of Shelton, South Carolina, he earned a bachelor's degree in French from Johnson C. Smith University, a master's in communication arts (journalism) from Cornell University, and the doctor of philosophy in communication arts (radio-television-film) from the University of Wisconsin at Madison.

KEVIN L. KEENAN is on the faculty of the College of Journalism at the University of Maryland. His professional background includes work in the advertising agency and marketing research industries. He holds a Ph.D. in mass communication from the University of Georgia and an M.S. in advertising from the University of Illinois. Professor Keenan's writing and research have been published in *Advertising Age, Journalism Educator, Journalism Quarterly,* and the *Proceedings of the American Academy of Advertising.*

MARILYN KERN-FOXWORTH is an associate professor in the Department of Journalism at Texas A&M University where she has taught magazine writing. She is very active in the Public Relations Society of America and the Association for Education in Journalism and Mass Communication and has served as head of the Minorities and Communication Division of that organization. She has published in numerous trade, academic, and popular periodicals and has just completed a book titled *Aunt Jemima, Uncle Ben and Rastus: Blacks in Advertising, Yesterday, Today and Tomorrow.* Dr. Kern-Foxworth's research focuses on the psychological impact of stereotypical depictions of African Americans in the mass media, and articles about her research have appeared in various local, regional, and national publications.

KATHERINE C. McADAMS has coached professional and student writers for more than fifteen years while pursuing research on audience needs and perceptions. An assistant professor at the University of Maryland, McAdams holds three degrees from the University of North Carolina at Chapel Hill, including a bachelor's degree in English education, a master's degree in journalism, and a doctorate in mass communication research. She is creator of The Grammar

Slammer, a workshop in grammar and spelling for student journalists at UNC—CH and in the College of Journalism at Maryland. Her teaching interests are news, feature, and public relations writing and mass communication research methods. Her research involves techniques for reaching audiences and for improving journalism education. Recent work includes a 1990 study of newspaper readers for the American Society of Newspaper Editors and a program of evaluation and training for the National Rural Electric Editors' Association.

RANDY E. MILLER is an assistant professor in the School of Mass Communications at the University of South Florida. He worked as a sports writer and editor for six years for various newspapers in Texas, earning writing awards from UPI, the Texas Sports Writers Association, and the Texas Press Association. He earned a Ph.D. in journalism from the University of Texas in 1991 where his dissertation dealt with intermedia agenda setting in the drugs-in-professional-sports issue. At the University of South Florida, he is news-editorial sequence head and teaches a graduate class entitled "Sports and the Media." He has also served two years as the Teaching Standards chair in the Association for Education in Journalism and Mass Communication's Newspaper Division.

LAWRENCE N. REDD is a communication arts and sciences specialist at Michigan State University. He holds a B.A from Tennessee State University and an M.A. and Ph.D. from Michigan State University. He has contributed chapters on communication to several books and published articles in a variety of scholarly journals on music, educational technology, and telecommunication. He is the author of *Rock Is Rhythm and Blues* (1974). His dual career encompasses professional work in the record industry, radio, and television. In addition to his work with Al Green, he has produced two blues albums for his own company and is the owner/manager of a cable radio station.

M. KENT SIDEL is an associate professor in the College of Journalism and Mass Communications at the University of South Carolina. Professor Sidel holds a Ph.D. from Northwestern University in radio-TV-film. He served as a Fulbright Scholar at the University of Guyana and continues to do international consulting work. He recently completed a radio journalism training project for the U.S. Information Agency at the University of Bucharest (Romania). He has published book chapters and articles on international communication, policy planning, media development in the Third World, and educational broadcasting. He worked in radio journalism and programming in the Midwest.

LOWNDES F. STEPHENS is associate dean for graduate studies and research and professor, College of Journalism and Mass Communications, University of South Carolina at Columbia. Stephens, whose research has appeared in more than a dozen different academic journals including the *Journal of Consumer Research, Journal of Retailing,* and the *Journal of Advertising Research,* in the *New York Times,* and other popular media, is a fellow in the Inter-University Seminar on Armed Forces and Society and a frequent consultant to Department of Defense agencies, the Institute for Defense Analyses, the Academy for Educational Development, USIA, and corporate clients. He has served as a consultant for the Kentucky Educational Television Foundation and the South Carolina Educational Television Network. The author, who holds a Ph.D. in mass communications research from the University of Wisconsin at Madison, has been recognized for teaching excellence by Mortar Board and as a faculty leader by Omicron Delta Kappa.

ALICE A. TAIT is an award-winning associate professor of communication at Central Michigan University, Mt. Pleasant, Michigan. In 1989, Central Michigan University awarded her a teaching fellowship and in 1990 a Teaching Excellence Award. Butler University, Indianapolis, Indiana, awarded her a 1991–1992 Visiting African-American Scholar's position. The Butler award allowed her to teach one course per semester and pursue research. She cochaired the Placement Service for the Broadcast Education Association, 1989–1992, and was chairperson of the Communication Division of the Michigan Academy of Arts and Sciences (1991–1993) and for four years directed Central Michigan University's High School Journalism Workshop. Tait graduated from Wayne State University in 1969 with a B.A. in speech and received her M.A. in mass communications and communications theory from Wayne State University in 1974. She received her Ph.D. in mass communication research and theory, and a cognate in interpersonal and public communication from Bowling Green State University in 1985.

ERWIN K. THOMAS is the former acting chair, coordinator of Graduate Studies, and associate professor in the Department of Mass Communications at Norfolk State University. He has published in the *Journal of Ethnic Studies, Studies in Latin American Popular Culture, Gazette,* and the *Dictionary of Literary Biography.* He has authored *Make Better Videos with Your Camcorder* (1991) and various book chapters. Dr. Thomas was secretary/treasurer (1989–1990) and director, Overseas Book Project (1990–1991), of the International Division of the Association for Education in Journalism and Mass Communication.

RONALD J. ZBORAY is assistant professor of history, Georgia State University, and the author of *A Fictive People: Antebellum Economic Development and the Reading Public* (1993). His articles and essays have appeared in *Essays in Economic and Business History* (1992), *Dime Novel Round-Up* (1991), *Libraries and Culture* (1991), *Studies in Bibliography* (1990), *Publishing History* (1989), *Documentary Editing* (1989), *American Quarterly* (1986, 1988), *Book Research Quarterly* (1987), *American Archivist* (1987), *Journal of American Culture* (1987), *Southwest Review* (1986), *Film and History* (1980), and several edited books. He was microfilm editor of *The Emma Goldman Papers* (1991) at the University of California at Berkeley. He received his Ph.D. from New York University and his research interest is in the history of the book in America.

ISBN 0-313-27811-3

EAN

9 780313 278112

90000>

HARDCOVER BAR CODE